Water Policy in the Netherlands

Integrated Management in a
Densely Populated Delta

EDITED BY

Stijn Reinhard
Henk Folmer

RESOURCES FOR THE FUTURE
Washington, DC, USA

Printed in the United States of America.

An RFF Press book
Published by Resources for the Future
1616 P Street NW
Washington, DC 20036–1400
USA
www.rffpress.org

Library of Congress Cataloging-in-Publication Data

Water policy in the Netherlands : integral management in a densely populated delta.
    p. cm.
    ISBN 978-1-933115-73-3
    1. Water-supply—Government policy—Netherlands. 2. Water-supply—Management—Netherlands. I. Resources for the Future.
    HD1697.N4W364 2009
    333.91009492—dc22   2009016253

This book was typeset by Andrea Reider. It was copyedited by Joyce Bond. The cover was designed by Maggie Powell. Cover photo credits, © iStock International, Inc. all rights reserved. The Production Coordinator of this book was Ellen A. Davey, and the Marketing Coordinator was Andrea Titus.

ISBN 978-1-933115-73-3 (cloth)

About Resources for the Future *and* RFF Press

Resources for the Future (RFF) improves environmental and natural resource policymaking worldwide through independent social science research of the highest caliber. Founded in 1952, RFF pioneered the application of economics as a tool for developing more effective policy about the use and conservation of natural resources. Its scholars continue to employ social science methods to analyze critical issues concerning pollution control, energy policy, land and water use, hazardous waste, climate change, biodiversity, and the environmental challenges of developing countries.

RFF Press supports the mission of RFF by publishing book-length works that present a broad range of approaches to the study of natural resources and the environment. Its authors and editors include RFF staff, researchers from the larger academic and policy communities, and journalists. Audiences for publications by RFF Press include all of the participants in the policymaking process—scholars, the media, advocacy groups, NGOs, professionals in business and government, and the public.

Resources for the Future

Issues in Water Resource Policy

Ariel Dinar, Series Editor, University of California, Riverside

Series Advisory Committee
Tony Allan, King's College, London, UK
Carl J. Bauer, University of Arizona, USA
James Boyd, Resources for the Future, USA
Franklin M. Fisher, Massachusetts Institute of Technology, USA
Jerson Kelman, National Electric Energy Agency (ANEEL), Brazil
Jennifer McKay, University of South Australia, and Water Policy and Law Group,
    Australia
Sandra Postel, Global Water Policy Project, USA
Walter A. Rosenbaum, University of Florida, USA
R. Maria Saleth, Madras Institute of Development Studies, India
Aaron Wolf, Oregon State University, USA

Books in the *Issues in Water Resource Policy* series are intended to be accessible to a broad range of scholars, practitioners, policymakers, and general readers. Each book focuses on critical issues in water policy at a specific subnational, national, or regional level, with the mission to draw upon and integrate the best scholarly and professional expertise concerning the physical, ecological, economic, institutional, political, legal, and social dimensions of water use. The interdisciplinary approach of the series, along with an emphasis on real world situations and on problems and challenges that recur globally, are intended to enhance our ability to apply the full body of knowledge that we have about water resources—at local, country, and international levels.

For comments and editorial inquiries about the series, please contact *waterpolicy@rff.org*.

For information about other titles in the series, please visit *www.Rffpress.org/water.*

The *Issues in Water Resource Policy* series is dedicated to the memory of Guy LeMoigne, a founding member of the Advisory Committee.

Contents

Foreword

Margreeth de Boer

THE NETHERLANDS FACES enormous challenges with respect to its water management. Climate change, a rising sea level, soil subsidence, and urbanization all necessitate a rethinking of the Dutch approach toward water management. On July 2, 2003, representatives of the national government, provincial authorities, municipal councils, and water boards signed the National Administrative Agreement on Water (NBW). This agreement sets forth how, by what means, and according to which timetable those involved would organize Dutch water management between 2003 and 2015. It also elaborates on the relationship between the Dutch Water Policy for the 21st Century and the European Union Water Framework Directive. The agreement is based on the realization that the nature and magnitude of the national water policy are structurally changing as a result of the above-mentioned causes. Cooperative action is necessary to ensure that the water system remains in good shape by 2015 and on toward 2050. The NBW describes the objectives and responsibilities for the national and regional groundwater and surface water systems. In 2009, the first National Water Plan will be adopted.

The new Dutch water policy aims to help make the Netherlands safe and able to withstand the challenges it faces, both now and in the future. To achieve this goal, a healthy and resilient water system has to be created and built up in a way that guarantees sustainable use. One example is that it is necessary to "give water room," making acreage available for storage in the floodplains and towns. Streams are permitted to meander as they once did, and farmers and water boards use detention ponds to store excess rainwater. Lowering floodplains, moving dikes inland, and digging extra channels alongside the rivers all allow more room for water and reduce the threat of flooding. The Room for the River project must ensure that the Rhine River at the Dutch-German border can safely carry 16,000 cubic meters per second by 2015. Dutch water management focuses on not only quantity, but also quality of water. Research institutes have been developing new water sanitation techniques, and these are being implemented. Both quantitative and qualitative water management require an adequate governance structure. Although the Netherlands has a long tradition in this respect, its water governance structure is still developing.

Water Policy in the Netherlands: Integrated Management in a Densely Populated Delta examines virtually all the important aspects of Dutch water management—quantity, quality, flood protection, and water for nature—as set forth in the NBW. It also addresses economic aspects and the specific Dutch governance structures, approaching water management from the perspectives of various disciplines in an integrated (also known as integral) fashion and in close collaboration with governments, companies, stakeholder organizations, citizens, and knowledge institutions. Although most of the authors have a scientific background, the book should prove useful for practitioners and policymakers alike. It also contains important information for water management in other countries, both developed and developing, which may face similar challenges to those experienced by the Netherlands. The Dutch experiences may provide important lessons for implementation of integrated water management. The integration of water quantity and quality management, the transformation of a sectoral approach toward an interdisciplinary one, and taking into account the entire water basin will provide useful information.

Margreeth de Boer is vice chairwoman of the Dutch Water Advisory Committee. She is a member of the Governing Board of UNESCO-IHE (Institute for Water Education) and is chairwoman of Wetsus, Centre of Excellence for Sustainable Water Technology and the Wadden Sea Council. Ms. de Boer was minister of Housing, Spatial Planning and the Environment of the Netherlands from 1994 to 1998.

Editors and Contributors

Editors

Stijn Reinhard is head of the Spatial and Regional Policy unit of LEI Wageningen UR (Agricultural Economics Research Institute), the Hague. His current research focuses on water economics. He received the American Agricultural Economics Association best dissertation award for his work on environmental efficiency.

Henk Folmer is professor of research methodology and spatial econometrics at the University of Groningen and of general economics at Wageningen University. Among his research interests are microeconomics, including game theory and environmental and resource economics; and econometrics, including spatial econometrics. He is editor in chief (with Tom Tietenberg) of the *International Review* (formerly *Yearbook*) *of Environmental and Resource Economics* and coordinating editor in chief of *Letters in Spatial and Resource Sciences*. His other books include *Land and Forest Economics* (with Cornelis van Kooten). He is doctor honoris causa at the University of Gothenburg, Sweden.

Contributors

Marija Bočkarjova is an economist at the Free University, Amsterdam, and at the International Institute for Geo-Information Science and Earth Observation (ITC), Enschede, the Netherlands. Her research interests include damage modeling, risk perception, and risk valuation of major disasters in modern economies, such as potential major floods in the Netherlands. She has published in *Ecological Economics* and *Natural Hazard*.

Leontien Bos-Gorter is a policy advisor for the Ministry of Transport, Public Works and Water Management in the Netherlands. Currently she focuses on public participation in and communication on water management, specifically in relation to the European Union Water Framework Directive. She was previously affiliated with the Institute of Environmental Studies (IVM), Free University, Amsterdam.

Roy Brouwer is an environmental economist at the Institute for Environmental Studies (IVM), Free University, Amsterdam. His main research interests are economic valuation, risk and uncertainty, and integrated hydroeconomic modeling. He is coeditor of *Managing Wetlands: An Ecological-Economics Approach* and *Cost–Benefit Analysis and Water Resources Management*, and is on the editorial board of *Environmental and Resource Economics* and *Environmental Modeling and Software*. He has published in *Risk Analysis* and *Water Resources Research*.

Cees J.N. Buisman is part-time professor of environmental technology at Wageningen University and part-time scientific director of Wetsus, Centre of Excellence for Sustainable Water Technology in Leeuwarden. His recent research has focused on environmental water technology.

Victor N. de Jonge is professor of estuarine and coastal management at the University of Hull. His recent research has focused on functional environmental indicators, factors regulating biodiversity development, and linking of ecological and socioeconomic systems. His writing has been published in a wide variety of international and national outlets

Gerrit J.W. Euverink is deputy scientific director of Wetsus, Centre of Excellence for Sustainable Water Technology in Leeuwarden. In his research, he is looking for new opportunities on the border of different scientific disciplines—such as biotechnology, nanotechnology, sensor technology, chemical technology, and physics—to develop new water technology.

Joost (W.J.M.) Heijkers is a hydrologist at the water board de Stichtse Rijnlanden. He has specialized in modeling, monitoring, and using geographical information systems (GIS) for strategic water management. He is working on his PhD thesis at Wageningen University and the University of Utrecht. His research deals with water balance component estimation using advanced modeling and monitoring methods. He is editor of *Stromingen*, a technical journal for Dutch hydrologists.

Arjen Y. Hoekstra is professor of multidisciplinary water management at the University of Twente, where he specializes in integrated water resources planning and management, river basin management, policy analysis, and systems analysis. He is coauthor with Ashok K. Chapagain of *Globalization of Water: Sharing the Planet's Freshwater Resources*.

Dave Huitema is a senior policy scientist at the Institute for Environmental Studies (IVM), Free University, Amsterdam, where he is head of the cluster Water Governance and Economics. His research theme is "adaptive governance" and the institutional prescriptions that are embedded in it, such as public participation and experimentation. In 2004, Huitema won the G.A. van Poelje award for the best publication in Dutch public administration.

Stefan M.M. Kuks is chair of the water board Regge and Dinkel and professor of innovation and water policy implementation at the University of Twente, where he is affiliated with the School of Management and Governance and the Twente Water Centre. He specializes in institutional aspects of water management. He is coeditor of *The Evolution of National Water Regimes in Europe* and *Integrated Governance and Water Basin Management*.

Kris Lulofs is a senior research associate and assistant professor at the University of Twente. His recent research focuses on environmental policy strategies and instrumentation, especially in the fields of climate change and water management. His book publications include *Industrial Water Pollution in the Netherlands: A Fee-Based Approach*.

Erna Ovaa is program leader in strategic studies at the Centre for Water Management of Rijkswaterstaat (Ministry of Transport, Public Works and Water Management). She was previously a senior researcher and policy advisor in participatory processes in relation to the European Water Framework Directive (project "Limits to Participation").

Theunis Piersma is professor of animal ecology at the Centre for Ecological and Evolutionary Studies of the University of Groningen and senior researcher at the Royal Netherlands Institute for Sea Research. He is an editor of the *Journal of Avian Biology*, member of the editorial boards of *Current Ornithology* and the *Journal of Ornithology*, and vice chair of the International Wader Study Group (IWSG). His current research focuses on the distributional ecology of migrant shorebirds worldwide.

Jan Rouwendal is associate professor of spatial economics at Free University, Amsterdam. His research focuses on applications of microeconomic theory to housing market and transportation problems and on cost–benefit analyses. He is an academic partner of the Netherlands Bureau for Policy Analysis (CPB) and is a member of the editorial board of *Growth and Change*.

René A. Rozendal is a postdoctoral research fellow in the Advanced Water Management Centre at the University of Queensland, Brisbane, Australia. His PhD research focused on bioelectrochemical conversion processes for energy production at Wetsus, Centre of Excellence for Sustainable Water Technology in Leeuwarden.

Albert E. Steenge is professor of economics at Groningen University. He is coeditor of the journal *Structural Change and Economic Dynamics* and the series *Wirtschaft: Forschung und Wissenschaft*. He is a member of the editorial board of *Economic Systems Research*. His research interests include the economics of regulation and deregulation, and environmental and regional economics.

Hardy Temmink is assistant professor at the Department of Environmental Technology of Wageningen University and theme coordinator at Wetsus, Centre of Excellence for Sustainable Water Technology in Leeuwarden. His recent research focuses on biological as well as physical-chemical wastewater treatment technology with an emphasis on nutrient removal, membrane treatment, and membrane bioreactors.

Jan (P.J.T.) van Bakel is senior hydrologist at the Centre of Water and Climate of Alterra, Wageningen University and Research Centre. From 1990 to 1995, he was employed at the water management consultancy bureau TAUW. His present work focuses on agrohydrology and regional water management in the Netherlands. He has published recently in the *Journal of Water and Land Development* and *Agricultural Water Management*.

Marleen van de Kerkhof is a senior policy scientist at the Institute for Environmental Studies (IVM), Free University, Amsterdam, and is also affiliated with the Department of Research and Strategy of the Port of Amsterdam. She specializes in stakeholder dialogue processes and participatory methodologies in the fields of climate change, energy, and transition processes. She has recently published in *Policy Sciences* and *Technological Forecasting and Social Change*.

Rob van der Veeren is a policy advisor at the Centre of Watermanagement of Rijkswaterstaat (Ministry of Transport, Public Works and Water Management). His current research focuses on economic analyses for the European Union Water Framework Directive.

Wim van Leussen is professor of river basin management at the School of Management and Governance at the University of Twente and senior advisor on water management at the Ministry of Transport, Public Works and Water Management. He is a member of a number of committees on water management in the Netherlands, particularly for the implementation of European water directives and development of a new Dutch flood defense policy.

Marleen (H.F.M.W.) van Rijswick is professor of European and Dutch water law at the Faculty of Law, Institute of Constitutional and Administrative Law, University of Utrecht. She is a member of the Centre for Environmental Law and Policy/Netherlands Institute for the Law of the Sea (CELP/NILOS). Her current research focuses on legal aspects of water management based on the transnational river basin approach.

Henk Voogd was until his death in March 2007, a professor of planning and urban geography at the University of Groningen. He published on a wide range of issues related to environmental and infrastructure planning. His books include *Recent Developments in Evaluation in Spatial Infrastructure and Environmental Planning*, and *Evaluation Methods for Urban and Regional Plans* (with D. Shefer).

Johan Woltjer is associate professor of planning at the Faculty of Spatial Sciences, University of Groningen. His research focuses on spatial planning, regional governance, policy evaluation, and water. His publications have appeared in *Habitat International*, *International Development Planning Review*, *International Planning Studies*, and the *Journal of the American Planning Association*. His recent book is *New Principles in Planning Evaluation*.

Map of the Netherlands

North Sea

Groningen

Leeuwarden

Assen

Zwolle

Haarlem

Amsterdam

The Hague

Utrecht

Eurpoort

Amhem

Rotterdam

's-Hertogenbosch

Germany

Belgium

Maastricht

Introduction

Stijn Reinhard and Henk Folmer

*T*HE NETHERLANDS and water are very closely related. A large part of the country was created by river and sea sediments that were deposited in the delta of four European rivers: the Rhine, Meuse, Scheldt, and Ems. Thus it can be characterized as a delta area, with more than 75% of its water coming into the Netherlands from rivers that cross national boundaries. It is a small country, with a total area of 41,500 square kilometers, of which 7,500 square kilometers is water, including estuaries, main rivers, and lakes (Statistics Netherlands 2008a). The Netherlands was further shaped by its inhabitants as a result of centuries of water level management and land reclamation. It has hundreds of polders, areas of low-lying land in some cases reclaimed from water bodies and protected by dikes, and an extensive and complex system of ditches and waterways regulates groundwater levels in these polders at all times. About a quarter of the Netherlands is below mean sea level (Pilarczyk 2007), where 9 million inhabitants live and two-thirds of the GDP is earned (Deltacommissie 2008; TK 2006). Without flood protection structures in the form of dunes and dikes, about two-thirds of the country would be flooded during storm surges at sea or high discharges in the river (Pilarczyk 2007).

The Netherlands serves as a role model for water policy. The country is well known for its traditional water management in the form of dikes, popularized by the story of Hans Brinker, who put his finger in a dike to prevent a flood. A dramatic transformation in Dutch water policy has been taking place, however, with a move from *keeping the water out* toward *living with water* and *closing the water chain*. Because of the recent changes in objectives and institutional settings, the focus of water policy has shifted from preventing disasters by all technological means toward an approach in which technical and social sciences are combined in a multidisciplinary fashion to optimize the water system. The required changes have led to numerous problems and raised many questions. It is clear that these issues are not restricted to technical approaches; water policy, spatial planning, and social processes until recently have been badly attuned, and interaction with other fields is of utmost importance.

Water Policy in the Netherlands: Integrated Management in a Densely Populated Delta examines various aspects of this paradigm shift, showing that Dutch water management is far more complex than a boy with his finger in a dike. The lessons learned through the experiences of the Netherlands should be extremely useful for other countries, many of which are struggling with similar problems in managing the water system effectively and efficiently and closing the water chain to prevent water pollution. This book will be valuable for those who work in and study comprehensive water management in developed and developing countries. Its objective is to present detailed descriptions and analyses of the many aspects of Dutch water policy to an international audience. It encompasses various issues those involved in water policy and management face with respect to quantity, quality, systems, and chains. The contributors to this book are experts in their fields and include practitioners, policymakers, advisors, and academics from a broad range of backgrounds, covering a wide breadth of topics and disciplines related to water policy and management.

THE NETHERLANDS

Following are descriptions of the geography and population, climate and weather, and political system of the Netherlands to set the scene for the book.

Physical and Social Geography

The Netherlands is located in northwestern Europe and is bordered by the North Sea to the north and west, Belgium to the south, and Germany to the east (see fig. I.1). Although Holland is commonly used as a synonym for the Netherlands, the name actually refers to a region in the west of the country that has been the most important in economic terms for many centuries.

The Netherlands is denesely populated, with more than 16.4 million inhabitants, or 484 people per square kilometer of land (Statistics Netherlands 2008b). The country is popularly known for its windmills, cheese, wooden shoes, dikes, tulips, bicycles, and social tolerance. The country has an international outlook and is a member of the European Union (EU), North Atlantic Treaty Organization (NATO), and Organisation for Economic Co-operation and Development (OECD), among others, and has signed the Kyoto Protocol.

The Netherlands is divided into 12 administrative regions, called provinces. All provinces are divided into municipalities (gemeente), 443 in total (Statistics Netherlands 2008c). The country is also subdivided into water districts, governed by water boards (waterschap), of which 27 existed as of January 1, 2008, each having authority over regional and local water management. The creation of water boards actually predates that of the nation, with the first one established in 1196. In fact, the Dutch water boards are one of the oldest democratic entities in the world today.

Figure I.1 *Map of the Netherlands*

Many economic historians regard the Netherlands as the first thoroughly capitalist country in the world. In early modern Europe, it featured the wealthiest trading city, Amsterdam, and the first full-time stock exchange. As of 2008, the labor force consisted of 8.7 million people, the unemployment rate was 4.3%, and the gross domestic product per inhabitant was 34,600 euros (Eurostat 2008a, 2008b), compared with the European Union average of 24,800 per inhabitant in 2007. The Netherlands has a prosperous and open economy. The Netherlands is headquarters for major corporations involved in food processing (Unilever and Heineken), chemicals (DSM), petroleum refining (Royal Dutch Shell), and electronics and electrotechnical industries (Philips). Slochteren, a municipality in the province of Groningen, has a large natural gas field. A highly mechanized agricultural sector employs 3% of the labor force (LEI/CBS 2008), but provides large surpluses for the food-processing industry and exports. The Netherlands ranks third worldwide in value of agricultural exports, behind only the United States and Brazil. The country's location gives it prime access to markets in the United Kingdom and Germany, with the port of Rotterdam being the largest in Europe. Other important sectors of the economy are international trade and transport.

A remarkable aspect of the low-lying country is its flatness. Hilly landscapes can be found only in the southeastern tip of the country (Zuid-Limburg), where moraines of ancient glaciation still exist in the form of several hilly ridges. About half of its surface area is less than one meter above sea level, and much of it is actually below sea level. An extensive array of dikes and dunes protects these areas from flooding. Numerous massive pumping stations keep the groundwater level in check. A substantial part of the Netherlands, including all of the province of Flevoland and large parts of the provinces of Noord- and Zuid-Holland, have been reclaimed from the water. Such areas are known as polders.

The country is divided into two main parts: north and south of the Rhine, Waal, and Meuse rivers. These rivers function not only as natural barriers, but also as a cultural divide, as evidenced in the different dialects spoken north and south of these "big rivers" and the former religious dominance of Catholics in the south and Calvinists in the north.

Climate and Weather

The predominant wind direction in the Netherlands is southwest. Because of the country's proximity to the North Sea, the Gulf Stream gives it a moderate maritime climate, which is milder than average at latitude 52° north. Generally, summers are cool and winters mild. The annual average temperature in the center of the country is 9.8°C. Figure I.2 shows the averages across the year for De Bilt, a town in the central province of Utrecht that is the seat of the headquarters of the Royal Dutch Meteorological Institute (KNMI).

Precipitation distribution is highly variable. Although the spatial variation in precipitation is small, seasonal variation is more pronounced. The wettest months are in summer and autumn. The heaviest inland showers are in summer, when surface warming is greatest. In the coastal area, maximum precipitation occurs in October and November, as a result of showers developing above the relatively warm waters of the North Sea. Interannual variability is quite large, with the lowest annual amounts about 400 millimeters (mm) and the highest nearly 1,200 mm. The average annual precipitation in De Bilt is 793 mm (KNMI 2002).

The mean annual evapotranspiration for the entire country is approximately 560 mm, with values of 600 mm in coastal areas and 500 mm inland. The seasonal variation is very large, as a result of changes in temperature and solar radiation. The seasonal cycles of precipitation and evapotranspiration create a water surplus in winter and a moisture deficit in summer. In exceptionally dry years, the maximum summer deficit may be as great as 300 mm.

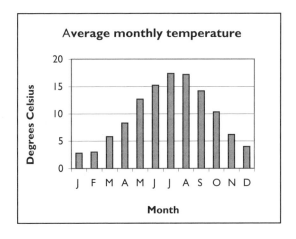

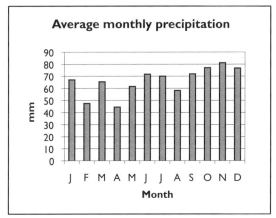

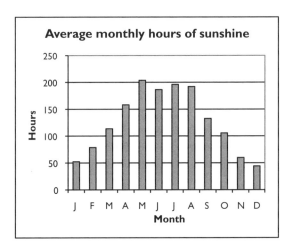

Figure I.2 *Average monthly temperature, monthly precipitation, and monthly hours of sunshine in De Bilt*

The Rhine and Meuse rivers are of great importance for the hydrology of the Netherlands. The characteristics of these two rivers differ greatly. The Meuse is rain-fed, with relatively high peak flows in winter (highest 3,100 cubic meters per second [m^3/sec]) and generally low flows in summer (lowest 0 m^3/sec). The mean discharge at the border is 230 m^3/sec. The Rhine is fed partly by rain and partly by snowmelt from the Swiss Alps. This produces two seasonal peak flows: one in winter (highest 12,500 m^3/sec) and a much lower one in summer originating from snowmelt. The mean discharge of the Rhine at the Dutch-German border is 2,200 m^3/sec.

Political System

The Netherlands has been a parliamentary democracy since 1848, with a monarch as the head of state; before then, it was a republic from 1581 to 1806 and then a kingdom until 1810. In addition, it was part of France between 1810 and 1813. Dutch politics and governance are characterized by a common pursuit of a broad consensus on important issues, both within the political community and in society as a whole. The Dutch government holds the executive power. With the multiparty system, no party has ever held a majority in Parliament since the 19th century, and for that reason, governments consist of political coalitions. The government is responsible to the Dutch Parliament, the Lower and Upper Chambers, or States General, which also has legislative powers. The 150 members of the Lower Chamber are chosen in direct elections every four years or after a government crisis. The members of the provincial assemblies also are directly elected every four years, and they elect the 75 members of the Upper Chamber, which has fewer legislative powers and can merely reject or accept laws, not propose or amend them, as the Lower Chamber can.

Both trade unions and employers' organizations are consulted beforehand in policymaking in the financial, economic, and social arenas. They meet regularly with government in the Social Economic Council. This body advises the government, and its advice cannot be put aside easily.

FRAMEWORK OF WATER SYSTEM MANAGEMENT

This section provides a framework to analyze various aspects of the Dutch water management system, which has to fulfill an array of competing requirements from different users. Governance of the Dutch water infrastructure is highly sophisticated, because many functions that compete with one another need to be reconciled. The presence of big harbors such as Rotterdam requires that waterways and canals be navigable. To this end, waterways were shortened to create effective water systems for shipping, which reduced their storage capacity in case of large discharges. Dutch arable farming, horticulture (e.g., flower bulbs), and dairy farming are intensive and require large quantities of high-quality water in rural areas. Since the 1980s, the importance of other functions in these regions has increased, and they compete with agriculture for water.

Environmental Aspects

The environment is an important issue. Initially, attention was restricted mainly to chemical water quality. Over time, the scope has broadened to now encompass virtually all environmental aspects, including ecological quality of surface water (as in the EU Water Framework Directive, for instance). Because the Netherlands is located downstream of a number of major rivers, it has encountered many water quality problems. These problems became manifest in the 20th century, when the large rivers were polluted by industrial emissions. The regional water system also suffered from a high concentration of nutrients in the form of phosphates from the drainage of household wastewater and water from agricultural land.

As a result of various innovations, such as sewage treatment plants, water quality has substantially improved. Restrictions on the application of manure (e.g., the EU Nitrate Directive) have led to a reduction in nonpoint-source pollution of phosphates and nitrates in canals and rivers, the capillaries of the system. Multiple relationships with the environment are present within policy concerning water quantity and quality, the water chain, and land use. Hence, although no one specific chapter is devoted to the environment, environmental topics are found throughout the entire book.

Competition for Water

In a modern society such as the Netherlands, water demands for human consumption, agriculture, nature, and recreation need to be met simultaneously, and it is necessary to weigh these competing, often conflicting demands for water by various functions. The value of water for the different functions has changed over time. The economic value attached to recreation and nature preservation has increased in recent decades compared with that of traditional activities such as agriculture. For instance, the Dutch nature reserve wetlands require high water levels, but this does not fit well with agricultural water requirements. Intensive agriculture requires fast drainage of water in times of abundant rainfall and needs to have some other form of water available during periods when precipitation is scarce. The various functions that compete for the use of water also have different requirements with respect to quality. For example, nature areas (e.g., the rare bluegrass fields) need water with a very low nutrient concentration, whereas high-quality fish for commercial fisheries require a relatively high phosphate concentration to provide enough food in the form of algae and plants.

From the above examples, it follows that Dutch water management has become increasingly complex. Table I-1 describes this complexity in terms of the effects of measures on the water level (a similar chart can be created for measures affecting water quality). The starting point is a change in functions or policies within the Dutch water system. One of these changes, regarding measures affecting the water level, is presented in the left-hand column of the table. The water system consists of the closely interrelated subsystems of surface water, groundwater, water soils, riverbanks, and vegetation. An intervention in one subsystem (e.g., changing the surface water level) will affect the others. In turn, the affected subsystems influence

Table I-I *Summary of water uses and services in the Netherlands*

Measures affecting water level

Regional water component affected	Water uses and services	Examples of water use
Surface water level	"Dry feet"	Inundation damage to houses, firms, and temporarily unusable infrastructure
	Transport	Shipment of goods
Groundwater level	Agricultural production	Crop production, yield loss of crops because of too-high or too-low groundwater level
Water quality	Industrial production	Groundwater or tap water used in production
	Waste transport	Chemical, biological, thermal water pollution
	Recreation	Aquatic recreation, other outdoor recreation
	Drinking water	Food, bathing
	Nature	Nature products, recreation, nonuse value
	Landscape	Experience value, historic value

Source: Reinhard et al. 2004.

the competition for water uses and services. The consequences of an intervention for all types of water uses and services need to be evaluated and compared, such as by analyzing the costs and benefits of the proposed intervention or change of functions.

The results of this valuation through cost–benefit analysis enable the ex-ante evaluation of the proposed activity or policy (Brouwer and Pearce 2005). Measures will normally affect multiple subsystems. For instance, holding water upstream will lead to higher groundwater levels upstream and a reduction of maximum surface water levels downstream. The construction of nature-friendly networks of ditches on agricultural land will result in a low nutrient concentration in the ditches, but they will hold water for a prolonged period of time in case of heavy precipitation and thus reduce the surface water level.

Current Problems

Climate change and soil subsidence are major threats to the Dutch water system and related subsystems, particularly soil. Sea level rise and increased rainfall over shorter periods of time are predicted (Deltacommissie 2008). Intensive agriculture and expanding urban areas have led to heavier drainage and a reduction of the storage capacity of the soil, causing rainwater to be transported toward surface water more quickly. This dramatically increases the chances of flooding and other problems caused by water. To handle this higher volume of excess water, greater pumping capacity is needed. In summer, however, less precipitation and more evaporation result in water depletion and salinization. The water system is also influenced by various claims on the available space and a changing use of this space. In recent decades, the amount of space available for water storage has been decreasing.

The technological approach to water system management has reached its limits (NRLO 2000). The total expenses of state, provinces, water boards, and municipalities with respect to water were 5.1 billion euros in 2007. The costs in 2007 for flood protection were 600 million euros, for quantitative water management 1.7 billion, and the remaining 2.8 billion was spent predominantly on water quality (LBOW 2008). Considerably larger investments in water management are expected in anticipation of climate change and to meet the objectives of the European directives to improve water quality (Deltacommissie 2008; Ligtvoet et al. 2008).

The dramatic changes in Dutch water management that have taken place can be summarized as a transformation from *keeping the water out* to *living with water* and *closing the water chain*. This shift has raised numerous questions and created many problems. It is clear that these themes are not restricted to a technical approach; the interaction with other disciplines is of utmost importance. Although economics has had a role in Dutch water management since the earliest flood protection, the focus has now shifted from a technological bias toward a situation in which the social sciences (economics as well as other branches) play a more important role.

The Dutch have understood that technological solutions alone will not be sufficient to win the battle against water problems in the long run. Also, in the international arena, particularly the EU and its Water Framework Directive (WFD), economics play a very important and explicit role in the design of river basin plans. The institutional setting of Dutch water policy has been innovative since the formation of water boards in the Middle Ages in order to prevent flooding more effectively and efficiently. The consensus-based decision process has to find new solutions for current problems and challenges, including the implementation of the EU Water Framework Directive. This requires new arrangements among the different institutions responsible for the various aspects of water policy.

OUTLINE OF THIS BOOK

To optimize the benefits for a broad readership, the book is organized into three main parts. The first part provides an overview of Dutch water system management, focusing on problems related to quantity. Water chain management—the management of the entire process of producing good-quality water and wastewater cleaning—is the subject of the second part, which mainly concerns water quality. The final part draws on institutional, governance, and management theories and practices to analyze and further the development of appropriate water policy in the Netherlands.

Part I: Key Issues in Dutch Water System Management

During its long history of combating high water levels and flood risks, the Netherlands developed a number of techniques, such as dikes, to withstand higher tides and defend lives and goods at lower costs. In Chapter 1, de Jonge shows that the sea level has risen and regressed over the last millennia as a result of natural fluctuations, particularly climate changes. From about 2500 BP, the inhabitants have shaped the country by water management. Originally, water policy started locally with the construction of mounds to safeguard properties against flooding. Gradually, this objective was extended to include the reclamation of land. Another major development in Dutch water management described by de Jonge is water quality improvement.

The Dutch control water not only at the macro level, as with dikes, but also at the micro level, such as the water quantity available for crops. The groundwater level has been made favorable for agricultural production over a large part of the Netherlands. Water quantity models were built to optimize water management in the agriculture areas by means of weirs and drains. The physical effects of possible measures are routinely estimated ex-ante to aid in policymaking. In Chapter 2, Heijkers and van Bakel describe a class of hydrological models that facilitate this highly sophisticated type of water management by the water boards. The use of numerical models in water management in the Netherlands is widely accepted because the need for verifiable results is high and many data are available. Another important feature of this class of models is that they offer the opportunity to gain insight into the interaction between water management and land use changes.

The concentration of chemicals in water adversely affects the natural habitat of migrating birds. Mechanical dredging for shellfish in the Dutch Wadden Sea also has caused ecological damage and the loss of shorebird populations dependent on these resources for food. Such losses are hard to reverse. In Chapter 3, Piersma discusses threats to intertidal soft-sediment ecosystems. He shows that mechanical harvesting methods in protected coastal reserves are unsustainable. Because a great positive value is attached to the protection of migrating birds in Dutch society, the government has prohibited mechanical dredging and offered compensation to shellfish fishermen in the Wadden Sea. This case study shows how changes in the valuation of different functions of water lead to changes in Dutch policy. The value of economic exploitation has declined compared with the value of water as a habitat for shorebirds.

Current technical solutions are inadequate for the expected rise in sea levels and land subsidence; new concepts must be developed to combat future floods. In Chapter 4, Bočkarjova et al. review this quintessential issue in Dutch water policy. Since the flooding disasters of 1953, flood control policy has mainly focused on investments such as dike fortification in coastal areas. During the 1990s, a risk of catastrophes due to river floods also became evident. The authors look at the management of such catastrophes, particularly through system risk analysis, which is of growing importance. They also assess a combination of technical, economic, legal, and administrative measures to improve risk control.

Water management in the Netherlands used to be largely technologically driven. Recently, however, the broader socioeconomic aspects of water policy and management are getting more attention. Consequently, knowledge, experience, and information about the economic costs and benefits of Dutch water policy and management have gradually increased. In Chapter 5, Brouwer and van der Veeren discuss these costs and benefits and examine the application of economic principles and methods in Dutch water policy research and integrated policy analysis, including flood control and water quality. They present a brief overview of the use and institutionalization of cost–benefit analysis in the Netherlands, followed by an example investigating costs and benefits of flood control policy for the Meuse. The systematic assessment and reporting of the interaction and dependency between water and the economy provide a starting point for the evaluation and prediction of changes in the water-economy relationship simultaneously

Part II: Water Chain Management and Water Quality

The water chain is made up of drinking-water extraction, production, distribution, and use, as well as wastewater collection, transport, and sewage treatment. Adequate management of the water chain is important from both environmental and economic points of view.

In the 1960s, polluted rivers attracted public attention. Since then, the disposal of chemical industrial waste into rivers has been regulated. A reduction in the discharge of toxic substances and nutrients in the Rhine River upstream of the Netherlands has substantially improved water quality in the country's main river system. Sewage plants further improved the water quality of the regional systems. In the Netherlands, virtually all houses in urbanized areas are linked to the sewage system, which consists of an extensive infrastructure and large-scale high-tech sewage treatment installations that work effectively and efficiently. New technologies expand the possibilities to reduce water sanitation problems and seem to be less expensive than the conventional systems.

Because of a decline in water quality and changing weather patterns, among other things, the efficient and equitable use of water is a subject of growing importance. In Chapter 6, Rouwendal presents an economic analysis of the water chain. He shows that it is useful to apply economic analysis tools to water supply and sewage plants. Water demand is closely related to the production of sewage. From a household perspective, the first can be interpreted as an input and the second as an output, one that cannot be freely disposed of. He introduces concepts of economic analysis and puts these together in a water chain model, covering water supply and sewage treatment, which in the Netherlands are in the hands of public utility companies.

In Chapter 7, Euverink et al. discuss the growing demand for fresh water for human consumption and agricultural and industrial applications in the Netherlands. They assert that this need can be met by recycling water and combining water treatment with the reuse of removed components or with energy generation. Many new water technologies have been developed in the Netherlands, but as yet only a few of these concepts have been put to use, partly because of high costs. Euverink et al. describe, among others, nitrogen and phosphorus removal and recovery and bioelectrochemical conversion processes. A reduction in costs may be achieved through the reuse of energy and minerals and the development of more economical treatment technologies. Demonstration sites are important to test the developed technology.

Part III: Institutional, Governance, and Management Theories and Practices

The governance of water resources has a long tradition in the Netherlands, with its origin in the continual struggle against water. Currently, almost all areas of water are under human control. Water boards were developed in the Netherlands as an efficient governance structure to combat flooding. Dutch governance structures regarding the water system and water chain have developed over time as a result of the increasing scale of control (from localities in the Middle Ages to the EU today) and the growing number of water functions that must be taken into account through integrated water management.

The Netherlands is a highly consensus-based community. In Chapter 8, Kuks examines the major conditions playing a role in the institutional evolution of the Dutch water board model. Water boards were primarily responsible for protection against flooding and management of water in the polders. In recent decades, they have also been combating water pollution. Water boards have a democratic structure and regulatory and taxation authority. The chapter also looks at the changing position of water boards in the Dutch administrative structure. In Chapter 9, van Leussen and Lulofs survey the governance of water resources in the Netherlands. They present a theoretical framework, describe the historical development of water resource governance, and show that changes in socioeconomic and political circumstances affected water policy and the institutional organization of water management. Water resource management is becoming increasingly complex, working with a greater variety of relevant policy fields and a larger number of stakeholders with dedicated governance structures at the international, national, regional, and local levels. Switching among these levels and coupling them for adequate results is one of the main challenges in water management today, requiring multilevel, multiactor, and multiresource governance approaches. Particularly the actual implementation of water policy amid so many interests and sometimes conflicting rules is at the heart of present-day water resource management.

Dutch spatial policy is well developed, and water plays an increasing role in spatial planning. As shown by Voogd and Woltjer in Chapter 10, spatial solutions are necessary to combat the growing water quantity problems. The government objective of spatial solutions is to minimize the chances of flooding downstream in the urbanized and capital-intensive western part of the country in the long term. To prevent flood problems downstream, the water policy document *A Different Approach to Water* (V&W 2000) introduced the quantitative strategy triplet retain-store-discharge. First, water should be held locally in the system by reducing the drainage capacity of land and cities. Second, each region has to expand its own storage capacity. Finally, the water may be discharged to downstream regions.

Water quality has improved since the 1970s, but in many regions, it is not yet sufficient to preserve endangered waterfowl, fish, amphibian, and plant species. The main impetus for a more stringent water quality policy is the EU Water Framework Directive (WFD). The WFD requires that each member state develop a water basin management plan in which it states what measures it will take in the period 2009–2015 to achieve the directive's goals. These goals are based on the potential ecological quality, determined by reference rivers. The way to manage water problems in the Netherlands is based on technical measures and cooperation, sharing responsibilities, money, and efforts. The legal arrangements to facilitate this cooperative and innovative way of working have been of great importance for the successful Dutch struggle against and with water. Van Rijswick looks at the interaction between European and Dutch water law in Chapter 11. She discusses the integration of water legislation in both the EU and the Netherlands, with special focus on the Water Framework Directive, and examines the preparation of new Dutch legislation to implement the WFD.

In Chapter 12, Huitema et al. discuss a wide range of possible methods for involving the public in water management, describing in detail the focus group and citizens' jury. The authors present differences in design and effectiveness, and show how these can be evaluated and integrated from a water manager's perspective. Public participation is increasingly regarded as an important element of a successful democracy. In water management, five goals can be distinguished: raised awareness; improved decisions; increased legitimacy of decisionmaking; better accountability of decisionmaking; and collective learning.

In Chapter 13, Reinhard and Folmer summarize the main conclusions that can be drawn from the various chapters. They also present the main lessons learned from the Dutch experiences in water management and discuss how these lessons can be used in other countries, including developing ones.

REFERENCES

Brouwer, R., and D. Pearce. 2005. *Cost–benefit analysis and water resources management*. Cheltenham, UK: Edgar Elgar.

Deltacommissie. 2008. *Samenwerken met water; Een land dat leeft, bouwt aan zijn toekomst: Bevindingen van de Deltacommissie* [*Working with water; A living country, building on its future: Conclusions of the Deltacommittee*]. Rotterdam: Deltacommissie.

Eurostat. 2008a. www.epp.eurostat.ec.europa.eu/extraction/evalight/EVAlight.jsp?A=1&language=en&root=/theme2/nama/nama_gdp_c (accessed September 18, 2008).

———. 2008b. www.epp.eurostat.ec.europa.eu/extraction/evalight/EVAlight.jsp?A=1&language=en&root=/theme3/lfsi/lfsi_act_a (accessed September 18, 2008).

KNMI (Koninklijk Nederlands Meteorologisch Instituut). 2002. *Klimaatatlas van Nederland; de normaalperiode 1971–2000* [*Climate atlas of the Netherlands in the period 1971–2000*]. Rijswijk, Netherlands: Elmar. www.knmi.nl.

LBOW (Landelijk Bestuurlijk Overleg Water). 2008. *Water in Beeld 2008: Voortgangsrapportage over het waterbeheer in Nederland* [*Water in Focus 2008: Annual report on water management in the Netherlands*]. www.waterinbeeld.nl/pdf/Wib_2008_rapport.pdf (accessed October 10, 2008).

LEI/CBS (Landbouw Economisch Instituut/Centraal Bureau voor de Statistiek). 2008. *Agricultural and horticultural figures 2006*. The Hague and Voorburg, Netherlands: LEI and CBS.

Ligtvoet, W., G. Beugelink, C. Brink, R. Franken, and F. Kragt. 2008. *Kwaliteit voor Later; Ex ante evaluatie Kaderrichtlijn Water* [*Quality for later; Ex-ante evaluation Water Framework Directive*]. Bilthoven, Netherlands: Planbureau voor de Leefomgeving (PBL).

NRLO (Nationale Raad voor Landbouwkundig Onderzoek). 2000. *Over stromen: Kennis- en innovatieopgaven voor een waterrijk Nederland* [*About flooding: Tasks for research and innovation for a water-rich Netherlands*]. NRLO-rapport 2000/4, AWT-advies 45, RMNO no. 147. The Hague: NRLO.

Pilarczyk, K.W. 2007. Flood protection and management in the Netherlands. In *Extreme Hydrological Events: New Concepts for Security*, ed. O.F.Vasiliev, P.H.A.J.M. van Gelder, E.J. Plate, and

M.V. Bolgov, 385–407. NATO Science Series IV: *Earth and Environmental Sciences*, vol. 78. London: Springer.

Reinhard, S., A. Gaaff, J. van Bakel, and K. van Bommel. 2004. *Waarderen van water in een regional watersysteem [Valuing water in a regional watersystem]*. LEI Report 4.04.03. The Hague: LEI.

Statistics Netherlands. 2008a. www.statline.cbs.nl/StatWeb/publication/?VW=T&DM=SLNL&PA= 70262ned&D1=0-1,5,11,18,24,27,31,41&D2=0-12&D3=a&HD=080924-1508& HDR=G2&STB=T (accessed September 18, 2008).

————. 2008b. www.statline.cbs.nl/StatWeb/publication/?VW=T&DM=SLNL&PA=37296 ned&D1=a&D2=0,10,20,30,40,50,(l-1)-l&HD=080918-1504&HDR=G1&STB=T (accessed September 18, 2008).

————. 2008c. www.cbs.nl/nr/exeres/260D1597-1004-42E3-A3E2-C7170220B436.htm? RefererType=RSSItem (accessed September 18, 2008).

TK (Tweede Kamer). 2006. *Second Chamber of Parliament, letter of the state secretary of the Ministry of Transport, Public Works and Water Management*. 27625 no. 79. The Hague: SDU.

V&W (Ministerie van Verkeer en Waterstaat). 2000. *Anders omgaan met water: Waterbeleid in de 21e eeuw; Kabinetsstandpunt [A different approach to water: Water policy in the 21st century; Cabinet's standpoint]*. The Hague: V&W.

Part I

KEY ISSUES IN DUTCH WATER SYSTEM MANAGEMENT

CHAPTER 1

From a Defensive to an Integrated Approach

Victor N. de Jonge

PRESENT WATER MANAGEMENT policy and practice in the Netherlands have been heavily influenced by a combination of the geological history of the country and the activities carried out by its inhabitants since about 2500 BP (years before present). The history of Dutch water policies began when the inhabitants of the coastal and floodplain areas tried to safeguard themselves and their livestock by building and living atop dwelling mounds. This was followed by the defensive and offensive periods, during which dikes were built, peat was excavated, and land was reclaimed for safety, living space, and agriculture. Quantitative water policy began in the 1200s, when farmers started organizing to combat flooding. Since then, local, and later also regional, water boards were formed. In the late 1960s, qualitative water policy was added to the existing quantitative policy. Two decades later, in the late 1980s, the focus of qualitative and quantitative water policies broadened to include the protection of aquatic ecosystems and sustainable economic development.

This chapter describes the geological history of the Netherlands, the impact of humans on its aquatic environments, and the history of water management in the country. It provides the foundation for more detailed discussions in the chapters to follow.

GEOLOGICAL HISTORY

For a full understanding of the development of the Netherlands' water policies, knowledge of the country's origin and recent geological history is necessary. A combination of erosion, transport, and sedimentation processes created the basis for what is now the Netherlands. These processes were governed by wind, rivers, and the sea and were active during periods of marine transgressions (inundation of land due to a relative sea level rise) and regressions, in concert with the formation of ice sheets during glaciations and their melting in interglacial periods.

During the Pliocene epoch, between 2,500,000 and 2,000,000 BP, the present area of the Netherlands was mainly a seabed. Around 200,000 BP, in the Saalian glaciation, the southern part of the region consisted of a polar desert (tundra), while the northern part was completely covered by an ice sheet. Important glacial depositions occurred during this period. After the melting of the gigantic Saalian ice sheet in the interglacial period known as the Eemian, an area was left containing drumlins (hills of glacial drift), small and large stones, gravel, sand, till, boulder clay, and glacial water basins (de Mulder et al. 2003). The coldest period occurred circa 18,000 BP, during the end of the last glaciation in the Weichselian period. The entire North Sea area was a polar desert where, in addition to the previous role of water, eolian sediment transport (carried by the wind) was important.

The European shoreline of the shallow North Sea area was shaped during the subsequent melting of the ice sheet and then inundation of seawater from what is now the northern North Sea and in the south through what is now the Strait of Dover (Ingólfsson n.d.). A relief-rich deltaic landscape developed, featuring rivers, moraine deposits, drumlins, gravel, sand, till, boulder clay, and loess derived from areas other than the Netherlands. The interaction among these elements, the wind, and the ongoing rapid sea level rise, a concomitant marine transgression, resulted in new marine and fluvial deposits. In addition, favorable conditions for the growth of wetland vegetations created the basis for future peat formation. The development of the North Sea shoreline between 9000 and 7800 BP, at the beginning of the Holocene, shows an ongoing fast marine transgression in the area now known as the Southern Bight. Between 8700 and 8300 BP, the British Isles became separated from the mainland of the European continent. The Dutch territory was then the area where the sea met some of the main European rivers.

It was here, under increasing human influence and circumstances of sea level rise, tides, and river discharges, in concert with the growth of vegetation, that the landscape evolved into a dynamic coastal and delta area consisting of peat bogs and moors. According to Zagwijn (1991), these developments (see fig. 1.1) occurred over a relatively short period of 7,000 years. The post–Weichselian Dutch area changed from an open coast, with islands and tidal inlets connected to tidal flat water basins (5300 BP), to the mainly closed sandy coastline of today. A sea level rise between 7000 and 4000 BP inundated the lowest parts of the present Dutch territory, creating large lagoon and tidal flat systems fringed by extensive salt marshes (7000 to 5300 BP). Because of the ongoing sea level rise, this period was followed by further inundations. In the meantime, large peat bogs and moors formed on top of the Pleistocene sediments (3000 BP). Often marine clay was deposited on top of the peat and salt marshes, serving as a basis for the development of new salt marshes.

Between 3000 and 2000 BP, the sea level showed stagnation and sometimes even a slight temporal decrease, indicating both regression and transgression periods. The reduction in the rate of sea level rise allowed for important sand depositions in the main tidal channels that connected the estuaries and lagoons with

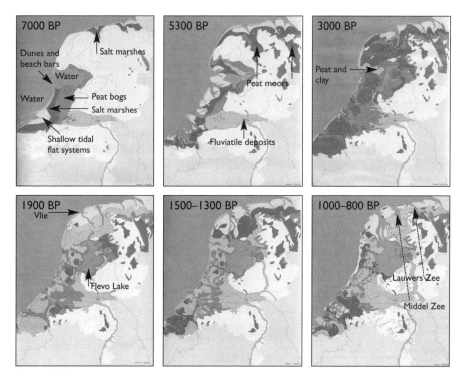

Figure 1.1 *Development of the Dutch area during the Holocene*

Source: Maps reproduced from Zagwijn 1991 with permission from Sdu Uitgeverij, 's-Gravenhage, the Netherlands.

the sea, diminishing the role of the tidal inlets. It also permitted the spread of vegetation to cover extensive coastal wetlands, contributing to the modification of the landscape and serving as the basis for later peat formations. Part of the former complex of estuaries and lagoons, such as the centrally situated Flevo Lake (later named the Almere; fig. 1.1), became completely isolated from the sea. At the same time, the western coast started to develop into one extensive single beach bar, extending to what is now the Vlie tidal inlet (fig. 1.1). The Wadden Sea was also created. While a long, dune-rich coastal barrier was forming in the western part of the country, a new breakthrough occurred in the north, by which the freshwater Flevo Lake became connected to the sea again (de Mulder et al. 2003). Permanent human habitation in the coastal area was presumably possible from 2700 BP onward.

After about 2000 BP, peat formation stopped as a result of drainage of the peat swamps both naturally, via the channel systems created during former sea inundations, and because of human activities related to cultivation and peat excavation (de Mulder et al. 2003). The ultimate result was that circa 1700 BP, the sea inundated deeply into the coastal part of the country. A combination of peat excavation to obtain sea salt, peat erosion, natural drainage, peat oxidation and compaction (surface lowering), and large-scale erosion changed the southwestern region of the Netherlands from a peat-rich area into a system poor in peat but rich in channels and intertidal sand- and mudflats (de Mulder et al. 2003).

WATER POLICY IN THE PAST

When the river floodplains and coastal areas were first inhabited, water policy was nonexistent. Any action to safeguard people from flooding was realized locally by small, solitary groups of people and on an event-to-event basis rather than following an agreed master plan. This situation changed in the Middle Ages, when step by step the first flood defense measures were developed.

The Dwelling Mound Period

The first inhabitants of the coastal and river floodplain areas had no means to defend themselves against the sea and therefore chose natural elevations in an attempt to find safe living areas. This was, however, difficult to realize when living in the middle of a river wetland or one consisting of coastal marshes and peat swamps. Initially, inhabitants actively elevated their own living areas for further protection. Around 2500 BP, they began to create dwelling mounds, basically human-made hills on which hamlets or small villages were often built. A marine transgression that started about 2550 BP served as the impetus for building this first generation of dwelling mounds. A second generation of mounds was built during another transgression in the late Roman period (1750 to 1400 BP). This was followed by two more generations of dwelling mounds, of which the last one dates from circa 1000 BP. These mounds basically consisted of every type of waste from their inhabitants. Very nice dwelling mounds can still be found along the coast in the north and on the river floodplains of the south and southeast where the Rhine River enters Dutch territory. The highest dwelling mound, part of which still exists, is the Frisian Hogebeintum in the north, which reached nearly 9 meters above the surface.

Remarkable contrasts existed in the Netherlands 2,000 years ago. In the north, the local inhabitants focused on basic agricultural activities and constructed technologically simple dwelling mounds as a safety measure. At the same time, in the south, the Romans modified the natural water network by connecting main rivers via newly dug canals. Although this was done chiefly for navigational purposes related to trade and transport of their legions, these technological modifications heavily influenced the water distribution over the area. The Roman Drusus and his son built the Drusus Canal, or Fossa Drusiana, which connected the lower Rhine with what was until then a very small stream flowing north, the present river IJssel (see fig. 1.2). Huisman (1995) believes that Drusus also constructed a canal connecting Flevo Lake with the coastal area in the north and what is now the Wadden Sea. The Romans also built a dam to increase the flow of the IJssel, which now discharges more than 10% of the total Rhine water to the north.

The importance of the Dutch part of the Rhine River significantly decreased in 70 AD, when Claudius Civilis wanted the Waal tributary (fig. 1.2) to become

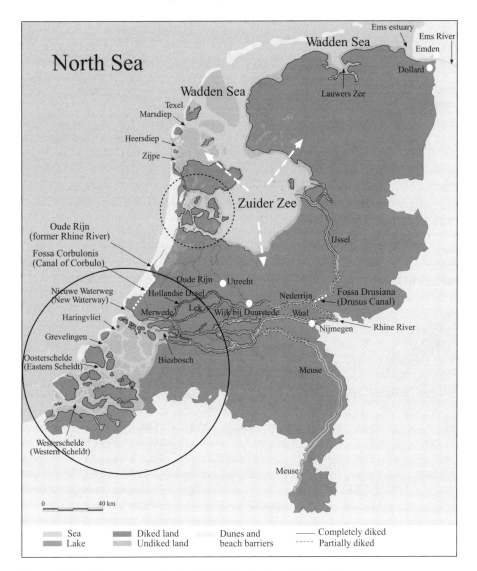

Figure 1.2 *Dike system in the Netherlands circa 1250 AD*

Notes: Dashed lines on the map indicate undiked areas around 1250 (750 BP), and arrows those hit by the 1916 storm surge in the Zuyder Zee. The large, solid circle encloses the area affected during the 1953 storm surge in the southwestern part of the Netherlands, and the smaller, dashed circle the region with big lakes that were emptied during the 17th century.

Sources: Information partly from www.livius.org. Geographic map reproduced from de Mulder et al. 2003 with permission from Wolters-Noordhoff BV, Groningen, Netherlands, and TNO.

more important than the lower Rhine. This decision might have been related to the place where Claudius Civilis lived, the civil settlement Noviomagum (Nijmegen), on the bank of the Waal River and also where the Roman legionary fortress was situated. The river flow was changed by the construction of a dam functioning as a water divider. Since then, the Waal has been the most important Rhine tributary in the Netherlands.

In 47 AD, the Roman general Gnaeus Domitius Corbulo ordered the construction of another navigation canal in the western part of the country, the Fossa Corbulonis (Canal of Corbulo). About 15 meters wide and 3 meters deep, this canal was built to connect the lower Rhine system (Oude Rijn) with that of the lower Meuse (fig. 1.2). Basically, part of this canal still exists as Vliet (Rijn-Schie Canal).

The Defensive Period

In 1999, an archaeological team lead by J.G.A. Bazelmans discovered in Peins (near Franeker in Friesland) the remains of a 40-meter-long dike dating to 2100–2200 BP, the oldest dike remnant ever found in the Netherlands. Created from sod, the dike was a small one, presumably made to protect a piece of low-lying agricultural land on a salt marsh. It demonstrates that the dike-building technique was already practiced on a small scale more than 2,000 years ago.

Large-scale and well-organized dike building started much later, circa 1100 BP. This process was primarily stimulated by widespread peat excavations and accompanying drainage activities necessary for access. Sovereign lords such as the Bishop of Utrecht gave out permits and encouraged extensive cultivation of the peat moor "wildernesses" in the western and northern parts of the country. The cultivation was accompanied by the excavation of large amounts of peat for fuel and resulted in major erosion of the former coastal and inland peat swamp areas. Facilitated by the human activities, the freshwater Flevo Lake extended to the east, while peat erosion in the north improved the lake's connection with the sea (see fig. 1.1; lower panels 1900–800 BP). Not only were lakes formed, but considerable surface lowering (up to three meters) occurred as well, because the human-driven dewatering of the peat swamps led to further compaction and consequent surface lowering and oxidation of the organic material. When this human activity started around 1100 BP, the average height of the peat layers was three meters above mean sea level; by about 500 to 600 years later, the average elevation had been reduced to mean sea level. This enormous human-induced decrease in surface level forced the inhabitants to further increase their efforts in building efficient drainage systems with free water runoff to the sea. The so-called cultivations of the peat moor "wildernesses" thus basically started a never-ending struggle to maintain dry land in what is now the Netherlands. The necessity to have dry land for human habitation and cattle grazing in combination with the ongoing oxidation and compaction of the peat-rich underground of most of the country created an imbalance. The present formation of new peat is close to zero and thus unimportant.

Initially, the water could run off freely. Starting around 500 BP, however, because of the ongoing surface lowering, watermills had to be built to pump the water out to the sea. This illustrates that the water problem in the Netherlands is not new and is mainly related to human activity and definitely not just due to climate change. The surface lowering of the area not only had consequences for the local water drainage systems, but also made the coastal zone of the country ever more vulnerable to inundations by the sea. Storm events led to fragmentation of the coastal area, a situation that was further worsened by socioeconomic circumstances and wars. The result of the fragmentation between 1000 and 800 BP can be seen in figure 1.1. Between 1100 and 1000 BP, three new breaches occurred in the previously closed coastline in the north—Marsdiep, Heersdiep, and Zijpe—and two new ones in the south, Haringvliet and Grevelingen (see fig. 1.2).

The Offensive Period

By around 1250 AD (750 BP; see fig. 1.2), large parts of the Netherlands were protected by dikes. Only in the higher elevated areas near the present German border were the rivers not diked. Yet despite the system of dikes, the country was not safeguarded from flooding. After 1250, flooding with dramatic effects still occurred on a frequent basis, including the years 1277, 1287, 1404, 1421, 1446, 1468, 1509, 1530, 1532, 1552, 1570, and 1584. These floods resulted in large areas of land being temporarily or permanently lost. Much of this can be attributed to bad or even improper technical dike maintenance; wrong priorities, in that dike maintenance was put too low on the agenda of the organizations responsible for a region's protection against flooding; and local quarrels or wars, as in the creation of the present Dutch Dollard area, part of the Ems estuary (fig. 1.2). In their historical treatment, Stratingh and Venema (1855, *68*) describe the factors leading to the formation of the Dollard: the ground on which the dikes were built was peaty and unstable, the seas sometimes rose very high, and governors responsible for dike maintenance disagreed with each other, resulting in poor dike condition. All these aspects led to the bursting of the Ems dike near Jansum opposite Emden (fig. 1.2) on January 13, 1277. A second catastrophic flood occurred later that year, on December 25. The local community was not able to restore the dike, and on December 14, 1287, a third big flood occurred. Within 10 years' time, an area of more than 300 square kilometers of land was lost, transformed into a tidal water body of which the present 100-square-kilometer Dollard is the remainder.

The large-scale peat excavations in the Netherlands changed the coastal parts of the country from a peat landscape into a brackish tidal, sand- and mud-containing area and the Zuider Zee, (fig. 1.2) which is the extension of the former Flevo Lake. Originally the Zuider Zee had very long channel connections to the sea (fig. 1.1) and a collection of islands that are partly based on or connected to the drumlins and boulder clay–rich areas. In the northeast, in Friesland, the Boorne Basin, Middel Zee, and Lauwers Zee were formed by sea inundations (see fig. 1.1, *1000–800* BP panel). By building dikes, the local population was able to reclaim bit by bit the Boorne Basin and Middel Zee before 1600, but not the large Zuider Zee and Lauwers Zee (fig. 1.2).

Over time, the area near the mouth of the Meuse River in the southwest also changed dramatically (see the changes in rivercourse in figs. 1.1 and 1.2). The extensive former peat swamp areas in the southwest were already replaced between

1500 and 800 BP by a collection of islands (see figs. 1.1 and 1.2). In between the islands, intertidal flat systems developed. The mouth of the Rhine River moved so far to the south that it joined that of the Meuse. On the order of the Bishop of Utrecht in the first part of the 12th century, the course of the Rhine near Utrecht was rerouted to prevent the yearly "wet feet" in the town and its surroundings (as is still happening in places such as Cologne, Germany). The Rhine was dammed near the present town of Wijk bij Duurstede, and the water diverted into what are now the Kromme Rijn (further seaward, the Oude Rijn) and Lek River (see fig. 1.2). As a result of these infrastructural changes, the former river course lost importance. These changes have been beneficial to the later development of Rotterdam's harbors (cf. figs. 1.2 and 1.4), because the Lek, the "modern Rhine," flows along this city.

The peat excavations for fuel and salt continued and not only affected the landscape further, but also led to disasters for the inhabitants. An example of mismanagement related to peat excavation was that in the southwestern part of the country, this activity was carried out up to the foot of the sea dike, thus directly undermining its foundations. This was the main reason for the catastrophic effect of the St. Elizabeth flood during a storm on the night of November 18–19, 1421. The storm and related flood drowned a low-lying area of 300 square kilometers near the town of Dordrecht (see fig. 1.4). Centuries later, this area acquired fame as one of the most important freshwater tidal systems in Europe, named Biesbosch.

Starting in the 13th century, centrally organized protection against flooding by the government became one of the most important issues in the Netherlands.

MODERN WATER POLICY

It became clear that the protection of the country against flooding had failed, and that a different organization and better measures were required to safeguard the country from this risk. Monasteries especially took the lead in this process, and this gave rise to the foundation of organizations that would later become water boards and an increasing role of the central administration. The continuing involvement of the central administration in combination with an improved organization to prevent flooding also resulted in strongly improved strategies and technical measures, which together ultimately led to the development of the Dutch water policy strategies of today.

Development of Quantitative Water Management

Because of frequent catastrophic flooding of both rivers and the sea, it became evident that coordinated actions were required to prevent further loss of land. After the main engineering works of the Romans about 2,000 years ago, the monasteries started to play a major role in organizing the local dike building and related land draining around 1200 AD. Small organizations of farmers, often managed by the monasteries, were active at this time to combat the storm-related flooding. This development of the organization and management of the flood defense can be considered the start of structural quantitative water management in the Netherlands. These small, local organizations also formed the historical basis for the present modern water boards. Large-scale and sophisticated dike building accompanied by small-scale land reclamations began during this period. After 1480, stimulated by economic developments and flourishing international trade, dike building was professionalized and was now done by specialists and no longer by local farmers.

The first real water board in the Netherlands was founded in 1255 under the name Rijnland. It consisted of rich and powerful inhabitants who were led by the baljuw, the local administrator and judge, on behalf of the duke, Graaf Willem II of Holland. This administrative body also managed lower organizations known as "trades," which collectively were responsible for maintenance of the local dike systems. The existence of such local water boards was, however, no guarantee for success. Often governors had to intervene to guarantee the implementation of the measures necessary for flood prevention. Starting in 1504, quantitative water control was centralized when Philip I ("the Handsome") of Habsburg and his son Emperor Karel V took charge of the process, because they considered flood defense and quantitative water control as too important to leave to local people or water boards. Local authorizations were taken over by the central national administration, although the water boards retained some influence in the decisionmaking process. When, in the 17th century, trade with the Baltic states, Asia, and the West became a financially successful enterprise, foreign cash flow allowed for a definite policy change from defensive to offensive water management. The need for new land, the enormous amount of trade activities with positive cash flow, the combination of land dewatering and increasing sea level, and the concomitant decrease in land surface elevation strongly stimulated technical developments for maintaining dry land. These activities were all related to water pumping by windmills, because much lower land level no longer guaranteed free runoff of surface water. During this period, windmills were used on a large scale.

After these technical innovations, because of economic factors at the national level during the eighteenth and early nineteenth centuries, little changed in terms of water management for a long period of time, and the landscape in the Netherlands remained basically the same. The foundation on May 24, 1798, of a very influential technical governmental authority, the Rijkswaterstaat, however, marked the start of a complete and thorough transformation of the Netherlands landscape. At the beginning of the 19th century, Rijkswaterstaat initiated drastic changes in the landscape with the planning and subsequent construction of new infrastructure in the form of railroads, canals, and roads (Bosch and van der Ham 1998; Lintsen 1998). The completed infrastructure immediately led to the local development of urban and industrial areas, which began the still ongoing fragmentation of the original Netherlands landscape.

Technical Developments between the 10th and 20th Centuries. Originally small dikes were built by piling up sods. Over time, several types of substratum for dike building were applied, including clay, mud, reed, eelgrass, wood, or combinations thereof. The facing of cylindrical wooden piles as a technique to defend the coast against any form of erosion by flowing water and waves was widely developed along the Dutch coast. From the 15th century onward, windmills were developed and used to create new land areas or reclaim lost land by emptying lakes. Large inland lakes such as the Schermer, Beemster, Purmer, and Wormer in the western part of the country (province Noord-Holland) were transformed into land by pumping out the water (the dashed circle indicates the lake area in fig. 1.2).

After the introduction of the shipworm (*Teredo navalis*) in 1725 by wooden vessels from Asia, an explosive population growth of the species occurred in the brackish and marine waters of the European and thus also the Dutch coastal zone. These wood-boring bivalves caused severe damage, and by 1730, their spread led to a real disaster, because all the wooden structures with a function in flood defense were completely perforated and had been dramatically weakened. This led to the replacement of wood by stone as a new, and still existing, element in the coastal defense. At the end of the 18th century, another novelty was the introduction of "mattresses," an underwater gauze network constructed from willow twigs and covered by stones, as a mean to protect the dike foundations from erosion by currents and waves. To reduce dike "washover" during storm surges, the wave energy was reduced by rows of poles placed in the dikes. In addition, between 1906 and 1936, small, concrete Muralt walls were built on top of existing dikes in some areas as further protection against washover. These measures were taken to avoid reconstruction of the entire dike, which would have led to a significant widening of its foot to maintain stability.

The Period of Big Closures. During a period when politicians and the private sector were discussing how to obtain more valuable land for agriculture and better protect the country from flooding, two politically critical storm surges occurred. The first flood was in 1916, hitting the former Zuider Zee area, and the second in 1953, in mainly the southwestern part of the country (see fig. 1.2). These two floods were determinants in the further geographic development of the Netherlands.

The Zuider Zee flood of January 14, 1916, led to the final decision to execute the reclamation of the entire area. On June 13, 1918, the Dutch Parliament passed a bill to start the reclamation, known as the Zuider Zee works. The process started in 1919 and was completed in 1932 after finalizing the main, 32-kilometer-long closure dam called Afsluitdijk (see fig. 1.3). In 1929, while the closure of the Zuider Zee was still in progress, the Department of Waterways and Public Works (Rijkswaterstaat, which is still part of the Ministry of Public Works, Transport and Water Management) started to investigate the reclamation of the Biesbosch, formed by the November storm surge in 1421 and now a magnificent freshwater tidal area.

A further study in 1934 showed, however, that this would have catastrophic consequences for the rest of the area, because the strength and height of the dikes were insufficient to cope with the expected increase in water height. A survey previously carried out in 1928 had led to the same conclusion. Both surveys indicated that something definitely had to be done about the condition of the dikes along the lower rivers. As an initial temporary measure, the Rijkswaterstaat decided to construct inexpensive concrete Muralt walls on top of dikes with insufficient waterholding capacity. Between 1906 and 1935, more than 120 kilometers of dikes in

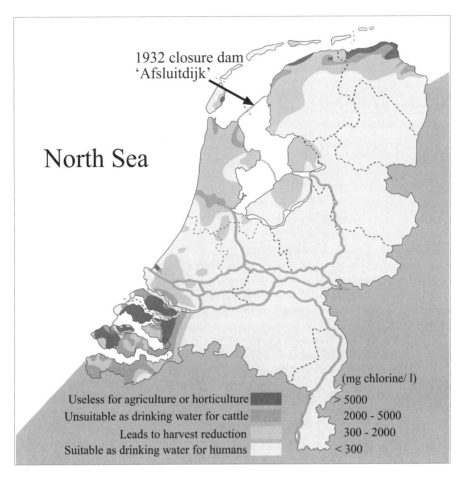

1932 closure dam 'Afsluitdijk'

North Sea

(mg chlorine/ l)

Useless for agriculture or horticulture	> 5000
Unsuitable as drinking water for cattle	2000 - 5000
Leads to harvest reduction	300 - 2000
Suitable as drinking water for humans	< 300

Figure 1.3 *Distribution of chlorinity in the groundwater of the Netherlands territory*

Source: Map reproduced with permission from Deltaworks Online Foundation, Sabine van Buuren, www.deltawerken.com.

Schouwen, Zuid-Beveland, and along the lower Rhine in Hollands Diep and Har-ingvliet (see fig. 1.4 for locations) were heightened.

The study service continued to emphasize the need to heighten the dikes but was unable to get political support. Meanwhile, in both the north and south (see fig. 1.3), the agricultural sector was coping with an increasing salt concentration in the groundwater, which was very costly to the farmers. Because of the importance of agriculture at that time, in an attempt to garner political support for the dike improvements, the study service changed its focus from flood defense to solving the agricultural salt problem. Interestingly enough, the solution for the agricultural sector was based on exactly the same plans as those for the dike improvements. The problem of increasing salt intrusion in the southwest was caused by the ongoing

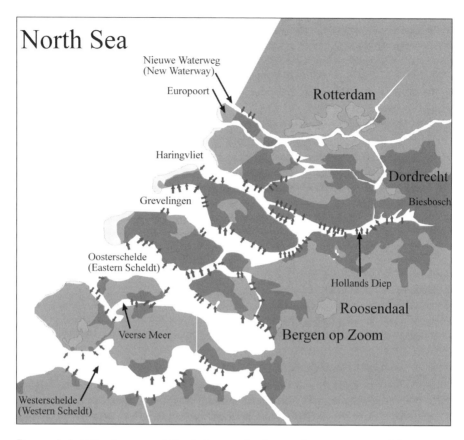

Figure 1.4 *Dike bursts and flooded areas in the southwestern part of the Netherlands as a result of the flood of January 31, 1953*

Note: Arrows indicate dike bursts, and flooded areas are in dark gray.
Source: Map reproduced with permission from Deltaworks Online Foundation, Sabine van Buuren, www.deltawerken.com.

deepening of the navigation channels, necessary for the further development of Rotterdam's harbors (fig. 1.4) but disastrous for arable farming.

Another problem, not recognized at the time, was that the deepening of navigation channels in estuaries affected the local gravitational water circulation. This in turn stimulated not only the upstream transport or flux of seawater, but also the transport and accumulation of seaborne mud in the river mouth at the low salinity zone. It was here, at the areas with the highest mud accumulation in the water, that Rotterdam's harbors developed (de Jonge and de Jong 2002).

The 1953 storm surge heavily affected the southwestern part of the Netherlands (the many dike bursts are indicated by arrows and the flooded areas by dark gray in fig. 1.4). Immediately after the extensive flooding, the first Delta Commission was created and charged with the task to safeguard this part of the country from future flooding (see de Haan and Haagsma 1984). The commission initially advised the construction of a movable storm surge barrier in the Hollandse IJssel (Dutch IJssel). It then developed a master plan to safeguard the area from further problems by closing all the tidal inlets except the Westerschelde (Western Scheldt) and Nieuwe Waterweg (New Waterway), the latter of which also got a movable barrier (see fig. 1.5; for locations of areas, see figs. 1.2 and 1.4).

In 1958, the government agreed on the Delta Law, which enabled the execution of the first Dutch Delta Plan and called for the reinforcement of all the national dikes and the closure of nearly all the former sea arms and estuarine areas

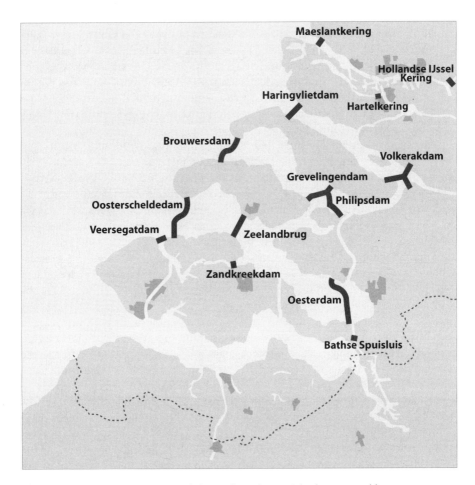

Figure 1.5 *The final design of the Delta Plan, with three movable storm surge barriers, one bridge, and nine dams*

Source: Map reproduced with permission from Deltaworks Online Foundation, Sabine van Buuren, www.deltawerken.com.

in the southwestern part of the country. This would lead to a dramatic shortening of the coastline, which, along with a nationwide increase in height and width of the sea dikes, would result in a much more effective coastal defense system than had existed before. Safety standards were dramatically strengthened to an accepted burst risk of the dikes up to 1 in 10,000 years. The closure of the sea arms would also greatly reduce the salt content of the lower rivers and groundwater by increasing the freshwater discharge via the Nieuwe Waterweg. Finally, as much land as possible would be reclaimed for agriculture.

The Delta Plan as implemented differed significantly from the original, however. Gaining more land for agriculture was no longer a goal, replaced by the formation of major freshwater basins: the Grevelingen and large parts of the Oosterschelde (Eastern Scheldt) (for locations of areas, see figs. 1.2 and 1.4). A powerful lobby consisting of scientists, environmentalists, recreational groups, bird societies, and fishermen ultimately led to the decision to keep the Grevelingen "salt" and not to close the Oosterschelde by a dam, but to build a storm surge barrier allowing the tide to go in and out. The final part of the Delta Plan was the construction in 1997 of the movable Maeslantkering (Maeslant barrier), in the mouth of the Nieuwe Waterweg (fig. 1.5). Once the plan had been implemented, the southern part of the Netherlands was declared protected against the marine influence, but only for the time being (see below).

The closures definitely provided safety against floods but also resulted in unforeseen environmental problems. With the disappearance of the tide, the Haringvliet–Hollands Diep area, upstream of the Haringvlietdam and Volkerakdam (for locations of areas, see fig. 1.5), became a sink for contaminated riverborne sediments and associated phosphorus. The Grevelingen area, between the Brouwersdam and Grevelingendam, initially showed an exponential increase in eelgrass (*Zostera marina*) beds. These beautiful underwater meadows were widely appreciated, but after some time they collapsed for still unknown reasons. The Oosterschelde area, between the storm surge barrier known as the Oosterscheldedam and the Oesterdam, exhibited large-scale erosion of intertidal flats, with a significant decrease in the primary production and widespread deterioration of the eelgrass there. The navigation route between Westerschelde and the Rhine, east of the Oesterdam, developed extensive blooms of blue-green algae (Cyanobacteria). In 2007, it was decided to flush this area again with Cyanobacteria-free estuarine water. The area between Veersegatdam and Zandkreekdam (Veerse Meer) had excessive growth of sea lettuce (*Ulva* sp.) and deterioration of eelgrass beds, in combination with strong eutrophication-related problems such as low oxygen values. This lake has recently been reconnected to the Oosterschelde to combat these unforeseen problems.

The original political attitude, before 1974, was that after the completion of the Delta Plan in the southwest, the next step should be the further protection of the Dutch population by closing off and reclaiming all or parts of the Wadden Sea in the north (the area between the barrier islands and main coast in figs. 1.2 and 1.3), which would provide additional coastal defense because of significant shortening of the coastline. In 1970, the Mazure Committee was appointed and commissioned to study all the possibilities. The committee's report (Waddenzeecommissie 1974) was negative on nearly every aspect related to possible dam building or closures in the Wadden Sea. One of the most important arguments was the value of the sea as a natural area, which should be maintained for nature itself as well as forthcoming human generations (cf. the goals of all the EU directives below). This advice was a milestone in Dutch history, resulting in the environment as an issue temporarily gaining in importance and attention, until 2000. Because of this decision, all the sea dikes in the north had to meet the delta requirements and therefore had to be heightened and broadened. The necessity of the first Delta Plan was proven on November 1, 2006, when the water in the Ems estuary, in the northeast, reached a level never before recorded, at 4.84 meters above Dutch ordinance level and about 30 centimeters above the former record of January 28, 1901.

Attention also has focused on the main rivers. Several recent high river floods and near floods demonstrated that the river dikes also need reinforcement. This led to the declaration of Arles in 1995, which was to draft an action plan on flood control measures in the Rhine River basin. During a new convention on the Rhine in 1998, an action plan on flood defense was presented, and it entered into force on January 1, 2003. In the Netherlands, it was called the Delta Plan Main Rivers. The main proposals were that the rivers be widened and deepened. Further, secondary channels would be created to increase the discharge capacity during high river discharges. Attention was not restricted to the Rhine and other main rivers; rather, the plan covered the entire water network, from these big flows to the smallest ditches, pivotal in the Dutch network. It called for the creation of new wetlands to serve as overflow systems during wet periods, local widening and deepening of small and large waterways, and large-scale dike improvements. Except for the widening of the Waal River near Nijmegen (for location, see fig. 1.2), all parts of the plan have been realized.

Since the completion of the first Delta Plan and the Delta Plan Main Rivers, debate has again centered on where to go with coastal defense. Several options have been considered. One is to further increase the height of the dikes. Another is not to increase the height of each primary sea dike, but to build another one behind it and use the space between the double dikes for retaining any water that washes over. An experiment with the double dike system started in 2007.

While the first Delta Plan was still under execution, the Rijkswaterstaat prepared the *First National Policy Memorandum on Water Management* (1968). Although this document strongly focused on quantitative water management, and considered the effects of deepening the navigation channels and how to reduce the salt intrusion for the sake of agriculture, it also made some remarks on water quality. At this time, water quality concerns mainly centered on adequate oxygen content, coli bacteria as a quality measure for bathing water, biological oxygen demand to indicate pollution with organic matter, and radioactive substances.

Development of Qualitative Water Management

Qualitative elements in coastal management issues can be subdivided into physical, chemical, biological, and ecological aspects. In this section, each will be treated in isolation as well as in combination. The physical and chemical components can be considered as setting the boundary conditions for ecological functioning, the results of which have to be judged by biological quality.

The Start of International Cooperation to Combat Pollution of the Rhine. The final act of the 1815 Congress of Vienna settled the future boundaries of the European continent. This act formed the legal basis for founding the Central Commission for Navigation on the Rhine and established the Rhine River internationally as a navigable waterway (Frijters and Leentvaar 2003). The first laws governing navigation on the Rhine date from 1831. As a regulatory body, this commission was not yet involved in real present-day water management, but it can be considered the start of it. Modern water management in western Europe, the Netherlands included, began in the early 1900s with some focus on quantitative physical aspects such as river discharges, water height, and current velocity.

Between 1831 and the early 1900s, little attention was paid to chemical and biological water quality aspects. But then, around 1935, salmon vanished entirely from the Rhine River. The water tasted salty and often had a carbolic acid smell. By the mid-20th century, the river had clearly lost all its original ecological functions and mainly served as a canal for navigation and a depository for the discharge of untreated organic waste, nutrients, and human-produced chemical compounds.

In 1950, the International Commission for the Protection of the Rhine against Pollution (ICPR) was established, and it was formalized during the Bern Convention of April 29, 1963. Its main tasks were to conduct research on pollution and define appropriate measures to the governments involved in order to reduce the pollution and prepare intergovernmental regulations. This led to the first Rhine Ministers' Conference in 1972, which resulted in charging the ICPR with elaborating conventions to reduce chemical and chlorine pollution. The ministers further decided to equip future power stations with cooling towers and instruct the ICPR to draft a long-term working program on pollution of the Rhine River. The European Economic Community (EEC) became a formal partner in 1976. In 1987, the ministers of the Rhine states adopted the implementation of the Rhine Action Program, and in 1998, a new, now EU-wide, treaty was adopted to protect the river. The document was ratified in 2000, and since then, the protection of the Rhine River system has been the full responsibility of the European Union.

Development of Water Quality Issues in Freshwater Systems. Until the *Second National Policy Memorandum on Water Management* (V&W 1984) was published, little interest existed in the quality of the majority of the Netherlands freshwater systems. This lack of interest held for all noninternational and thus relatively small water bodies.

The *First National Policy Memorandum on Water Management* (Rijkswaterstaat 1968) was concerned with water quality of the Rhine in terms of chlorinity, BOD_5 (biological oxygen demand in five days, measuring the amount of oxygen consumed during that period), and concentrations of ammonium, nitrate, oxygen, phenols, and radioactive compounds. For all the other water bodies in the Netherlands, based on the importance of agriculture at that time, only the chlorinity (salinity) of surface water and groundwater was an issue.

The *Second National Policy Memorandum on Water Management* covered both freshwater and marine systems, focusing not only on the quantitative distribution of surface water, but also on the excessive use of groundwater.

In a formal way, the situation changed with the publication of the *Third National Policy Memorandum on Water Management* (V&W 1989). This document paid attention to all the country's water bodies, with the aim of improving the water quality of its aquatic ecosystems.

Development of Water Quality Issues in Marine Systems. Just as for the freshwater systems, the history of water quality management of marine systems has been dictated by pollution events. In the northeast of the country, in the province of Groningen, the lack of interest in water quality led to one of the most dramatic organic waste problems in the world (Ribbius 1961). The pollution was estimated (Hopmans 1959) at about 15×10^6 inhabitant equivalents (ie, where 1 ie = 35 g BOD_5). Later, Eggink (1965) provided a maximum estimate of 12×10^6 inhabitant equivalents, of which about 50% were discharged to the Dollard (see fig. 1.2 for location). The problem was not only the discharges to the Dollard as the "end of the pipe," but also the enormous amounts of untreated organic waste from the potato flour and strawboard industries being discharged into small local canals as the first stage. From there, the mephitic water mass slowly flowed to the southeastern part of the Dollard, where it was sluiced out to the estuary. The odor in the area was unbearable during autumn and early winter, when huge quantities of potatoes were processed to make flour. As a contributor to the investigation of the effects of these discharges on the ecosystem of the Ems estuary, I witnessed the situation during the 1970s. The strawboard problem was solved as the market changed between 1977 and 1990, leading to closure of the factories. The number of potato flour factories was reduced from 21 to just 1 now, and 100% cleaning of the process water took place, heavily supported financially by the government.

According to de Jong (2006), who used the political life cycle developed by former Planning, Housing and Environment minister Pieter Winsemius, the history of water quality management was subdivided into four periods. During the period 1970–1975, and strongly based on the negative developments in freshwater systems, marine pollution was recognized as an issue by scientists and put on the political agenda. This was then followed by a relatively long period of monitoring and investigations to assess water quality and its relation to the discharges of polluted fresh water (1975–1984). The next important period, 1984–1990, was characterized by decisionmaking at the governmental level. The final one, 1990–present, has seen the implementation of strategies and management measures prepared earlier.

The introduction into the Netherlands of monitoring of nutrient levels and BOD_5 as quality aspects occurred nine years after the First International Conference on Water Disposal in the Marine Environment took place in 1959 at Berkeley, California, in the United States. Before 1970, pollution was internationally a subject only for disposal engineers and scientists (de Jong 2006). Despite the increasing pollution of the Netherlands' freshwater systems, estuaries, and coastal area, less than 5% of the 200-page *First National Policy Memorandum on Water Management* (Rijkswaterstaat 1968) was devoted to water quality.

During the early 1970s, however, awareness of the deterioration of the aquatic ecosystems was increasing. The environmental situation at this time was exemplified by large kills of plankton, fish, and bottom fauna following spills. Causes ranged from the effects of increased nutrient levels (de Jonge and Postma 1974) to pollution by heavy metals such as copper sulfate (Roskam 1966) and pesticides such as dieldrin (Koeman 1971). The Dutch Pollution of Surface Waters Act (WVO) was adopted in 1970. Since then, strongly driven by international meetings, developments have been considerable.

In 1971, the Ramsar Convention on Wetlands took place in Ramsar, Iran, with the aim of conservation and wise use of wetlands and their resources. Several international events were held in 1972. An important one was the International United Nations Conference of the Human Environment (UNCHE) in Stockholm, Sweden. Also that year were the London and Oslo Conventions, on the prevention of marine pollution by dumping of wastes and other matter. During a summit of the nine EEC states that same year, the basis for a European environmental policy was created. An Environmental Action Program was formulated for 1973 to 1976, with the objectives of preventing, reducing, and eliminating pollution. It also introduced the "polluter pays" principle, which has successfully led to increased efforts by companies to reduce their waste loads. In 1974, the Paris Convention on land-based sources of marine pollution was held. Despite the developments, however, by 1985, the focus was still mainly on how to maintain the 1970 Dutch Pollution of Surface Waters Act (WVO).

In the early 1980s, the nutrient loads in the Rhine River and all other fresh waters in the Netherlands reached their maximum. This was due to the increasing use of artificial fertilizers and detergents since the mid-1960s. The ecological status of the majority of fresh waters had deteriorated. As a consequence of the natural seaward-flowing direction, the seas also suffered. In the North Sea and Baltic areas, large-scale oxygen depletion was reported for the German Bight, Kattegat, Belt Seas, and Kiel Bight (Gerlach 1984). These events alarmed society, and politicians decided to take action, resulting in a series of political conferences of the littoral North Sea states. The first three meetings, in 1984, 1987, and 1990, strongly stimulated the further development of the so-called science-policy network (de Jong 2006) in the Northeast Atlantic Ocean, the North Sea included. Based on the reference year 1985, a 50% load reduction was agreed upon for nutrients and harmful substances by 1995. The second set of conferences, in 1993, 1995, 1997, and 2002, were held mainly to discuss the progress and consequences of the reduction measures. The reduction was not achieved well for phosphorus and not at all for nitrogen.

Other international meetings also took place during that time period. The Paris Commission, held in 1988, recommended a 50% reduction in the concentrations of phosphorus and nitrogen for the entire Northeast Atlantic Ocean. In 1992, the Oslo and Paris Commissions decided to join and operate as the Oslo-Paris Commission (OSPAR), with the task of protecting the marine environment of the Northeast Atlantic Ocean. Also in the 1990s, the European Commission adopted the Nitrates Directive (91/676/EC) and Urban Waste Water Directive (91/271/EEC) as legal instruments to improve the environmental quality. Many more directives followed in the subsequent years. Meeting the goals on water quality is dependent not only on reducing human-driven pollution, however, but also on continental freshwater discharges and, for nutrients, global variations in ocean current patterns.

The Netherlands finally took a big step forward in 1988, when the Dutch government decided to change from simply maintaining the 1970 Dutch Pollution of Surface Waters Act (WVO) to considering all aspects of water management. Ecologists explained to the environmental engineers that concentrations of compounds had to be translated into a certain biological or ecological quality of the system under consideration, and thus integrated water management was introduced. This means that physical conditions and chemical concentrations are related to the structure and functioning of the aquatic ecosystem, and the quality of the ecosystem is considered along with the desired socioeconomic developments.

The preparations for what became the *Third National Policy Memorandum on Water Management* (V&W 1989) started in 1987 and took two full years. The main document was titled *Water for Now and Later* and was based on the exploration of several environmental options, among them the *Ecological Development Directions of Marine Waters* (Ten Brink and Colijn 1990). Covering a time period up to 2010, the document described historical trends in a large number of relevant aspects, including surface areas of salt marshes, occurrence of fish diseases, and a range of 32 species from algae to mammals. It also gave the outlook for all the above elements, depending on the developing direction or policy option. Finally, it presented a method describing and assessing the different coastal ecosystems, called the AMOEBA approach because it visualized the situation per factor in a radar plot resembling an amoeba in shape. For six different policy options, the ecological expectations or prognoses were described and compared with each other in what resembled an ecological Dow Jones index.

Based on this approach, the document concluded that a general 50% reduction measure for pollutants and nutrients would offer no improvement of the marine system in terms of sustainability. Even a general 90% decline was predicted not to result in the required improvement. The solution presented was the selective reduction of loads of compounds in combination with supplementary local measures, both physical (stimulating habitat-providing conditions) and biological (e.g., the rehabilitation of eelgrass beds). An insufficiently addressed general problem when assessing the effects of changes in water quality is that other resources and environmental factors besides nutrients are responsible for the production of organic material and a certain biodiversity. Among the most important of these are light, temperature, and the dilution rate of the water, including the nutrients, in the system.

The *Fourth National Policy Memorandum on Water Management* (V&W 1998) basically reconfirmed the previous one, with the addition of some further detailing.

Effects of Political Decisionmaking on the Quality of the Environment. At present, and from both a national and international perspective, there are two main streams of thought on environmental quality. One claims that the environmental successes in countries adjacent to the North Sea and Atlantic Ocean are so clear that, as for the Netherlands, the focus should now be more on economic development and slightly less on the environment. The other is that the necessary environmental quality levels have not yet been achieved, so we cannot become complacent.

Neither is completely true, although the situation has definitely changed. The countries sharing the river basins of, for instance, the Scheldt, Meuse, Rhine, Ems, Weser, and Elbe have been successful in reducing the main well-known pollutants, although we do not know all the new ones that have emerged more recently. In terms of eutrophication, these states have been successful in reducing the phosphorus loads and part of the nitrogen loads. But other issues have become evident that were overshadowed in the past by more problematic factors. One is the underwater light climate, with light reduction caused by turbidity resulting from suspended materials such as detritus, living plankton, clay, and other minerals. Since the phosphorus and nitrogen concentrations, which encouraged algal growth, have decreased, turbidity is emerging as a problem. Under excess nutrient conditions, algal growth may be high even under low light conditions. When, however, the nutrient concentrations are decreasing, the algal growth can maintain a relatively high level only when the light conditions are optimal. The present light conditions are not optimal, being much lower than the natural background situation (see de Jonge and de Jong 2002). This is largely due to human activities such as channel maintenance dredging (de Jonge 1983) and the disposal of harbor sludge in estuaries and the coastal zone (de Jonge and de Jong 2002).

Important remaining issues in the Netherlands are thus related to activities that disturb the light climate and further reduction of nutrients. Some people and economic sectors such as the fisheries are concerned about the decline of fish stocks, macrozoobenthos, low recruitment, and protection measures. Part of the fishery sector, for instance, blames the declining fish stocks on the reduction in nutrient loads as the main cause, rather than the actions of the fishery sector itself. Nevertheless, evidence on the role of additional factors apart from nutrients, such as light, indicate that other common environmental conditions deserve much more attention than they have received so far.

EUROPEAN UNION DIRECTIVES

The EU has adopted a large number of directives meant to protect the environment and stimulate an integrated ecosystem approach to water management. Two important existing directives with respect to this are the EU Wild Birds Directive (79/409/EG) on the conservation of wild birds and EU Habitats Directive (92/43/EEC) on the conservation of natural habitats and wild fauna. Based on these two directives, an initiative to set up a network of nature conservation areas across Europe, called Natura 2000, has been started. This Natura 2000 network is meant to conserve natural habitats and species diversity. This is the biggest initiative so far on protection and conservation of nature in Europe. The Netherlands has designated 79 Birds Directive areas and 141 Habitats Directive areas. In combination with the National Ecological Network and Robust Corridors, the Natura

2000 areas contribute to combat the fragmentation of natural areas by coupling all terrestrial and wetland areas.

At the end of 2000, the EU Water Framework Directive (EC 2000) was introduced (see Chapter 11). In general terms, the requirements of the Water Framework Directive (WFD) are an analysis of the ecological characteristics of the different water types, a review of the impact of human activity on the status of surface waters and groundwater, and an economic analysis of water use. Ecologically, the WFD is one of the best directives produced so far; founded on a scientific theory and approach known as systems ecology, it has a very clear and understandable basis and goals.

Several years later, the EU Marine Strategy Directive (EC 2005) was published. Its aim is to "promote sustainable use of the seas and to conserve marine ecosystems." According to the directive:

> This will be achieved by control and reduction of pressures and impacts on the marine environment by a sector by sector approach which then should result in a patchwork of policies, legislation, programmes and actions plans at national, regional, EU and international level, which contribute to the protection of the marine environment. At the EU level, while there are a number of policies affecting the marine environment, and while a reflection has begun on a future all-encompassing Maritime Policy for the Union, there is no overall, integrated policy for the protection of the marine environment.

This strategy has resulted in the introduction of the term the "ecosystem approach," which is meant to follow in practice the Driver-Pressure-State-Impact-Response (DPSIR) model as an analysis framework for the development of management strategies. Like the Dutch Natura 2000 designations, this is all meant to contribute to ensuring quality of life for nature and humans and also provides chances for socioeconomic developments. Just as in the WFD (Annex V), it aims to protect structure and functioning of aquatic ecosystems in an ecosystemwide approach based on a sound scientific foundation. Here, structure refers to species, and functioning to processes such as the production, consumption, and degradation of organic carbon, fluxes of organic material among species groups within the food web. Although the idea has been presented, a clear basic concept of how and what to use, further develop, or implement is lacking at the moment. Thus the Netherlands still has a long way to go before the foreseen policy and management instrument is operational at the required levels of quality and detail. An additional step in applying measures to control human impact at sea can be found in the EU Maritime Development, whose goals are continued technical development while at the same time taking measures to safeguard coastal and marine ecosystems.

TOOLS TO JUDGE THE QUALITY OF AQUATIC SYSTEMS

Ecological quality objectives (EQOs) have to be defined for nearly every regulation today, both for national purposes and for legislation in international frameworks such as the Trilateral Wadden Sea Cooperation and the EU directives. EQOs can vary widely from vague development directions, as in the EU Habitats Directive, to precisely defined concentration levels to be reached, as in the Dutch policy on nutrient reduction. In Dutch national policy, the first time a real objective was defined was during the preparation of the *Third National Policy Memorandum on Water Management* in 1987–1989. Since then, EQOs have been part of environmental and international policymaking and management.

The most important EQOs at the moment are those dictated by the European Union, which are under development with OSPAR (e.g., OSPAR Commission 2005) and the International Council for the Exploration of the Sea (ICES) as advisory body to OSPAR (ICES 2004). When going through the recent documents of these organizations, it is evident that despite all the directives and regulations produced nationally and at EU level, the discussion on EQOs has just begun. The current discussion is more focused on starting points than on how to judge success, and it thus has not yet been finalized by the production of a suitable applicable instrument or technique for judging the system's condition objectively. It is also apparent that at all levels, advisors are struggling with hard and rational objectives in terms of an index or a clear value or number. This all indicates that people worldwide are on the way to another sort of rational or soft decisionmaking that should be based on an ecosystem approach, of which the contours are as yet vague and unclear.

Monitoring is generally acknowledged as a suitable means to collect the data for assessing the status of an aquatic system. These data may be helpful in establishing a coherent and comprehensive overview of water status within each river basin district. From a biological and ecological point of view, however, and considering what we know about the structure and functioning of coastal and marine aquatic food webs, the WFD monitoring requirements include a rather arbitrary set of factors (see Chapter 11) and a frequency schedule that does not make sense (de Jonge et al. 2006). For the Dutch situation, organism groups such as microalgae cells are monitored twice a year, but the species composition may change completely within one to two weeks. It also does not make sense to monitor the species composition of these algal cells without taking into account their activity (growth expressed in organic carbon) or considering the most important removal process, done by grazing organisms such as copepods. These aspects are listed in table 1-1 and illustrate that against the background of an ecosystem or integrated ecological approach, with required quality objectives, ecological potential, and ecological status, the fact that the microbial food web and everything smaller than one millimeter mesh size, notably the grazing zooplankton, are not monitored seriously handicaps both the WFD and the ecosystem approaches.

In the Netherlands, the monitoring of marine waters is more extensive and also more intensive (high frequency) than required by the WFD (see de Jonge et al. 2006). Nevertheless, for coastal and marine waters, it is still not possible to fulfill the ecological requirements of the EU's ecosystem approach. For freshwater systems with a long history of monitoring quality, this does not seem to be a real problem. Based on the above-mentioned uncertainties as well as the often strong interannual variation in species composition and abundance, de Jonge et al. (2006) proposed to work on an integrated index or set of indices covering both the func-

Table 1-1 *Environmental elements, means and symptoms, and parameters to be measured during monitoring programs as required by the WFD*

Quality elements	Means and symptoms	Parameter and frequency
Morphology		
Geomorphology of system	Means for realizing optimal habitat providing conditions	Soundings once per six years
Physicochemical conditions		
Temperature, oxygen, salinity, nutrients, pH	Means for realizing optimal habitat providing conditions	Water sampling once per three months
Other pollutants		Sampling once per three months
Priority substances		Sampling once per month
Biology		
Phytoplankton	Toxic blooms	Species composition and countings twice per year
Macroalgae	Algal mats	Species composition and countings every three years
Macrophytes	Loss of habitat	Surface area of eelgrass beds and salt marshes every three years
Macrobenthos	Anoxia	Species composition and countings every three years
Fish (transitional waters)	Migration barrier	Species composition and countings every three years

tioning and species structure, or biodiversity, of the aquatic ecosystems. Such an approach may be possible when we are able to integrate, for instance, a flux analysis of marine food webs with the species responsible for these fluxes. A suitable basis could be to apply and further develop ecological network analysis as developed by Ulanowicz (1980, 1986, 1997).

When applying the implementation requirements of the WFD to the ecological reality, it is evident that the directive fails to follow its own clear starting points, because in practice, only parts of the systems' ecological principles are applied. The directive also neglects to set the scene for a real ecosystem or holistic approach. This is an extremely important point, as the EU Marine Strategy (EC 2005) builds further on the fundamentals of the WFD. In addition, politicians ask for indicators that are easy to measure and understand, inexpensive, representative of the system's condition, and appealing to decisionmakers and the general public. This is asking a great deal when working with such a complex system. Moreover, the government bodies serving the politicians often find it difficult to translate the political aims into practice and to handle the associated concepts or principles, and also may have a hard time convincing the responsible politicians that achieving these aims requires sufficient funding for the scientific community.

CLIMATE CHANGE EFFECTS AND WATER MANAGEMENT

Apart from direct human impact at local and regional levels, we are also dealing with large-scale natural changes that cannot easily be regulated. It has widely been accepted that because of widespread global changes in land use and related activities resulting from increased population, humans are contributing to climate change. This term can be defined as an alteration in the state or condition of the climate system. The present climatic changes are ascribed to increased concentration of trace gases, such as carbon dioxide (CO_2) and chlorofluorocarbons (CFCs), in the atmosphere, resulting mainly from the oxidation and burning of fossil organic material and industrial production of CFCs. These alterations in gas composition affect the amount of radiation absorbed by the atmosphere because of a depletion of the ozone layer. The most important aspects related to climate change are global warming, with an expected increase in temperature of 2.0° to 4.5°C by circa 2050; more precipitation at the Netherlands' latitude, resulting in higher freshwater discharges; a changed wind climate, which at this latitude may lead to greater average wind speed; and more frequent occurrences of extreme weather conditions. One of the main results of the expected temperature increase is a sea level rise due to the thermal expansion of oceanic water. The rise projected by the Intergovernmental Panel on Climate Change (IPCC) varies from 0.09 to 0.88 meters over the period 1990 to 2100. The consequences of this sort of forecasting for safety against flooding have prompted the Dutch government recently to commence a new, second Delta Commission with the task of briefly formulating what has to be done to safeguard the Netherlands from problems related to increased future sea level rise (Deltacommissie 2008).

The recorded steady increase in the tidal range around the North Sea, which influences the semidiurnal variations in water height, is an issue that is not clearly attributable directly or indirectly to climate change. For the Netherlands, the most important anticipated short-term changes are the expected increases in precipitation and wind speed, on top of which the country has to be prepared for an unknown sea level rise and increased tidal range.

Some of the necessary management measures related to the expected increase in precipitation and consequently higher water discharges are those discussed earlier: widening and deepening of waterways, from ditches and canals to the main rivers; creation of wetlands as overflow systems; and reinforcement of the dikes. Not yet mentioned is the need to enlarge the sluices in the sea defenses, channels that allow free runoff of fresh water during low tide, and create large freshwater basins just in front of these sluices. The rising sea and lowering land have already led to big problems, as the difference in elevation between the freshwater and seawater levels during low tide is decreasing. In the short term, this problem can be solved by enlarging the sluices in conjunction with providing for sufficient water storage in front of them. As a long-term solution, large-scale infrastructural adaptations are necessary and pump capacity must be increased significantly.

From a safety management point of view, an increase in the mean wind speeds will lead to longer and higher waves, with a greater risk of washover during storm surges. In combination with a higher sea level, measures are needed to reduce the size of the waves. This is technically possible by building structures in the sea to diminish the fetch and consequently reduce the capacity for gigantic waves to build up. These structures may be used for economic purposes (e.g., airport, wind power, harbors, or fish culturing) or recreation (e.g., boating or bathing in a sheltered lagoon system).

From mainly a technical point of view, the second Delta Commission (Deltacommissie 2008) formulated 12 recommendations. Some of these are interesting. Sand is essential for the morphological developments along the coast and in the Wadden Sea. A presently ongoing technique in coastal defense is beach nourishment, actively transporting sand to compensate for any sediment deficit in front of the coast. The Delta Commission recommends extending these activities on a very large scale, termed "foreshore nourishment," to let the vertical morphological growth of the Dutch coastal zone, the Wadden Sea included, keep pace with the sea level rise in a seminatural way. Another recommendation is to build dikes that are not necessarily able to keep all the water out, but are technically "unbreachable," so that the damage caused by any flooding due to extensive washovers will be restricted.

Ecologically, more fresh water, increased wind, higher temperatures, and a sea level rise may result in complex changes in the functioning of estuarine and coastal ecosystems, which includes the majority of Dutch territorial waters. Changes in wind climate may result in wind-induced resuspension of mud, creating greater water turbidity. This turbidity as well as the rising temperatures may stimulate the production of organic matter by mainly benthic microalgae instead of phytoplankton, which then serve as an alternative source of food for the other aquatic organisms (de Jonge et al. in preparation). An increase in temperature may also trigger changes in the biogeographic distribution of species and thus lead to the introduction of invaders, something that has taken its toll already. The use of coastal areas and rivers for navigation necessarily is accompanied by dredging activities, and the disposal of the dredged material may be another cause of turbidity of the water column (de Jonge 1983; de Jonge and de Jong 2002). The decrease in the light climate as a function of suspended material (SPM) follows a power function. This means that a slight increase in SPM in basically productive and clear coastal waters will strongly reduce the total light penetration in the water column and thus the production of food by algae. With respect to the WFD, light (SPM) is acknowledged only as a natural boundary condition and not as a pollutant that reduces the functioning of the ecosystem. This should be corrected, because the effects of climate change on the functioning of coastal ecosystems may be dramatic, with a complex mixture of human-induced and natural changes. On top of that, we are dealing with often nonlinear feedback systems that are not all known and whose outcomes cannot be predicted.

NATURAL VERSUS HUMAN-DRIVEN SIGNALS

The concept of integrated water management is a complicated one. Depending on the factor we are interested in, the data we collect may be a mixture consisting of a natural trend, including its natural variation, and a human-driven signal (see fig. 1.6).

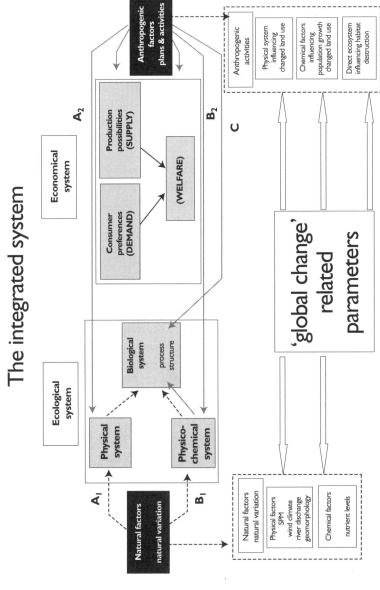

Figure 1.6 *The structure of the integrated system*

Notes: Dashed lines indicate natural influences, and solid lines denote anthropogenic influences. A_1 and A_2 refer to influences of the physical system, B_1 and B_2 to those of the physicochemical system, and C to direct human impact on the biological system. SPM = suspended material.

Source: Modified after de Jonge et al. 2003.

Examples of such trends in physical factors are the sea level rise, the development of the tidal range (including low and high water levels), and temperature (represented by A_1 and A_2 in fig. 1.6). A trend may be partly natural (A_1) and partly caused by human activities (A_2), as is the case with estuarine tidal range, where low and high water levels can be influenced by channel maintenance dredging (de Jonge 1983) or engineering works.

Comparable influences hold for physicochemical factors, such as the natural discharges of river water and society-related discharges of nutrients and contaminants. Changes in these factors may indirectly influence the biological subsystem (B_1 and B_2 in fig. 1.6), resulting in a change of the ecological quality of the ecosystem under consideration. It is also possible to change the biotic subsystem directly, as fisheries do (C line in fig. 1.6). This all illustrates that a good basis exists for the use of the term "biocomplexity" in these sorts of systems.

It is a challenge to society to manage the whole integrated system as visualized in figure 6. This is possible only when the scientific basis is solid and concepts have been developed that are suitable for application in the policymaking and management arena. Before developing measures to effectively combat undesired situations or developments, we need to know how our systems function. We also need to know how they will respond when basic conditions change (e.g., changes to SPM and thus light by dredging, eutrophication by nutrients, temperature by trace gas production, and residence time by engineering) and how important the relative contribution of human-related changes is to the total change.

Considerable improvements have been made in our understanding of aquatic systems. It is clear that we need to continue to manage these environments with the information we have while striving for better understanding of their functioning. With reference to all available national and international agreements, legislation, and directives, the ecological and biological quality of these systems currently has to be judged against ecological quality objectives that often seem unsuitable. The big management issue is how to determine suitable indicators and their levels. This will be possible only when we have sufficient knowledge about the complex, nonlinear responses of our aquatic ecosystems to changes in environmental factors.

CONCLUSIONS

Water management in the Netherlands has transformed from the simple flood protection of the past into a combination of managing water in terms of its quantity, quality, and biocomplexity. The history of coastal defense and water management in this country spans more than 2,000 years and is therefore among the longest in Europe. Large-scale peat excavations since the beginning of the 12th century, with related dewatering, peat oxidation, and sediment compaction, caused a dramatic decrease in surface elevation all over the country, and the combination of sinking land and a rising sea hampered the free runoff of fresh water to the sea and dramatically increased the risk for flooding.

Several milestones in water management can be recognized. The first were the decisions in 1974 not to reclaim the present Wadden Sea and not to close the

Oosterschelde by a dam, but to build a storm surge barrier instead. The second was the presentation in 1989 of the *Third National Policy Memorandum on Water Management*, which introduced integrated water management after ecologists explained successfully to the environmental engineers that concentrations of compounds had to be translated into a certain biological or ecological quality of the system under consideration. This decision brought the Netherlands a strong and well-respected reputation in the fields of coastal defense and integrated water management, which included both water quantity and quality.

Despite the significant advances to the coastal engineering works, some new problems arose. The large closures of the Zuider Zee and southwestern part of the Netherlands provided a greater level of safety against flooding. Environmentally, however, the country has largely failed to manage these waters according to plan. Every closed former estuarine system in the southwest now has at least one major environmental problem, ranging from large-scale erosion of intertidal flats to massive algal blooms.

The Water Framework Directive, based on systems ecology, is in practice a fragmented approach, because only portions of the system's ecological principles are applied. The directive also neglects to set the scene for a real ecosystem or holistic approach. Policymakers have failed to understand that complex coastal ecosystems cannot be represented by simple indicators.

The present water policy developed step by step, from flood defense to quantitative and then qualitative water management, and on to integrated water management in the late 1980s. It is notable that every new topic addressed built on an existing program, which led to integrated water management. Since about 2000, water management has been returning to a sector approach, exemplified by the recent presentation of the new second Delta Plan, in which coastal defense strongly prevails. Nevertheless, increasing internationalization has strongly stimulated debate on quantitative and qualitative aspects of water management, including the complex functioning of its biology.

ACKNOWLEDGMENT

The author acknowledges the Water Service of Rijkswaterstaat for its support.

REFERENCES

Bosch, A., and W. van der Ham. 1998. *Twee eeuwen Rijkswaterstaat 1798–1998* [*Two centuries Rijkswaterstaat 1798–1998*]. Zaltbommel, Netherlands: Europese Bibliotheek.

de Haan, H., and I. Haagsma. 1984. *De Deltawerken. Techniek, politiek, achtergronden* [*The Delta Works. Technique, politics, background information*]. Delft, Netherlands: Waltman.

de Jong, F. 2006. *Marine Eutrophication in Perspective. On the Relevance of Ecology for Environmental Policy*. Berlin: Springer-Verlag.

de Jonge, V.N. 1983. Relations between annual dredging activities, suspended matter concentrations, and the development of the tidal regime in the Ems estuary. *Canadian Journal of Fisheries and Aquatic Sciences* 40 (Suppl. 1): 289–300.

de Jonge,V.N., and D.J. de Jong. 2002. "Global change" impact of inter-annual variation in water discharge as a driving factor to dredging and spoil disposal in the river Rhine system and of turbidity in the Wadden Sea. *Estuarine Coastal Shelf Science* 55:969–91.

de Jonge,V.N.,W.F. de Boer, D.J. de Jong, andV.S. Brauer. In preparation. Air temperature induced effect on interannual variations in microphytobenthos chlorophyll-a. Submitted to Limnology & Oceanography.

de Jonge,V.N., M. Elliott, andV.S. Brauer. 2006. Marine monitoring: Its shortcomings and mismatch with the EU Water Framework Directive's objectives. *Marine Pollution Bulletin* 53:5–19.

de Jonge,V.N., M.J. Kolkman, E.C.M. Ruijgrok, and M.B. de Vries. 2003.The need for new paradigms in integrated socio-economic and ecological coastal policy making. Proceedings of 10th International Wadden Sea Symposium, Ministry of Agriculture, Nature Management and Fisheries, Department North, Groningen, Netherlands, 247–70.

de Jonge,V.N., and H. Postma. 1974. Phosphorus compounds in the Dutch Wadden Sea. *Netherlands Journal of Sea Research* 8:139–53.

Deltacommissie. 2008. *Samen werken met water. Een land dat leeft, bouwt aan zijn toekomst. Bevindingen van de Deltacommissie 2008* [*Collectively working with water. A living country building on its future. Conclusions of the Deltacommittee 2008*]. Rotterdam: Deltacommissie.

de Mulder, E.F.J., M.C. Geluk, I.L. Ritsema,W.E.Westerhoff, and T.E.Wong. 2003. *De ondergrond van Nederland* [*The underground of the Netherlands*]. Groningen/Houten, Netherlands:Wolters-Noordhoff.

EC (European Commission). 2000. Directive 2000/60/EC of the European Parliament and of the Council of 23 October 2000 establishing a framework for community action in the field of water policy. *Official Journal of the European Communities* L 327:1–72.

———. 2005. *Framework for community action in the field of marine environmental policy.* Marine Strategy Directive. Proposal for a Directive from the European Commission. 24.10.2005, COM(2005)505 final. Brussels: EC.

Eggink, H.J. 1965. *Het estuarium als ontvangend water van grote hoeveelheden afvalstoffen* [*The estuary as receiving water body for large amounts of waste*]. RIZA-Mededeling No. 2. Lelystad, Netherlands: RIZA.

Frijters, I.D., and J. Leentvaar. 2003. Rhine case study. UNESCO-IHP Publications, No. 17. Delft, Netherlands: UNESCO-IHP.

Gerlach, S.A. 1984. *Oxygen depletion 1980–1983 in coastal waters of the Federal Republic of Germany.* Berichte aus dem Institut für Meereskunde Nr. 130. Kiel, Germany: Institut für Meereskunde.

Hopmans, J.J. 1959. De waterhuishouding van Nederland. De waterverontreiniging in Nederland en de bestrijding daarvan [Water management of the Netherlands.Water pollution in the Netherlands and its combat]. *De Ingenieur* 4:1–7.

Huisman, K. 1995. De Drususgrachten: een nieuwe hypothese [The Drusus Canals: A new hypothesis]. *Westerheem* 44:188–94.

ICES (International Council for the Exploration of the Sea). 2004. Report of the Study Group on Ecological Quality Objectives for Sensitive and for Opportunistic Benthos Species. ICES Advisory Committee on Ecosystems ICES CM 2004/ACE:01 Ref. E,WGECO, BEWG, March 22–24, 2004, ICES, Copenhagen.

Ingólfsson, O. No date. Quaternary Geology. www.hi.is/~oi/quaternary_geology.htm (accessed May 25, 2007).

Koeman, J.H. 1971. Het voorkomen en de toxicologische betekenis van enkele chloorkoolwaterstoffen aan de Nederlandse kust in de periode van 1965 tot 1970 [The occurrence and toxicological meaning of some chlorinated organic compounds along the Dutch coast in the period 1965–1970]. Master's thesis. Utrecht, Netherlands: University of Utrecht.

Lintsen, H.W. 1998.Twee eeuwen Rijkswaterstaat. Een geschiedenis van drie golven van op- en neergang [Two centuries of Rijkswaterstaat. A history of three waves up and down]. *Tijdschrift voor Waterstaatsgeschiedenis* 7 (webversion 2006): 116–24.

OSPAR Commission. 2005. Towards Finalisation of Ecological Quality Objectives (EcoQOs) for the North Sea, Biodiversity Series, OSPAR Stakeholder Workshop. December 13–14, 2004, Oslo.

Ribbius. F.J. 1961.The biggest waste problem in the world. *Land en Water* 5:24.

Rijkswaterstaat. 1968. *De Waterhuishouding van Nederland* (*Eerste nota Waterhuishouding*) [*First National Policy Memorandum on Water Management*]. The Hague: Staatsuitgeverij.

Roskam, R. Th. 1966. Kopervergiftiging in zee [Copper pollution at sea]. *Water Bodem Lucht* 56:19–23.

Stratingh, G.A., and G.A. Venema. 1855. *De Dollard of geschied-, aardrijks- en natuurkundige beschrijving van dezen boezem der Eems* [*Historical, geographical and physical description of the Dollard as part of the Ems drainage system*]. Repr., Groningen, Netherlands: J. Oomkens, J. Zoon en R.J. Schierbeek, 1979.

ten Brink, B.J.E., and F. Colijn. 1990. *Ecologische ontwikkelingsrichtingen zoute wateren. Ecologische toestandsbeschrijving en toekomstverwachting 1985–2010* [*Directions of the ecological development of the marine waters. Description of ecological status and its possible developments*]. Notanummer GWWS-90.009. The Hague: Ministerie van Verkeer en Waterstaat, Rijkswaterstaat, Dienst Getijdewateren.

Ulanowicz, R.E. 1980. An hypothesis on the development of natural communities. *Journal of Theoretical Biology* 85:223–45.

———. 1986. *Growth and development: Ecosystems phenomenology*. New York: Springer-Verlag.

———. 1997. *Ecology, the ascendent perspective*. New York: Columbia University Press.

V&W. 1984. *Tweede nota Waterhuishouding* [*Second National Policy Memorandum on Water Management*]. The Hague: Staatsuitgeverij, Ministry of Transport, Public Works and Water Management.

———. 1989. *Derde nota Waterhuishouding* [*Third National Policy Memorandum on Water Management*]. The Hague: Ministry of Transport, Public Works and Water Management.

———. 1998. *Vierde nota Waterhuishouding* [*Fourth National Policy Memorandum on Water Management*]. The Hague: Ministry of Transport, Public Works and Water Management.

Waddenzeecommissie. 1974. *Advies inzake de principiële mogelijkheden en de voor- en nadelen van inpolderingen in de Waddenzee* [*Recommendation on the possibilities and the advantages and disadvantages of reclamations in the Wadden Sea*]. Report of the Mazure Committee. Z 58355 (STCRT 1970, 234). The Hague: Ministerie van Verkeer en Waterstaat.

Zagwijn, W.H. 1991. *Nederland in het Holoceen* [*The Netherlands in the Holocene*]. The Hague: SDU Uitgeverij.

CHAPTER 2

Hydrological Models

Joost (W.J.M.) Heijkers and Jan (P.J.T.) van Bakel

THE HYDROLOGICAL SITUATION in the Netherlands is typical for a deltaic region. Many parts of the country are below sea level (mainly the Holocene portion), and without flood protection measures, they would be inundated frequently by either the sea or the Rhine and Meuse rivers. Thanks to highly sophisticated management by special authorities—the water boards (see Chapter 8), which have existed for centuries—people are able to live and work here. But flood protection is not the only aim of water management. Upward seepage of seawater contains salt and nutrients, which can result in undesirable water quality, so qualitative management is also necessary to ensure that people can drink or enjoy the water, farmers can use it to irrigate their land, and it will foster the biodiversity of nature, both aquatic and terrestrial.

In the areas not affected by flooding (mainly the higher Pleistocene part of the country), the annual surplus of water during winter, when evapotranspiration decreases, requires proper drainage. In summer, a water shortage usually occurs, causing damage to crops and nature areas. Thus adequate, integrated water management is an essential prerequisite for life in many parts of the Netherlands, most tellingly illustrated by the situation in the polders, where the land would be flooded if the water were not pumped away.

To create favorable conditions for agriculture, the groundwater must be maintained between certain levels. This is achieved by installing tile drains and manipulating surface-water levels through the use of weirs and inlets. These structures are also essential for stable roads and to prevent houses from getting too wet. But insufficient groundwater levels can lead to drought, which also can cause damage to building foundations, as well as crops and nature areas.

Another major problem is that, generally speaking, water management that is suitable for nature areas differs considerably from that suitable for housing or agriculture.

A complicating factor is that nature areas tend to be small and are scattered all over the country, and the mutual influence through the thick aquifers or surface-water system is high, so the different interests are in conflict. This calls for the weighing of interests and methods in order to cope with this interdependency, a major task for all parties involved in water management—not just the water boards, but provinces, nature foundations, and civilians too.

The situation sketched above illustrates the complexity of water management in the Netherlands. The country is unique in its specific hydrological situation combined with a dense population and high level of economic activity. This calls for an extremely demanding water management system employing every possible method, one of which is the use of numerical hydrological models, the main subject of this chapter.

Since the 1970s, hydrological models have been used for system analysis, policymaking, and decisionmaking. Because the hydrological situation in the Netherlands is very distinctive, typical modeling approaches have emerged. Many models were developed based on typical Dutch hydrological concepts, and different types of numerical models have been applied for nearly 40 years, varying from stationary for one hydrological subsystem (such as the unsaturated zone only), to nonstationary and all relevant subsystems integrated (atmosphere, unsaturated zone, saturated groundwater system, and surface water system). The scale of application ranges from local (one parcel) to catchment areas and polders, to nationwide. This chapter provides a review of most types of hydrological models that have contributed or still contribute significantly to the planning, design, and operation of the Netherlands' water management system. Although we are aware that other modeling approaches exist, we will focus on physically based, distributed modeling systems because of their importance for strategic water management, both for surface water management (water boards) and groundwater managers (provinces, drinking-water companies), and because it is widely recognized that these types of models are capable of scenario analysis and can serve as a basis for water quality assessment.

CONCEPTUAL FRAMEWORK

A concept is a way to look to a phenomenon such as water flow. For example, groundwater flow is nonturbulent and can be modeled with an image of the reality, viz. Darcy's law, expressing a linear relation between the magnitude of the flow and the gradient in hydraulic head. A numerical model is a specific image of reality using a computer code with which the mathematical expressions of water flow are discretized in space or time and solved with specified boundary conditions such as precipitation. In modeling the hydrology of a parcel, catchment area, or entire country, simplifications must always be applied, in the form of division in subsystems and simplifying the mutual interdependencies. For the land phase of the hydrological cycle, the usual subdivision in subsystems is depicted in figure 2.1, together with their mutual boundaries.

For each subsystem, the relevant processes (depending on the concepts used) are defined and expressed in mathematical expressions. The hydrological behavior can

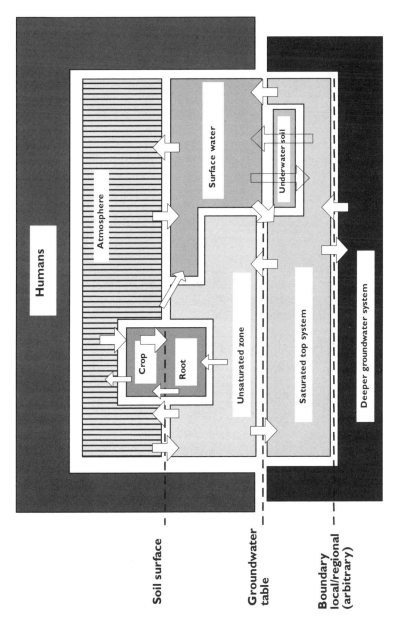

Figure 2.1 *Schematic representation of the hydrological subsystems and their interrelations*

Note: "Mondriaan," by Piet Groenendijk, personal communication.

be known by solving the mathematical expression. A numerical model is an image of reality created by simplifying the hydrological processes and discretizing the spatial or temporal variation in properties and behavior, using a computer code. Simulation is applying the model and producing meaningful results.

A BRIEF HISTORY OF NUMERICAL HYDROLOGICAL MODELING

This section presents a brief history of both water quantity and water quality modeling in the Netherlands, in light of the development of computer science and water policymaking.

Water Quantity Modeling

Before the emergence of computers and computer models, water management in the Netherlands was based to a large extent on organized experience. The water boards were established to bring private interests together to better manage the resource. Their authority can be predicated only on professional knowledge and a more efficient way to perform the task of water management. This calls for a systematized way of learning through practical experience and evaluating hydrological events. But the experimental method has serious limitations: extreme events cannot be fully experienced, and exogenous circumstances can change. Therefore, scientific methods came into use for the planning and design of water management systems. The essence of scientific methods is reproductivity and their verification possibilities. Early examples include time series analyses of high river floods and high sea levels and the use of mathematical formulas to calculate drain depth and intensity (Hooghoudt 1940). Daily water management remained based on experience.

The rapid increase in computing capacity with the emergence of commercially usable computers in the early 1960s led to the development of numerical models. The essence of a numerical model is the translation of hydrological concepts and mathematical expressions for water flow and water-related processes into numerical schemes in which space, time, or both are discretized. By specifying boundary conditions such as precipitation, the schemes can be solved. The result is a reproduction of the dynamics of hydrological variables such as groundwater and surface water levels.

With the first generation of computer codes, only one subsystem of the hydrological system could be modeled. For the unsaturated zone, de Laat (1980) developed the model MUST, based on a quasi-steady-state approach (succession of steady states) and a subdivision of the unsaturated zone into a root zone and a subsoil. This model was used frequently, such as to produce a metamodel (a model of the results of a model) for the relation between groundwater depth and the reduction in evapotranspiration for different combinations of soil types and crops (HELP-tabel 1987). The computer code SWAP, based on a more detailed discretization of the unsaturated zone, has de facto become the standard for one-dimensional vertical water flow, including root water uptake and soil evaporation (Kroes and van Dam 2003). For modeling saturated groundwater flow, different computer codes are used, such as MICROFEM (Hemker and Nijsten 1996) and MOD-FLOW (Harbaugh et al. 2000). The most commonly used computer codes for flow of water in open watercourses in the Netherlands are DUFLOW (DUFLOW 2006) and SOBEK-CF (WL | Delft Hydraulics 2001).

The strength of numerical models becomes very clear with the modeling of situations where the subsystems for flow of water in the unsaturated zone, saturated groundwater, and surface water are mutually dependent and vary spatially. This is the most common situation in the Netherlands, with shallow groundwater tables and a strong dependency between the flow to the surface water system and the water level in surface waters. The model of Freeze (1971) is one of the first codes to combine hydrological processes in the unsaturated zone and the saturated groundwater system, which could be applied regionally. Today the SHE model (Beven 2002) is a generally recognized example of the possibilities of physically based distributed modeling.

In the Netherlands, the Commission for Water Management of the province of Gelderland promoted the development of a number of integrated models for operational use. The most well-known product is the computer code GELGAM, which integrates a model for saturated groundwater flow with a model for water flow in the unsaturated zone (Awater and de Laat 1980).

In cooperation with the RAND Corporation, Delft Hydraulics developed a sophisticated palette of computer codes for the planning and operation of the National Water Management System, consisting of the main rivers and big lakes. The Netherlands is divided into small catchments or polders, connected to the national system. Each catchment area discharges water into the main system and fulfills water demand during periods of prolonged drought. When a shortage of water occurs, a distribution model helps optimize water distribution (Abrahamse et al. 1982). The calculations with this so-called PAWN instrument also formed the basis for the *Second National Policy Memorandum on Water Management* (V&W 1984), which marked a "water divide" between "one custom serving" and integrated water management.

Based on the philosophy that integration of the hydrological subsystems into one model is essential for solving water management problems, at the Institute for Land and Water Research (ICW), the code UNSAT-2 (Neuman et al. 1974) was made suitable for regional application, which resulted in the model code SIMGRO, the main modeling tool for regional water management of Wageningen University and Research Centre (van Walsum et al. 2004). Recent developments are to couple this code with MODFLOW and SOBEK-CF, using Open Modelling Interfaces (Moore et al. 2005), and to generate metamodels, thereby using results from sophisticated models of one subsystem, such as the unsaturated zone. For example, the sophisticated unsaturated zone model code SWAP (van Dam 2000) was used to create MetaSWAP. See van Walsum and Groenendijk (2006) and Veldhuizen et al. (2006) for more details.

With the availability of GIS-based pre- and post-processing tools, the possibilities of data-driven modeling have dramatically increased. This emphasizes the need for proper model calibration and verification with Bayesian probability, which is supposed to measure the degree of belief an individual has in an uncertain proposition, and is in this respect a subjective investment in the development of stochastic methods for parameter estimation and uncertainty analysis using the Kalman filter principles (see, e.g., van Geer and Te Stroet 1990; Van Geer et al. 1990). Ultimately this resulted in an adjoint-representer approach, implemented in the MODFLOW code (Valstar et al. 2004).

Another, more Bayesian, statistics-based approach has been adopted by the University of Amsterdam, which resulted in the SCEM-UA and MOSCEM-UA (the multiobjective version of SCEM-UA) algorithms (Vrugt et al. 2003a, 2003b). This approach, which has been tested on a wide variety of models and data sets, appears to be very useful for calibration and uncertainty analysis of rainfall–runoff models as well as unsaturated zone models and is therefore complementary to the Representer approach as implemented in the MODFLOW code.

In recent years, data assimilation (see, e.g., McLaughlin 2002 for an overview of existing methods) has been used for state estimation, both for forecasting and reanalysis applications. An example for a Dutch situation is provided in Schuurmans et al. (2003). In this study, an existing SIMGRO model of the Drentse Aa area was updated using data assimilation. SEBAL-based estimates of evapotranspiration were assimilated in the model, which resulted not only in improved results, but also in a clearer understanding of existing model errors, mainly in the geohydrological portion.

Water Quality Modeling

The basis of modeling water quality is a correct model of the water balance. But for modeling water-related processes, we also need to know the fate of water particles. This requires some kind of post-processing where water particles are tracked. For this purpose, particle tracking codes such as the MODFLOW-based MODPATH can be used.

In the Netherlands, the fate of nutrients in the unsaturated zone and the upper part of the saturated groundwater system is of major concern, because surface water quality is unacceptable with regard to nutrient contents. National and European environmental policies demand a reduction in nutrient loads, a major source of which is the nitrogen (N) and phosphorus (P) leaching from agricultural land. The effects of all kinds of source-oriented measures have been evaluated on a national scale, using 6,405 models for the flow of water and the fate of nutrients, incorporated in the STONE simulation tool (Groenendijk et al. 2005; Overbeek et al. 2001; Wolf et al. 2003, 2005a, 2005b). Each model is a quasi-two-dimensional image of the water flow in the upper 15 meters of one plot, using a version of the code SWAP extended with an interaction with the surface water system and a simple reservoir for the surface water system itself. A plot consists of a number of more or less homogeneous parcels of land with respect to hydrology and land use, each with an area of 6.25 hectares. The relation with the regional groundwater system is established with a sine-shaped lower boundary flux, which is calculated by an at-distance coupling with the NAtional GROundwater Model, NAGROM (de Lange 1996). The calculated upward or downward seepage fluxes, showing considerable spatial differences, are tested with measured water balances.

Other determining hydrological factors for the nutrient loads to the ground-water and the surface water are the precipitation surplus, the water supply, and the groundwater depth dynamics. The nutrient input varies with different policy scenarios regarding manure used by farmers. For example, the mean nitrate concentration in shallow groundwater is computed for two scenarios (Wolf et al. 2005a). MINAS, in the first scenario, is a system where farmers must annually provide figures to the government concerning the nutrient balance of their farms. The concentration especially in the southern and eastern sandy regions is more than 50 milligrams of NO_3 per liter and can be classified as too high. Despite strong restrictions in the second scenario, the calculated nitrate concentrations are reduced further, but remain too high, in the aforementioned regions.

PRESENT SITUATION

The use of numerical modeling in water management is now common practice. Almost all water boards have employed numerical hydrological models to determine the measures to be taken to face the increase of water damage as a result of climate change. Furthermore, they have adopted a new method to weigh different interests in proper water management, called the Waternood approach (Projectgroep Waternood 1998). With this approach, the most desirable situation with respect to groundwater and surface water in a region is established in a structured manner. An essential element is a comparison of different hydrological regimes in order to find the most desirable one. As these regimes cannot be experienced in reality, numerical models are applied.

The Ministry of Transport, Public Affairs and Water Management uses elements of the previously mentioned PAWN instrument for a study called the Droogtestudie Nederland (2005), quantifying the effects of changes in land use and climate on water shortages and the economy. The Ministry of Agriculture and the Ministry for the Environment apply STONE on a regular basis for prognosis and evaluation of their policy with respect to nature and environment.

The Netherlands Environmental Assessment Agency applies several numerical models, or results of these models, in the Waterplanner, a decision support system that calculates the environmental pressure on surface water quality. This system can be used to evaluate environmental policy on a national or catchment scale and assess measures to fulfill the EU Water Framework Directive demands to achieve a good ecological status of surface water and groundwater bodies by 2015.

The Netherlands recently decided to develop a national hydrological model as a basis to support water management and environmental policy on both national and regional levels. It will integrate the modeling experiences of the main water research institutes: TNO (MODFLOW), Alterra (SIMGRO and MetaSWAP), and Delft Hydraulics (SOBEK-CF). With close cooperation between policymakers and researchers from the main hydrological institutes, this will constitute a shift from research-driven to data- and demand-driven modeling of the hydrology on a very detailed scale. Flexible upscaling techniques will make it possible to apply the model on different levels, so both the ministries and the water boards will be able to use the model, or parts of it. Additionally, it will serve as a basis for the major task of water management in the near future: modeling hydrology and water quality to determine the measures to take to meet the demands set by the EU Water Framework Directive. Integration with socioeconomic models is necessary to find the most cost-effective measures that would also be accepted by society.

The Dutch experience with numerical modeling of the unsaturated zone and the upper part of the saturated zone, including interaction with the surface water system, is recognized worldwide and will be emphasized by linking the typical modeling concepts with the international standard for groundwater modeling, the MODFLOW package.

CONCLUSIONS

People nowadays ask for transparency with respect to decisions in the public domain, including water management. Numerical models can be very helpful, because results are reproducible and can be presented in almost any desired spatial and temporal detail. Still, these models are not commonly employed in the field of water management in the Netherlands. A reason that is often mentioned is a lack of data. The use of numerical models is indeed strongly correlated with data availability; the expression "modeling is collecting data" is very true. Limited data should not be an excuse not to use numerical models in the Netherlands, however, as many data are available, although data mining has not yet been fully applied.

Another trend is the interaction between water management and changes in land use. Increased land use has put greater pressure on the water supply. This requires not only reliable and reproducible model results, but also proper communication about the hydrological results, making presentation more significant. GIS is already widely used as a pre- and post-processing tool and will become even more important.

To conclude, the use of numerical models in water management in the Netherlands is widely accepted today, because the need for verifiable results is great and many data are available.

REFERENCES

Abrahamse, A.H., G. Baarse, and E. van Beek. 1982. *Model for regional hydrology, agriculture and damages from drought and salinity.* Vol. 13 of *Policy analysis of water management for the Netherlands.* RAND note N-1555/12-NETH. Santa Monica, CA: Rand.

Awater, R.H.C.M., and P.J.M. de Laat. 1980. *Groundwater flow and evapotranspiration, a simulation model.* Part 1: *Theory.* Arnhem, Netherlands: Commissie Bestudering Waterhuishouding Gelderland.

Beven, K. 2002. Towards an alternative blueprint for a physically based digitally simulated hydrologic response modelling system. *Hydrological Processes* 16 (2): 189–206.

de Laat, P.J.M. 1980. Model for unsaturated flow above a shallow water table, applied to a regional subsurface flow problem. PhD thesis. Wageningen, Netherlands: Pudoc.

de Lange, W.J. 1996. Groundwater modelling of large domains with analytic elements. PhD thesis. Delft, Netherlands: Technical University Delft.

Droogtestudie Nederland. 2005. *Aard, Ernst en omvang van watertekorten in Nederland.* [*Water shortage in the Netherlands: Its nature, seriousness and scope*]. Eindrapport. RIZA Report 2005.016. Lelystad, Netherlands: RIZA.

DUFLOW. 2006. www.duflow.nl (accessed February 2, 2009).

Freeze, R.A. 1971. Three-dimensional, transient, saturated-unsaturated flow in a groundwater basin. *Water Resources Research* 7 (2): 347–66.

Groenendijk, P., L.V. Renaud, and J. Roelsma. 2005. *Prediction of Nitrogen and Phosphorus leaching to groundwater and surface waters.* Process descriptions of the ANIMO 4.0 model. Report 983. Wageningen, Netherlands: Alterra.

Harbaugh, A.W., E.R. Banta, M.C. Hill, and M.G. McDonald. 2000. MODFLOW-2000, the U.S. Geological Survey modular ground-water model: User guide to modularization concepts and the ground-water flow process. U.S. Geological Survey Open-File Report 00-92.

HELP-tabel. 1987. *De invloed van de waterhuishouding op de landbouwkundige productie.* [Impact of the water balance on the Agricultural production]. Report of the working group HELP-tabel. Mededelingen Landinrichtingsdienst 176. Utrecht: Landinrichtingsdienst.

Hemker, C.J., and G.J. Nijsten. 1996. Groundwater flow modelling using MicroFem, manual version 3. Amsterdam: Hemker Geohydroloog.

Hooghoudt, S.B. 1940. *Algemeene beschouwing van het probleem van de detail ontwatering en de infiltratie door middel van parallel loopende drains, greppels, slooten en kanalen* [*General discussion concerning the problem of drainage and infiltration by means of parallel tile drains, furrows, small watercourses and canals*]. Verslagen van landbouwkundige onderzoekingen 46 (14) B. The Hague: Algemeene Landsdrukkerij.

Kroes, J.G., and J.C. van Dam. 2003. *SWAP 3.0.3 reference manual.* Report 773. Wageningen, Netherlands: Alterra.

McLaughlin, D. 2002. An integrated approach to hydrologic data assimilation: Interpolation, smoothing, and filtering. *Advances in Water Resources* 25:1275–86.

Moore, R., I. Tindall, and D. Fortune. 2005. Update on the HarmonIT Project: The openMI standard for model linking. In *Proceedings of the 6th International Conference on Hydroinformatics*, ed. S.Y. Liong, K. Phoon, and V. Babovic, 1811–18 Singapore: World Scientific Publishing Company.

Neuman, S.P., R.A. Feddes, and E. Bresler. 1974. *Finite element simulation of flow in saturated-unsaturated soils considering water uptake by plants.* Third Annual Report, Project No. A10-SWC-77. Haifa, Israel: Hydraulic Engineering Lab, Technion.

Overbeek, G.B.J., A. Tiktak, A.H.W. Beusen, and P.J.T.M. van Puijenbroek. 2001. Partial validation of the Dutch Model for Emission and Transport of Nutrients (STONE). *Scientific World* 1(S2)]:194–99.

Projectgroep Waternood. 1998. *Grondwater als leidraad voor het oppervlaktewater* [*Groundwater guidance for surface water*]. DLG publicatie 98/2. Utrecht and the Hague: Dienst Landelijk Gebied en Unie van Waterschappen.

Schuurmans, J.M., P.A. Troch, A.A. Veldhuizen, W.G.M. Bastiaanssen, and M.F.P. Bierkens. 2003. Assimilation of remotely sensed latent heat fluxes in a distributed hydrological model. *Advances in Water Resources* 26 (2): 151–59.

V&W. 1984. *Tweede nota Waterhuishouding* [*Second National Policy Memorandum on Water Management*]. The Hague: Ministry of Transport, Public Works and Water Management.

Valstar, J.R., D.B. McLaughlin, C.B.M. te Stroet, and F.C. van Geer. 2004. A representer-based inverse method for groundwater flow and transport applications. *Water Resources Research* 40:W05116.

van Dam, J.C. 2000. SWAP model concepts, parameter estimation, and case studies. PhD thesis. Wageningen, Netherlands: Wageningen University.

van Geer, F.C., and C.B.M. te Stroet. 1990. A Kalman filter approach to the quantification of the reliability of a groundwater model. In *Calibration and reliability in groundwater modelling. ModelCare '90*, ed. K. Kovar, 467–76. IAHS Publication 195. Washington, DC: International Association of Hydrological Sciences.

van Geer, F.C., C.B.M. te Stroet, and M.F.P. Bierkens. 1990. Groundwater modelling in relation to the system's response time using Kalman filtering. In *Proceedings of the Eighth International*

Conference on Computational Methods in Water Resources and Surface Hydrology, Part A, ed. G. Gambolati, A. Rinald, C. A. Brebbia, W. G. Gray, and G.F. Pinder, 23–30. Venice: Computational Mechanics Publication.

van Walsum, P.E.V., A.A.Veldhuizen, P.J.T. van Bakel, F.J.E. van der Bolt, P.E. Dik, P.Groenendijk, E.P. Querner, and M.F.R. Smit. 2004. *SIMGRO 5.0.1:Theory and model implementation.* Alterra Report 913.1. Wageningen, Netherlands: Alterra.

van Walsum, P.E.V., and P. Groenendijk. 2006. *Dynamic metamodel for the unsaturated-saturated zone.* Proceedings of MODFLOW 2006. Golden, Colorado: International Groundwater Modeling Center (IGWMC).

Veldhuizen, A.A., P.E.V. van Walsum, A. Lourens, and P.E. Dik. 2006. *Flexible integrated modelling of groundwater, soil water and surface water.* Proceedings of MODFLOW 2006. Golden, Colorado: International Groundwater Modeling Center (IGWMC).

Vrugt, J. A., H.V. Gupta, L.A. Bastidas, W. Bouten, and S. Sorooshian. 2003a. Effective and efficient algorithm for multi-objective optimization of hydrologic models. *Water Resources Research* 39 (8): 1214–32.

Vrugt J. A., H.V. Gupta, W. Bouten, and S. Sorooshian. 2003b. A shuffled complex evolution metropolis algorithm for optimization and uncertainty assessment of hydrologic model parameters. *Water Resources Research* 39 (8): 1–16.

WL | Delft Hydraulics. 2001. *SOBEK Rural, managing your flow.* Manual version 2.07. Delft, Netherlands: WL | Delft Hydraulics. www.delftsoftware.wldelft.nl.

Wolf, J., A.H.W. Beusen, P. Groenendijk, T. Kroon, R. Rötter, and H. van Zeijts. 2003. The integrated modelling system STONE for calculating emissions from agriculture in the Netherlands. *Environmental Modelling and Software* 18:597–617.

Wolf, J., M.J.D. Hack-ten Broeke, and R. Rötter. 2005a. Simulation of nitrogen leaching in sandy soil in the Netherlands with the ANIMO model and the integrated modelling system STONE. *Agriculture, Ecosystems and Environment* 105:523–40.

Wolf, J., R. Rötter, and O. Oenema. 2005b. Nutrient emission models in environmental policy evaluation at different scales: Experience from the Netherlands, Agriculture. *Ecosystems and Environment* 105:291–306.

CHAPTER 3

Threats to Intertidal Soft-Sediment Ecosystems

Theunis Piersma

O NE OF THE MANY FACTORS threatening the ecological integrity of the Wadden Sea, a coastal shallow water ecosystem in the northern part of the Netherlands, is bottom disturbance due to fishing, particularly mechanical dredging for shellfish. Because of its far-reaching national and international ecological impacts, fishing has been a major policy issue for several decades.

Tidal flats occur along the edges of shallow seas with soft-sediment bottoms, in areas where the tidal range is at least a meter or so (Eisma 1998; van de Kam et al. 2004). The lowest intertidal areas are largely barren, except for seagrass meadows (*Zostera*) and reefs formed by shellfish such as oysters (*Ostrea*) or tubeworms (e.g., *Sabellaria*). Intertidal areas are inundated at least once per day; higher up are salt marshes, which are more rarely and irregularly inundated. In tropical regions, and even some benign temperate areas such as northern New Zealand, the upper parts of intertidal areas may be covered by mangrove forests rather than salt marsh. Mangroves also have a tendency to cover the regularly inundated parts of intertidal soft sediments, thus reducing the extent of mudflats in many tropical areas. No intertidal deposits occur at high latitudes, farther north than 70° to 73°, as coastlines are either ice covered for most of the year or disturbed by moving ice too frequently for soft-sediment deposits to build up.

Soft-sediment systems worldwide provide living space for a group of highly specialized migrant shorebirds, relatively long-legged small to medium-size birds that breed spread out over boreal to arctic areas in the Northern Hemisphere during June and July and migrate considerable distances to much smaller coastal intertidal ecosystems the world over. From August to May, the birds are found in large concentrations in the Wadden Sea. Long-distance migrant shorebirds are particularly susceptible to the effects of human encroachment on coastal habitats, overexploitation of marine resources, and global climate change (Piersma and Baker 2000;

Piersma and Lindström 2004). A recent survey by the International Wader Study Group showed that of 207 shorebird populations with known population trajectories (out of a total of 511 known shorebird populations), almost half (48%) are in decline, whereas only 16% are increasing (International Wader Study Group 2003). With three times as many populations decreasing as increasing, shorebirds belong to the most globally endangered segment of migrant birds of the world.

This chapter focuses on the role of intertidal ecosystems such as the Wadden Sea in supporting intricate networks of intercontinental shorebird flyways, phenomena for which the Dutch government has pledged responsibility through international agreements such as the Ramsar Convention on Wetlands and the European Union's Habitats and Birds Directives. Nevertheless, the Dutch government has also allowed mechanical dredging for shellfish. The main objective of this chapter is to show that permitting this activity undermines the government's commitment to the international agreements.

Signed in 1971 in Ramsar, Iran, the Ramsar Convention on Wetlands (www.ramsar.org) is an intergovernmental treaty that provides the framework for national action and international cooperation on the conservation and wise use of wetlands and their resources. Presently, the convention has 153 contracting parties, with 1,631 designated wetland sites covering a total of 145.6 million hectares on the Ramsar List of Wetlands of International Importance. The Habitats Directive of the European Union (EU) is much more recent, dating from 1992, and aims to ensure biodiversity through the conservation of natural habitats and wild fauna and flora in the continent. Under this directive, EU member states have agreed to design, maintain, or restore natural habitats and species of wild fauna and flora, including the establishment of a coherent European ecological network of special protection areas (SPAs). This network, known as Natura 2000, should enable the natural habitats of the species concerned to be maintained or, where appropriate, restored to a favorable conservation status. The Birds Directive of 1994 embodies a far-reaching protection scheme for all of the continent's wild birds, particularly those that are threatened and in need of special conservation measures. Under this directive, member states are required to establish SPAs not only for the 194 species designated as threatened, but for *all migratory* bird species. SPAs, such as wetlands, are scientifically identified areas critical for the survival of the targeted species and form part of Natura 2000. The designation of an area, such as the intertidal flats in the Netherlands' Wadden Sea, as an SPA gives it a high level of protection from potentially damaging developments.

Of the many factors threatening the ecological integrity of coastal shallow water ecosystems, sustained bottom disturbance from fishing appears to be the most overlooked yet pervasive (Coleman and Williams 2002; Jackson et al. 2001; Worm et al. 2006). Building on the lines of argument developed in Bakker and Piersma (2005) and Piersma (2006), this chapter will outline in some detail how mechanical dredging for shellfish in the Dutch Wadden Sea has led to long-term ecological damage and the loss of shorebird populations dependent on shellfish resources. We begin by describing the geophysical and ecological nature of soft-sediment habitats, especially those in the coastal zone. Then we examine the nature of human disturbances and human-related threats to the integrity of soft-sediment ecosystems in order to

develop the argument in detail for a well-researched case study of a protected intertidal area in the Netherlands where dredging for shellfish led to a cascade of ecological consequences and the disappearance of a significant part of a fully protected
wintering shorebird population. The chapter concludes with a more general discussion of the incompatibility of bottom-disturbing harvesting practices and the
proper protection of seabed systems.

SOFT-SEDIMENT ECOSYSTEMS

Soft-sediment shores in general, and intertidal sand- and mudflats in particular, in
contrast to rocky shorelines, are in dynamic flux. The nature of the sediments is
determined by the sediment types available, currents, tides, and wind-generated
waves, as well as the presence or absence of ecosystem-engineering organisms (such
as reef-building oysters or mussels, but also subsurface-dwelling species producing
fecal pellets that help consolidate sediments; e.g., Risk and Moffatt 1977; Rothschild et al. 1994) and human activities such as bottom-fishing and dredging. Good
general introductions to the nature of intertidal soft-sediment habitats can be found
in Eisma (1998), Little (2000), Raffaeli and Hawkins (1996), and Reise (1985).

Coarse-grained sediments mostly occur on wave-exposed shores but may even
be found in sheltered places if currents are strong enough. Fine-grained sediments
accumulate in areas that have some shelter, with lower currents and less wave
action. Biofilms of microscopic algae and bacteria, which produce polymeric substances, trap and bind sediments, producing a surface that is more resistant to ero-
sive forces (Austen et al. 1999; Paterson 1997). The presence of seagrass meadows
not only suppresses erosion, but also increases the accretion rate relative to unveg-
etated areas (Fonseca and Fisher 1986; Gleason et al. 1979; Ward et al. 1984).

Mussel and oyster beds have similar roles in providing shelter and enhancing
accretion rates by their capacity to increase particle size of flocculate matter (Verweij 1952), but they are prone to erosion by the forces of wind and currents. For
the Wadden Sea, Nehls and Thiel (1993) concluded that the longest-living mussel
beds occurred in areas where they had some degree of protection from storms. In
general, wind and tidal stress factors seem to influence benthic community structures quite strongly (e.g., Emerson 1989; Thistle 1981; Warwick and Uncles 1980).
Thus one of the most interesting phenomena affecting the appearance and biodiversity of intertidal flats is the mutual interaction between abiotic factors (wind
and currents) and the organisms present (Bruno and Bertness 2001; Verweij 1952).
The establishment on bare intertidal flats of species that influence the complexity
of the habitat, such as seagrasses, oysters, mussels, or tubeworms, typically generates
even greater habitat complexity, more variations in sediment structure, and
increased biodiversity.

Intertidal soft-sediment systems are among the most productive natural ecosystems, even those in terrestrial habitats on earth (e.g., Beukema 1975; van de Kam
et al. 2004). To a large extent, this is because the waters and sediments are nutrient
rich and because sunlight has easy access, both in the shallow water layer and on
the mud surface at low tide, enabling high primary productivity, which is then

channeled to the higher trophic layers according to the principle of the food pyramid. Food chains are rather like pyramids, with less numerous predators at the top and a great abundance of sunlight-catching plants at the bottom. For instance, one shark will eat many big fish, each of which eats a lot of little fish. These little fish might eat crustaceans that feed on zooplankton, which in turn graze on algae, unicellular plants. In this example, the food chain has six links, but in reality, most have fewer. In every food chain, 10% of the organic matter produced at one link is eaten by the next level. The production of 1 kilogram (kg) of shark meat requires 10 kg of big fish, which requires 100 kg of little fish. Working back through the chain, it therefore requires 100,000 kg of algae for a shark to gain 1 kg in mass (a good summary is presented in Pauly and MacLean 2003).

Food chains in European tidal flat systems such as the Wadden Sea usually consist of four levels, with the fourth level composed of seals and fishermen. Birds and fish form the third level and eat invertebrates such as shellfish, worms, and crustaceans (the second level), which feed on algae (the first level). Thus one could say that invertebrates transfer the nutrients and energy from algae into bite-size food portions for the birds (van de Kam et al. 2004).

HUMAN-INDUCED THREATS TO INTERTIDAL ECOSYSTEMS

Although rich in principle, coastal marine ecosystems have suffered very badly at the hand of humans over the last few hundred years (Jackson et al. 2001; Pauly and MacLean 2003; Worm et al. 2006). Upon discovering the Americas for the Spanish king, Christopher Columbus found it hard going in the Caribbean because the passage of his ships was obstructed by the presence of sea turtles, grazers of seagrass meadows that have since been decimated by humans greedy for their meat and eggs. In most parts of the world, certainly in Europe, intertidal flats have experienced human exploitation from the mid-Holocene onward. Most of the human exploitation of intertidal flats was relatively unintrusive for a long time, as it consisted of small-scale fishing and the taking of shellfish by hand. With the advent of motorized power in the last century, however, as well as the use of large nets and dredges, human exploitation of intertidal flats has come to influence the natural processes a great deal. For example, mussels have been farmed in the western Dutch Wadden Sea since specialists from the province of Zeeland moved in during the early 1960s. This industry not only involves the filling up and dredging out of artificial subtidal mussel beds, but also entails the bringing together of mussel spat from much larger areas, including the nearby intertidal zone as well as outside the Netherlands (Kamermans and Smaal 2002). These mussels may be replaced several times during their lives before final transport to the market, and each replacement involves bottom dredging.

In response to the development of markets for bait used in sport-fishing (angling), techniques to mechanically dredge for lugworms (*Arenicola marina*) were developed in the Netherlands in the early 1980s. Given the considerable depth at which they live (30 to 40 centimeters), dredging for lugworms is very invasive, leaving 40-centimeter-deep gullies, with considerable consequences for the intertidal biota (Beukema 1995). In a four-year dredging period, lugworm densities over a square kilometer declined by half. Simultaneously, total biomass of benthic organisms declined even more with an almost complete local disappearance of the large sand gaper (*Mya arenaria*), a bivalve that initially constituted half of the biomass. Recovery took several years.

Edible cockles *(Cerastoderma edule)* have not been a popular food in the Netherlands, but the demands of foreign markets nevertheless made this fishery profitable, albeit on a limited scale, from the early 1900s onward. With the discovery of new markets, notably in countries in the Mediterranean region, and the development of mechanical harvesting techniques, this fishery has seen a large expansion over the past decades. Starting in the late 1970s, the dredging for cockles became a veritable industry. Ecological studies have shown long-term, near decadal, effects on rates of recruitment of cockles and another bivalve called the Baltic tellin (*Macoma balthica*) (Piersma et al. 2001). Also, in the shorter term, mechanical cockle-dredging practices appear to be having strong negative ecological impacts (see below).

In the Wadden Sea, reclamation, pollution of various kinds (organochlorines and heavy metals in the 1960s, fertilizers such nitrates and phosphates in the 1970s, and many rare and exotic organic compounds since), as well as the release and subsequent invasion of exotic species can be counted as threats (van de Kam et al. 2004). As emphasized by Jackson et al. (2001) in their review, however, among the many threats to coastal ecosystems, fishing has always been the most significant human disturbance. Especially in modern times, when fishing involves the use of capital- and energy-intensive mechanical harvesting devices rather than manual or wind power, this activity plays a primary role in the deterioration of coastal ecosystems. This is particularly so in the Wadden Sea, where industrial forms of fishing that include bottom nets, scrapes, and dredges induce serious habitat transformation (Bakker and Piersma 2005). When intertidal structures change as a result, local biodiversity and its generative processes are greatly reduced. The scenario outlined by Jackson et al. (2001) certainly applies to the intertidal flats in the Dutch Wadden Sea.

Summarizing detailed faunistic information from the Wadden Sea dating back to 1869, Reise (1982) concluded that whereas bivalves and some other groups of invertebrate animals show long-term decreases in species diversity, the smaller polychaete species with short life spans (e.g., *Scoloplos armiger*) are doing well, as they can take rapid advantage of environmental disturbances that lead to depletions of other fauna. Reise attributed the disappearance of 28 common macroinvertebrate species to the loss of the many microhabitats provided by complex physical structures such as oyster beds, tubeworm reefs, and seagrass meadows. When mussel beds and seagrass meadows that have provided shelter, nutrition, and other benefits to various species disappear, so does the fauna associated with them.

In summary, the evidence that trawling, digging, and dredging have serious negative effects on the sediment characteristics and community structure of intertidal flats and other sea bottoms is now overwhelming and paramount (e.g., Collie et al. 2000; Dayton et al. 1995; Hall and Harding 1997; Hall et al. 1990; Jackson et al. 2001; Kaiser et al. 2000; Roberts 1997; Watling and Norse 1998; comprehensive review in Dieter et al. 2003). Hall (1994, *194*), in an early review of physical disturbance and marine benthic communities, summarized this by saying: "There is increasing recognition of the role man plays in physically disturbing marine sediment environments, the most obvious and widespread being commercial fishing."

Effects of Dredging on Shorebirds in a Protected Ecosystem

The intertidal flats of the Dutch Wadden Sea are a state nature monument and are protected under the Ramsar Convention and EU's Habitats and Birds Directives (Reneerkens et al. 2005). Despite the high-level conservation status and widespread scientific concerns about the damaging effects of shellfish dredging on marine benthic ecosystems, three-quarters of these intertidal flats were open to mechanical dredging for edible cockles until 2004. A direct, immediate effect of dredging is the complete removal of all organisms larger than 19 millimeters in the 5-centimeter top layer. As the dredged sites are usually the most biodiverse (Kraan et al. 2007), the activity may also affect smaller cockles; other bivalves such as blue mussels (*Mytilus edulis*), Baltic tellins, and sand gapers; polychaetes; and crustaceans such as shore crabs (*Carcinus maenas*). More indirectly, and over longer time frames, sediments lose fine silts from dredging, which leads to long-term reductions in settlement success in both cockles and Baltic tellins (Hiddink 2003; Piersma et al. 2001). Between 1997–1998 and 2002–2003, the numbers of wintering red knots (*Calidris canutus*) in Northwest Europe declined by about 25%, from approximately 330,000 to 250,000 (unpublished data of the British Trust for Ornithology [BTO], Dutch Centre for Field Ornithology [SOVON], and others), and in the Wadden Sea by some 80%, from about 100,000 to 20,000 or fewer (van Roomen et al. 2005). Before we examine whether these declines in red knot numbers can be attributed to the mechanical downfishing of the intertidal food webs in the Wadden Sea, a few words about this shellfish-eating shorebird are necessary.

Red knots are highly specialized with respect to feeding and habitat use. Outside the breeding season in the High Arctic, their occurrence is restricted to open coastal intertidal wetland habitats and their diet to hard-shelled mollusks and crustaceans (fig. 3.1). These birds are sandpipers that breed on High Arctic tundra *only*, but move south from their disjunct, circumpolar breeding areas to nonbreeding sites on the coasts of all continents (except Antarctica) between latitudes 58° north and 53° south. Because of their specialized sensory capabilities (Piersma et al. 1998), red knots generally eat hard-shelled prey found on intertidal, mostly soft, substrates (Piersma et al. 1995, 2005). As a consequence, ecologically suitable coastal sites are few and far between, so the birds must routinely undertake flights of many thousands of kilometers. Each of the six separate tundra breeding areas hosts a population with a sufficiently distinct appearance in body size and plumage during the breeding season to have been assigned a subspecies names (Piersma and Davidson 1992; Tomkovich 2001). Red knots shared a common ancestor as recently as within the last 20,000 years or so (Buehler and Baker 2005; Buehler et al. 2007), and as a result, the subspecies show little genetic divergence.

In an area of roughly 250 square kilometers in the western Dutch Wadden Sea, we annually sampled knot foods and studied the densities and quality in great detail (e.g., Piersma et al. 2001; van Gils et al. 2006b). Each year from early September into December, immediately after completion of our sampling program, mechan-

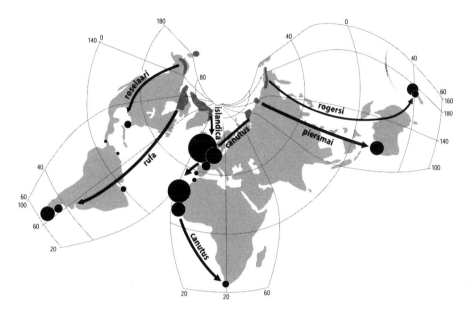

Figure 3.1 *Worldwide connectedness: the flyways of the six identified subspecies of red knots (Calidris canutus)*

ical dredging took place at some of the intertidal flats previously mapped for benthos. Using the black-box GPS data on dredging activity that fishery organizations must present annually to the Dutch government (Kamermans and Smaal 2002), we could categorize one-square-kilometer sample blocks as dredged or undredged (this was partially verified based on observations of damaged sediment surfaces; see Kraan et al. 2007). During the years of our study, red knots consumed mostly first-year cockles (58%, based on 174 samples of between 50 and 100 droppings), and for this reason, we focused our analysis on the effects of dredging on freshly settled first-year cockles, known at this stage as spat (see van Gils et al. 2006a).

In dredged areas, densities of cockle spat remained stable, whereas in undredged areas, they increased by a marginal amount (2.6%) per year (van Gils et al. 2006a). This result is consistent with a previous assessment that showed that dredged areas become unattractive for cockles to settle in, perhaps because such sediments have lost silt and good structure (Piersma et al. 2001). In addition, the *quality* of cockle spat, indicated by the ratio between the mass of the flesh inside the shell and that of the shell itself, declined by 11.3% per year in dredged areas but remained stable in undredged areas, something we explain by the fact that coarser sediments may lead to worse feeding conditions (Drent et al. 2004) and therefore to reduced body condition in deposit-feeding bivalves such as freshly settled cockles (Rossi et al. 2004). Thus both the abundance and quality of the food of red knots decreased in areas where dredging took place.

We quantified the consequences of these declines by calculating, for each year, the percentage of the intertidal area that would yield insufficient intake rates for knots to maintain a positive energy balance. In the Wadden Sea, only a limited part of the available intertidal flats is rich enough in suitable prey to be of any use to foraging red knots in the best of years (Piersma et al. 1995; van Gils et al. 2006b). From 1998 to 2002, however, the percentage of one-square-kilometer blocks that were too poor for red knots to obtain a threshold intake rate of 4.8 watts, based on food requirements at that time of year (see Piersma et al. 1995), increased from 66% to 87% (van Gils et al. 2006a). This loss was entirely due to an increase in previously suitable blocks that were dredged; the number of previously unsuitable (and undredged) blocks did not increase.

As a consequence of the widespread dredging in the most biodiverse areas of intertidal flat (Kraan et al. 2007), diet quality in terms of the flesh-to-shell mass ratios declined by 11.7% per year. To compensate for such reductions in prey quality, red knots should increase gizzard mass (Dekinga et al. 2001; van Gils et al. 2003), and they did (van Gils et al. 2006a). This allows them to process the larger amounts of shell material that are necessary in order to maintain a sufficient intake of meat. Despite increasing gizzard size over the years, resightings of individually color-banded birds whose gizzards were measured with ultrasonography before release demonstrated that birds not seen in our study area within a year after release had undersize gizzards; individuals that we did see again had gizzards large enough for a balanced daily energy budget (van Gils et al. 2006a). Local annual survival rate, calculated from resighting rates of banded birds, increased with year-specific food quality. This means that birds arriving from the tundra breeding areas with gizzards that were too small needed more time for their gizzards to adjust than their energy stores allowed them, and thus they faced starvation unless they left the area.

Banded knots that disappeared from our study area may have died or, perhaps more likely for a wide-ranging migrant, emigrated to other areas such as the estuaries in the United Kingdom. Here they probably paid a mortality cost as a result of the extra travel or uncertainties in the food supply at their new destination. Whatever happened to them, the stark decline in numbers of red knots wintering in the Wadden Sea can be explained satisfactorily by these documented population effects of declining food conditions (van Gils et al. 2006a). The local disappearance can also account for much of the 25% decline of the entire Northwest European wintering population over the same period. This leads us to conclude that the industrial forms of commercial exploitation allowed by the Dutch government in one of the country's best legally protected nature reserves have been directly responsible for the population decline of an also fully protected long-distance migrant shorebird species. Studies on the declines of both another fully protected shellfish-eating shorebird, the Eurasian oystercatcher (*Haematopus ostralegus*), in the Wadden Sea (Verhulst et al. 2004) and a nearby UK estuary, the Wash (Atkinson et al. 2003), and a strictly molluscivore sea duck, the common eider (*Somateria mollissima*) (Camphuysen et al. 2002), have reached precisely the same conclusion.

Obeying an order of the European Court that mechanical dredging for cockles is a new economic activity that has to be evaluated in the context, the EU's Habitats and Birds Directives, the Netherlands State Court (Raad van State) destroyed the existing governmental permits for the procedure issued by the Dutch Ministry for Agriculture, Nature and Food Quality. This forced the ministry to prohibit the mechanical forms of cockle dredging from 2004 onward, and the international companies affected received a generous compensation sum of more than 100 million euros (Wilde Kokkels n.d.). Although this may have meant the end of industrial dredging for cockles in the Wadden Sea, the ministry has since issued new permits for mechanical dredging for lugworms, worked toward an increase in the number of permits for hand cocklers and harvesting intertidal mussels, and failed to examine the degree to which the negative effects of shrimp fishing on bottom communities warrant fresh examination (e.g., Buhs and Reise 1997; Buschbaum and Nehls 2003).

CONCLUSIONS

One of the many factors threatening the ecological integrity of the Wadden Sea is bottom disturbance from fishing, particularly mechanical dredging for shellfish. Because of its far-reaching ecological impacts, it has been a major policy issue for several decades.

In view of the commitments made by the international community to safeguard the flyway populations of shorebirds such as the red knot, the direct and indirect effects of bottom trawling and dredging on intertidal ecosystems are a major concern. The probability that damaged intertidal flat communities will recover has not been determined, but it is likely to be even lower than the probability of the recovery of fish stocks after overfishing (Hutchings 2000). Little doubt exists that the time course of any recovery will be a function of the spatial scale at which the disturbance took place (Lenihan and Micheli 2001). The time constant of general processes in the coastal zone is quite tightly correlated with their specific spatial scale. Given the extent of dredging for cockles on the intertidal flats of the Wadden Sea, the time to the beginning of recovery would be rather longer than a year (Piersma et al. 2001). Using data from the literature for minimum recovery times after disturbance for intertidal and subtidal soft-sediment habitats, we can make a preliminary quantitative assessment of time to the beginning of a recovery; it would be semiquantitative, however, as only datapoints from studies where recovery was positive could be included (Versteegh et al. 2004). Affecting up to 100 square kilometers of intertidal flats, mechanical dredging for cockles alone is predicted to require at least 30 years for full recovery. We regard this as the most optimistic assessment, as recovery times may be much longer still if mechanical dredging moves the intertidal ecosystem toward a different, and much less biodiverse and productive, stable state (Scheffer et al. 2001).

In summary, mechanical dredging for shellfish in the Dutch Wadden Sea has caused long-term ecological damage and led to the loss of shorebird populations dependent on shellfish resources. After dredging, soft-sediment systems are left greatly impoverished in both biomass and biodiversity, with serious negative effects for the birds, fish, and humans living off these coastal ecosystems. Such losses are easy to predict but hard to reverse: large-scale mechanical disturbance of intertidal flats and other sea bottoms has been shown to lead to irreversible, or at least very long-term, negative changes in ecosystem properties. It follows that industrial, mechanical harvesting methods such as those allowed by the Dutch government in protected coastal nature reserves under its management are unsustainable (Gross 2006). Only handpicking and some limited forms of gillnetting may qualify as sustainable forms of intertidal exploitation.

REFERENCES

Atkinson, P.W., N.A. Clark, M.C. Bell, P.J. Dare, J.A. Clark, and P.L. Ireland. 2003. Changes in commercially fished shellfish stocks and shorebird populations in the Wash, England. *Biological Conservation* 114:127–41.

Austen, I., T.J. Andersen, and K. Edelvang. 1999. The influence of benthic diatoms and invertebrates on the erodibility of an intertidal mudflat, the Danish Wadden Sea. *Estuarine, Coastal and Shelf Science* 49:99–111.

Bakker, J.P., and T. Piersma. 2005. Restoration of intertidal flats and tidal salt marshes. In *Restoration ecology: The new frontier*, ed. J. van Andel and J. Aronson, 174–92. Oxford: Blackwell Science.

Beukema, J.J. 1975. Biologische productie in zee [Biological production in the sea]. In *Produktiviteit in biologische systemen* [*Productivity in biological systems*], ed. G.J. Vervelde, 243–62. Wageningen, Netherlands: Pudoc.

———. 1995. Long-term effects of mechanical harvesting of lugworms *Arenicola marina* on the zoobenthic community of a tidal flat in the Wadden Sea. *Netherlands Journal of Sea Research* 33:219–27.

Bruno, J.F., and M.D. Bertness. 2001. Habitat modification and facilitation in benthic marine communities. In *Marine community ecology*, ed. M.D. Bertness, S.D. Gaines, and M.E. Hay, 201–18. Sunderland, MA: Sinauer Publishers.

Buehler, D.M., and A.J. Baker. 2005. Population divergence times and historical demography in red knots and dunlins. *Condor* 107:497–513.

Buehler, D.M., A.J. Baker, and T. Piersma. 2007. Reconstructing palaeoflyways of the late Pleistocene and early Holocene red knot (*Calidris canutus*). *Ardea* 94: 485–98.

Buhs, F., and K. Reise. 1997. Epibenthic fauna dredged from tidal channels in the Wadden Sea of Schleswig-Holstein: spatial patterns and a long-term decline. *Helgoländer Meeresuntersuchungen* 51:343–59.

Buschbaum, C., and G. Nehls. 2003. Effekte der Miesmuschel- und Garnelenfischerei [Impact of mussel and shrimp fishing]. In *Warnsignale aus Nordsee und Wattenmeer* [*Warning signals from the North Sea and Wassen Sea*], ed. J. Lozán, E. Rachor, K. Reise, J. Sündermann, and H. von Westernhagen, 250–55. Hamburg, Germany: Wissenschaftliche Auswertungen.

Camphuysen, C.J., C.M. Berrevoets, H.J.W.M. Cremers, A. Dekinga, R. Dekker, B.J. Ens, T.M. van der Have, R.K.H. Kats, T. Kuiken, M.F. Leopold, J. van der Meer, and T. Piersma. 2002. Mass mortality of common eiders (*Somateria mollissima*) in the Dutch Wadden Sea, winter 1999/2000: Starvation in a commercially exploited wetland of international importance. *Biological Conservation* 106:303–17.

Coleman, F.C., and S.L. Williams. 2002. Overexploiting marine ecosystem engineers: potential consequences for biodiversity. *Trends in Ecology and Evolution* 17:40–44.

Collie, J.S., S J. Hall, M.J. Kaiser, and I.R. Poiner. 2000. A quantitative analysis of fishing impacts on shelf-sea benthos. *Journal of Animal Ecology* 69:785–98.

Dayton, P.K., S.F. Thrush, M.T. Agardy, and R.J. Hofman. 1995. Environmental effects of marine fishing. *Aquatic Conservation: Marine and Freshwater Ecosystems* 5:205–32.

Dekinga, A., M.W. Dietz, A. Koolhaas, and T. Piersma. 2001. Time course and reversibility of changes in the gizzards of red knots alternately eating hard and soft food. *Journal of Experimental Biology* 204:2167–73.

Dieter, B. E., D. A. Wion, and R. A. McConnaughey. 2003. *Mobile fishing gear effect on benthic habitats: A bibliography.* Seattle: NOAA, Department of Fisheries.

Drent, J., P.C. Luttikhuizen, and T. Piersma. 2004. Morphological dynamics in the foraging apparatus of a deposit feeding marine bivalve: Phenotypic plasticity and heritable effects. *Functional Ecology* 18:349–56.

Eisma, D. 1998. *Intertidal deposits: River mouths, tidal flats, and coastal lagoons.* Boca Raton, FL: CRC Press.

Emerson, C.W. 1989. Wind stress limitation of benthic secondary production in shallow, soft-sediment communities. *Marine Ecology Progress Series* 53:65–77.

Fonseca, M.S., and J.S. Fisher. 1986. A comparison of canopy friction and sediment movement between four species of seagrass with reference to their restoration and ecology. *Marine Ecology Progress Series* 29:15–22.

Gleason, M.L., D.A. Elmer, N.C. Pien, and J.S. Fisher. 1979. Effects of stem density upon sediment retention by salt marsh cord grass *Spartina alterniflora* Loisel. *Estuaries* 2:475–82.

Gross, L. 2006. Mixing exploitation and conservation: A recipe for disaster. *Public Library of Science Biology* 4:4418.

Hall, S.J. 1994. Physical disturbance and marine benthic communities: life in unconsolidated sediments. *Oceanography and Marine Biology Annual Review* 32:179–239.

Hall, S.J., D.J. Basford, and M.R. Robertson. 1990. The impact of hydraulic dredging for razor clams *Ensis* sp. on an infaunal community. *Netherlands Journal of Sea Research* 27:119–25.

Hall, S.J., and M.J.C. Harding. 1997. Physical disturbance and marine benthic communities: the effects of mechanical harvesting of cockles on non-target benthic infauna. *Journal of Applied Ecology* 34:497–517.

Hiddink, J.G. 2003. Effects of suction-dredging for cockles on non-target fauna in the Wadden Sea. *Journal of Sea Research* 50:315–23.

Hutchings, J.A. 2000. Collapse and recovery of marine fishes. *Nature* 406:882–85.

International Wader Study Group. 2003. Waders are declining worldwide. *Wader Study Group Bulletin* 101/102:8–12.

Jackson, J.B.C., M.X. Kirby, W.H. Berger, K.A. Bjorndal, L.W. Botsford, B.J. Bourque, R.H. Bradbury, R. Cooke, J. Erlandson, J.A. Estes, T.P. Hughes, S. Kidwell, C.B. Lange, H.S. Lenihan, J.M. Pandolfi, C.H. Peterson, R.S. Steneck, M.J. Tegner, and R.R. Warner. 2001. *Historical overfishing and the recent collapse of coastal ecosystems.* Science 293:629–38.

Kaiser, M.J., K. Ramsey, C.A. Richardson, F.E. Spence, and A.R. Brand. 2000. Chronic fishing disturbance has changed shelf sea benthic community structure. *Journal of Animal Ecology* 69:494–503.

Kamermans, P., and A.C. Smaal. 2002. Mussel culture and cockle fisheries in the Netherlands: Finding a balance between economy and ecology. *Journal of Shellfish Research* 21:509–17.

Kraan, C., T. Piersma, A. Dekinga, A. Koolhaas, and J. van der Meer. 2007. Dredging for edible cockles (*Cerastoderma edule*) on intertidal flats: Short-term consequences of fisher patch-choice decisions for target and non-target benthic fauna. *ICES Journal of Marine Science* 64:1735–42.

Lenihan, H.S., and F. Micheli. 2001. Soft-sediment communities. In *Marine community ecology,* ed. M.D. Bertness and S.D. Gaines, 253–88. Sunderland, MA: Sinauer Publishers.

Little, C. 2000. *The biology of soft shores and estuaries.* Oxford: Oxford University Press.

Nehls, G., and M. Thiel. 1993. Large-scale distribution patterns of the mussel *Mytilus edulis* in the Wadden Sea of Schleswig-Holstein: Do storms structure the ecosystem? *Netherlands Journal of Sea Research* 31:181–87.

Paterson, D.M. 1997. Biological mediation of sediment erodibility: Ecology and physical dynamics. In *Cohesive sediments,* ed. N. Burt, R. Parker, and J. Watts, 215–29. Chichester, UK: Wiley.

Pauly, D., and J. MacLean. 2003. *In a perfect ocean: The state of fisheries and ecosystems in the North Atlantic Ocean.* Washington, DC: Island Press.

Piersma, T. 2006. Migration in the balance: Tight ecological margins and the changing fortunes of shorebird populations. In *Waterbirds around the world,* ed. G.C. Boere, C.A. Galbraith, and D.A. Stroud, 74–80. Edinburgh: HM Stationery Office.

Piersma, T., and A.J. Baker. 2000. Life history characteristics and the conservation of migratory shorebirds. In *Behaviour and conservation,* ed. L.M. Gosling and W.J. Sutherland, 105–24. Cambridge: Cambridge University Press.

Piersma, T., and N.C. Davidson. 1992. The migrations and annual cycles of five subspecies of Knots in perspective. *Wader Study Group Bulletin* 64 (Suppl.): 187–97.

Piersma, T., A. Koolhaas, A. Dekinga, J.J. Beukema, R. Dekker, and K. Essink. 2001. Long-term indirect effects of mechanical cockle-dredging on intertidal bivalve stocks in the Wadden Sea. *Journal of Applied Ecology* 38:976–90.

Piersma, T., and Å. Lindström. 2004. Migrating shorebirds as integrative sentinels of global environmental change. *Ibis* 146 (Suppl. 1): 61–69.

Piersma, T., D.I. Rogers, P.M. González, L. Zwarts, L.J. Niles, I. de Lima Serrano do Nascimento, C.D.T. Minton, and A.J. Baker. 2005. Fuel storage rates before northward flights in red knots worldwide: Facing the severest constraint in tropical intertidal environments? In *Birds of two worlds: The ecology and evolution of migration*, ed. R. Greenberg and P. P. Marra, 262–73. Baltimore: Johns Hopkins University Press.

Piersma, T., R. van Aelst, K. Kurk, H. Berkhoudt, and L.R.M. Maas. 1998. A new pressure sensory mechanism for prey detection in birds: The use of principles of seabed dynamics? *Proceedings of the Royal Society of London B* 265:1377–83.

Piersma, T., J. van Gils, P. de Goeij, and J. van der Meer. 1995. Holling's functional response model as a tool to link the food-finding mechanism of a probing shorebird with its spatial distribution. *Journal of Animal Ecology* 64:493–504.

Raffaeli, D., and S. Hawkins. 1996. *Intertidal ecology*. London: Chapman and Hall.

Reise, K. 1982. Long-term changes in the macrobenthic invertebrate fauna of the Wadden Sea: Are polychaetes about to take over? *Netherlands Journal of Sea Research* 16:29–36.

———. 1985. *Tidal flat ecology: An experimental approach to species interactions*. Berlin: Springer-Verlag.

Reneerkens, J., T. Piersma, and B. Spaans. 2005. *De Waddenzee als kruispunt van vogeltrekwegen. Literatuurstudie naar de kansen en bedreigingen van wadvogels in internationaal perspectief* [*The Wadden Sea as a crossroad of shorebird flyways. A literature study on the chances and threats of shorebirds in an international perspective*]. NIOZ Report 2005-4. Texel: Netherlands Institute for Sea Research (NIOZ).

Risk, M.J., and J.S. Moffat. 1977. Sedimentological significance of fecal pellets of *Macoma balthica* in the Minas Basin, Bay of Fundy. *Journal of Sedimentary Petrology* 47:1425–36.

Roberts, C.M. 1997. Ecological advice for the global fisheries crisis. *Trends in Ecology and Evolution* 12:35–38.

Rossi, F., P.M.J. Herman, and J.J. Middelburg. 2004. Interspecific and intraspecific variation of delta^{13}C and delta^{15}N in deposit- and suspension-feeding bivalves (*Macoma balthica* and *Cerastoderma edule*): Evidence of ontogenetic changes in feeding mode of *Macoma balthica*. *Limnology and Oceanography* 49:408–14.

Rothschild, B.J., J.S. Ault, P. Goulletquer, and M. Héral. 1994. Decline of the Chesapeake Bay oyster population: A century of habitat destruction and overfishing. *Marine Ecology Progress Series* 111:29–39.

Scheffer, M., S. Carpenter, J.A. Foley, C. Folke, and B. Walker. 2001. Catastrophic shifts in ecosystems. *Nature* 413:591–96.

Thistle, D. 1981. Natural physical disturbances and communities of marine soft bottoms. *Marine Ecology Progress Series* 6:223–28.

Tomkovich, P.S. 2001. A new subspecies of red knot *Calidris canutus* from the New Siberian Islands. *Bulletin British Ornithologists Club* 121:257–63.

van de Kam, J., B. Ens, T. Piersma, and L. Zwarts. 2004. *Shorebirds: An illustrated behavioural ecology*. Utrecht, Netherlands: KNNV Publishers.

van Gils, J.A., T. Piersma, A. Dekinga, and M.W. Dietz. 2003. Cost–benefit analysis of mollusc-eating in a shorebird. 2. Optimizing gizzard size in the face of seasonal demands. *Journal of Experimental Biology* 206:3369–80.

van Gils, J.A., T. Piersma, A. Dekinga, B. Spaans, and C. Kraan. 2006a. Shellfish-dredging pushes a flexible avian top predator out of a protected marine ecosystem. *Public Library of Science Biology* 4: e376.

van Gils, J.A., B. Spaans, A. Dekinga, and T. Piersma. 2006b. Foraging in a tidally structured environment by red knots (*Calidris canutus*): Ideal, but not free. *Ecology* 87:1189–1202.

van Roomen, M., C. van Turnhout, E. van Winden, B. Koks, P. Goedhart, M. Leopold, and C.J. Smit. 2005. Trends in benthivorous waterbirds in the Dutch Wadden Sea 1975–2002: Large differences between shellfish-eaters and worm-eaters. *Limosa* 78:21–38.

Verhulst, S., B.J. Ens, K. Oosterbeek, and A.L. Rutten. 2004. Shellfish fishery severely reduces condition and survival of oystercatchers despite creation of large marine protected areas. *Ecology and Society* 9:17.

Versteegh, M., T. Piersma, and H. Olff. 2004. Biodiversiteit in de Waddenzee: mogelijke implicaties van de verwaarlozing van kennis over zeebodemverstoringen [Biodiversity in the Dutch Wadden Sea: Possible consequences of ignoring the evidence on ecological effects of mobile fishing gear]. *De Levende Natuur* 105:6–9.

Verweij, J. 1952. On the ecology of distribution of cockle and mussel in the Dutch Waddensea, their role in sedimentation and the source of their food supply, with a short review of the feeding behaviour of bivalve mollusks. *Archives Neerlandaises de Zoologie* 10:171–239.

Ward, L.G., W.M. Kemp, and W.R. Burton. 1984. The influences of waves and seagrass communities on suspended particles in an estuarine embayment. *Marine Geology* 59:85–103.

Warwick, R.M., and R.J. Uncles. 1980. Distribution of benthic macrofauna associations in the Bristol Channel in relation to tidal stress. *Marine Ecology Progress Series* 3:97–103.

Watling, L., and E.A. Norse. 1998. Disturbance of the seabed by mobile fishing gear: A comparison to forest clearcutting. *Conservation Biology* 12:1180–97.

Wilde Kokkels. No date. www.wildekokkels.nl (accessed May 25, 2007).

Worm, B., C. Folke, B.S. Halpern, J.B.C. Jackson, H.K. Lotze, F. Micheli, S.R. Palumbi, E. Sala, K.A. Selkoe, J.J. Stachowicz, and R. Watson. 2006. Impacts of biodiversity loss on ocean ecosystem services. *Science* 314:787–90.

CHAPTER 4

Management of Flood Catastrophes
An Emerging Paradigm Shift?

Marija Bočkarjova, Albert E. Steenge,
and Arjen Y. Hoekstra

THE NETHERLANDS has witnessed quite a number of water-related disasters in its history. In fact, catastrophes have been recorded from the 15th century on. The last major flood dates to 1953, when large parts of the southwestern part of the country were flooded, and about 1,835 people lost their lives. More recently, in 1995, 250,000 people were evacuated because a polder along the Rhine River was in danger of being inundated.

In the European spectrum of countries, the Netherlands occupies a special place, with a number of distinguishing factors. Probably the most important one is its geography along the North Sea coast, with a quarter of its territory below sea level and two-thirds vulnerable to flooding. The country is a delta where four of Europe's rivers reach the sea: the Rhine, Meuse, Ems, and Scheldt. In combination with the uncertain dynamics of possible climate change, with its implications of a rising sea level, increasing peak flows in the rivers, and a growing frequency and intensity of extreme rainfall events (MNP 2005), as well as a greater amount of precipitation and a gradually subsiding ground level, the Netherlands faces a continuous, probably increasing risk.

For a long time, the Netherlands has addressed the problems posed by the sea and rivers in an essentially technocratic way. This basically meant raising the dikes according to the latest calculations regarding the frequency of critical peak flows. The 1953 flood was a decisive event in the formulation of flood protection policy as it currently exists. The country responded to this event by a combined strategy of building higher dikes and developing an integrated structural approach for the entire delta area, known as the Delta Plan.[1] The major outlets to the sea were cut off by dikes or a storm surge barriers (with the exception of the Scheldt, motivated by the interests of Antwerp Harbor). The Delta Plan was completed in 1997 with the building of the Maeslant Barrier (Maeslantkering), a storm surge barrier in the

New Waterway (Nieuwe Waterweg), near Rotterdam (see Deltawerken 2006). The idea was not new. In 1932, a closure dam called the Afsluitdijk was finalized, cutting off the Zuider Zee, which then became an interior lake, the IJsselmeer. This was combined with other large infrastructural works such as creating new polders to provide room for new towns, farming, nature, and recreation.

Since the 1960s, the policy of raising the dikes aimed at reducing the probability of a flood to close to zero. This was supported through model calculations based on standards such as one flood in 10,000 years at the utmost for the most vulnerable areas in the western part of the country. The high standards applied have created a general feeling of security and an expectation that public authorities can always guarantee safety. This permitted phenomenal economic growth in the protected areas behind the dikes, which rapidly transformed into a highly urbanized economy that claimed a significant role in the "global village," reflecting a near absolute faith in the physical, geographical, and climatological foundations of the underlying (model) calculations. Policy mainly focused on managing the probability of flooding, meaning that less attention was given to policies for controlling and reducing the consequences of such an event. This has resulted in the current situation in which the *risk of a flood*, defined as the product of the probability of a flood and the expected loss in case of a flood, is addressed one-sidedly by looking only at the first term of the product.

It is increasingly recognized, however, that the state cannot completely control natural variability or changes therein—which means that extreme situations will remain possible. Because flooding frequency standards during the past 50 years have not changed and economic expansion behind the dikes was exponential, expected risks actually have increased (RIVM 2004). In other words, although the probability of flooding is relatively low at present, potential damage is enormous. Against this background, insight is developing that the current strategy cannot be sustained ad infinitum and that new solutions have to be found (see, e.g., Commissie WB21 2000).

A corresponding development in this context is the growing importance of system risks (see, e.g., OECD 2003; Hoekstra 2005), which threaten the stability of the entire social system. For the Netherlands, this means that the relevant question has become which combination of technical, economic, legal, and administrative measures can contribute to improved risk control and, in particular, to decreasing the economic and social vulnerability of flooding. This includes attention to the governance structure that can assist in creating the political conditions and reaching the necessary consensus for effective choices.

Here we shall not discuss related developments such as the establishment of modern systems for data storage and retrieval in water monitoring. We should mention, however, the Netherlands' High Water Information System (HIS) (V&W 2005b), recently developed by the Dutch Ministry of Transport, Public Works and Water Management. This system has been designed to monitor flood defenses and present inundation and loss calculations. Several stakeholder organizations are involved, with a central role for the ministry. We will only briefly touch on international dimensions in flood cooperation, where several highly interesting developments have occurred.

This chapter focuses on developments in water policy and management in the Netherlands, including a discussion of currently circulating methodologies on economic flood consequence estimation, which differ significantly in background philosophy, objective, and scope. We will briefly go into such issues as the choice of time horizon and the demarcation between individual and state responsibility. Some main trends are evident, but for the most part, the debate is just beginning.

THE SHIFT FROM PROBABILITY TO RISK MANAGEMENT

The practice of guaranteeing public safety in the Netherlands by raising and strengthening the dikes in combination with land claim policies has a long history. It reached its culmination in the Delta Plan after the catastrophic 1953 flood. The decisions made in that context fixed Dutch policy for the next 50 years. Certain elements of safety standard differentiation according to the relative economic importance of the area were included in the design of the plan.

Central focus was to ensure safety under the motto "never such a flood again." The Delta Commission asked van Dantzig, a well-known statistician, to address the problem of calculating the optimal investment strategy in flood protection. He developed a general formula for the optimal height of the dikes in a dynamic context in which investments at regular intervals are required (van Dantzig 1956). His formula gives a fixed exceedance probability after each investment in the relevant safety structure.[2] The method is still in use today in cost–benefit analysis of flood-protection measures.

The high protection levels permitted accelerating socioeconomic development behind the dike system. The increasing growth of human and economic interests behind the dikes slowly created a problem in itself, however. In fact, the protective system and that which it is protecting are bound together in a seemingly endless action–reaction system with ever-increasing stakes and potential damage. This means that lowering the probability of a particular flood, such as protection against a 10,000-year flood, is not sufficient to guarantee sustainable development for the country in the long run, as flood risk is continuously increasingly because of population growth and economic expansion.

The conclusion has emerged that not only decreasing the probability of flooding should be considered, but also the possible consequences of a flood (RIVM 2004). The new question has become how to balance lowering both the probability of a flood *and* potential damage. This means an entirely different conceptual basis, reflecting the paradigm shift in Dutch thinking and policymaking about protection strategies. The concept of risk is being rediscovered and is the key to understanding the future direction water policy in the Netherlands should take.

We can observe the revival of the concept of risk in flood management, which is the product of the probability of flooding and its consequences (i.e., the costs inflicted). If we denote the flooding probability by the symbol P and potential loss (potential economic consequences) by E, the risk R can be defined as $R = P \times E$. Acknowledging the fact that full flood risk is the sum of different flood scenarios, it is more precise to write $R = \Sigma_i (P_i \times E_i)$, with $i = 1$ to n, where n denotes a number of flood scenarios. For many years, public policy aimed at lowering P as much as possible. Simultaneously, however, the country experienced a period of rapid growth, which meant that E, the potential flood effects, in the risk formula became larger and larger. The Netherlands is thus now confronted with a low probability of a flood and potentially extremely high consequences. In the coming decades, this must be translated into a policy aimed at decreasing *overall risk* (RIVM 2004), evidently a formidable task, because it requires insight into not only the risk equation and its dynamics, but also the relation between the two terms constituting risk. This clearly is the place where the water management specialist and the social scientist meet.

The part of the country vulnerable to flooding from sea or rivers is subdivided into a number of regions called dike-ring areas. Each is surrounded by a ring of natural or man-made water defenses, such as dikes, dunes, concrete structures, or high grounds, and may consist of one or more polders or low-lying areas. Ninety-nine such dike-ring areas exist in the country (V&W 2005a, *13*). One of the largest comprises the densely populated western part of the Netherlands, covering important parts of the provinces of Noord-Holland, Zuid-Holland, and Utrecht and including several major cities: Amsterdam, Rotterdam, and the Hague. In the western coastal area, the standard for exceedance probability is most stringent, once per 10,000 years, followed by the southern and northern coastal areas at once per 4,000 years. Several dike-ring areas with lower population and economic significance, such as in Limburg, have exceedance probabilities in the neighborhood of once per 150 or 200 years. The standards differ among regions because of variations in population and capital densities. All these standards are laid down in the Flood Defence Act (1996).

One element of the new risk thinking is that risk analysis is about the probability not only that the rivers or sea will reach a certain critical water level, but also that a particular link in the entire defense line will succumb (TAW 2000; Vrijling 2001). That is, one should be looking for possible dike failure mechanisms, stability of dike closing mechanisms (such as sluices), and more generally, the weakest links in the entire system.[3] The real probability of a flood is thus equal to the probability of the water reaching a particular level in conjunction with other processes.

The first comprehensive study presenting an evaluation of flood safety policy was *Dutch Dikes and Risk Hikes* (RIVM 2004), which concludes that although the water barriers have never been as strong as now, the country's vulnerability has increased significantly and potential loss can be very large, not only in material terms, but also in terms of the population at large. The report signals a discrepancy between the legal standards regarding dike height and socioeconomic growth over the past decades. A second study, *Flood Risks and Safety in the Netherlands* (V&W 2005a), by the Ministry of Transport, Public Works and Water Management, focuses on safety within the Dutch system of interconnected polders. It presents a series of calculations based on an adapted framework that accounts for not only dike overtopping, but also several other causes of dike breaching.

The signaled awareness is causing a gradual shift in thinking about water policy, with increasing attention paid to the possible effects of flooding and measures to prepare the country for the new situation. New ideas such as "room for water" or "room for the river" fit very well in this context (Silva et al. 2001), combined with fresh views on concepts such as vulnerability, resilience, and minimizing system risks. All this presumes integration among spatial planning, economic development, and water management, as the "room for water" strategy means the creation of retention areas available for controlled inundation in case it becomes necessary. Such an approach will require a revision of spatial patterns for land use, and adjustments that may cause changes in economic structure and infrastructure in the long run.

The above clearly signals a paradigm shift in water and flood management in the Netherlands—that is, a shift from focusing on the probability of flooding to thinking in terms of the risk of flooding. The essence of the old thinking in this sense was to keep the probability of flooding constant in conformity with the accepted standards. The new thinking takes into account the risk connected to the event of a flood, which implies balanced attention to both flooding probabilities *and* effects. A further step in this direction would focus the attention of politicians and decisionmakers particularly on managing the potential effects of a flood. The accumulation of assets and accelerated urbanization in the flood-prone areas of the Netherlands dictate these new rules. The probabilities of a flood set by the National Flood Defence Act (1996) actually are minuscule, especially in comparison with the standards imposed around the globe, averaging once per 100 years.

The signaled shift in perspective furthermore implies that it is increasingly important to properly account for the economic consequences of any particular decision, as the country now has to weigh these against the costs of a possible flood. Thinking in terms of risk also implies that the ultimate decision about the acceptable level should be made by society at large. That is, flood protection is not solely a matter of engineering anymore, but must be decided in public debate and compromise. The question is whether everyone, wherever he or she lives, has a right to the same protection level, or whether protection levels should be a function of population and capital densities. In the former case, the safety level in each dike-ring area should be of the same order of magnitude. In the latter case, different safety levels should be accepted, with the final choice of staying in a higher risk area left up to its residents. Reaching a compromise requires that many parties become involved in the decisionmaking process, which in turn may result in a significant rise of political transaction costs. Increasingly, analysis of the social, environmental, and economic costs and benefits should be performed to determine the most cost-effective measures (such as allowing more "room for the rivers," compartmentalizing existing dike rings, creating emergency inundation areas, adjusting building methods, or rearranging spatial patterns of living and economic activity) that would correspond to the accepted level of risk.

A next question concerns the responsibility issue. Up to now, the Dutch government had full responsibility for flood safety, at least as perceived by the public, but can that continue in the future? One aspect is that no government can guarantee perfect safety from natural hazard; residual risks will always remain. Here the question appears to be how to cover this residual risk. Public or private initiatives are needed, as well as mixed solutions. So far, government has always provided aid to the victims of natural disasters based on the solidarity principle, which needed reinterpretation for each particular case (see the Decision and the Law on Compensation of Damage in Case of Disasters and Serious Accidents, both from 1998). Recent years, however, have seen an intensification of the debate over private insurance against flooding. Addressing this issue touches immediately on the future scope of governance, which brings entirely new elements into the debate. In any case, the role of the Dutch water boards, the age-old public bodies governing water safety, will have to be reconsidered. On the economic side, cost–benefit analysis will be a central element, combined with willingness-to-pay explorations (see Chapter 5).

CONCEPTUAL ISSUES

This section addresses a number of problems in assessing flood damage. It does not put forward any new views about best practices, as the wide variety of problems requires a corresponding wide set of methodologies. Rather, this section is meant to draw attention to the existence of some of the fundamental choices involved, highlighting the issues that are essential in constructing consistent frameworks for disaster modeling. The discussion is limited to economic damage.

Defining Economic Damage

Important questions concerning economic damage caused by a disaster are what precisely should be measured, and to what purpose. A whole range of issues are involved here. Above all is the issue of human health or life. Many studies recognize the fact that nonmaterial issues are involved but skip the emotional or psychological ones, which require separate attention. We will also leave those aspects out of our current discussion. The reason for doing so is twofold. Valuation in economic terms of emotional or psychological effects, as well as human life itself, is an extremely intricate task that involves indirect valuation methods, as one cannot estimate such losses directly by assigning monetary values to them. Additionally, by engaging in such valuations, one enters a gray area of ethical issues, involving questions of whether human lives and emotional aspects of disasters can or should be valued at all. We leave it to the discretion of the individual researcher to decide whether to include such valuations. What can be done, however, is to view the loss in terms of human capital, which can be analyzed economically. Because many of the issues discussed here have appeared in international disaster studies, we refer to both Dutch and international expertise.

A first observation is that no uniformity exists in the use of damage concepts (Mitchell 2000; NRC 1999). This is reflected in the treatment of *loss* (in concepts such as direct, indirect, primary, secondary, or induced damage), the role of substitution effects, and the statistical databases. With respect to damage classification, however, one may notice a certain tendency toward the direct-indirect loss distinction. Here two main approaches can be discerned. According to the *spatial criterion*, all losses attributable to the affected area are direct, and losses incurred elsewhere are indirect (Bočkarjova et al. 2007; Chang 1998; Cochrane 1997a; Cole et al. 1993;

Rose and Lim 2002). According to the *stock-flow differential criterion*, on the other hand, losses that refer to physical damage are considered stock losses and are direct. All losses associated with production curtailment, whether within or outside the affected area, are indirect and measured as a flow (Booysen et al. 1999; BTRE 2001; Messner and Meyer 2006; Parker et al. 1987).[4] In this context, depending on the chosen framework, direct losses may refer to the costs to replace the lost assets based on their market value or on their restoration or rebuilding value.

For the purposes of our discussion, we do not need to make a choice in favor of one of these definitions. We therefore will refer broadly to indirect damage as loss of connectivity and interruption of flows in the production network and the losses due to it. In applied studies, however, it is important to state which definition is chosen, for transparency as well as comparability purposes.

Second, a study on disaster effects requires a clear delineation of its spatial and temporal dimensions. Whether the analysis is performed for a part of the country or the country as a whole makes quite a difference in terms of analysis. A recent example is provided by Hurricane Katrina in New Orleans in 2005. In relative terms, effects evidently are much more serious at the level of the state of Louisiana than at the federal level. In terms of the time dimension, damage assessment requires a clear insight into what precisely is meant by the term "recovery period" (ECLAC 2003); that is, at which point in time should damage be measured? In one respect, the answer is quite simple: direct damage—that to the constructed environment, physical assets, and property—is best recorded immediately after the calamity. One should also account for indirect damage, however, which involves interruptions to the flows of goods and services. Dealing with these effects requires a broader time horizon, extending several years after the catastrophe.

Here a fundamental issue arises: in establishing the effects of a flood, one should take into account not only losses as a result of the disturbance, but also emerging sequential effects, such as possibilities for product substitution and adjustments in the production and consumption markets. Such accommodations to the new situation, often referred to as "resilience," make the economy reach a new equilibrium faster, thereby moderating the initial negative effect. For the country as a whole, other effects may occur, such as businesses outside the affected area increasing their production if spare capacities are present or consumers adjusting their consumption patterns during the emergency situation. In many respects, the disaster aftermath can be viewed as a new situation with new underlying conditions; what is lost cannot be recovered anymore, and in this sense lost assets essentially are sunken costs. Thus decisions such as whether to resume production should be made based on the new realities without undue reference to the predisaster situation.

Third, damage is a multidimensional concept, because it serves various purposes. Multiple groups of stakeholders have their own views about the aims disaster analysis and damage assessment should serve (NRC 1999). Some of these can be easily identified, such as governments or industry representatives; insurers or reinsurers, including their associations and government insurance regulators; business corporations; individuals; and research analysts and experts in disaster analysis. A range of analyses is needed to cover the multiple aspects of disasters, because each of the parties that have a stake in damage estimation generally is interested in a specific aspect.

Fourth, a clear distinction should be made between financial and economic appraisals. The former type deals with the financial and accounting aspects, and the latter deals with alternative or opportunity costs. Many insurance companies' or governmental expenditure reports on damage are based on financial considerations. Using the economic concept of opportunity cost in valuations requires a quite different approach. When both economic and financial concepts are used at the same time, methodologically inconsistent results may be obtained, which makes assessments difficult to compare or interpret (Benson 1997).

Costs and Double Counting

In economic appraisal studies for damage assessment, one is immediately confronted with the notion of opportunity or alternative costs. Standard alternative costs represent anything that has to be sacrificed to obtain some specific commodity or service. Conventionally, this means, for example, that government may have to decide between two options, such as dike strengthening and a public campaign on raising flood-risk awareness. The alternative cost of investing in dike strengthening in this case would be forgone investment in public campaigning.

Unfortunately, the concept of alternative costs is a complex one, and its application in disaster damage assessment offers many conceptual problems. Because assets are lost as a result of the hazard, we have to deal with the loss of resources. Losses due to flooding are not a choice; in other words, no trade-off can be made between various ends on which money could be spent (opportunity costs). This is a problem in itself: it is not straightforward how to define disaster losses in terms of alternative costs. Because of this difficulty, the methodological underpinnings of the damage concept, and consequently damage estimation, remain disputable.

In addition, another issue to consider is that when accounting for the various categories of damage, the risk of double counting exists as a result of the failure to make a correct distinction between stock and flow concepts (Riddell and Green 1999; van der Veen et al. 2001). In economic terms, the value of capital goods, a stock measure, must be equal to the discounted value of the flow of outputs that a capital good can produce during its lifetime. The problem of double counting arises when one has to assess the value of lost capital goods involved in the production of goods and services, such as machinery, various types of equipment, or the industrial installations involved in the production process. In this situation, adding direct losses, which refer to the stock value of lost assets, and indirect losses, which refers to the loss of the flow of goods and services that are not produced anymore by these assets, implies double counting.

A second source of double counting is accounting for both loss of income and expenditure. Cochrane (in NRC 1992, *101*) observes that the level of economic activity can be measured by counting expenditures or incomes. On the consumption side, income is spent on the goods and services supplied throughout the economy. On the production side, expenditures are made in providing these goods and services. Price of a good or service in this case reflects the value of overall production and covers all costs incurred in the production process, including raw materials, wages, taxes, and profits. This means that when a good or service is consumed, an accounting balance is fulfilled: income is equal to expenditure. Thus, theoretically, accounting for either of them should result in the same outcome.

RESPONSIBILITY FOR FLOOD PROTECTION

For a long time, responsibility for flood protection in the Netherlands has lain solely with the government. Recently, however, opinion has shifted toward more interactive decisionmaking involving more parties. Lately, government has also expressed its views on a more deregulated mode of dealing with flood risks.

Public versus Private Responsibility

The National Policy Agreement on Water (2003) puts forward that issues should be addressed at the level where they appear. This principle, in practice, should mean that individuals, municipalities, and provinces should show more initiative in taking care of their own safety without relying solely on the protection provided by the national government. This is a remarkable development, marking a shift in the approach to flood risk. Up to now, flood prevention has been a 100% public good. The observed shift signals a change in the nonexcludability characteristic of a public good. That is, the producer of the good, here the national government, may gradually introduce a policy of excluding particular parties from consuming it. One can thus observe here a tendency toward growing institutional diversity, thereby attributing more direct influence and responsibility to the parties involved. This may be interpreted in terms of a Williamson-type alignment in which governance structure and product (or transaction) are aligned such that total transaction costs are minimized (Williamson 2000).[5]

A related point concerns flood insurance. At present, private insurance against flooding is not available in the Netherlands. This has historical grounds. After the flood of 1953, insurers basically refrained from selling policies covering flood damage, arguing that flooding is an uninsurable catastrophic risk (see Kok 2005). Recently, however, the issue of private insurance has been surfacing more and more. Herein lies a fundamental problem: insurance is based on diversification and generally covers events with a reasonably known frequency distribution. As a rule, insurance companies collect insurance premiums that should cover the payments of claims over a fixed period. Premiums are calculated on the basis of the average expected replacement value of the insured asset and the probability of the event against which the asset is insured. This means that incurred costs in case of a calamity are spread among the policyholders on a periodical basis, with premiums reflecting average expected loss plus a markup.

A disaster, however, especially flooding in the Netherlands, is typically characterized by uncertain low frequency and very high cost. Large numbers of people inhabiting a polder as well as property may be affected, leading to substantial claims.

Covering claims associated with such a disaster would require access to a large amount of capital. This leaves basically two options: either premiums would have to be so high to cover the costs of low-frequency, high-consequence events that insurance would be virtually inaccessible for consumers, or insurance companies would need access to supplementary emergency capital sources in case a major calamity occurs. To this end, Jaffee and Russel (2006) point to the possibility of the government providing insurance companies with loans to guarantee smoothness of accounting and prevent bankruptcy, but they say that even this may not be enough.[6] Because residual risk is high and hard to measure, reinsurers covering insurance company losses may be reluctant to provide this type of financial service, and the available ones may be expensive.

Nevertheless, this may be the way future developments evolve. A central issue will be that all agents on the insurance market should have appropriate incentives. In the Netherlands, the government, though it is not obliged to provide assistance in case of a disaster, often does so based on the solidarity principle. This serves as a disincentive for citizens to buy insurance, as they rely on government support in case a flood does take place. Eventual transition to the principle of shared responsibility and the emergence of a market for private insurance will demand clear roles of each participant.

Government Involvement in the Economy

The role of government in economic policymaking in the aftermath of a disaster is of predominant interest. If a region where important production facilities are located is hit, that specific part of the established economic network is lost, temporarily or forever, and the system suddenly is not able to keep on functioning as before. The problem is that often various production sectors may suffer damage to a different extent, which implies asymmetry of effects. This creates imbalances among sectors in the economy, leading to supply and demand shortages in diverse markets. We cannot rely on such imbalances being automatically restored. This in turn means that economic policy is required to provide appropriate incentives for all agents and parties concerned. To be prepared in emergency situations, the government thus needs to have full knowledge of its options, and above all to have insight into how the economy may respond to a variety of stimuli.

A time horizon issue clearly exists for proactive policy formation for the risk-averse policymaker. Short-and medium-term approaches should be conceptually distinguished from, yet compatible with, those with a long-term perspective. When talking about long-term policy, often Hicksian sustainability concepts enter, in the sense that the choices of future generations should not be compromised. The case of flooding presents an intertemporal choice dilemma: whereas the present generation needs to invest in flood protection, most of its benefits will be reaped by the next generations in the form of greater safety and lower expected losses. This implies that we have to think of ways to enhance the robustness and resilience of the systems in question in the long run. It also implies a different set of concepts and variables in making today's decisions than in cases where policymakers are aiming only at a short-term horizon.

PREPARATION EFFORTS

In the debate about long-term effects of flooding and society's capability to recover, a number of concepts are gaining increasing attention in disaster analysis, among others, *resilience* and *adaptation*. A problem is that neither multidisciplinary literature covering disaster modeling nor economic literature has developed generally accepted definitions. They certainly deserve more elaboration (Alexander 1997). Nevertheless, some tendencies can be observed.

Taking into account a wider temporal span in disaster analysis, resilience becomes an essential matter, as it has direct implications for total damage sustained. Resilience reflects a system's capacity to adjust in the face of tribulation and respond to it in a way that cushions the immediate negative impact, maintaining its main characteristics (Allenby and Fink 2005; Gunderson and Holling 2001). Some authors, especially from the socioecological field, attribute learning and adaptive capacity to resilience as well (see Kendra and Wachtendorf 2003; RA 2005). In connection with this, it is assumed that a higher resilience level can make an economy recover faster and with fewer costs (Rose 2004a). Recently, in disaster consequence studies, resilience has played a more prominent role, becoming a goal in itself (de Bruijn 2004). Besides, a prudent policymaker would wish to link this goal to the sustainability principle, providing resilience with normative contents (Tobin 1999).

To enhance the resilience of a system, one has to think in terms of disaster preparedness. In this sense, it is connected to the concept of adaptability. Adaptation is directed at the preparation of the system to the expected adversity and may cover local, national, and even global aspects. Adaptation is intended to reduce the inherent vulnerability of a system to a calamity, as well as improve its response capacity, or resilience. It differs from the widely used *mitigation* strategies in that, contrary to adaptation, which is aimed at the system under attack, mitigation is seen as the entirety of strategies that address the source of adversity.

We may distinguish here a number of efforts to make adaptability more tangible. Essentially, these are aimed at the definition of critical system characteristics that should guarantee the continuity of operation in the face of calamity. Pingali et al. (2005) offer the following strategies to augment the food system's resilience and apply these to a more general case: strengthening diversity, rebuilding local institutions and traditional support networks, reinforcing local knowledge, and building on economic agents' ability to adapt and reorganize. Such a strategy signifies the importance of an integrated approach to flood management, where the multiple dimensions of contemporary society overlap.

Besides, a more proactive approach can be positioned for the risk-averse policymaker. According to the precautionary principle (COMEST 2005), an activity should not be undertaken if one might expect that it will bring substantial or irreversible negative effects. In the case of flood protection, one can also interpret this in a slightly different manner, in terms of activities or policies that have to be implemented, because idleness may lead to an incident whose consequences cannot be precisely estimated in advance but can be expected to have serious negative or even irreversible effects on the entire economy or society, such as in the form of system and group risks. This represents a fundamental break with the past, when progress typically was a matter of trial and error within a particular vision on growth and development.

INTERNATIONAL COOPERATION

International cooperation has been gaining prominence in the last decade. Two intergovernmental initiatives in this context are the International Commission for the Protection of the Rhine against Pollution (ICPR) and the Convention of the International Meuse Commission (IMC).[7] Founded in 1950, ICPR currently unites the efforts of five countries from the Rhine basin, ensuring sustainability of one of the largest river basins in Europe. It includes cooperation in protection against floods and provisions for ecological amelioration of the Rhine and its floodplains. IMC was established in 1994 with the goal of achieving sustainable and integrated water management of the international river basin of the Meuse. In recent years, both ICPR and IMC have been showing signs that they intend to build more cooperation in the area of flood protection and monitoring (see, e.g., ICPR 2002).

At the EU level, the European Commission's Communication on Flood Risk Management (2004) aims to foster cooperation among the member countries in the field of flood protection in the wider context of sustainable development. Among recent important developments is a Directive on the Assessment and Management of Flood Risks (2007), an initiative that fills the gap since the Water Framework Directive (2000) was adopted, with the goal of developing integrated management plans for river basins in order to achieve a good ecological and chemical status.

FLOOD DAMAGE MODELING

In looking at recent modeling efforts in flood damage assessment in the Netherlands, it appears that no unique methodology exists; rather, researchers employ different types of models depending on the kind of questions they wish to address. Some models focus on the micro or sectoral level, others on the macro level. Additionally, new research lines have been developed in the macroeconomic sphere.

In some of the studies, we may recognize the difference between *measurement* and *inference*. We can observe, and measure to a certain extent, direct damage caused by the hazard, such as loss of human life or production capacity. Much more difficult to observe or measure are the *consequences* of this loss—the indirect effects. These have to do with business and production activity interruptions within an interconnected network. A temporary or persistent disappearance of suppliers or consumers from an established system has significant effects on the welfare of society at large. It is here that modeling claims its place.

One model is the standard method, developed by HKV Consultants in a study for the Dutch Ministry of Transport, Public Works, and Water Management (Vrisou van Eck and Kok 2001). This method is based on specific standardizations and is also used in the Netherlands' High Water Information System (HIS), which provides information about high-water developments in the primary dikes system to professionals and policymakers. The standard method addresses various types of direct physical damage, as well as loss of life. It uses extensive GIS data by zip code and detailed unit loss functions for direct damage estimation per dike ring, depending on the inundation level. Each loss function includes the maximum damage value, based on replacement value, as well as damage factors, which are determined in scenario simulations using hydrodynamic calculations and GIS maps, thereby taking into account intermediate defenses, differences in elevation and water levels, and building types. This method determines damage functions per activity sector: agriculture and recreation, pumping stations, means of transport, infrastructure, companies, and housing. It pays relatively little attention, however, to indirect losses throughout the economy. The classification of losses underwent some changes, and in a recent version of the standard method (see V&W 2005a), direct material damage is defined as damage caused to objects, capital goods, and movable goods as a result of direct contact with water; direct damage due to business interruption refers to losses resulting from interrupted production of businesses in the flooded area; and indirect damage is viewed as damage to business suppliers and customers outside the flooded area and travel time losses because of the inaccessibility of roads and railways in the flooded area.

The Netherlands Economic Institute (NEI) (Briene et al. 2003) presents a method to assess the maximum damage caused by a flood in a dike ring, including the calculations of indirect effects of production loss throughout the country (following the classification of damage as put forward in the standard method), using a study by the Tebodin consultancy group (van den Berg et al. 2000) as a background document. In that study, the intraindustry economic effects of shutting down part of a productive sector in the country are estimated in a way that attempts to avoid the rigidity of the standard input–output multiplier in favor of "corrected" coefficients for each industry, thereby accounting for substitution effects in the reconstruction period. This correction ratio is multiplied by the sectoral input–output multiplier to obtain losses due to business interruption. Furthermore, both Briene et al. and van den Berg et al. do not account for the market value of the lost assets, but take the replacement value (after accounting for depreciation) as a threshold for direct damage, which is basically a financial concept. Methodologically, this may suggest disparity in the chosen concepts for the estimation of direct and indirect effects.

The Netherlands Bureau for Economic Policy Analysis (CPB) has published several studies on water management and policy assessment. In a recent study, it presented a cost–benefit analysis rooted in economic welfare theory; an example is the analysis for infrastructural alterations of rivercourses, *Giving Room for Water* (CPB 2000), with only limited attention to typical indirect effects. In two other studies (Ebregt et al. 2005; Eijgenraam 2005), the CPB presents a further developed methodology based on cost–benefit analysis, focusing at the macroeconomic level rather than using standard damage calculations for a particular dike ring. It aims at providing a more complete picture of the overall effects among the constituent parts of the entire economic system under study. Eijgenraam (2005) dis-

cusses optimal safety standards for dike-ring areas, correcting the 50-year-old contribution of van Dantzig (1956), and gives the formulas for the optimal investment
in the heightening of dikes, where key questions are "when" and "how much." The
basic principle is the aforementioned balancing of P and E in the risk equation for
each dike-ring area. Using the year 2015 as a reference point, the study provides
the calculated time paths of the first investment in the protection structures and
the resulting factual flood probabilities.

These are the concepts currently in use in the Netherlands, along with their
interpretation and justification. The methodologies on economic cost assessment
are still being developed and are rarely described in detail. This is one factor that
may explain the difficulty in comparing the relative merits of the various methodologies, as well as the fact that the underlying concepts often vary in dimensions. At
best, we may conclude that at the moment, many studies in the form of partial
analyses are available. These, however, do not easily add up to provide a single picture. In future work, convergence to clarify and possibly create uniform definitions
of the concepts, as well as make explicit choice of the modeling framework, will
be a priority.

Although a number of studies have focused, broadly speaking, at the micro and
meso levels, so far macroeconomic studies are relatively underrepresented. New
research lines are being pursued in several directions, however. An overview of damage evaluation methods as a result of flooding is provided in the study of the Erasmus University of Rotterdam Centre for Sustainable Development and
Management team (van Ast et al. 2004). The report outlines ample possibilities for
establishing the value of assets, also including indirect monetary assessment strategies for nonmarket goods (including revealed and stated preference, cost avoidance,
and other methods).[8] Ultimately, the authors develop a risk assessment approach,
based on a discounted cost–benefit analysis framework, acknowledging the non-
monetary damage aspects (e.g., damage to the nature and environment, emotional
damage, as well as uncertainty) and the risk perception of policymakers.

Some recent Dutch work in the macroeconomic sphere (Bočkarjova et al. 2004;
van der Veen and Logtmeijer 2005) concentrates on the effects of large-scale calami-
ties in highly industrialized economic systems. Bočkarjova et al. (2004) offer a three-
stage procedure using an adjusted input–output framework with a geography
component. The first stage is accounting for the immediate postdisaster disequilibrium situation when an essential part of a socioeconomic network is suddenly not
available anymore. The second stage concerns the design of recovery scenarios and
an investigation of possible new equilibria. The aftermath of a calamity is often
accompanied by complex adjustments in the system, which may require government involvement in steering economic recovery. Clearly a number of options exist
here, and these should be studied as well. For example, the country may wish to
reestablish the status quo as soon as possible. On the other hand, it may wish to use
the occasion to renew selected parts of its physical infrastructure. Finally, the model
offers a cost–benefit analysis of various policy options when the outcomes of multiple preventive measures and recovery paths can be compared.

Other existing analytical frameworks circulating internationally contain computable general equilibrium (CGE) and input–output (I–O) models, including their

linear programming variants and social accounting matrices (SAMs). All have their strong and weak points. I–O models offer a transparent structure of an economy by sector, allow concentrate specifically on the physical side of the problem at hand, and are temptingly simple, but they seem to be somewhat underutilized or underdeveloped as a methodology for dealing with disruptions of the type we are discussing. In fact, standard I–O methodology, stressing interaction and equilibrium, does not offer a very flexible set of tools to deal with postdisaster situations that are characterized by disruption and disequilibrium. The problem here is partially shared by CGE methodology. Standard I–O, however, being limited by fixed production functions, is an antipode of CGE models, which are deemed to be intricate, involve multiple actors and markets, and be overflexible, allowing markets to adjust elastically through the price mechanism to the new circumstances. One thus is confronted with trade-offs between complexity and flexibility when choosing a model for situations where an economy is facing an entirely new set of circumstances and decisions have to be made in a nonstandard way in the light of suddenly restricted or unavailable resources (Steenge and Bočkarjova 2007).

Up to now, the economic analysis of flood disasters is a field that to a large extent is still developing. One issue to be explored concerns policies in countries differing in political and economic structure. In a pure market economy, calamity consequences and policy priorities can be expected to differ from those in a more regulated country such as the Netherlands. In the United States, for example, a number of market-based approaches have been put forward recently focusing on short- and medium-run disequilibria (see, e.g., Cochrane 1997b, 2003; Cole 1998; Cole et al. 1993; Okuyama 2004; Okuyama et al. 2004; Rose 2004b; Rose and Lim 2002). To apply the experience in disaster modeling from other countries to the Dutch situation, one has to bear in mind that the Netherlands requires a quite different approach. Here we have to look for novel solutions that would address the entire range of preconditions. First of all, we should decide on the level of analysis: at the moment, a macro-oriented framework is needed that would provide insight into the working of the entire socioeconomic system. Next, efforts should aim at modeling a wide range of effects inflicted by a disaster, in particular covering the extent of direct and indirect economic losses throughout the system. Finally, it is essential that models be capable of covering available policy options. Whether proactive or recovery-oriented, policy measures should be tested with an appropriate (statistical) reliability level for the response that these might cause throughout the economy. Such models, being able to assess relative costs and benefits of various policy options, will be indispensable means for policy analysis.

CONCLUSIONS

This chapter has looked at recent developments in Dutch water management and policy, signaling a paradigm change in thinking about flood risks. For many years, both sea and rivers have continuously been a source of danger. The Delta Plan, which came into being after the disastrous 1953 flood, has for decades set the stage for flood protection. It was based on the concept of a very strong sea defense, organized to withstand extreme situations. For the highly developed and populated central part of the Netherlands, this amounted to the chance of a flood on average once per 10,000 years.

This permitted a spectacular economic growth in the provinces below sea level, which ultimately made the country a world player on many markets. The discrepancy between the infinitesimal probability of dike overtopping and the high and ever-growing risk of flooding requires, however, a different type of calculation. The country has to prepare for future challenges, finding a balance between expected risks and growth and development desires.

Several issues stand out. Many of these are a consequence of the way Dutch spatial structure has developed. The country is a patchwork of interconnected polders, each of which has different characteristics, such as population, economic value, and safety standards. This means that probability calculations should be based on the much more complex concept of systemic risk, where a number of dike-rings should be seen as an interdependent system.

This also implies other questions, such as whether everyone has the same right to protection from water, which is not the case right now. In fact, there also is a discrepancy between safety standards as fixed by Dutch law and the actual situation as it has developed. Here *the country faces the task of redistributing safety in a reasonable and acceptable way*. This relates to other issues. At the moment, the Dutch government has full responsibility for protection against threats posed by the water, coming from either outside (the sea) or inside (the rivers). In the next decade, however, this may evolve into a more decentralized policy. For example, if people want to settle in low-lying areas, they also may have to bear a part of the involved responsibilities. This can take various forms, all of which have to be sorted out.

The wealth of issues concerns the present spatial distribution of activities. It is a big question whether the western part of the country can remain as prominent in Dutch society as it is now. Systemic factors do not look favorable, with a sea level rise, subsiding ground level, increased precipitation, and peak river discharges. The Netherlands has to decide how it will develop in the next decades. Should it keep its core economic activities located in the areas directly behind the dikes, or should it adopt a policy of spreading these activities to the higher areas in the eastern and southern parts of the country? It is here that further research is needed.

In this chapter, we have drawn attention in particular to the effect constituent of the risk equation. A number of fundamental issues with respect to potential damage assessments were outlined as a part of disaster consequence analysis. The models and methods for economic damage evaluation currently circulating in the Netherlands represent a spectrum of possibilities and have the potential to mature as damage estimation techniques are further explored. Opportunities to use international experience and expertise in this field should be well considered.

Finally, we are not proposing that any single model should be capable of covering all the outlined aspects that are relevant in the economic analysis of flood disasters. Rather, we would welcome the emergence of a multiplicity of models aiming at the achievement of the ultimate goal of providing better knowledge about the impacts of large-scale catastrophes on a 21st century economy and how best to prepare for them. We recognize that the diversity of models may create a selection problem. Simultaneously, however, this should act as a challenge and stimulate modelers to propose integrated multi- or interdisciplinary approaches, which are often lacking at the moment.

NOTES

1. The first comprehensive study of the Delta Plan was presented by Maris (1954), Tinbergen (1954), and Zeegers (1954) and discussed its engineering, economic, and social aspects.

2. The term "exceedance probability" refers to the chance that the water level will exceed the crest of the dike, resulting in overflow and breaking of the dike and thus flooding of the land behind it.

3. Nine dike failure mechanisms are distinguished by RIVM (2004, *110*): overtopping, instability through infiltration and erosion after overtopping, piping, heave, macroinstability at land side, macroinstability at river side, microinstability, instability of dike cover, and sliding off at riverside.

4. In addition, some authors advise conducting analysis at the macroeconomic level (ECLAC 2003; Murlidharan and Shah 2003; Freeman et al. 2004; Mechler 2004; Linnerooth-Bayer et al. 2005). ECLAC notes, however, that macroeconomic analysis acts as complementary statistics that reflects the impacts of a catastrophe in terms of macrovariables.

5. Transaction costs are interpreted here in a broad sense, including information, bargaining, and monitoring costs.

6. In cases where governments are not able to absorb the losses and provide help to the population, international organizations such as the World Bank and International Bank for Reconstruction and Development (IBRD) may provide loans to prevent bankruptcy of a state; see, for example, Parker (2000) and Arnold (2006).

7. For more information, see the ICPR and IMC websites, www.iksr.org and www.meuse-maas.be.

8. Other models estimating nonmarket goods include loss of human or animal life (e.g., Jonkman et al. 2002) or loss of landscape, natural, or historical values (Nieuwenhuizen et al. 2003).

REFERENCES

Alexander, D. 1997. The study of natural disasters, 1977–97: Some reflections on a changing field of knowledge. *Disasters* 21:284–304.

Allenby, B., and J. Fink. 2005. Toward inherently secure and resilient societies. *Science Journal* 309 (5737): 1034–36.

Arnold, M. 2006. *Overview of 5 ProVention recovery case studies.* The 6th IIASA-DPRI Forum Integrated Disaster Risk Management. Istanbul, Turkey.

Benson, C. 1997. *The economic impact of disasters: Current assessment practices.* Assessment of the economic impact of natural and man-made disasters: Expert consultation on methodologies. Brussels: Centre for Research on the Epidemiology of Disasters (CRED).

Bočkarjova, M., A.E. Steenge, and A. van der Veen. 2004. On direct estimation of initial damage in the case of a major catastrophe: Derivation of the "basic equation." *Disaster Prevention and Management* 13 (4): 330–36.

Bočkarjova, M., A.E. Steenge, and A. van der Veen, A. 2007. Flooding and consequent structural economic effects: A methodology. In *Flood risk management in Europe: Innovation in policy and practice*, ed. S. Begum, M.J.F. Stive, and J.W. Hall, 131–54. New York: Springer.

Booysen, H.J., M.F. Viljoen, and G.T. de Villiers. 1999. Methodology for the calculation of industrial flood damage and its application to an industry in Vereeniging. *Water* 25:41–46.

Briene, M., S. Koppert, A. Koopman, and A. Verkennis. 2003. *Financial foundations for indicators of flood damage: Final report*. Rotterdam: NEI.

BRTE (Bureau of Transport and Regional Economics). 2001. *Economic costs of natural disasters in Australia*. Disaster Mitigation Research Working Group. Canberra, Australia: Paragon Printers.

Chang, S.E. 1998. Direct Economic Impacts. In *Engineering and socioeconomic impacts of earthquakes: An analysis of electricity lifeline disruptions in the New Madrid area*, ed. M. Shinozuka, A. Rose, and R.T. Eguchi, 75–94. Buffalo, NY: Multidisciplinary Center for Earthquake Engineering Research.

Cochrane, H.C. 1997a. Economic impact of a Midwest earthquake. *NCEER Bulletin* 11:1–15.

———. 1997b. Forecasting the economic impact of a Midwest earthquake. In *Economic consequences of earthquakes: Preparing for the unexpected*, ed. B.G. Jones, 223–48. Buffalo, NY: National Center for Earthquake Engineering Research.

———. 2003. Economic Loss: Myth and Measurement. In *In search of a common methodology for damage estimation: Joint NEDIES and University of Twente Workshop Proceeding*, ed. A. van der Veen, A.L. Vetere Arellano, and J.-P. Nordvik, 11–19. Delft, Netherlands: Office for Official Publications of the European Communities.

Cole, S. 1998. Decision support for calamity preparedness: Socioeconomic and interregional impacts. In *Engineering and socioeconomic impacts of earthquakes: An analysis of electricity lifeline disruptions in the New Madrid area*, ed. M. Shinozuka, A.Z. Rose, and R.T. Eguchi, 125–53. Buffalo, NY: Multidisciplinary Center for Earthquake Engineering Research.

Cole, S., E. Pantoja, and V. Razak. 1993. *Social accounting for disaster preparedness and recovery planning*. Technical report. Buffalo, NY: National Center for Earthquake Engineering Research.

COMEST (World Commission on the Ethics of Scientific Knowledge and Technology). 2005. *The precautionary principle*. Paris: UNESCO.

Commissie WB21 (Commissie Waterbeheer 21e eeuw). 2000. *Waterbeleid voor de 21e eeuw; Geef water de ruimte en de aandacht die het verdient [Water policy for the 21st century; Give water the space and attention it deserves]*. The Hague: WB21.

CPB (Centraal Planbureau). 2000. *Ruimte voor water; kosten en baten van zes projecten en enige alternatieven [Giving room for water: Costs and benefits of six projects and some alternatives]*. Werkdocument 130. The Hague: CPB.

de Bruijn, K.M. 2004. Resilience and flood risk management. *Water Policy*, 6 (1): 53–66.

Deltawerken. 2006. Deltaworks. www.deltawerken.com (accessed October 30, 2008).

Ebregt, J., C.J.J. Eijgenraam, and H.J.J. Stolwijk. 2005. *Kosteneffectiviteit van maatregelen en pakketten: Kosten-batenanalyse voor Ruimte voor de Rivier, deel 2 [Cost efficiency of measures and policies: Cost–benefit analysis for giving room for the river]*. CPB Document 83. The Hague: CPB.

ECLAC (UN Economic Commission for Latin America and the Caribbean). 2003. *Handbook for estimating the socio-economic and environmental effects of disasters*. Santiago, Chile: ECLAC.

Eijgenraam, C.J.J. 2005. *Veiligheid tegen overstromen: Kosten-batenanalyse voor Ruimte voor de Rivier, deel 1 [Cost–benefit analysis for giving room for the river flooding safety]*. CPB Document 82. The Hague: CPB.

Freeman, P., L. Martin, R. Mechler, and K. Warner. 2004. A methodology for incorporating natural catastrophes into macroeconomic projections. *Disaster Prevention and Management* 13(4): 337–342.

Gunderson, L.H., and C.S. Holling. 2001. *Panarch*. Washington, DC: Island Press.

Hoekstra, A.Y. 2005. *Generalism as specialism: Water management in the context of sustainable development, globalisation, uncertainties and risks*. Inaugural address. Enschede, Netherlands: University of Twente.

ICPR (International Commission for the Protection of the Rhine). 2002. *Non-structural flood plain management: Measures and their effectiveness*. Bern, Switzerland: ICPR.

Jaffee, D.M., and T. Russell. 2006. Should governments provide catastrophe insurance? *Economists' Voice* 3 (5), article 6. www.bepress.com/ev/vol3/iss5/art6.

Jonkman, S.N., P.H.A.J.M. van Gelder, and J.K. Vrijling. 2002. Loss of life models for sea and river floods. *Flood Defence* 1:196–206.

Kendra, J.M., and T. Wachtendorf. 2003. Elements of resilience after the World Trade Center disaster: Reconstituting New York City's Emergency Operations Center. *Disasters* 27:37–53.

Kok, M. 2005. *Insurance in the Netherlands: Possible and desirable?* Lelystad, Netherlands: HKV Consultants.

Linnerooth-Bayer, J., R. Mechler, and G. Pflug. 2005. Refocusing disaster aid. *Science Journal* 309 (5737): 1044–46.

Maris, A.G. 1954. Het waterstaatkundig aspect van het Deltaplan [Water management perspective on the Delta Plan]. In *Het Deltaplan, afdamming zee-armen* [*The Delta Plan: Closing the sea arms with the dike*]. The Hague: Nederlandse Maatschappij voor Nijverheid en Handel.

Mechler, R. 2004. *Natural disaster risk management and financing disaster losses in developing countries.* Karlsruhe, Germany: VVW GmbH.

Messner, F., and V. Meyer. 2006. Flood damage, vulnerability and risk perception: Challenges for flood damage research. In *Flood risk management: Hazards, vulnerability and mitigation measures,* ed. J. Schanze, E. Zeman, and J. Marsalek, 149–67. New York: Springer.

Mitchell, J.K. 2000. What's in a name? Issues of terminology and language in hazards research. *Environmental Hazards* 2 (3): 87–88.

MNP (Milieu en Natuur Planbureau). 2005. *The effects of climate change in the Netherlands.* Bilthoven, Netherlands: MNP.

Murlidharan, T.L., and H.C. Shah. 2003. *Economic consequences of catastrophes triggered by natural hazards.* Palo Alto, CA: John A. Blume Earthquake Engineering Center and Department of Civil and Environmental Engineering, Stanford University.

Nieuwenhuizen, W., H.P. Wolfert, L.W.G. Higler, M. Dijkman, H.J. Huizinga, J. Kopinga, A. Makaske, B.S.J. Nijhof, A.F.M. Olsthoorn, and J.H.M. Wösten. 2003. *Standaardmethode schade aan LNC-waarden als gevolg van overstromingen; Methode voor het bepalen van de gevolgen van overstromingen voor de aspecten opgaande begroeiing, vegetatie, aquatische ecosystemen en historische bouwkunde* [*Standard method for predicting damage to the LNC-values as a result of floods*]. Alterra Report 709. Wageningen, Netherlands: Alterra.

NRC (National Research Council, Committee on Earthquake Engineering, Division of Natural Hazard Mitigation, Commission on Engineering and Technical Systems). 1992. *The economic consequences of a catastrophic earthquake: Proceedings of a forum.* Washington, DC: National Academies Press.

NRC (National Research Council, Committee on Assessing the Costs of Natural Disasters, Board on Natural Disasters, Commission on Geosciences, Environment, and Resources). 1999. *The impacts of natural disasters: A framework for loss estimation.* Washington, DC: National Academies Press.

OECD (Organisation for Economic Co-operation and Development). 2003. *Emerging risks in the 21st century: An agenda for action.* Paris: OECD.

Okuyama, Y. 2004. Modelling spatial economic impacts of an earthquake: Input–output approaches. *Disaster Prevention and Management* 13 (4): 297–306.

Okuyama, Y., G.J.D. Hewings, and M. Sonis. 2004. Measuring economic impacts of disasters: Interregional input–output analysis using sequential interindustry model. In *Modelling spatial and economic impacts of disasters: advances in spatial science,* ed. Y. Okuyama and S.E. Chang, 77–103. New York: Springer-Verlag.

Parker, D.J. 2000. *Floods.* London and New York: Routledge.

Parker, D.J., C.H. Green, and P.M. Thompson. 1987. *Urban flood protection benefits: A project appraisal guide.* Aldershot, UK: Gower.

Pingali, P., L. Alinovi, and J. Sutton. 2005. Food security in complex emergencies: Enhancing food system resilience. *Disasters* 29:5–24.

RA (Resilience Alliance). 2005. Research on resilience in social-ecological systems: A basis for sustainability. www.resalliance.org (accessed October 30, 2008).

Riddell, K., and C. Green. 1999. *Flood and coastal project appraisal guidance: Economic appraisal.* London: Ministry of Agriculture, Fisheries and Food, Flood and Coastal Defence Emergencies Division (MAFF).

RIVM (Rijksinstituut voor Volksgezondheid en Milieu). 2004. *Risico's in bedijkte termen een thematische evaluatie van het Nederlandse veiligheidsbeleid tegen overstromen* [*Dutch dikes, and risk hikes:*

A thematic policy evaluation of risks of flooding in the Netherlands]. RIVM Report 500799002. Bilthoven, Netherlands: RIVM.

Rose, A.Z. 2004a. Defining and measuring economic resilience to disasters. *Disaster Prevention and Management* 13 (4): 307–14.

———. 2004b. Economic principles, issues, and research priorities in hazard loss estimation. In *Modelling spatial and economic impacts of disaster*, ed.Y. Okuyama and S.E.Chang, 13–36. New York: Springer-Verlag.

Rose, A.Z., and D. Lim. 2002. Business interruption losses from natural hazards: Conceptual and methodological issues in the case of the Northridge earthquake. *Environmental Hazards* 4:1–14.

Silva, W., F. Klijn, and J. Dijkman. 2001. *Room for the Rhine branches in the Netherlands*. Lelystad, Netherlands: RIZA.

Steenge, A.E., and M. Bočkarjova. 2007. Impact and recovery after a big disaster: Input-output methodology revisited. *Economic Systems Research* 19 (2): 205–23.

TAW (Technische Adviescommissie voor de Waterkeringen). 2000. *Van overschrijdingskans naar overstromingskans [From overtopping probability to flooding probability]*. Delft, Netherlands: Technische Adviescommisie voor de Waterkeringen.

Tinbergen, J. 1954. Economisch aspect van het Deltaplan [Economic perspective on the Delta Plan]. In *Het Deltaplan, afdamming zee-armen [The Delta Plan: Closing the sea arms with the dikes]*. The Hague: Nederlandse Maatschappij voor Nijverheid en Handel.

Tobin, G.A. 1999. Sustainability and community resilience: The Holy Grail of hazards planning? *Environmental Hazards* 1:13–25.

V&W (Ministerie van Verkeer en Waterstaat). 2005a. *Flood risks and safety in the Netherlands: Full report*. Delft, Netherlands: V&W.

———. 2005b. *HIS Hoogwater Informatie Systeem voor de rampenbestrijding bij overstromingen [HIS: High Water Information System for the prevention of disasters caused by flooding]*. Delft, Netherlands: V&W.

van Ast, J., J.J. Bouma, and D. François. 2004. *Final report on the evaluation of risks due to flooding*. Rotterdam: Erasmus Centre for Sustainable Development and Management, Erasmus University of Rotterdam.

van Dantzig, D. 1956. Economic decision problems for flood prevention. *Econometrica* 24:276–87.

van den Berg, K., L. Sluijs, M. Snuverink, and A. Wiertz. 2000. *Damage curves for industry as a consequence of a flooding*. The Hague: V&W/Tebodin Consultancy.

van der Veen, A., N. Groenendijk, N. Mol, C.J.J. Logtmeijer, and A.J. Wesselink. 2001. *Kosten-Baten analyse en evaluatie van maatregelen tegen overstromingen [Cost–benefit analysis and evaluation of flood control measures syllabus]*. Delft, Netherlands: Delft Cluster.

van der Veen, A., and C.J.J. Logtmeijer. 2005. Economic hotspots: Visualizing vulnerability to flooding. *Natural Hazards* 36 (1–2): 65–80.

Vrijling, J.K. 2001. Probabilistic design of water defence systems in the Netherlands. *Reliability Engineering and Systems Safety* 74:337–44.

Vrisou van Eck, N., and M. Kok. 2001. *Standaardmethode Schade en Slachtoffers als gevolg van overstromingen [Standard method for predicting damage and casualties as a result of floods]*. Lelystad, Netherlands: HKV Consultants.

Williamson, O.E. 2000. The new institutional economics: Taking stock, looking ahead. *Journal of Economic Literature* 38 (3): 595–613.

Zeegers, G.H.L. 1954. Planning and sociological perspectives on the Delta Plan. In *Het Deltaplan, afdamming zee-armen [The Delta Plan: Closing the sea arms with the dikes]*. The Hague: Nederlandse Maatschappij voor Nijverheid en Handel.

Legal Acts

Besluit tegemoetkoming schade bij rampen en zware ongevallen [Decision on Compensation of Damage in Case of Disasters and Serious Accidents] (1998), Staatsblad 648, Netherlands.

Communication from the Commission to the Council, the European Parliament, the European Economic and Social Committee and the Committee of the Regions Flood Risk Management Flood Prevention, Protection and Mitigation. COM(2004)472, Brussels.

Directive 2000/60/EC of the European Parliament and of the Council of 23 October 2000 establishing a framework for Community action in the field of water policy. *Official Journal of the European Communities L 327:1–72.*

Directive 2007/60/EC of the European Parliament and of the Council of 23 October 2007 on the assessment and management of flood risks. *Official Journal of the European Union L 288:27-34.*

Wet op de Waterkering [*Flood Defence Act*] (1996), Netherlands.

Wet toegemoetkoming schade bij rampen en zware ongevallen [*Law on Compensation of Damage in Case of Disasters and Serious Accidents*] (1998), Staatsblad 325, Netherlands.

Nationaal Bestuursakkoord Water [*National Administrative Agreement on Water*] (2003), Netherlands.

CHAPTER 5

Costs and Benefits of Water Policy

Roy Brouwer and Rob van der Veeren

*W*ATER ECONOMICS DEVELOPS more and more into a new interdisciplinary research theme and as such also plays an increasingly important role
in water policy in the Netherlands. Water policy is guided by economic principles
such as cost recovery and the "polluter pays" principle, and economic instruments
are commonplace in the institutional organization of Dutch water management.
For example, charges are made for groundwater abstraction when threshold values
are exceeded and for the discharge of pollutants into surface water, the latter going
back to the Surface Water Pollution Act established in 1970. More recently, economic methods such as cost–benefit analysis (CBA) have become an integrated
part of water policy decisions, such as those related to flood control policy and the
implementation of the European Water Framework Directive (WFD) (EC 2000).

Investment expenditures in water management in the Netherlands by central
and local government, water boards, and industry are around 5 billion euros annually (LBOW 2005). This corresponds to 1% of annual gross domestic product
(GDP). These investments relate to flood control, sewerage works, wastewater treatment, ecological restoration of water bodies, and the maintenance (dredging) of
waterways. A key question is what are the corresponding benefits associated with
these investments (Brouwer et al. 2003)? The Fourth National Policy Memorandum on Water Management, published in 1998, was the first to ask, "What are the
financial and economic consequences of investments in water management for
society as a whole?" The Advisory Committee for Water Management for the 21st
Century concluded in its report published two years later that policymaker and
public awareness of the benefits of water management is low, and benefits should
be addressed more explicitly in the future (Commissie WB21 2000). A recurring
problem is that the goods and services provided by a well-managed water system,

including good water quality and public safety in the context of climate change and flooding, often are (quasi) public goods for which no market prices are available and whose benefits are therefore not directly comparable to the relatively easy computable investment costs. These costs are published and accounted for explicitly in annual reports and therefore more liable to public scrutiny, whereas the corresponding benefits are much less visible.

The main objective of this chapter is to illustrate the application of economic principles and methods in Dutch water policy and integrated policy analysis, covering the policy's two main pillars: flood control and water quality management. We start off with a brief overview of the use and institutionalization of CBA in flood control policy in the Netherlands (based on Brouwer and Kind 2005), followed by a contemporary case study example investigating the costs and benefits underlying alternative long-term flood control policy in one of the largest Dutch river basins, the lower Rhine-Meuse Delta (based on Brouwer and van Ek 2004). This chapter then presents NAMWARiB, a new integrated water and economic information system that links economic activities to water use, such as surface and groundwater abstraction and the emission of water polluting substances (based on Brouwer et al. 2005). The systematic assessment and reporting of water and economy interactions and dependencies provide an important starting point for integrated modeling of these relationships and the evaluation and prediction of changes in the water economy as a result of policy interventions in physical and monetary terms. Integrated hydroeconomic models can be used, for example, to inform decisionmaking about so-called disproportionate costs in the WFD (based on Brouwer et al. 2008). The chapter concludes with a future water economics research agenda for the Netherlands.

COSTS AND BENEFITS OF FLOOD CONTROL POLICY

One of the first CBAs carried out in the Netherlands for a large-scale water management project was in the 1960s for the Delta Plan, drawn up by the Delta Commission (Tinbergen 1960) after the flood disaster in 1953 when about 1,835 people died (see Chapter 1 for more information on this flood). The Delta Plan aimed to protect the vulnerable coastline by closing off the gateways to the southwestern estuaries in the Netherlands, except the Rotterdam Waterway and Western Scheldt (see Chapter 4 for the technical aspects). The implementation costs of this plan were estimated at about 1.1 billion Dutch guilders (price level 1955).[1] This amounted to 4% of the net national income (NNI). Although the total costs of the Delta Plan were only 200 million Dutch guilders higher than the alternative plan of further dike strengthening, the plan was expected to result in considerably more indirect gains, including drought damage reduction and recreation. The study concluded that the incremental costs of the Delta Plan were justified compared with the material damage costs of the 1953 floods. Although the study did not include a probabilistic analysis of future flooding events and their impact with respect to future economic damage because of insufficient knowledge and information at that time, Tinbergen acknowledged the importance of such an analysis for the outcome of the CBA, as well as the fact that the expected economic value of future damage avoided diminishes at positive discount rates.

Knowledge and information about the risks of flooding were very limited in the 1950s and 1960s, and Tinbergen was therefore unable to quantify these risks. Nevertheless, the study was amazingly comprehensive in those early years in its coverage of the relevant issues. The concept of risk is central to CBA of alternative flood control options and scenarios (see Chapter 4). Reductions in flood risk are the main economic benefit in a CBA in the context of flood control. It was not until the end of the 1990s, however, that these benefits could actually be quantified in CBA of large-scale flood control projects based on advanced hydraulic and flood probability models and a new national information system that enables assessment of the damage costs of flooding with the help of damage cost functions (DWW 2000).

Besides the estimation of the material damage costs, nonpriced benefits of recently introduced flood control measures such as land use changes and floodplain restoration as an alternative to traditional dike strengthening receive increasingly more attention. Examples include biodiversity conservation and recreation. The inclusion of the economic value of these nonpriced benefits plays an important role, as this economic value is expected to be decisive in favor of these new flood control alternatives. In the policy document *A Different Approach to Water*, the government states that "*alternative flood control measures will have to be tested based on their costs and benefits. In this test also non-priced costs and benefits will be taken into account, such as costs and benefits related to nature and spatial quality*" (V&W 2000, 31). Benefit–cost ratios based on property damage costs may furthermore substantially underestimate the total benefits if public risk aversion is not accounted for. These well-being effects, measured in economics through the concept of society's willingness to pay (WTP) to avoid a risk or for risk protection should be added to the expected damage costs (Pearce and Smale 2005).

The estimation and valuation of these nonpriced public good benefits is not without problems, however. The ecological functions of floodplains, fluvial wetlands, and intertidal salt marshes, such as the provision of wildlife habitat and nutrient assimilation, and spatial (landscape) quality and diversity are difficult to translate into economic terms. Although various economic methods and techniques have been developed over the past decades to value nonpriced public goods in monetary terms, few studies exist in the Netherlands that have estimated the nonpriced public benefits of floodplain restoration compared with traditional dike strengthening. Economic valuation of these benefits can be a costly and time-consuming undertaking. In practice, benefits transfer is often used as a cost-effective alternative to value these benefits. An example of a CBA including the wider socioeconomic impacts of flood control, including the expected nonmarket benefits, is presented in the next section.

Case Study Example

Between 1998 and 2000, a regional government working group (GWG) investigated alternative flood protection options, including a variety of land use change and floodplain restoration schemes in the Lower River Delta (LRD) along the rivers Lek, Merwede, Meuse, and Waal in the Netherlands. The LRD consists of the estuaries of the international rivers Rhine and Meuse. The river system in the LRD is influenced by the tides. The high water levels in 1993, 1995, and 1998, when polders were threatened and tens of thousands of people were evacuated, demonstrate how real the risk of flooding is in this area. Awareness is growing that alternative measures have to be taken besides raising the dikes to protect the LRD against flooding in the future (see Chapter 10 for the spatial aspects of these alternative measures).

Following the floods in 1993 and 1995, the existing dike defenses were strengthened (see also Chapter 4). In order to ensure public safety levels in the longer term, however, and anticipating an expected water level rise between 20 and 115 centimeters over the next 50 years based on different climate change scenarios, alternative land use changes and floodplain restoration measures were identified in the area. These measures will be implemented stepwise between 2000 and 2050. The identified sets of alternative flood protection measures are part of a planning strategy designed to prevent, where possible, new rounds of dike reinforcement and encourage multifunctional land use and biological diversity (SIVB 2000 and Chapter 10).

The aggregate effects of these sets of measures were examined and evaluated in detail in an environmental impact assessment (EIA) and CBA. The expected impacts of the proposed land use change and floodplain restoration measures are shown in table 5-1. In the table, distinctions are made between priced and nonpriced effects and between direct and indirect effects. The most important welfare effects are changes in the water system's discharge capacity, and consequently safety levels and public perception thereof, and the enhancement of biodiversity as a result of floodplain restoration. These welfare effects are, however, typically nonpriced.

The investment costs needed to implement the flood protection measures and consequently the material damage costs avoided are direct priced effects. The total

Table 5-1 *Expected impacts of alternative flood protection measures such as land use changes and floodplain restoration compared with traditional dike strengthening*

Priced effects	Nonpriced effects	Redistribution effects
Direct	**Direct**	Income losses in agriculture and
Investment costs	Change in discharge capacity,	industry as a result of relocation
Damage costs (avoided)	surface water and	
Market revenues from sand	groundwater levels	
extraction	Public perception of safety	
Indirect	Public perception of dislocation	
Business interruption	of inhabitants and farmers	
Increased recreation	Biodiversity conservation	
Change in water infrastructure		
and effects on commercial		
and recreational shipping		

economic costs of the set of alternative flood protection measures were estimated at about 5.5 billion euros (price level 2000), while the total costs of dike strengthening to achieve the same level of safety are approximately 800 million euros (for a more detailed discussion of the total costs, see Brouwer and van Ek 2004). The most important reason for the much higher costs of the proposed alternative measures is that they consist of land use changes in one of the most densely populated and economically developed areas in the Netherlands, with an enormous complex network infrastructure that would be substantially affected if these changes are implemented. The direct investment costs would be borne by the government, which would carry out the project, but a large share of the costs would also be borne by farmers, industries, and local residents, who would have to be compensated by the government for the loss of their land and livelihoods, including farms, houses, and industrial estates.

The direct beneficiaries would be the inhabitants, farmers, and industries that are able to stay in the area. Their properties and other economic interests in the order of magnitude of 300 billion euros would be protected by the proposed measures, at the expense of the relocation of a small number of houses and businesses. Indirect, third parties benefiting from the proposed flood protection measures would include the sand and grit exploitation companies in the area (< 200 million euros) and possibly the construction industry and dredging companies as a result of increased sedimentation in the longer term caused by the land use change and floodplain restoration measures.

In view of the positive effects on nature and landscape, the area is expected to become more attractive for recreational activities. The attraction of extra visitors (not a redistribution of recreational visitors) is anticipated to increase income in the region by approximately 100 million euros over the next 50 years. These recreational benefits are considered an important indirect effect. The possible impacts of the proposed alternative flood control measures on commercial shipping are also indirect effects, which can be valued with the help of market prices (e.g., change in loading depth and corresponding prices per ton load). The net effect on commercial shipping could be either positive or negative. The deepening of riverbeds and creation of additional watercourses would increase commercial and recreational shipping possibilities. The change in the water infrastructure may also enhance the accessibility of the area. On the other hand, widening the rivers also would lower water levels throughout parts of the river basin, in which case the shipping possibilities would decrease.

Redistribution effects do not influence the economic output of a region or country, measured in terms of regional or national income. Examples are the loss of income and employment in agriculture and industry in one area as a result of the implementation of the proposed land use changes and floodplain restoration measures, which are offset by income generation elsewhere as a result of the relocation of farms and businesses.

Implementing the proposed set of alternative flood protection measures would result in the long term (next 50 years) in a net welfare loss to the economy as a whole of 2 billion euros. Traditional dike strengthening clearly is more beneficial from a cost-effective point of view. The socioeconomic value of the nonpriced social and environmental benefits related to public safety and biodiversity restoration was expected to be decisive in the decisionmaking process and therefore assessed using the results from a meta-analysis carried out by Brouwer et al. (1999). The 30 international studies Brouwer et al. examined generate more than 100 WTP values. These values were related to the main hydrological, geochemical, and biological ecosystem functions performed by wetlands and floodplains: floodwater retention; surface water and groundwater recharge; nutrient retention and export; nursery and habitat for plants, animals, and microorganisms; and landscape structural diversity. The average economic values found in the international literature associated with these functions are presented in table 5-2.

The economic values in this table are expressed in euros per household per year. Often these values are related to the size of the environmental change involved, such as euros per hectare. This suggests that the average values can be transferred unconditionally over large and small sites irrespective of the number of people who benefit from these sites. An example is the study carried out by Costanza et al. (1997), in which the total economic value of the world's ecosystem goods and services was estimated based on average values per hectare. Not only has the average value used to estimate the value of nonpriced environmental benefits caused discussion about the "right" price, but the determination of the "market size," the number of beneficiaries, also has contributed to the controversy over using monetary estimates in CBA (e.g., Bateman et al. 2000). Expressing average values per household per year implies that the user of the average values has to think carefully about the exact market size in order to be able to calculate a total economic value, which can then be used in the CBA. In this case study, the market size was determined in terms of number of households that are expected to benefit from the proposed set of flood protection measures. Together with the GWG, it was

Table 5-2 *Economic values of wetland and floodplain ecosystem functions (price level 2000)*

Wetland and floodplain characteristics	Average economic value (WTP in € /household/year)
Ecosystem function	
Floodwater retention	120
Surface water and groundwater recharge	30
Nutrient retention and export	70
Wildlife habitat and landscape diversity	95
Value type	
Use value	85
Nonuse value	45
Use and nonuse value	80
Continent	
North America	90
Europe	40

Source: Adapted from Brouwer et al. 1999.

agreed that the whole population of the province Zuid-Holland, 1.5 million house-holds, would benefit.

The fact that the function of floodwater retention is valued highest in table 5-2 conforms to expectations, considering the possible risks to life and livelihood and the capacity of wetlands and floodplain restoration to reduce flood risks. Use values for wetland ecosystems are significantly higher than nonuse values. This is partly due to the high value attached to floodwater retention. The table also shows that use and nonuse values cannot simply be added in order to get a total economic value (see, e.g., Hoehn and Randall 1987). The economic value of use and nonuse values together (80 euros/household/year) is a factor 0.62 lower than the sum of the use (85 euros/household/year) and nonuse (45 euros/household/year) values. The economic value of the nonpriced benefits related to public perception of safety against flooding, biodiversity preservation, and landscape diversity is calculated based on the economic value for floodwater retention (120 euros/household/year) and wildlife habitat and landscape diversity (95 euros/household/year). An important assumption here is that the economic value of floodwater retention found in the international literature and presented in the table refers to the same reduction in risk level as in this specific case study. The values are adjusted for the income differences found between Europe and North America and a correction for the summation of use and nonuse values. First, the average values, 120 and 95 euros, are multiplied by 0.61 to correct for income differences.[2] Second, the income adjusted average values are added and multiplied by the above-mentioned factor of 0.62 (80 euros/130 euros = 0.62) to account for the fact that use and nonuse values cannot simply be added. These corrections result in an average WTP for floodwater retention and wildlife and land-scape amenities of around 80 euros/household/year. Multiplying this by 1.5 million households results in a total economic value of 120 million euros per year. Discounted at the prescribed 4% discount rate by the Dutch Treasury over the next 50 years yields a present value of 3.1 billion euros. Including this economic value in the CBA, a net welfare gain is found of 1.1 billion euros (table 5-3).[3]

Using half the economic value per household per year, to conform to results found in a contingent valuation study carried out in 1995 (Brouwer and Slangen 1998) looking specifically at the economic value of biodiversity preservation and landscape amenities on agricultural land in the province Zuid-Holland, or reducing the number of beneficiaries by half in a sensitivity analysis, the net present value

Table 5-3 *Present value of costs and benefits of alternative land use changes and floodplain restoration measures in the LRD in billion euros (price level 2000)*

Costs		Benefits	
Investment costs	2.4	Expected value material damage costs avoided	3.3
Production loss agricultural land	1.8	Revenues sand extraction	0.2
Operation and maintenance costs	1.3	Economic value public safety, biodiversity,	3.1
Net welfare gain	1.1	and landscape amenities	
Total	6.6	Total	6.6

becomes negative (–450 million euros). This suggests not only that the transfer values have to be applied and interpreted with the necessary care, but also that the economic value of the nonpriced benefits may indeed play a decisive role in the final decisionmaking based on the economic efficiency criterion.

INTEGRATED WATER AND ECONOMIC ACCOUNTING INDICATORS

Over the last several years, the demand for information about the economic value of water and the wider economic consequences of water policy and management has increased rapidly. The introduction of the European Union Water Framework Directive has provided an important impetus, as it requires that river basins across Europe be described in both physical and economic terms. According to article 5, the economic characterization of river basins should include an assessment of the economic significance of current and future water use up to 2015.

In order to meet this growing demand, the possibilities of linking existing water information systems to the economic accounting system were investigated. This research resulted in the creation of a new integrated water economics information system called the National Accounting Matrix Including Water Accounts for River Basins (NAMWARiB). NAMWARiB provides information about the interconnections between the physical water system and the economy at national and river basin scale. NAMWARiB is an extension of the National Accounting Matrix (NAM) and National Accounting Matrix Including Environmental Accounts (NAMEA). The NAM presents the system of national accounts in one overall matrix framework, providing information about the flows of goods and services in the national economy in a particular year and the related money flows. As such, the NAM is an official account of the economic transactions in a country, following the internationally adopted methodology of the European System of Accounts (Eurostat 1996), which in turn is based on the worldwide System of National Accounts (UN 1993). The use of an internationally accepted methodology allows for international comparability. The NAMEA is a satellite account extension of the NAM (de Haan and Keuning 1996; de Haan et al. 1993) and includes the environmental pressures related to the production of goods and services and household consumption. NAMWARiB is a further specification of the NAMEA for water, using the same basic structure. Within this structure, each column represents the supply of a good or service, and the rows describe the demand for those goods and services. The monetary flows are in exactly the opposite direction: columns represent receipts, and rows show expenditures. The totals of the columns equal the totals of the corresponding rows. Together, rows and corresponding columns make up an account for a specific good or service, reflecting where it comes from and where it goes. Basically, the structure of NAMWARiB consists of three parts:

- an economic account (in millions of euros per year);
- an emission account (in kilograms per year);
- a water extraction and discharge account (in millions of cubic meters per year).

Whereas the economic accounts are monetary (millions of euros), the emission accounts are expressed in physical units (kilograms). NAMWARiB describes the emissions of 78 substances from economic activities to the aquatic environment. The list of substances includes the most important ones identified in the WFD. The emission data for these substances are supplied by the Dutch National Emission Registration. The water flow account, water extraction and discharge, is expressed in millions of cubic meters (m^3) and is based on a National Water Survey carried out once every five years by Statistics Netherlands. About 7,500 companies participate in the survey, providing information about their water consumption: how much fresh, brackish, and salt water they use and for what purposes.

A key feature of NAMWARiB is that it presents information at the level of the four main river basins in the Netherlands: Rhine, Meuse, Scheldt, and Ems. As the Rhine basin covers approximately 70% of the entire Dutch territory, making it difficult to carry out any meaningful analysis, this basin is further split up into four districts: Rhine North, Rhine West, Rhine East, and Rhine Centre.

The data from the economic, emission, and water flow accounts are aggregated to the level of the seven river basin districts using geographical information systems (GIS). The economic data are based on the regional accounts, which in turn are based on geographical economic units (COROPs), whereas regional water flow data are based on the business-level data from the survey. The regional water flows add up to the total of the national water flow. Emission data are available at the level of individual plants, including their exact locations, which are used to allocate the data to the different districts (van der Veeren et al. 2004).

The allocation of economic data to river basin districts enables a detailed description of their economic structure. Most economic value, as of 2000, is generated in the river basin district Rhine West (50%), followed by the Rhine North (21%) and Rhine East (10%). These are the three largest river basin districts in the Netherlands. Rhine West is economically a very important area in the Netherlands and the most densely populated, covering a large part of the province Zuid-Holland. The contribution of each of the other basins to total GDP is less than 5%.

The economic structure is fairly similar across the various river basin districts. The service sector dominates in each river basin, but especially in Rhine West and Rhine Centre. Almost 60% of total value added is generated in the service sector in these districts, compared with approximately 50% in the rest of the Netherlands. The share of agriculture in total value added is relatively low here (< 5%), compared with other sectors, but agriculture is especially important in Rhine North and Rhine East. Industry consists of many subsectors. Of those that are generally believed to have an important impact on water—the mining, food, chemical, metal, and energy subsectors—mining (oil and gas) is particularly important in Rhine North and the Ems, while the shares of the chemical and food industries are relatively high in the Scheldt basin. No substantial differences can be found in the case of the energy sector. The metal industry is slightly more important in the Meuse basin than in the rest of the country.

Most wastewater is produced in Rhine West, followed by the Meuse and Rhine East. Total wastewater production in 2000 was 27 million inhabitant equivalents (ie). This is slightly lower than in 1996 (−0.5%).[4] When relating wastewater production to the total number of inhabitants in the river basins, the highest wastewater production per capita ratio in 2000 is found in the Scheldt (2.4 ie/inhabitant), followed by Rhine East (2.0 ie/inhabitant) and the Ems (1.9 ie/inhabitant). Average wastewater production per capita in the Netherlands is 1.8 ie. Wastewater discharge per sector does not differ significantly across the river basin districts. Most wastewater is produced by households, about 60%. The food and transport sector each contribute about 7%. The contribution from agriculture, the metal industry, and the service sector is relatively low, less than 1%. Unknown sources account for 15% of all wastewater.

NAMWARiB is a descriptive tool, presenting information about the pressures exerted on the water system in some past period, such as indicating which river basins have had excess amounts of nutrients enter surface waters. It does not, however, describe the extent to which these pressures actually result in environmental damage. An impact analysis of whether environmental pressures result in environmental damage requires the use of appropriate models. The data presented in NAMWARiB can be used as input into these models.

On the other hand, NAMWARiB offers opportunities to carry out time series analysis for environmental pressures. This allows us to evaluate the effectiveness of environmental policies aimed at reducing environmental pressures exerted by specific economic sectors or activities. Figure 5.1 provides an example. By means of trend analysis, the potential decoupling of economic activities and pressures such as water consumption, wastewater production, and the emission of polluting substances (nutrients, metals, etc.) can be examined.

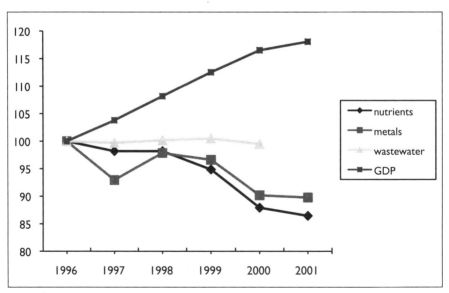

Figure 5.1 *Economic growth, wastewater production, and emission of nutrients and metals in the Netherlands, 1996–2001 (1996 = 100)*

At the national level, real economic growth (in terms of GDP in constant prices) over the period 1996–2001 was 18% (on average 3% per year). Total wastewater production remained more or less the same over that same period, whereas the emission of nutrients decreased significantly, by approximately 15%, and the emission of metals by about 10%. Similar diagrams can be made for specific substances per sector at river basin level. These types of indicators are helpful in assessing the success or failure of environmental (sector) policy, as they provide important insight into the environmental efficiency of economic activities.

INTEGRATED MODELING AND VALUATION OF THE COSTS AND BENEFITS OF IMPLEMENTING THE WFD

The integrated accounting work presented in the previous section provides an important starting point for integrated river basin modeling. Such models aim to evaluate and predict the impacts of policy interventions on both economic and water systems. Integrated river basin modeling is based on the recognition that aquatic ecosystems perform valuable functions in economic consumption and production processes. Water is used as an input factor (source) in economic production processes (food processing, electricity production, and so on) and at the same time also as a sink for the unwanted by-products of economic production processes (e.g., emission of pollutants to water).

Water–economy interactions are characterized by complex linear and nonlinear feedback mechanisms. Water has public good characteristics and can be used simultaneously or consecutively in different economic activities as a result of recycling, such as when water for electricity production or cooling is discharged again after it has been used. One challenge in integrated river basin modeling is to integrate the complexity of these important feedback mechanisms into economic models. Degradation and depletion of water systems affect economic production directly and indirectly, such as through the extra costs of cleaning polluted water used in food processing or drilling new nonpolluted or nonexhausted drinking-water bore holes. Nonproductive activities can also be affected, such as the loss of recreational fishing or swimming opportunities as a result of pollution upstream.

Research in this area in the Netherlands is ongoing (see Brouwer et al. 2008). Using an existing static-comparative applied general equilibrium (AGE) model of the Dutch economy, including 27 economic sectors (see Hofkes et al. 2004 for a detailed description), the emission of nutrients (nitrogen and phosphorus) and ecotoxicological substances (e.g., arsenic, cadmium, copper, chromium, mercury, nickel, lead, zinc, and polycyclic aromatic hydrocarbon, or PAH) to water has been linked to the economic sectors in the AGE model. Emission units are included as input factors in a constant elasticity of transformation (CET) production function in the AGE model, meaning that a certain (relative) quantity of emission units is needed, just as are labor and capital, to be able to produce economic output. A reduction of an emission unit implies a reduction of output, with constant labor and capital input. Emission units thus are valuable input to production. An auxiliary emission abatement producer is introduced into the model as a separate economic sector, producing abatement goods, which can substitute for emissions as input of production. Economic sectors can reduce their emission levels through the purchase of these intermediate abatement goods (i.e., best available techniques) or by reducing their production or consumption level. The model is calibrated for the year 2000 using data from the NAMEA.

The AGE model was used to evaluate the direct and indirect economic consequences of the implementation of the WFD for the 27 sectors in the Dutch economy. For this purpose, three hypothetical emission reduction policy scenarios were developed and calculated with the AGE model.[5] These hypothetical WFD policy scenarios involve a reduction of 10%, 20%, and 50% of the national emission levels in the year 2000. Imposing these emission reduction levels on the national economic system, under the assumption that they are immediately and fully implemented, the AGE model estimates the minimum economic costs for the Dutch economy as a whole to reach these emission levels. The total direct and indirect economic effects are found by comparing GDP with and without implementing the emission reduction scenarios. A reduction in GDP implies that the total economic effect is negative and the economy suffers a loss.

Depending on assumptions about possible corresponding changes in world market prices, a 10% reduction of the 2000 emission levels of nutrients and ecotoxicological substances results in a decrease of net national income (NNI) of around 0.2% (700 million euros), a 20% emission reduction in a decrease of NNI between 0.5% and 0.6% (1.6–1.9 billion euros), and a 50% reduction in a decrease of NNI between 3.1% and 9.4% (10.5–32.1 billion euros). In the case of variant 1, world market prices are assumed constant, making it more attractive to import relatively cheaper polluting goods and services. In the case of variant 2, world market prices are assumed to change in the same way as domestic price levels as a result of the imposed emission reduction scenarios, and import–export ratios remain the same.

Relative changes in world market prices appear to have almost no influence on the total economic costs under the 10% and 20% emission reduction policy scenarios. In the case of a 50% reduction, however, the total costs under variant 2 are three times higher than under variant 1.

The economic costs differ substantially across economic sectors, but the same sectors appear to bear the largest part of the total costs under the various emission reduction scenarios (fig. 5.2).[6] In the case of a 50% reduction of the emission levels, especially commercial shipping, the metal, chemical, rubber, and plastic industries have a relatively large share in the total costs. Each of these sectors faces a decrease in value added of more than 15% to 20% compared with the base year 2000. A remarkable finding is the reduction in value added in the primary agricultural sector, which becomes significant only when imposing a 50% nutrient emission reduction scenario.

In order to assess to what extent the estimated costs of the implementation of the WFD are considered disproportionate, as outlined in article 4 of the directive, households were asked in a large-scale contingent valuation (CV) survey for their WTP for additional water quality improvements in the Netherlands (Brouwer 2004). Currently, Dutch households pay on average 200 euros per year for wastewater collection and treatment (LBOW 2005). Including also the other water-related expenses (water quantity management, flooding, and so on), the total "water bill" is

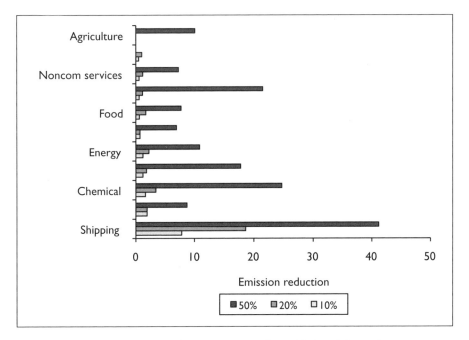

Figure 5.2 *Economic costs (relative loss in value added in %) in the most important economic sectors under 50%, 20%, and 10% emission reduction scenarios, assuming fixed world market prices (variant 1)*

about 500 euros per household per year. Between 2005 and 2010, a further increase in household taxes and levies related to wastewater collection and treatment is expected between 1.5% and 3% annually because of current policies (Gerritsen and Sterks 2004). It was expected that the estimated public WTP value could serve as a benchmark for affordable and thus acceptable future price and tax increases, and hence inform the discussion about what constitutes a disproportionate cost to those who will pay a large share of the costs of WFD implementation as taxpayers.[7]

In the CV study, 5,000 questionnaires were sent in October 2003 to a random selection of Dutch households, asking them about their knowledge, perception, and opinion of, and attitudes toward, current water quality and the introduction of future standards as a result of the implementation of the European WFD. A distinction was made between the quality of coastal waters and inland freshwater bodies. Although the response was 27%, the sample is representative for the total Dutch population.

Overall, a third of the population considers the quality of water in the Netherlands insufficient. Only 20% are of the opinion that water quality is sufficient. A significant difference can be detected between public perception of coastal and inland waters. About 40% perceive inland waters as polluted, whereas just over a quarter of the population feels the same about coastal water.

Corresponding with the actual development of water quality, a quarter of the population believes that coastal water quality has improved over the past 10 years, whereas 45% think that inland freshwater quality has improved. A minority of 15% feel that surface water quality has deteriorated over the past 10 years. One-third do not know what has happened to water quality in the Netherlands over this time period.

When asked how important it is to improve surface water quality in the Netherlands, 97% of all households consider this important or very important. Reasons given include concerns about public health and clean drinking water, the conservation of a healthy water environment for plants and animals, followed by the ability to swim safely in open water and the preservation of clean water for future generations. Hence, although there is no evidence that a majority perceives water quality as a problem in the Netherlands, most people believe that water quality should be improved.

A majority of 70% of the population is aware of the fact that citizens already pay for surface water and groundwater quality. In response to a dichotomous choice WTP question, 65% of the population agree to pay one of the presented bid amounts in the CV study over and above their current income tax for the foreseen benefits of implementing WFD and reaching a good ecological status for all water bodies in the Netherlands, but 15% refuse to pay the proposed bid amounts because of low preferences for water quality improvements or income constraints.[8] A third of these respondents are, however, willing to pay a lower amount than the proposed original bid. Another 15% protest against paying, because they believe the polluter should pay and lack trust that the money will actually be spent on water quality improvements and not something else. This group is usually referred to as protest bidders. Finally, 5% are not sure if they are willing to pay.

The 95% confidence interval around average WTP for achieving the WFD objective of good status for all water bodies in the Netherlands is between 90 and 105 euros per household per year over the next 10 years. This corresponds with about a 20% increase of what households currently pay for water.[9] Aggregated across the whole population from which the sample was drawn, a total economic value results of 600 to 700 million euros per year. Discounted at the official rate of 4% from 2004 through 2015, the present value equals about 6.3 billion euros. Comparing this with the total economic costs calculated with the AGE model, the 10% and 20% emission reduction scenarios can be justified in benefit–cost terms, assuming that these scenarios deliver the benefits for which households are willing to pay derived from good water status, but not the 50% emission reduction policy scenario.

Finally, besides uncertainty about the relationship between the emission reduction scenarios and the associated benefits from good water status, another important source of uncertainty in the comparison is how costs and benefits will evolve after adaptation to the new situation when the emission reduction scenarios are implemented. Flows of costs and benefits will occur after the WFD has been implemented and the environmental objectives have been achieved in 2015, but their size and distribution across different sectors are unknown. Currently, there is no insight into these longer-term economic effects of WFD implementation.

CONCLUSIONS

In this chapter, we provided a few examples of the practical application of economic methods to underpin decisionmaking in Dutch water policy and management. These examples illustrate the direction of water economics as a new inter-disciplinary policy research theme in the Netherlands. Standard economic methods and models are not always directly applicable because of the specific characteristics of the water economy. Carrying out economic analysis at river basin scale introduces a whole range of challenges, including up- and downscaling procedures of economic costs and benefits both up- and downstream.

Given the country's downstream location in Europe, an international river basin perspective in future economic research programs is paramount. Performing economic analysis at international river basin scale instead of local water body or subregional level is expected to be economically beneficial, as it may result in substantial cost savings. Preventive measures at an upstream source are usually cheaper than damage repair and remediation downstream.

Future research questions relate to a further investigation and elaboration of how economic and water systems interact and the ways water adds value in regional, national, and international economic production processes as a source (extraction) and a sink (emission). Long-term research programs have to be set up, focusing on how these interactions can be formalized in integrated transboundary river basin models to facilitate integrated assessment of the impacts of future policy scenarios on both the water system and the economy. Besides spatial up- and downscaling procedures, dynamic feedback and adaptation mechanisms should play a central role in this research.

From a consumption point of view, the economic value of water at micro or household level is another key research question, including nonextractive use and nonuse. Here the main focus is the further development and methodological testing of stated and revealed preference methods, including choice experiments. The estimated economic water values are expected to provide the basis for alternative future payment structures for watershed services and environmental liability based on firmly institutionalized economic principles in Dutch water policy, such as the polluter or beneficiary pays principle and cost recovery.

NOTES

1. In 1955, 1 guilder equaled approximately $3.60.

2. The regression in the meta-analysis (see Brouwer et al. 1999) shows that while accounting for floodplain and methodological study characteristics, studies carried out in the United States nevertheless produce systematically higher economic values than those done in Europe because of income differences. The estimated regression coefficient used to modify the average value estimates for this income difference is 0.61; in other words, the economic values found in Europe are 61% of the average values presented in table 5-2.

3. To avoid double counting, the economic value of additional recreational opportunities is not included in table 5-3.

4. The discharge of wastewater from different sources (household and industry) is expressed in inhabitant equivalents (ie) so that it can be compared across sectors. One ie is related to the amount of oxygen used to decompose the organic compound content of wastewater, also referred to as chemical oxygen demand (COD) or biological oxygen demand (BOD).

5. The policy scenarios are hypothetical because the WFD environmental objectives were unknown at the time of writing of this chapter. Moreover, the objectives are related to water

quality. The translation of these water quality objectives to corresponding emission reduction levels is a complex scientific problem.

6. The noncommercial services sector in figure 5.2 includes environmental services such as sewerage and wastewater treatment plants.

7. Individual household WTP is influenced by household income levels. The WTP values presented here therefore incorporate individual household ability to pay. In the CV study, households were asked to trade off part of their income in order for the proposed WFD water quality improvements to reach good ecological status by 2015.

8. Income tax was the most preferred payment vehicle by a majority of households. Fourteen bid amounts were used in the study to elicit WTP: 1, 5, 10, 15, 20, 25, 30, 40, 50, 60, 75, 100, 150, 200 euros. These bid amounts were based on open-ended WTP questions used during the pretest of the survey. Bid amounts were randomly allocated across respondents, so each respondent answered the WTP question based on one of the above amounts.

9. For a comparison of the economic value of the nonmarket benefits of the WFD presented here with other economic water valuation studies carried out in the Netherlands, see Brouwer (2006). For instance, public WTP for bathing water quality improvements as a result of the implementation of revised European bathing water quality standards (EC 2006) is 25 to 30 euros per household per year.

REFERENCES

Bateman, I.J., I.H. Langford, N. Nishikawa, and I. Lake. 2000. The Axford debate revisited: A case study illustrating different approaches to the aggregation of benefits data. *Journal of Environmental Planning and Management* 43 (2): 291–302.

Brouwer, R. 2004. *De economische waarde van schoner water* [*The economic value of cleaner water as a result of the implementation of the EU Water Framework Directive*]. RIZA Report 2004.013. Lelystad, Netherlands: RIZA.

———. 2006. Valuing water quality changes in the Netherlands using stated preference methods. In *Valuing the environment in developed countries,* ed. D.W. Pearce, 132–47. Cheltenham, UK: Edward Elgar Publishing.

Brouwer, R., J. de Boer, R. van Ek, and M. Hisschemoller. 2003. *Baten van water in geld, groen en gevoel. Leidraad voor integrale beleidsevaluaties* [*Guidelines for integrated water policy analysis*]. RIZA Report 2003.026. Lelystad, Netherlands: RIZA.

Brouwer, R., M. Hofkes, and V. Linderhof. 2008. General equilibrium modelling of the direct and indirect economic impacts of water quality improvements in the Netherlands at national and river basin scale. *Ecological Economics* 66 (1): 127–40.

Brouwer, R., and J. Kind. 2005. The costs and benefits of flood control policy in the Netherlands. In *Cost–benefit analysis and water resources management,* ed. R. Brouwer and D.W. Pearce, 93–123. Cheltenham, UK: Edward Elgar Publishing.

Brouwer, R., I.H. Langford, I.J. Bateman, and R.K. Turner. 1999. A meta-analysis of wetland contingent valuation studies. *Regional Environmental Change* 1 (1): 47–57.

Brouwer, R., S. Schenau, and R. van der Veeren. 2005. Integrated river basin accounting and the European Water Framework Directive. *Statistical Journal of the United Nations Economic Commission for Europe* 22 (2): 111–31.

Brouwer, R., and L.H.G. Slangen. 1998. Contingent valuation of the public benefits of agricultural wildlife management: The case of Dutch peat meadow land. *European Review of Agricultural Economics* 25:53–72.

Brouwer, R., and R. van Ek. 2004. Integrated ecological, economic and social impact assessment of alternative flood protection measures in the Netherlands. *Ecological Economics* 50 (1–2): 1–21.

Commissie WB21 (Commissie Waterbeheer 2le Eeuw). 2000. *Waterbeleid voor de 21ste eeuw: geef water de ruimte en de aandacht die het verdient* [*Water policy for the 21st century: Give water the space and attention it deserves*]. The Hague: Commissie WB21.

Costanza, R., R. d'Arge, R. de Groot, S. Farber, M. Grasso, B. Hannon, K. Limburg, S. Naeem, R.V. O'Neill, J.U. Paruelo, R.G. Raskin, P. Sutton, and M. van den Belt. 1997. The value of the world's ecosystem services and natural capital. *Nature* 387:253–60.

de Haan, M., and S.J. Keuning. 1996. Taking the environment into account: The NAMEA approach. *Review of Income and Wealth* 42 (2): 131–48.

de Haan, M., S.J. Keuning, and P.R. Bosch. 1993. *Integrating indicators in a national accounting matrix including environmental accounts (NAMEA).* Statistics Netherlands, National Accounts Occasional Paper NA-060. Voorburg: Statistics Netherlands.

DWW (Dienst Weg- en Waterbouwkunde). 2000. *Schade na overstroming: Een verkenning [Damage after flooding: An exploration].* Delft, Netherlands: Ministerie van Verkeer en Waterstaat.

EC (European Commission). 2000. Directive 2000/60/EC of the European Parliament and of the Council of 23 October 2000 establishing a framework for community action in the field of water policy. *Official Journal of the European Communities* L 327:1–72.

———. 2006. Directive 2006/7/EC of the European Parliament and of the Council of 15 February 2006 concerning the management of bathing water quality and repealing Directive 76/160/EEC. *Official Journal of the European Communities* L 64:37–51.

Eurostat. 1996. *European System of Accounts ESA 95.* Luxembourg: Office for Official Publications of the European Communities.

Gerritsen, E. and C.G.M. Sterks. 2004. *Kostenontwikkeling in de waterketen 1990–2010 [Cost development in the water chain 1990–2010].* COELO Report 04-03. Groningen: COELO.

Hoehn, J.P., and A. Randall. 1987. A satisfactory benefit cost indicator from contingent valuation. *Journal of Environmental Economics and Management* 14:226–47.

Hofkes, M.W., R. Gerlagh, and V. Linderhof. 2004. *Sustainable national income: A trend analysis for the Netherlands for 1990–2000.* IVM Report R-04/02. Amsterdam: Institute for Environmental Studies.

LBOW (Landelijk Bestuurlijk Overleg Water). 2005. *Water in Beeld 2005: Voortgangsrapportage over het waterbeheer in Nederland [Water in focus 2005: Annual report on water management in the Netherlands].* www.waterinbeeld.nl (accessed September 9, 2008).

Pearce, D.W., and R. Smale. 2005. Appraising flood control investments in the UK. In *Cost–benefit analysis and water resources management,* ed. R. Brouwer and D.W. Pearce, 71–92. Cheltenham: Edward Elgar Publishing.

SIVB (Stuurgroep Integrale Verkenning Benedenrivieren). 2000. *Vergroting van de afvoercapaciteit en berging in de benedenloop van Rijn en Maas [Enlargement of the discharge capacity and retention of stormwater in the Lower River Delta of Rhine and Meuse].* Rotterdam: Rijkswaterstaat, Directie Zuid-Holland.

Tinbergen, J. 1960. *De economische balans van het Delta Plan [The economic balance of the Delta Plan].* The Hague: Deltacommissie.

UN (United Nations). 1993. *1993 System of National Accounts.* Washington, DC: Statistics Division, UN.

V&W (Ministerie van Verkeer en Waterstaat). 2000. *Ruimte voor de rivier [Room for the river].* The Hague: V&W.

van der Veeren, R., R. Brouwer, S. Schenau, and R. van der Stegen. 2004. *NAMWA: A new integrated river basin information system.* RIZA Report 2004.032. Lelystad, Netherlands: RIZA.

Part II
WATER CHAIN MANAGEMENT AND WATER QUALITY

CHAPTER 6

Efficient and Equitable Use of Water Resources

Jan Rouwendal

*E*CONOMIC ANALYSIS of the water sector is useful, even if water might be regarded as an elementary need for human life that should be available at zero or negligible cost. Water is often thought of as being freely available, with the main tasks of public utilities to bring it to the locations of the demanders and return the sewage, after appropriate treatment, into the environment. The efficiency of the distribution system and how to deal with fluctuations over time in demand for and availability of fresh water so as to serve the needs of society in an optimal way are important issues, as is the determination of the appropriate degree of treating the sewage before it is disposed into the natural environment. In fact, water supply is much more complicated than just bringing fresh water to demanders through pipelines. The production process used to reach and maintain a high quality level can be quite complicated and may require large investments. A similar remark can be made with respect to sewage treatment. This suggests that it may be useful to apply the tools of economic analysis to the water supply and sewage treatment industries.[1] It is the purpose of this chapter to show that such an analysis can provide fruitful insights into the efficient use of water resources.[2]

To achieve this goal, the chapter focuses on some aspects of the organization of the market for water. In particular, it examines how the institutional framework in which water supply and sewage treatment are placed affects welfare. Even though it would be possible to treat water supply and sewage treatment as separate industries, it seems natural to study their mutual relationship. Water demand is closely related to the production of sewage. From a household production perspective, the former can be interpreted as an input and the latter as a (secondary) output that cannot be freely disposed. Decisions about water demand are therefore often also decisions about sewage supply. Moreover, the use of natural water for consumption or production activities starts by withdrawing water from nature and ends with disposing sewage back into the environment. By considering water supply as well as sewage treatment, the complete chain can be studied.

Focusing on water supply and sewage treatment implies that we ignore other relevant economic aspects of water resources, such as their use for recreational purposes. This choice does not reflect a judgment on the relative importance of these other aspects. It is simply the result of the necessity to concentrate on one or a few aspects for reasons of available space.

The analysis carried out below is of a general nature, but the situation in the Netherlands is the primary frame of reference. In this country, water supply and sewage treatment are public utilities, for two main reasons: (1) fresh water is a primary need for every household, and public control is thought necessary to ensure its availability for everyone; and (2) the market provides insufficient possibilities for competition because of the network structures involved.

Even though these are—at least at first sight—strong arguments, water is supplied by private companies in some countries, the United Kingdom being the most important example. Economic analysis is helpful for finding the pros and cons of these two polar cases of external organization of the industry. More generally, economic theory highlights the consequences of external effects and other types of market failure on resource allocation and provides important suggestions for the development of policy measures to deal with them.

Although the Netherlands is a country with abundant water resources, supply of fresh water to all households is not a trivial issue. For instance, household water demand is especially high during the summer, when dry periods of several weeks are common. When this happens, rivers carry a much smaller flow of higher-temperature water, but approximately the same amount of pollutants. Moreover, the groundwater table tends to be lower during such an event, and additional pumping causes relatively severe environmental damage. Current practice is to store enough water to serve demand during these periods at constant prices, but storage capacity is expensive, and the efficiency of this policy may be questioned. This motivates interest in the study of capacity choice of water supply. The subsequent discussion focuses attention on the role of prices in allocating the scarce resources involved.

This chapter first introduces some concepts of economic analysis that are relevant for the study of the economics of water supply and sewage treatment industries. These are put together into a model of the water industry, covering water supply as well as sewage treatment. The organization of the industry as a (regulated) monopoly is compared with a public utility, and the question of cost coverage and analyze capacity choice is considered. Thereafter, flesh is put onto the bones of the model by a discussion of some relevant empirical evidence. Details of the formulas are given in a mathematical appendix at the end of this chapter.

BASIC CONCEPTS

This section introduces some useful elements from the economist's toolbox. It starts with a brief discussion of consumer surplus, then deals with costs and revenues of water supply and sewage treatment, taking into account environmental damage. It also defines the social surplus as the social welfare function.

Consumer Surplus

A central concept in the analysis of efficient pricing is consumer surplus. In the paragraphs that follow, we introduce this concept and illustrate its usefulness for the analysis of water supply.

A Single Good. Applying the concept to a single good, intuitively, the idea is that a consumer is willing to pay a high price for the first unit of a commodity he or she consumes. The difference between the consumer's willingness to pay for this unit and the actual market price is his or her benefit. The next units of the commodity are less valuable for the consumer and give a smaller, but still positive, benefit. The consumer stops buying the product when the benefit of an additional unit is smaller than the cost. The total benefits can then be measured as the sum of the differences between the willingness to pay and the market price over all units that are bought. This sum is equal to consumer surplus.

A question that arises naturally in many cases, perhaps especially in the context of water demand, where there is often no immediate relation between consumption and payment, is whether the view on consumer behavior involved in the derivation of consumer surplus is realistic. This question will be addressed later in this chapter on the basis of the empirical evidence.

Figure 6.1 illustrates consumer surplus for a commodity that is available in continuous quantities. Consumer surplus is the area under the (inverse) demand curve

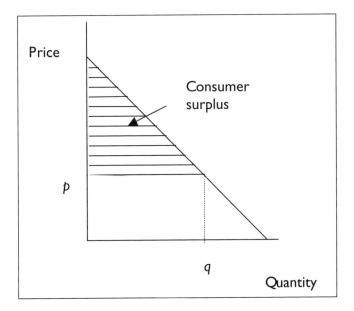

Figure 6.1 *Consumer surplus*

above the market price. The change in consumer surplus that occurs when the price changes by one unit is the demand for the good at that price.

The usefulness of consumer surplus as a welfare measure can be illustrated by the explanation it provides for the "paradox of value." This is the phenomenon that some products of crucial importance for human well-being—water being a prominent example—nevertheless can have a very low price, which suggests that these products are almost worthless. The paradox is explained by pointing out that the total value of the commodity is indicated by the consumer surplus associated with it, whereas the price indicates only the value of the marginal unit that is consumed.

A convenient property of consumer surplus is that it can be easily aggregated over consumers. Total demand for water is the sum of all individual demands, and it follows easily from figure 6.1 that total consumer surplus from water is the sum of the individual consumer surpluses.

Generalization to Multiple Goods. It is sometimes necessary to analyze welfare effects in situations where more than one commodity must be considered. An example is the effect of the provision of bottled drinking water on the demand for fresh water provided through a pipeline. In such cases, we need to generalize the concept of consumer surplus to the situation of multiple goods.

In this case, we can no longer use graphs and need to work with mathematical equations. In the interest of readability, most of these equations and the associated analyses have been placed in an appendix at the end of this chapter. The main text contains a description and discussion of the results.[3]

If the number of commodities to consider is arbitrary, say n, consumer surplus is a function of the prices of all of them. In this more general situation, the relationship between the general consumer surplus and the demand for each of the n commodities remains similar to that in the case of a single commodity: the quantity demanded is equal to the change in surplus that results from a small change in the price of that particular commodity.

Although the demand for each commodity is in general a function of the prices of all the n commodities considered, such interdependencies are not always present. For instance, if we treat water consumed in different time periods (say months) as separate commodities, it is reasonable to assume that the demand in a given month is independent of the price to be paid in the other months. As this is the main application in the analysis that follows, we will usually assume that demand is a function of its own price and ignore dependence on the price of other water supply products. In this special case of *independent demands*, the total consumer surplus of all commodities *is* equal to the sum of individual consumer surpluses.

The Price of Water. Throughout this chapter, the unit price of water of type i consists of three elements, some of which may be zero: the price of supplied water π_i, the price of sewage treatment ρ_i, and a (Pigovian) environmental tax τ_i. The price p_i is the sum of these three elements:

$$p_i = \pi_i + \rho_i + \tau_i, \quad i = 1,...,I \tag{6-1}$$

This equation is based on the assumptions that (a) all the water supplied to a consumer is also deposited by him or her after use as sewage and (b) this quantity can be observed and therefore be priced. This is not necessarily true. In many countries, not all households are metered, and most countries have no direct information about the amount of sewage deposited by a household. We will discuss the consequences of such limited information for optimal allocation of resources later. When the firm supplies only one product, the equation is simplified somewhat, as the suffix i is superfluous.

In the standard case, water has a constant unit price, but this is not always the actual situation. For instance, in reality, a flat rate sometimes is charged for water supply, sewage treatment, or both, which implies that the cost of an additional unit of water is effectively zero, whereas the average price per unit of water is decreasing in the quantity consumed. Under such a flat rate, no direct correlation exists between the amount of water consumed or waste deposited by the household and the amount of money that has to be paid for it. A flat rate is the only possibility where no metering is done, as happens frequently even in developed countries.[4] In the presence of metering, an entrance fee or block rate pricing may mean a difference between average and marginal price of a unit of water. In the discussion that follows, we usually assume the standard case in which the marginal and average price per unit are equal to each other, but we occasionally discuss other pricing practices.

WATER SUPPLY

Water is usually supplied by a local monopoly; this subsection examines the profits and costs of such a firm. Costs are a function of the outputs of the firm. We consider the general case with an arbitrary number of outputs, say n. These outputs can be interpreted in various ways, such as water supplied during different periods of the year or to residential customers and firms. Costs are increasing in the quantities of the commodities supplied. This implies that marginal costs—that is, the costs of producing an additional unit of a particular output, which play an important role in market analysis—are positive.

An important characteristic of the cost function is the development of average cost when output increases. In order to explain this, we will use as a basic example a firm that produces just one product ($n = 1$).[5] The average cost of this firm is the ratio of total cost and output. If the average cost decreases when output increases, the firm is said to operate under increasing returns to scale. It is not difficult to verify that for such a firm, marginal cost will be lower than average cost.[6] If the price of the product is equal to its marginal cost, as is suggested by economic theory, the firm therefore will be unable to cover its cost completely.

Increasing returns to scale are probably relevant in many industries, at least when taking into account the short-run cost function, and water supply is no exception. A very stylized description of the production process involved in water supply is that groundwater or water from a river or lake is collected in a basin that is connected to an infrastructure of pipelines through which the water flows to the consumers. The costs of constructing and maintaining the basin and infrastructure are fixed in the short run, whereas the costs of operating the system are variable. If operating costs are proportional to output, the marginal cost of water supply is equal to the average variable cost. If the price of water would be equal to the marginal cost, revenues would be sufficient to pay the total variable cost, but the fixed cost would remain uncovered.

An industry is called a "natural monopoly" if the long-run average cost of a single firm is decreasing until market demand is completely served. In a natural monopoly, total costs of production are necessarily higher if two or more firms are present in the market instead of only one. The cost structure just discussed suggests that water supply and sewage treatment are natural monopolies at a local level.

Even in a natural monopoly, capacity restrictions can cause increasing average costs in the short run. For instance, in situations of high demand, during a period of drought in the summer, the limits of capacity may be approached. In such a situation, the short-run economies of scale are exhausted, and it can be very costly to increase the supply of water. The marginal cost of water supply may then increase considerably and become much higher than average cost. We will look at this situation later.

In the long run, capacity is also an endogenous variable. The capacity of the basin and that of the pipeline network are both related to the maximum amount of water that the firm expects to supply. In a long-run setting, the costs associated with these facilities are therefore also related to demand or, more precisely, its expected maximum level. This implies that, from a long-run perspective, marginal cost will be higher than average variable cost. If the price of water is based on long-run marginal cost, it will therefore also cover part or all of the costs associated with the basin and the network.

In the discussion above, we have informally introduced the revenues and profits of the firm. Revenues are the product of output and the price per unit. Profits are the difference between revenues and total costs. Losses are negative profits.

Environmental Damage and Sewage Treatment

Water supply is intimately related to sewage treatment. The firm or utility that provides this service has a cost function that is qualitatively similar to that of a water supply industry, implying that much of the discussion in the previous section is also relevant for sewage treatment. The simplest technique of such a firm is to collect the sewage in a pipeline system and discharge it outside residential areas. This results in a minimum level of waste quality and a maximum of environmental damage. To improve the quality of the sewage that is discharged requires other, more costly techniques. Here we concentrate on this aspect of sewage treatment.

In order to take the environmental damage of the water industry into account, we introduce an environmental damage function D. The value of this function is the total environmental damage, which is the sum of the damage done by the extraction of fresh water and the sewage returned to the natural environment. It is determined by output levels for each of the n products of the water supply industry and by the quality r of the sewage that is returned to the natural environment after treatment.

The environmental damage that occurs when fresh water is extracted from the natural environment should not be neglected. Even in the Netherlands, where water from natural resources such as rivers and groundwater is abundantly available, concern exists in some parts of the country about low levels of groundwater associated with extraction of fresh water for consumption by households and firms.

The function D is increasing in the quantities of the n outputs. We adopt the convention that a high quality of the sewage that is returned to the environment (after treatment) implies that relatively little damage is caused, so that D is decreasing in r.

The damage is expressed in monetary terms, because the value attached to environmental quality becomes clear only when it can be compared with that attached to other things, and money is a commonly used yardstick of value. In practice, however, it may be difficult to determine the value of environmental damage in monetary terms. Extractions of fresh water and disposal of sewage have many effects on the environment, and some of them are difficult to evaluate. An elaboration of this important issue is outside the scope of this chapter, but it should be stressed that all aspects of environmental damage should be included in the function D. Their valuation in monetary terms depends on the willingness to pay for avoiding this damage. For the purposes of this discussion, we assume that this willingness to pay is known, but the determination of this trade-off between money and environmental quality is certainly not a trivial issue, and in fact, a substantial part of environmental economics is concerned with this question.

Environmental damage associated with the discharge of sewage can be diminished by abatement activities. Here we assume that these activities are an integrated part of the production process of the sewage treatment industry. We denote the cost of the sewage treatment firm as K. When sewage remains untreated, it is returned to the environment at the minimum quality level r^*. Abatement cost K will increase when more water is used and when sewage has to be treated until a higher quality is reached.

The profits associated with sewage treatment are defined in the same way as those of water supply: the difference between revenues and costs. The revenues are equal to the sum of the products of p_i, the price of treating one unit of sewage of type i and the quantity q_i.

The Social Welfare Function and Social Surplus

In order to evaluate the effects of changes in, for instance, the institutional structure of the water supply and sewage treatment industry, a social welfare function is necessary. Such a function relates the welfare of a country or region to that of its inhabitants. The use of consumer surplus can be justified by a particular form of the social welfare function, one that ignores distributional issues. This does not necessarily reflect the view that distributional issues are unimportant. Usually it results from the pragmatic point of view that economic policy with respect to the water supply and sewage treatment industries should be aimed primarily at the improvement of efficiency in this sector, and other policies, such as income taxation, should be used to address equity issues.

Accepting this argument, we can use the social surplus as our welfare function. The social surplus is defined as follows: (a) consumer surplus, plus (b) the profits of the water supply and sewage treatment industries, minus (c) the environmental damage, plus (d) the revenues of a possible regulatory tax imposed on one or both industries. The first three concepts mentioned have already been introduced above, and the potential usefulness of a tax is discussed later.

To see how the evaluation of water policy works, consider an increase in profits of the sewage treatment industry caused by employment of a less expensive method that became available through technological progress. Greater profits provide a higher income for the shareholders of this industry, and this increases their welfare and therefore social surplus.

THE WATER SUPPLY AND SEWAGE TREATMENT INDUSTRY

In this section, we develop an analytical model of the water industry from the elements discussed in the previous one. We introduce social surplus as our principal welfare indicator, consider the market when water supply and sewage treatment are provided by monopolies, investigate welfare maximization and point out a problem associated with this goal, and examine two practical solutions to that problem. Finally, we investigate the issue of capacity choice. Throughout this section, the standard situation to which the model applies is that in which the n products refer to water supply during different periods of the year.

Social Surplus

In the previous section, we presented the elements of water supply and sewage treatment that are important for a social cost–benefit analysis. In order to carry out such an analysis, they have to be put together into a consistent framework. This framework is provided by the social surplus, defined above and denoted as SS.

Social surplus can be defined in an alternative, but equivalent, way by writing out the two profits as the difference between total revenues and costs. The second formulation is sometimes easier to handle. An example is the situation in which one government agency runs the whole industry (water supply and sewage treatment) and charges consumers a single price, which may include a Pigovian tax, for its services. This single price is the p in equation (6-1) above, and its decomposition in terms of costs of supply and sewage treatment and tax is unimportant for the consumer.

The Market Solution: Monopolistic Water Supply and Sewage Treatment

The solution the market provides for organizing the water industry is local monopolies for water supply and sewage treatment. The reason for this organization of the market is that competition among firms in either activity is wasteful because of the costly networks involved. We therefore take it for granted that both activities are natural monopolies, which implies that the total costs are always lowest when only one firm is in operation.

Water Supply. The water supply monopoly maximizes its profits, which were defined above as the difference between revenues and costs. This behavior implies that the price of water (that is, in equation (6-1) above) will be set in such a way that marginal revenues will be equal to the marginal cost. It is shown in the mathematical appendix that this implies that the price will be higher than the marginal cost. The difference is often referred to as the markup. When it is expressed as a share of the price charged to the consumer, it is equal to the inverse of the price elasticity of demand.

The prices set by the monopoly thus are determined by marginal costs as well as by the characteristics of demand. This contrasts with a Pareto-optimal situation in which prices are equal to marginal costs and therefore independent of demand. In order to understand the price-setting behavior of the monopoly a bit better, consider the situation in which the marginal cost is equal for all its products. This happens, for instance, when the same water is supplied to different groups of consumers, such as firms and households. If the price sensitivity, as measured by the price elasticity, of the two groups differs, the monopoly will set different prices. In particular, its markup will be larger for the group of customers whose demand is less price elastic. These customers are "captives" of the monopoly. Such discriminatory behavior is easily regarded as inequitable. We will show below that it is also inefficient, in a first-best sense, but that things become more complicated in a second-best world.

Sewage Treatment. Even though sewage treatment is in reality always the task of a government agency, it seems possible, at least in principle, that a private firm could treat sewage by connecting households to its pipeline system.[7] As all households have a clear incentive to get rid of the waste they produce, there seems no reason why this service could not be provided by a private firm. In order to arrive at a benchmark case in which both water supply and sewage treatment are taken care of by the market, we will assume the existence of such a firm that is concerned only with profits. Hence it does not care about environmental quality and has set up no abatement facilities. All the firm does is collect the sewage by means of its pipeline system and discharge it into the environment at a location where its presence and stench will not discomfort the human population.[8] This elementary, minimal treatment results in a quality r^* of the waste that is returned to the environment.

Implications for Social Surplus. Profit-maximizing monopolies are concerned only with the consequences of their behavior for their own profits and disregard the effects on the other components of social surplus. Many analyses have considered situations in which social surplus is the sum of consumer surplus and profits, and environmental considerations are absent. It is well known that monopolistic behavior results in a welfare loss in comparison with marginal cost pricing, because the markup implies a decrease in consumer surplus that is larger than the associated increase in profits. In other words, the sum of consumer surplus and profits will be smaller than would be possible with marginal cost pricing.

The presence of environmental damage complicates this analysis. Even though a monopoly has no incentive to decrease this damage, its markup will nevertheless have a beneficial effect in this respect, as it discourages the consumption of water. Two distortions are therefore involved: the markups tend to make the price higher than is socially optimal, but the neglect to consider environmental damage tends to make it lower. The sign of the difference between the total price of water charged by the monopolies and the socially optimal price is therefore indeterminate.

Finally, as the monopoly has no incentive to engage in sewage treatment activities that improve the quality of the water that is discharged, the indicator r^* will therefore have the lowest possible value.

Maximization of Social Surplus

If water supply and sewage treatment are left to the market, entrepreneurs will maximize their profits. Except for the special case of perfect markets, this does not result in maximization of social welfare. We have already seen that the markets for water and sewage treatment are imperfect: there are increasing returns to scale at the industry level and external effects on the environment. It is thus useful to consider the difference between the organization of the industry that can be provided by the market and the one that would result when social welfare is maximized by a benevolent planner. In this subsection, we therefore investigate the organization of the water supply and sewage treatment industry that would result from maximization of social surplus—the sum of consumer's surplus associated with water use, the profits of the water supply, and sewage treatment industries minus the environmental externalities involved. In particular, we ask how the prices and the quality of treated sewage must be set so as to reach the maximum possible value of this surplus.

The First-Best Optimal Water Price. It is shown in the mathematical appendix that maximization of the social surplus implies that the total price per unit of water should be equal to (a) the social marginal cost of water consumption, which is equal to the supplier's marginal cost, plus (b) the marginal cost of abatement activities, plus (c) the marginal cost of environmental damage.

This pricing rule thus implies that the component π in equation (6-1) also is equal to the marginal cost of the water supplier, the component ρ to the marginal cost of the sewage treatment industry, and the tax component τ to the marginal environmental damage. The same pricing structure would result if the companies that supplied the water and treated the waste charged consumers their marginal cost, and a Pigovian tax was introduced to cover the cost of environmental damage.

Because of the tax component, the socially optimal price of water is higher than the sum of the marginal costs of the water supply and sewage treatment. It is therefore clear that in the situation examined here, environmental considerations cause a kind of markup on this marginal cost. It must be noted, however, that the determinants of this markup are completely different from that used by the profit-maximizing economist.[9] Only by coincidence will the profit-maximizing monopoly charge the socially optimal price for water.

Maximization of the social surplus is in general incompatible with returning the sewage into the environment without any treatment. It is shown in the mathematical appendix that maximization of social surplus requires that the marginal cost of additional sewage treatment be equal to the benefits of the associated reduction in environmental damage. Note that this condition implies that it will in general not be optimal to remove *all* environmental damage. Environmental damage will be diminished only as long as the cost of doing so is lower than the benefits it provides. This is a result of a trade-off among the various components of the social surplus. None of them has priority over the others, and for this reason the optimal solution usually takes the form of a balance between costs and benefits. The condition also implies that lower marginal abatement costs, such as because of improved sewage treatment technology, will result in a higher optimal quality of the treated sewage.

First-Best Solution to Cost Coverage. The first-best solution to cost coverage maximizes the value of social surplus, but if the water supply and sewage treatment industries operate under increasing returns to scale, their profits will be negative. For these utilities to continue to operate in such a case, they must be subsidized. Many politicians do not regard this as an attractive option, however. The main reason seems to be that it is considered desirable that these utilities cover their own costs unless this would have substantial social costs. Thus we will examine two possible solutions to satisfy this requirement: Ramsey-Boiteux pricing, and entrance fees and block rates.[10]

Ramsey-Boiteux Pricing. One possibility to meet the requirement that water supply and sewage treatment industries at least break even is to add this as a side condition to the maximization problem. This extension implies the derivation of *second-best* prices—that is, prices that maximize social welfare under restrictions that do not follow from the technology of the resource allocation problem alone. The requirement that the firms should break even is clearly such an additional constraint, as it is possible to subsidize them.[11]

The literature contains some studies that investigate the welfare gains that can be realized if water prices are changed from average costs to optimal second-best values. For instance, Garcia and Reynaud (2004) studied water utilities in France, whereas Kim (1995) provided an analysis for the United States. Both studies concluded that these gains are small.

Entrance Fees and Block Rates. As a solution to the cost coverage problem, Coase (1946) suggested introducing an entrance fee that is independent of the amount of water consumed. The marginal price of water is set equal to marginal cost, and if the entrance fee for each consumer is lower than his or her individual consumer surplus, this solution is first-best optimal. This condition is crucial: if consumers are heterogeneous, the fixed entrance fee may induce some to abstain completely from consumption. In developing countries, where water consumption from rivers and wells is common, fixed fees may well have this effect.[12] In a developed country like the Netherlands, however, this is unlikely to happen.

Block rates can be regarded as a generalization of this solution. Under a block rate, the price of an additional unit of water depends on the quantity already consumed; at some critical quantities, the marginal price jumps to a different value, where it stays until the next critical quantity is reached. An entrance fee is a special case with only one critical value, which is associated with the first unit consumed. The price of that first unit equals the entrance fee plus the unit price that is charged for all additional units of water consumed.

Figure 6.2 illustrates block rate structures and the consequences they have for the consumer's budget line. Associated with every critical value of consumption is a kink in the budget line. When block rates are increasing, the budget line is concave, but with a decreasing price structure, it becomes convex. In the latter case, a small increase in marginal price can result in a jump in consumption.

An extensive analysis of pricing schedules and their welfare implications can be found in Wilson (1993), to which we refer the interested reader for further details. Decreasing block rates imply that the producer takes part of the consumer surplus from the consumers and uses it to cover the part of the costs that remains after the revenues of the lower marginal price have been taken into account.

Even though economic theory suggests the use of decreasing block rates, in reality increasing rates are also used. One possible reason for this practice is equity con-

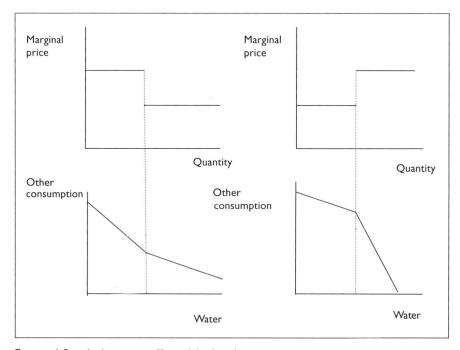

Figure 6.2 *Block rate tariffs and budget lines*

Notes: The left-hand side of the figure shows a decreasing block rate structure. The price of an extra unit of water is initially high, but it drops to a lower value when a threshold value is exceeded. The jump in the price of an extra unit creates a kink in the budget line, which is shown in the lower panel of the figure. The right-hand side shows an increasing block rate structure. Now when a threshold value is exceeded, the price of an extra unit of water is higher and the budget line becomes steeper.

siderations. The presumption is then that high-income households consume more water than low-income households (see Rietveld et al. 2002 for an example).

For the achievement of a first-best Pareto optimum, the important point is that all consumers pay the marginal price of the water supplied to them. This situation can be attained simultaneously with the coverage of all costs if a decreasing marginal price is used. Under increasing returns to scale, it cannot be realized with an increasing marginal price.

From a welfare economic point of view, the most attractive aspect of block rate pricing is its potential compatibility with a first-best optimum. In the Netherlands, water companies charge a fixed entrance fee (called vastrecht in Dutch) in combination with a fixed price per unit.[13]

Capacity Choice

The choice of capacity of water supply and sewage treatment systems is an issue receiving increasing attention. Because of changes in climate, regularities in rainfall and water supply from rivers are also changing, and the result is increased uncertainty about the availability of fresh water. For instance, at the end of February 2006, residents in southeast England were advised not to wash their cars, because extreme drought had caused the water companies' supply to shrink to alarmingly low levels. Eleven years earlier, a similar situation occurred during a summer drought. Also in the Netherlands, during dry periods in summer months, households are exhorted not to water their gardens because of the threat of a shortage of water.

An obvious way to deal with this problem is to build larger basins to provide sufficient water for periods of drought. The cost involved in constructing such basins or other additional storage capacity can be enormous. These investments are extremely long-lived, however, and their cost can therefore be spread out over many years, during which huge quantities of water can be supplied to households and firms. Their great durability makes the discount rate an important variable, and because the government is able to borrow at a lower interest rate than private parties, this provides an argument for involvement of the local or national authorities in financing these investments.[14]

A related question is who should pay for the cost of the extended capacity. To see what economic analysis suggests, we consider a simple further specification of the cost function. Suppose that the water-supplying firm is able to serve demand up to a critical value when it has storage capacity *cap*. A fixed cost is associated with water supply that is proportional to the capacity of the firm. In other words, the supplier has to pay a given amount of money for each unit of capacity the firm has available in each year. Since capacity is fixed, at least in the short run, this is referred to as a fixed cost. In addition, other, variable costs are associated with water supply. This means that the supplier has to pay a given amount of money for each unit of water it provides to its customers. As long as the quantity of water supplied does not exceed capacity, the sum of the fixed and variable costs gives the total cost of the supplier. When demand exceeds storage capacity, however, the supplier has to use more costly methods to serve demand, and in these circumstances, additional costs per unit supply have to be made. These costs are also variable, because they increase with the amount of water supplied whenever capacity is exceeded. It seems reasonable to assume that these additional variable costs increase when the difference between demand and capacity becomes greater. This is because the cost of serving demand increases more than proportionally when the difference between demand and capacity is greater, and it becomes increasingly difficult to supply a sufficient amount of water. The additional cost associated with surpassing the supplier's capacity may be the cost of transporting additional fresh water to the region in order to serve demand. Alternatively, it may refer to the cost associated with temporarily increasing short-run capacity.

The company can try to avoid situations in which demand exceeds capacity by choosing the value of *cap* high enough to make it very unlikely that this will ever happen. Indeed, such behavior appears to be common practice in many countries. The question we consider here is whether this behavior with respect to capacity choice coincides with the suggestions provided by economic theory.

To answer this question, the remainder of this subsection concentrates on the part of the social surplus associated with water supply separately. In the mathematical appendix, we show that optimal prices are still equal to marginal costs. This means that the price of water increases whenever capacity is exceeded. More surprising is the conclusion that the optimal capacity of the water supplier is *smaller* than the maximum demand. In other words, it is not optimal to choose capacity so large that it will never be exceeded. The difference between optimal capacity and peak demand becomes greater when the fixed cost per unit of capacity is higher, and smaller when the additional cost associated with supplying water beyond capacity increases. Note also that marginal cost pricing implies that the unit price of water should be high in the period during which demand peaks. Indeed, the price in the peak period may be much higher than that in other periods when the additional cost of providing water during the peak period is large—that is, when ac_i is high.

It is also shown in the appendix that the additional revenues that result from the higher prices in situations where demand exceeds capacity cover the total cost of capacity as well as the higher variable costs necessary to serve demand when it exceeds capacity. Indeed, a profit remains. We can therefore conclude that in the social optimum, the combination of peak load pricing and optimal capacity choice results in revenues for the water supplier that completely cover its costs. This is possible only if capacity is chosen in such a way that it is exceeded in at least one period. We have already seen that this is indeed optimal. Even though there are economies of scale in all other periods, the diseconomies that are relevant when demand exceeds supply result in a price that is sufficiently high to cover the total fixed cost of capacity and double the additional costs of supplying water in excess of capacity.

The analysis just carried out strongly suggests that from the point of view of optimal allocation of water resources, peak load pricing should be regarded as an important element of water policy. This conclusion is reinforced if sewage treatment and environmental damage are also considered. Capacity choice is also a problem in sewage treatment, and economic analysis shows that it can be solved in the same way—that is, by peak load pricing. It is also probable that the marginal environmental damage costs are highest in exactly those periods when water demand peaks.

The capacity variable does not indicate an upper bound on the possible supply of water, only on the supply at the standard level of variable costs. It is assumed in this analysis that the supplier can also serve demand when this normal capacity is exceeded. Indeed, it is of crucial importance that the company is able to do this, because only in this way can total costs be covered.

In practice, it is highly unusual that water suppliers increase their prices when the limits of their ability to serve their customers are approached, as is suggested by the previous analysis. Rather, suppliers rely on exhortations to their clients to limit their demand. Introduction of peak load pricing policy would predictably result in protesting consumers, as they are forced to pay more for water just when they need it most. It is probably for this reason that most water suppliers (and politicians) are inclined to increase the normal capacity to such a level that it becomes improbable that it will be exceeded. The analysis just carried out suggests that this will result in overinvestment in the capacity of water supply and prices that are too low in periods when demand is high.

In order to implement the first-best solution, it is not necessary to allow the regulated monopoly that supplies the water to make positive profits. Just as the revenues of this water supplier operating under increasing returns can be increased by introducing a block rate tariff, they can also be decreased by such a tariff when the supplier is operating under decreasing returns. The appropriate block rate is now an increasing one.

APPLICATIONS AND EMPIRICAL EVIDENCE

The theoretical concepts that have been discussed in the previous sections provide important qualitative insights. Their usefulness becomes even more apparent when they are employed as guides for setting up and interpreting the results of empirical work. This is demonstrated in the following review of a number of empirical studies of the water supply and sewage industries.

Elasticities of Demand

Estimating the price elasticity of water supply is not an easy task. In order to estimate a price elasticity, one needs data with variation in prices, and because water prices often change little over time, reactions to these changes are difficult to measure. Block rate pricing offers the ability to observe consumer demand under different marginal prices in a single cross section, and this opens new possibilities for demand analysis. With such a pricing structure, however, consumers choose not only the quantity they consume, but also the marginal price. As a consequence, the marginal prices are endogenous, and ordinary least squares (OLS) estimates are inconsistent. An ingenious solution to this problem, which combines the implications of utility maximizing behavior with statistical theory, was proposed by Hausman (1985).[15] An application to water demand analysis can be found in Hewitt and Hanemann (1995). Unfortunately, the intimate relationship between economics and statistics in this approach implies restrictions on the estimated parameters of the demand functions (see MaCurdy et al. 1990).

The issues just mentioned are related to the concern about the validity of the standard assumptions of economic theory that is expressed repeatedly in the water demand literature. It may, for instance, be doubted that consumers know the marginal price of water and increase consumption only when the benefit of doing so exceeds the costs. One problem is that water expenses are usually a small part of total consumer expenditure, and a large time interval often occurs between consumption and payment. This makes it probable that the marginal costs of water consumption are unclear to many consumers. It is unlikely that such inattentive consumers react to a price change unless it is explicitly brought to their attention.

The fact that many consumers do not know the relevant marginal price of water has led some researchers to adopt the hypothesis that the average price of water is the relevant price variable. Presumably, the idea behind this practice is that consumers have a somewhat vague notion of the price of water, being aware of the total amount used and how much money they had to pay for it, but ignorant of the exact pricing schedule. It is not always appreciated, however, that under block rate pricing, the average price is also an endogenous variable whose value depends on the amount of water used.[16] In other words, knowledge of the relevant average price requires as much information and the same computational abilities as knowledge of the marginal price schedule. Moreover, the fact that the average price is not a constant implies that standard welfare analyses that assume a given and constant unit price are not applicable.

Carter and Milon (2005) tried to deal with this problem by using a model in which some consumers compute the marginal price but others are unaware of it. Consumers place themselves into one of these two groups on the basis of global knowledge of, among other things, the price of water. An alternative possibility is to adopt the more robust approach to demand estimation with nonlinear budget sets developed in Blomquist and Newey (2002), as in the recent paper of Nauges and Blundell (2005).

A large number of studies on water demand have been conducted over the years, and recent surveys of the literature can be found in Arbués Gracia et al. (2003) and Dalhuisen et al. (2003) or Dalhuisen (2002). Kooreman (1993) and Linderhof (2001, Chapter 4) provided analyses for the Netherlands.[17] With few exceptions, these studies conclude that demand for residential water is price inelastic. Since it was shown above that at the profit-maximizing price of a monopoly, demand is elastic, this finding confirms the conjecture that actual behavior of water suppliers differs from optimizing behavior of a monopoly.[18] Most demand curves imply that the absolute value of the price elasticity increases with the price, so the demand becomes more elastic when the price goes up. This finding therefore strongly suggests that actual prices are lower than those that would be charged by a profit-maximizing monopoly. It also implies that firms engaged in water supply and sewage treatment can easily increase their revenues, when needed, by increasing their prices.[19] This sheds some light on the surprisingly high interest among stock investors in the United Kingdom for the privatized, but regulated, water companies: even though the regulation implies a ceiling on expected profits, it also provides a floor, as the companies are allowed to at least break even, and they will be able to do so because demand is price inelastic.

Price elasticities are usually estimated on annual water demand. Because water suppliers in the Netherlands calculate their bills once a year on the basis of metering, and information about demand is often derived from their administration, disaggregation over time is problematic.[20] The analysis of the previous section clearly suggests, however, that it may be beneficial—at least from the perspective of resource allocation—to differentiate prices over the year, and in particular, to charge a higher price during periods of peak demand. This is possible only with a more refined metering system than is commonly used. If one were introduced, the higher price during peak load periods could have potentially great consequences for capacity choice. It is probable that the relevant price elasticities are different from those based on annual data, as water demand is closely related to the weather and consumers' activity patterns, which may differ substantially from their average value during the summer months, when water demand peaks. Not much seems to be known about variations in the price sensitivity of water demand over the year. Pint (1999) uses bimonthly figures to estimate the effect of increases in the marginal price of water during a dry period. Even though her estimated price elasticities are low (that is, negative and close to zero), price increases were sufficient to induce a substantial (16%) decrease in water demand. This suggests that investments in the capacity of water supply can be reduced substantially by an appropriate peak load pricing scheme.

Apart from the problems associated with metering facilities, which must be able to support such a pricing scheme, gaining acceptance of peak load pricing may be a tough issue. Two recent papers by Hensher et al. (2004, 2005) suggest that households attach value to high service levels in the provision and disposal of water but are unwilling to pay to avoid drought restrictions. Consumers tend to prefer nonprice instruments.[21]

Finally, it should be noted that long-run price elasticities may differ from their short-run values. One reason is that water consumption is closely related to household appliances and fixtures such as washing machines, dishwashers, and showers. The technology incorporated into these items is an important determinant of total water consumption and is sensitive to consumer considerations with respect to price and environmental damage. It therefore may well be the case that long-run responses to price changes are more substantial than appears from the low short-run elasticities. A recent study by Martínez-Espiñeira and Nauges (2001) does not confirm this intuition, but more research in this area is needed.[22]

Empirical studies on the supply of sewage by households, let alone its price elasticity, seem to be scarce, if they exist at all. Because metering of sewage discharge seems to be absent, at least in the household sector, often there is no direct relation between the charge and the amount of sewage conveyed. Given the intimate economic and physical relationships between water demand and sewage treatment, the best way to improve incentives seems to be to connect the two charges.

The Cost Function for Water Supply

In the Netherlands, fresh water is supplied by 10 regional companies. Because the only shareholders are local governments, the water industry is in fact a public utility. In the past, the number of water suppliers used to be much larger, but the 20th century saw a gradual movement toward concentration.[23] Privatization of the industry was contemplated in the 1990s but ultimately rejected. Efficiency is a cause for concern, and a benchmarking system has been introduced and appears to work well (see Dijkgraaf and Varkevisser 2004). In recent years, the efficiency of the industry has improved substantially. This did not result in lower prices, however, but only in increased profits and financial reserves for the companies.

Even though groundwater is the major source of fresh water, a substantial amount is derived from the Meuse and Rhine rivers. Variation in the quality of water in the rivers necessitates a large storage capacity. Moreover, water originating from the rivers requires more, and costly, purification. Groundwater is generally of a good quality. Sources are spread over the country and used by industries and agriculture as well as by water suppliers. The provincial government issues licenses on the basis of competition.

Dijkgraaf et al. (1997) estimated a cost function for water companies in the Netherlands.

The marginal cost is found by taking the first derivative of this function with respect to output. A 1% increase in output will increase costs by only 0.7%. This means that there are substantial economies of scale. In the literature, this measure of scale economies is often referred to as economies of density, as it assumes that output increases while the number of clients and the length of the network are kept constant.

Another interesting result from this analysis is that the coefficient for total output is—slightly, but significantly—larger than 1. It implies that cost would increase by 1.1% if output, the length of the network, and the number of connected clients all increased by 1%. The estimated cost function therefore indicates that the geographical scale at which Dutch water suppliers operate is roughly adequate.

Efficiency of the water supply industry is a cause of concern in the Netherlands, as elsewhere. Because privatization is no longer an issue, attention is now focused on a benchmarking system that allows the determination of the relative efficiency of the various companies. In recent years, substantial shifts have occurred in the composition of the total cost of these companies. For instance, between 1997 and 2003, the share of distribution costs decreased from almost 30% to 20% (VEWIN 2004). A recent international comparison suggests that the Dutch water supply industry is on average somewhat less efficient than that of the United Kingdom, but more efficient than that of Belgium (de Witte 2006).

The Cost Function for Sewage Treatment

In the Netherlands, sewage treatment is a task of the provincial governments, which have the possibility of delegating this to special institutions, the water boards (see Chapter 8). Many companies treat their own sewage, and approximately 40% of total sewage produced is treated privately. In order to do so, a license is required. One of the reasons for making the license obligatory is the fear that the large investments in the public utility would become partly superfluous if a large sewage company decided to switch to private treatment. Another is that the public infrastructure usually would be needed for conveying privately treated sewage to the point where it is disposed. Even though this practice can be questioned from the point of view of economic efficiency, it may also be defended from the same viewpoint. Because treatment of all sewage from households and industries is a public task, the public utility cannot refuse to treat it, even in circumstances when this requires large investments with a long economic life. Therefore, some asymmetry is involved in this market. Firms that exploit this asymmetry will not necessarily act in the public interest. For instance, if technological progress enables less expensive treatment, it may not be in the public interest to abandon the existing capital immediately.

It is probably the case, however, that improvements in the efficiency of the Dutch sewage industry would be possible through better use of pricing measures. One elementary idea would be to replace the currently popular flat rate with a system that links the charges for sewage treatment and water demand. The efficiency of the sewage treatment industry tends to attract less attention from politicians and the public at large than that of the water supply industry, even though it is not clear that its performance is better.

Dijkgraaf et al. (1997) also have estimated a cost function for the sewage treatment industry. In contrast with their cost function for water supply, here they include capacity as an explanatory variable. They use a log-linear (Cobb–Douglas) cost function and estimate an elasticity of 0.38 with respect to sewage input and of 0.42 with respect to capacity. This indicates substantial economies of scale as long as capacity is not reached: an increase in input of 1% would increase cost by only 0.38%. Even if capacity has to be expanded to deal with increased input, scale economies appear to be present: when capacity and input both increase by 1%, costs increase by only 0.8% (0.38% + 0.42%).

It seems fair to say that in the Netherlands, as elsewhere, the sewage treatment industry has attracted less attention from economists than the water supply industry, even though large capital investments—in both replacement of outdated infrastructure and development of new and enlarged production units, the latter often in the interest of the natural environment—have been made in this industry. It seems worthwhile to take a closer look at the efficiency aspects of this sector and improve its pricing practices.[24]

CONCLUSIONS

We conclude this chapter with a discussion of some implications of economic analysis for the organization of the water supply and sewage treatment industry. First, regulation appears to be successful in preventing water suppliers (and sewage treatment firms) from charging prices that are compatible with monopolistic behavior. Estimated price elasticities for the Netherlands, and elsewhere, are almost always below 1 (in absolute value), which is incompatible with profit-maximizing behavior of a monopoly.

This does not imply, however, that actual pricing behavior is close to the first-best social optimum. A potentially important suggestion of economic theory is that prices should be equal to marginal costs. If the marginal cost is higher in some periods of the year, as is likely to be the case, this implies that the unit price of water should also vary over the year. One possible reason for the absence of this practice in the present circumstances is that acceptance of such a varying price may be problematic. It seems likely that marginal costs are highest during dry periods, especially in the summer, when demand peaks. Nevertheless, charging a higher price during the summer months may be regarded as unjustified, because this is when the water is needed most.

The analysis also suggested that normal capacity should not be chosen at such a high level that it will never be exceeded, but at such a level that capacity constraints become binding during at least one period. Marginal cost pricing then implies a high price during these periods. Indeed, the price should be so high that revenues are sufficient to cover the complete capacity cost as well as the variable cost. The obvious benefit of such a pricing policy is that it limits the cost of capacity and realizes maximal downward pressure on peak demand. The acceptability problems noted above will probably be even higher, however, when such a "minimal sufficient capacity" combined with peak load pricing is introduced.

The analysis was carried out in a framework that ignored uncertainty of demand and supply levels, whereas in practice, it seems difficult to predict bottlenecks in the supply of water. A more complete analysis, which is outside the scope of this chapter, would pay attention to this problem and probably result in a capacity level that is sufficiently high to be able to act as a buffer for this uncertainty. Nevertheless, endogenous capacity choice will also in this case result in peak load pricing that may imply considerably higher prices (compared with the average) in periods when the probability of surpassing capacity is relatively large.

The previous sections did not include sufficient detail to provide a complete analysis of the welfare loss involved in the current practice of uniform pricing and the choosing of a level of capacity that will in practice never be surpassed, but it would be interesting to carry out such an exercise. Changes in rainfall and water supply from the rivers, which may or may not be caused by global climate change, seem to create increasing uncertainty about the capacity needed, and the costs involved are certainly not negligible.

The remarks made above referred especially to water supply, but similar remarks can be made with respect to the sewage treatment industry. Also here, the provision of sufficient capacity is a major issue, and uncertainty about the required level seems to increase. A specific issue for this industry is that maximum capacity is determined in large part also by rainfall, which is insensitive to pricing measures. In recent years, however, attention has been increasingly focused on keeping a large amount of rainfall outside the sewage infrastructure, in order to avoid peak load problems. When successful, capacity can be chosen at a lower level, and having more rain fall on the soil may also be beneficial for the environment, implying that these policies can be regarded at least partly as abatement activities.

Summarizing, it may be said that economic analysis of the water industry offers a number of suggestions about the efficient provision of this primary commodity. Some of them can be interpreted as affording a justification for current practice. For instance, the combination of an entrance fee and a fixed price per cubic meter is compatible with a first-best pricing scheme as put forth by Coase (1946). Others are more controversial, the proposal for peak load pricing being a notable example. The controversial suggestions may be the most interesting ones, however, as they provide food for thought and will perhaps open the way for further improvements in the efficient provision of water.

NOTES

1. The technological aspects of sewage treatment are dealt with in Chapter 7; cost–benefit analysis is elaborated in Chapter 5.

2. See Hanemann (2006) for an elaborate exposition on the economic conception of water.

3. Also in some notes, mathematical symbols are used.

4. More than 90% of the houses in the Netherlands are metered, but in some cities this percentage is substantially lower.

5. Increasing returns to scale can also be studied in the context of a multiproduct firm, but for the purpose of this chapter, such a generalization does not have to be considered explicitly.

6. If average cost is decreasing in output $\partial(C/q)/\partial q < 0$. Elaboration of this inequality gives $(\partial C/\partial q - C/q)/q < 0$. The expression in parentheses is the difference between marginal cost and average cost, which must therefore be negative whenever q is positive.

7. An important background of the practice is that, for technical reasons, sewage treatment is closely connected with the drainage system for rain, and the same network is used for both.

8. This was actual practice in the Netherlands (and other countries) until the 1960s.

9. With the organization of the industry as in the previous section, the total price of water can be written as $p_i = (\partial C/\partial q_i + \partial K/\partial q_i)(\varepsilon_i/(\varepsilon_i - 1))$. This shows that the deviation from the sum of the marginal costs is multiplicative rather than additive, and it depends on the price elasticity of demand, not on environmental damage.

10. Another, more fundamental drawback of subsidizing a natural monopoly is that it removes the incentives for cost efficiency.

11. Strictly speaking, this argument is valid only when no welfare costs are involved in providing the subsidy.

12. See, for instance, the discussion in Hanemann (2006) of households in developing countries that state a higher preference for electricity than for water or sewer.

13. Entrance fees also can be used as a charge for connecting a house to the pipeline system. In the Netherlands, the owners of existing houses (mainly located in the countryside) that are not hooked up to the pipeline system have to pay the full connection cost. This practice favors an efficient choice between connection to the pipeline systems and alternative possibilities for water supply or sewage treatment.

14. See Hanemann (2006) for a discussion.

15. This article summarizes a number of earlier analyses. See Moffit (1986) for a relatively nontechnical introduction to the subject.

16. See Taylor et al. (2004) for a discussion of this issue.

17. Kanne (2005) provides an informative overview of residential water use in the Netherlands but does not discuss price sensitivity.

18. See also equations (6-12) and (6-14).

19. Revenue is the product of price and quantity, and it is easy to verify that its derivative with respect to the price is positive if the absolute value of the price elasticity of demand is smaller than 1.

20. In the United States, metering is more frequent (often on a monthly basis).

21. It is possible that this changes if the higher price charge for water during periods of drought is offset by a lower price during the rest of the year, but such a trade-off was not the subject of this research.

22. See also Linderhof (2001, chapter 4), who includes dummies for water-consuming durables in his demand function for water.

23. This was especially the case in the 1990s, when privatization was considered a real possibility. In 1988, the Netherlands had 73 water supply companies; by 2008, their number was reduced to 10.

24. Experiences in related activities, such as the collection of household waste, suggest that substantial effects are possible. See, for instance, Linderhof (2001) and Dijkgraaf (2005).

25. Note that this implies that *cap* must be interpreted as the maximum possible amount of water that can be supplied *under normal conditions*. It is not an absolute upper bound.

26. Note that the summation disappears because capacity is exceeded in only one period.

27. When demand exceeds capacity, the price must be increased by f, with f the first derivative of f. Additional revenues are $q_i f = (q_i\text{-}cap) f + cap f$. The first term to the right of the equal sign is at least equal to the additional cost $f(q_i\text{-}cap)$ because of the convexity of f. Optimal choice of capacity implies that f is equal to the cost per unit of capacity, and hence the second term is equal to the cost of capacity.

REFERENCES

Arbués Gracia, F., M.A. García-Valiñas, and R. Martínez-Espiñeira. 2003. Estimation of residential water demand: A state-of-the-art review. *Journal of Socio-Economics* 32:81–102.

Baumol, W.J., J.C. Panzar, and R.D. Willig. 1982. *Contestable markets and the theory of industry structure.* New York: Harcourt Brace Jovanovich.

Blomquist, S., and W. Newey. 2002. Nonparametric estimation with nonlinear budget sets. *Econometrica* 70:2455.

Carter, D.W., and J.W. Milon. 2005. Price knowledge in household demand for utility services. *Land Economics* 81:265–83.

Coase, R.H. 1946. The marginal cost controversy. *Economica* 13:169–82.

Dalhuisen, J. 2002. The economics of sustainable water use. PhD thesis. Amsterdam: Free University.

Dalhuisen, J.M., R. Florax, H. de Groot, and P. Nijkamp. 2003. Price and income elasticities of residential water demand: A meta-analysis. *Land Economics* 79:292–308.

de Witte, K. 2006. Efficiëntieprikkels in de drinkwatersector [Incentives for efficiency in the water supply industry]. *Economisch Statistische Berichten* 91:201–4.

Dijkgraaf, E. 2005. Regulating the Dutch waste market. PhD thesis. Rotterdam: Erasmus University.

Dijkgraaf, E., R. de Jong, E.G. van de Mortel, A. Nentjes, M. Varkevisser, and D. Wiersma. 1997. Mogelijkheden tot marktwerking in de Nederlandse watersector [Possibilities for market functioning in the Dutch water sector]. Report OCFEB. Rotterdam: OCFEB.

Dijkgraaf, E., and M. Varkevisser. 2004. Kosten en baten van toezicht op de doelmatigheid van drinkwaterbedrijven [Costs and benefits of controlling the efficiency of water supply companies]. Report OCFEB. Rotterdam: OCFEB.

Garcia, S., and A. Reynaud. 2004. Estimating the benefits of efficient water pricing in France. *Resource and Energy Economics* 26:1–25.

Hanemann, W.M. 2006. The economic conception of water. In *Water crisis: Myth or reality?* ed. P.P. Rogers, M.R. Llamas, and L. Martinez-Cortina, 61–91. London: Taylor & Francis.

Hausman, J.A. 1985. The econometrics of nonlinear budget sets. *Econometrica* 53:1255–82.

Hensher, D., N. Shore, and K. Train. 2004. Households' willingness to pay for water service attributes. Working paper.

———. 2005. Water supply security and willingness to pay to avoid drought restrictions. Working paper.

Hewitt, J.A., and W.M. Hanemann. 1995. A discrete/continuous choice approach to residential water demand under block rate pricing. *Land Economics* 71:173–92.

Kanne, P. 2005. *Watergebruik thuis 2004 [Water use at home 2004]*. Report TNS NIPO. Amsterdam: TNS NIPO.

Kim, H.Y. 1995. Marginal cost and second-best pricing for water services. *Review of Industrial Organization* 10:323–38.

Kooreman, P. 1993. The price sensitivity of residential water use: Evidence from aggregate panel data. Working paper. A shortened version appeared as de prijsgevoeligheid van huishoudelijk waterverbruik in *Economisch Statistische Berichten* 78:181–83.

Linderhof, V.G.M. 2001. Household demand for energy, water and the collection of waste: A microeconometric analysis. PhD thesis. Groningen, Netherlands: Groningen University.

MaCurdy, Th., D. Green, and H. Paarsch. 1990. Assessing empirical approaches for analyzing taxes and labor supply. *Journal of Human Resources* 25:415–90.

Martínez-Espiñeira R., and C. Nauges. 2001. Residential water demand: An empirical analysis using co-integration and error correction techniques. Working paper.

Moffit, R. 1986. The econometrics of piecewise-linear budget constraints: A survey and exposition of the maximum likelihood method. *Journal of Business Economics and Statistics* 4:317–28.

Nauges, C., and R. Blundell. 2005. Estimating residential water demand under block rate pricing: a nonparametric approach. Working paper.

Pint, E.M. 1999. Household responses to increased water rates during the California drought. *Land Economics* 75:246–66.

Rietveld, P., J. Rouwendal, and B. Zwart. 2002. Block rate pricing of water in Indonesia: An analysis of welfare effects. *Bulletin of Indonesian Economic Studies, Taylor and Francis Journals* 36 (3): 73–92.

Taylor, R.G., J.R. McKean, and R.A. Young. 2004. Alternate price specifications for estimating water demand with fixed fees. *Land Economics* 80:463–75.

Tirole, J. 1985. *The theory of industrial organization*. Cambridge, MA: MIT Press.

Train, K.E. 1991. *Optimal Regulation*. Cambridge, MA: MIT Press.

VEWIN (Vereniging van Waterbedrijven in Nederland). 2004. *Water in zicht 2003 [Water in sight 2003]*. Rijswijk, Netherlands: Vewin.

Wilson, R.B. 1993. *Nonlinear pricing*. New York: Oxford University Press.

MATHEMATICAL APPENDIX

The main text of this chapter frequently made use of the results of a formal analysis, which has been relegated to this appendix to improve readability. This appendix is intended to accommodate readers who are interested in the derivations. It also provides further references to the more technical literature. Readers looking for a more extensive discussion of the issues addressed below are referred to works such as Tirole (1985) or Train (1991).

Consumer Surplus

Formally, we can define consumer surplus of a single commodity sold at a price p on the basis of a Marshallian demand curve $q(p)$, with $q(p)$ the quantity demanded at price p as

$$CS(p) = \int_p^{\infty} q(z)dz \tag{6-2}$$

and we have $q(p) = -\partial CS/dp$.

If there are n commodities, consumer surplus is

$$CS = CS(p_1,...,p_n) \tag{6-3}$$

with p_i, $i = 1,...,n$ the price of commodity i.

Demand for each of these commodities is equal to minus the partial derivative of the consumer surplus function:

$$q_i(p_1,...,p_n) = -\frac{\partial CS(p_1,...,p_n)}{\partial p_i}, \quad i = 1,...,n \tag{6-4}$$

With independent demands, we have

$$CS(p_1,...,p_n) = \sum_{i=1}^{n} \int_{p_i}^{\infty} q_i(z)dz \tag{6-5}$$

Costs, Profits, and Social Surplus

In this subsection, we introduce a number of concepts and the associated notation, which will be analyzed below.

The costs of water supply are given by a function C that has the quantities of all water types supplied by the firm as its arguments:

$$C = C(q_1,...,q_n) \tag{6-6}$$

with q_i the amount of water type i supplied by the firm. We assume that all marginal costs $\partial C/\partial p_i$ are positive.

Scale effects are easiest to study for a single profit firm. We say that there are increasing returns to scale when the average cost $C(q)/q$ is decreasing in production volume q. For generalization to multiproduct firms, see, for instance, Baumol et al. (1982).

The profits ZS of the water supplier are defined as the difference between revenues and costs:

$$ZS = \sum_{i=1}^{n} \pi_i q_i - C(q_1,...,q_n) \tag{6-7}$$

with π_i the unit price for supplied water. Losses are negative profits.

The environmental damage function is D, where

$$D = D(q_1,...,q_n,r) \tag{6-8}$$

with r the quality of the sewage returned to the environment.

The costs K of the sewage industry are

$$K = K(q_1,...,q_n,r) \tag{6-9}$$

The profits ZS of this industry are defined similarly:

$$ZT = \sum_{i=1}^{n} \rho_i q_i - K(q_1,...,q_n) \tag{6-10}$$

with ρ_i the unit price of sewage treatment.

Social surplus SS has been defined in the main text as

$$SS = CS + ZS + ZT - D + T \tag{6-11}$$

Using the definitions of the two profits, we can rewrite this as

$$SS = CS + R - C - K - D \tag{6-12}$$

where R denotes total revenues, including those from tax:

$$R = \sum_i p_i q_i$$
$$= \sum_i (\pi_i + \rho_i + \tau_i) q_i \tag{6-13}$$

Monopolistic Water Supply or Sewage Treatment

This section begins by considering monopolistic behavior of the water supplier, and then looks at similar behavior of the sewage treatment industry.

The profits of the monopoly were defined in equation (6-7) above, which we repeat here:

$$ZS = \sum_{i=1}^{n} \pi_i q_i - C(q_1,...,q_n) \tag{6-7}$$

We will consider only the case of independent demands. The first-order conditions for the profit-maximizing prices are

$$\left(\frac{\partial Z}{\partial \pi_i} = 0 \Rightarrow\right) \quad q_i + \pi_i \frac{\partial q_i}{\partial \pi_i} - \frac{\partial C}{\partial q_i}\frac{\partial q_i}{\partial \pi_i} = 0 \quad i = 1,...,n \tag{6-14}$$

These conditions lead to the familiar markup (or Lerner) rule:

$$\frac{\pi_i - \partial C/\partial q_i}{\pi_i} = \frac{1}{\varepsilon_i} \qquad (6\text{-}15)$$

Here, ε_i is the absolute value of the price elasticity of demand $\varepsilon_i = -(\partial q_i/\partial p_i)(\pi_i/q_i)$.

When sewage treatment is carried out by a monopoly, the analysis is similar. The profits of the monopoly are equal to

$$Z^* = \sum_{i=1}^{n} \rho_i q_i - K(q_1,...,q_n, r^*) \qquad (6\text{-}16)$$

with r^* the minimum quality of the sewage returned to the environment. The first-order conditions are similar to those of the water supplier and result in the markup rule:

$$\frac{\rho_i - \partial K/\partial q_i}{\rho_i} = \frac{1}{\varepsilon_i^*} \qquad (6\text{-}17)$$

where ε_i^* denotes the elasticity of water demand with respect to the price of waste treatment.

Maximization of Social Surplus

Here we want to find the prices p_i of water that maximize the social surplus (6-11). After substitution of the revenue and cost functions in this expression, we can calculate the partial derivatives of social surplus with respect to these prices.

The first-order conditions for a maximum are

$$\left(\frac{\partial SS}{\partial p_i} = 0 \Rightarrow\right) \quad -q_i + q_i + p_i \frac{\partial q_i}{\partial p_i} - \frac{\partial C}{\partial q_i}\frac{\partial q_i}{\partial p_i} - \frac{\partial K}{\partial q_i}\frac{\partial q_i}{\partial p_i} - \frac{\partial D}{\partial q_i}\frac{\partial q_i}{\partial p_i} = 0 \quad i=1,...,n \qquad (6\text{-}18)$$

The first term on the left-hand side of the equation $(-q_i)$ results from consumer surplus, the next two from the revenues, and the last three from costs of water supply, sewage treatment, and environmental damage, respectively. The first two terms cancel each other out. The next four terms are all multiples of $\partial q_i/\partial p_i$ which is negative when the demand for water is downward sloping, as we assume.

After rearrangement of terms, we can therefore conclude

$$p_i = \frac{\partial C}{\partial q_i} + \frac{\partial K}{\partial q_i} + \frac{\partial D}{\partial q_i} \qquad (6\text{-}19)$$

Because the first term to the right of the equal sign refers to the cost of water supply, the second to the cost of sewage treatment, and the third to the environmental damage, it is natural to interpret them as π_i, ρ_i and τ_i, respectively:

$$\pi_i = \frac{\partial C}{\partial q_i}, \rho_i = \frac{\partial K}{\partial q_i}, \tau_i = \frac{\partial D}{\partial q_i} \qquad (6\text{-}20)$$

By taking the first-order partial derivative of social surplus with respect to r and setting it equal to zero, we derive the first-order condition for the quality of treated sewage as

$$\frac{\partial K}{\partial r} = -\frac{\partial D}{\partial r} \tag{6-21}$$

Peak Load Pricing

We assume the following simple specification of the cost function:

$$C(q_1,\dots,q_n;cap) = c_0\, cap + \sum_{i=1}^{n} c_i q_i + \sum_{i=1}^{n} \delta_i ac_i\left(q_i - cap\right)^2 \tag{6-22}$$

The coefficient c_0 in the first term to the right of the equal sign is the annual cost of one unit of capacity. The next term tells us that there are constant variable costs c_i for each unit of water supplied. The third term refers to additional costs associated with the situation in which demand exceeds the water supplier's own capacity cap.[25] The variables δ_i take on the value 1 when demand exceeds the supplier's capacity and are equal to zero otherwise. The additional marginal cost equals $2ac_i(q_i - cap)$.

It is easy to verify that maximization of the social surplus implies optimal prices that are still equal to marginal cost; that is,

$$p_i = \begin{cases} c_i & \text{if } q_i < cap, \\ c_i + 2ac_i\left(q_i - cap\right) & \text{if } q_i \geq cap \end{cases} \tag{6-23}$$

The capacity is now an additional choice variable, and the first-order condition associated with it is

$$c_0 = \sum_{i=1}^{n} \delta_i 2ac_i\left(q_i - cap\right) \tag{6-24}$$

This condition can be used to determine the optimal capacity if demand exceeds capacity for at least one period. To simplify the discussion, we will consider only the case in which demand exceeds capacity for exactly one period. Denoting this period as j, we find for the optimal capacity

$$cap = q_j - \frac{c_0}{2ac_j} \tag{6-25}$$

These conclusions continue to hold when demand exceeds capacity in more than a single period.

The additional revenues that are associated with the higher price of water in the peak period are equal to $2ac_j\left(q_j - cap\right)q_j$, and this expression can be elaborated as follows:

$$2ca_j\left(q_j - cap\right)q_j = 2ac_j\left(q_j - cap\right)^2 + 2ac_j\left(q_j - cap\right)cap$$
$$= 2ac_j\left(q_j - cap\right)^2 + c_0\, cap \tag{6-26}$$

where the second line uses (6-24).[26] The expression shows that the additional revenues are equal to the sum of capacity cost and twice the additional variable costs, the first and third terms to the right of the equal sign in equation (6-22), respectively. Total revenues are therefore equal to total cost plus the cost associated with exceeding the capacity during one period.

The example considered here is admittedly a rather specific one, but this conclusion holds for more general cost functions as long as they exhibit decreasing returns to scale for demand that is sufficiently high relative to capacity. For instance, consider a water supplier whose fixed costs are proportional to capacity and who can serve demand at a constant variable cost c_i as long as it does not exceed capacity. When demand exceeds capacity, the additional costs are $f(c_i - cap)$, with f an increasing convex function. This generalizes (6-22) but leaves the conclusion unchanged that the water supplier makes a profit under socially optimal pricing.[27]

CHAPTER 7

Policies to Encourage the Development of Water Sanitation Technology

Gerrit J.W. Euverink, Hardy Temmink, René A. Rozendal, and Cees J.N. Buisman

IN THE NETHERLANDS, wastewater is treated in plants with the sole purpose of meeting the water standards specified by the Pollution of Surface Waters Act (see Chapters 1 and 11), which prohibits the discharge of polluting or harmful substances into surface waters without a license. As a consequence of this act, sewage treatment plants were built, mainly to reduce chemical oxygen demand (COD) and the amounts of phosphates and nitrogen present in wastewater. Since 1998, all water in Dutch sewage networks is treated, and almost all households have been connected to municipal sewage treatment (EEA 2005).

Wastewater is treated, not purified. Recalcitrant compounds such as hormones, medicine residues, and detergents are still present in the effluents of wastewater treatment plants. These compounds eventually will contaminate the groundwater reserves because of their slow degradation in nature. Higher production of wastewater by the growing world population and increased use of degradation-resistant chemicals led to the awareness that the natural cleaning capacity of the environment is no longer sufficient to deal with the removal of very slow-degrading pollutants. Small amounts of recalcitrant pollutants may be degraded before they come in contact with the groundwater reserves, but larger amounts are not completely degraded in time, and the residue slowly seeps into the groundwater reserves.

Development of new and sensitive analytical equipment as well as optimization of existing measurement methods showed that human-made chemicals contaminated the groundwater reserves. In the past, we were not able to measure these compounds satisfactorily or were unaware that monitoring for them was important. More and more stable compounds are added to consumer and industrial products to increase their lifetime or safety (e.g., flame retardants, plastic stabilizers, or antifouling chemicals). Some of these products end up in wastewater treatment plants. The present large-scale treatment plants are not designed to remove these recalcitrant compounds, and they harm the natural waters and spoil the ground-water reserves. Continuation of this discharge practice inevitably leads to problems in the natural environment. Consequently, drinking water and irrigation for food production will become more expensive because of the necessity for additional purification of intake water from surface water or groundwater reserves. For this reason, the European Union issued new and stricter guidelines in the Water Frame-work Directive (WFD) in 2000 (see Chapter 11).

Current methods are not sufficient to deal with these new demands either tech-nologically or economically. Therefore, new sustainable technology that enables reuse of water and recycling of minerals must be developed. Closing the loop in industrial, agricultural, and household water cycles is necessary to maintain the quantity and quality of the natural water resources, because the reuse of water will lead to a decrease of fresh water extracted from the environment and wastewater discharged. Recycling of wastewater also contributes to the agreements in the Kyoto Protocol and the legislation according to the WFD's environmental objec-tives that are to be met by 2015.

A relatively new but extremely important issue concerns the observation that wastewater pollutants often represent valuable and renewable resources. For instance, bulk organic compounds in wastewater can be recovered as methane by anaerobic processes and as electricity by biofuel cells or converted into valuable products (Reis et al. 2003). Another example is the mineral phosphorus, present in domestic, agricultural, and industrial wastewaters. Economically exploitable phos-phorus ores are expected to be depleted within 50 years. This period can be extended if phosphorus is recovered from wastewater. Current treatment technolo-gies were developed with discharge limits in mind and not for recycling of water, energy, and minerals. Development of new technology for the removal of bulk components such as organic compounds, nitrogen, and phosphorus from waste-water allows for the extraction of energy and fertilizers.

New concepts for water purification start at the source of wastewater produc-tion. Traditionally, wastewater from different sources is collected, combined, and transported via the sewage system to central treatment plants. The dilution and mixing of different wastewaters decreases cleaning efficiency, however, and extrac-tion of valuable reusable components becomes impossible. Changing the traditional way of thinking how to treat wastewater using new concepts is a challenging task that cannot be carried out without help of national and local governments. Stim-ulation and financing of research programs that focus on the development of sus-tainable water technology are needed, but research alone is not sufficient. Most important are demonstration sites where the developed technology can be tested and proven on a larger scale, using more realistic conditions than are possible in the laboratory. These sites must be made available by the government, but often exist-ing regulations do not allow for their establishment. For example, a "separation at source" project in the Netherlands city of Sneek was delayed because the govern-ment did not permit the vacuum toilets necessary for the process to be connected to the water supply lines. Thus it is important that the government change the reg-ulations, either temporarily or permanently, so that the necessary research can be carried out.

This chapter examines innovations in water technology, policies to develop technologies that will contribute to a sustainable economy, and the introduction of the new concepts to society. In Chapter 6, Rouwendal elaborated on the optimal capacity of sewage treatment, based on costs and benefits. We discuss our views on how wastewater treatment may be performed in the future in such a way that the WFD guidelines are met economically. Preventing the mixing and diluting of different wastewater streams would enable reuse of valuable components (energy, minerals, and water). This chapter also describes nitrogen removal and recovery techniques that can convert ammonia and nitrates into dinitrogen gas. At present, industrial ammonia synthesis from dinitrogen gas is more economically feasible than reuse of ammonia from wastewater. Chemical and biological methods to remove phosphorus are examined as well. Phosphorus is a good potential target for reuse, as the natural reserves of the ore are limited. Removal of phosphorus from wastewater would also decrease eutrophication of natural waters. Membrane bioreactors are very promising in the treatment of special industrial wastewater or enhanced treatment of municipal wastewater. The chapter then looks at bioelectrochemical conversion processes—microbial fuel cells and biocatalyzed electrolysis—new techniques to recover energy from wastewater that require less energy than conventional techniques. Therefore, more energy is left in the wastewater and conversion into methane, electricity, or hydrogen becomes possible.

SEPARATION AT SOURCE

Removal of bulk pollutants already was an important issue, but today micropollutants have become equally important. Micropollutants include, among others, heavy metals, medicine residues, pesticides, and hormones. The problem with micropollutants is twofold: they are difficult to remove and environmentally dangerous even at very low concentrations. The efficient removal of these priority micropollutants is hindered by the fact that different streams of wastewater are mixed before treatment. For example, in the Netherlands, 150 liters of wastewater are produced per person per day. The majority of this, 120 liters, is so-called gray water, originating from kitchen sinks, bathroom sinks and tubs, washing machines, and dishwashers. The remainder is black water, produced by flushing toilets. These wastewater streams are collected in the sewage system and are mixed with other water streams, such as industrial wastewater, sometimes groundwater as a result of leakage of the sewage system, and occasionally rainwater. This dilution makes the removal of micropollutants even more difficult. A possible solution to overcome these problems is to separate the different streams of wastewater at the source, which has some additional benefits.

It is in the black water that most of the COD, nitrogen, phosphorus, hormones, and medicine residues are found, and using vacuum toilets with low water consumption prevents dilution of the concentrated black water stream. This results in a 95% saving of water used for toilet flushing, which represents about 30% saving in total water use. Biodegradation of hormones and medicine residues in these concentrated streams is much more efficient. After treatment of black water and isolation of all the reusable material, only a small volume of water contaminated with nonbiodegradable compounds (e.g., medicine residues) and pathogens such as viruses and microorganisms is left. This small volume allows for highly efficient removal of these compounds by adsorption in combination with more expensive oxidation techniques (e.g., ozone, UV, H_2O_2). Oxidation will also kill the pathogens before the water is discharged into the environment.

The large volume of gray water makes reuse of water from this stream attractive, although hormone-disturbing chemicals are present in gray water. These originate from household chemicals containing, for example, surfactants, plasticizers, and perfumes that are partly biologically degraded (Eriksson et al. 2002; Palmquist and Hanaeus 2005). New bioconversion technologies in combination with removal of pollutants via membrane separation or adsorption and subsequent oxidation of the concentrates are required before sustainable reuse of gray water is possible.

Separation at source is also an option for treatment of industrial and hospital wastewater streams, which can have major effects in central treatment plants because of high concentrations of chemicals or large volumes. Special dedicated treatment technologies need to be developed for these wastewater streams. A promising technology with high potential is the membrane bioreactor, where a bioreactor is used in combination with separation via membranes.

POLICIES IN THE NETHERLANDS

In the Netherlands, several organizations are active in wastewater technology. Among the key players are the various levels of government. The central government issues laws and regulations concerning discharge of water into the environment in order to safeguard the quality and quantity of the surface water. The regional water boards implement and control the corresponding legislation by maintaining treatment plants for the communal wastewater and inspecting discharge points at different locations. The local governments (municipalities) are responsible for the transportation of wastewater from the cities to the treatment plants via the sewage system.

The government, in several memoranda, has been paying increasing attention to the quality of the effluent from wastewater treatment plants. One policy is that wastewater from industrial sewage systems as well as from tourism (e.g., boats and campers) must be cleaned according to more stringent discharge guidelines to meet the WFD objectives for 2015. As a result of this policy, new technology must be developed and implemented.

The government has provided stimulus for this technology through a number of subsidy programs wherein industries, universities, and knowledge institutions cooperate in water purification and other projects. Examples of successful cooperation in other research areas are Technological Top Institutes (TTI), with industry, knowledge institutions, and government all contributing (25%, 25%, and 50% of the budget, respectively) to the research. A business proposal for a TTI Water Technology was approved by the Dutch government and the research started in 2007, with a total budget of 70 million euros available. The research program is focused on development of new water technology for drinking-water preparation, wastewater treatments for consumer and industrial needs, sensors for water, and water interaction with the environment.

To implement the introduction of developed technology into the market, a new subsidy program called InnoWATOR was launched in September 2006 by the Ministry of Economic Affairs. This program promotes and subsidizes demonstration sites where the new technology is tested in real situations. These sites are indispensable for proper market introduction and acceptance by the general public. From 2006 to 2008, 5 million euros per year was available.

In the Netherlands, several "separation at the source" demonstration projects in houses were started. The local government subsidizes these programs indirectly by decreasing the costs for wastewater treatment for the people occupying the houses. We will describe two examples. The first one was started in 2000 in Waterland, Groningen. Gray water, black water, and rainwater are separated in these communities. The gray water is successfully purified by two helophyte filters. The effluent of this filter bed is kept in ponds and not distributed outside the area to minimize the risk that surrounded surface waters would be contaminated in case of failure of the helophyte filters. Contamination by seeping pond water into the groundwater reservoirs is not prevented. The soil's cleaning capacity by sand filtration and bacterial degradation is sufficient to safeguard the groundwater quality if the ponds become contaminated with gray water. In winter, these helophyte filters are closed because the lower temperatures reduce cleaning efficiency. The gray water is then discharged into the sewage system, diminishing the advantages of separation at the source. Clearly, new robust technology is needed to purify gray water throughout the year. Such technology does not exist at the moment and is part of the research program of Centre of Excellence for Sustainable Water Technology (Wetsus), the new TTI Water Technology Institute.

In the second example, 30 houses were built in 2006 in Sneek, Friesland, and installed with vacuum toilets. Household wastewater is separated at the source, and the black water is treated according to the newest available technologies: anaerobic digestion using highly concentrated black water to recover energy, followed by struvite production to recover nitrogen and phosphorus. This black water stream is 400 to 800 times more concentrated than normal Dutch sewer water. Industry, Wageningen University, local government, the water board Wetterskip Fryslân, and Wetsus supported the development of this demonstration site, where the focus is on energy and nutrient recovery and pathogen removal. The presence of these and other pilot sites facilitates innovations in water technology.

NITROGEN REMOVAL AND RECOVERY

Available technologies to recover nitrogen from wastewaters include ammonia stripping, membrane filtration, electrodialysis, struvite precipitation, and ion exchange. It is generally recognized, however, that these physicochemical processes are expensive and consume a great deal of energy and chemicals (Mulder 2003) and therefore are not competitive with traditional fertilizer production by the

Haber-Bosch process. Only recovery of struvite, a slow-release fertilizer, could be a viable option when applied in decentralized wastewater treatment systems.

In contrast to recovery of nitrogen, in the Netherlands much attention has been devoted to biological nitrogen removal, converting nitrogen in wastewaters to dinitrogen gas. According to EU regulations, Dutch treatment plants should remove, on average, at least 75% of the nitrogen present in sewage. To achieve this objective, large investments were made by Dutch water boards in the last decade, but already they are facing a new challenge. The new, more stringent guidelines that are expected in implementing the WFD require sewage treatment plants in certain regions to remove nitrogen to levels below 2.2, or even below 1, milligrams per liter ($mg \cdot l^{-1}$). It is believed that these guidelines cannot be met with conventional nitrogen removal technology based on nitrification (conversion of ammonium to nitrite and nitrate) and denitrification (conversion of nitrate to dinitrogen gas using a carbon source), because the concentration of carbon sources in sewage is too low to sustain a sufficient degree of denitrification.

Some water boards anticipated this new challenge by installing denitrifying sand filters as a post-treatment at their sewage treatment facilities; however, this requires an expensive external (i.e., not present in the sewage) carbon source such as methanol. Recently, the Netherlands has developed more promising biological nitrogen removal technologies that are less dependent on external carbon sources and have lower energy consumption than traditional nitrification–denitrification. Examples are the single-reactor high-activity ammonia removal over nitrite (SHARON) and completely autotrophic nitrogen removal over nitrite (CANON) processes. The nitrogen pathways of all three processes are depicted in figure 7.1.

SHARON combines partial nitrification of ammonium to nitrite with denitrification of nitrite to nitrogen gas using an external carbon source (van Kempen et al. 2001). This saves methanol and 56% energy (for aeration) compared with traditional nitrification–denitrification followed by post-denitrification with methanol. An even more promising concept is CANON, which couples partial nitrification to anaerobic ammonium oxidation by the use of anammox bacteria (Sliekers et al. 2003). Less energy is consumed for aeration, and CANON is completely independent from carbon sources. The carbon sources present in wastewater would no longer have to be saved for denitrification, but could be converted in anaerobic reactors to methane, a valuable energy source. Thus sewage treatment could even be transformed from an energy-consuming to an energy-producing process. A full-scale application of partial nitrification of ammonium to nitrite with the SHARON concept and anaerobic ammonium oxidation with nitrite (anammox) already is being implemented to remove nitrogen from the recirculation water of the sludge treatment facilities of Sluisjesdijk in Rotterdam. The CANON process is successfully being applied at full scale for the treatment of a number of industrial wastewaters.

Two other recent Dutch developments in the field of biological nitrogen removal are the bioaugmentation batch enhanced (BABE) and Nereda processes. BABE is a batch process nitrifying the relatively warm recirculation water, typically 30°C, of sludge digesters that contain high concentrations of ammonium, typically 700 $mg \cdot l^{-1}$ (Berends et al. 2005). Particularly under winter conditions, BABE boosts the nitrification process, resulting in higher average nitrogen removal effi-

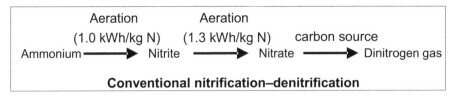

Conventional nitrification–denitrification

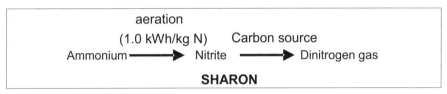

SHARON

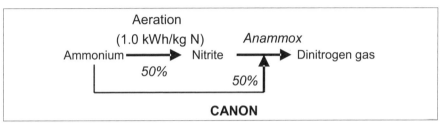

CANON

Figure 7.1 *Nitrogen removal from wastewater according to conventional nitrification–denitrification, SHARON, and CANON*

ciency. The nitrifying bacteria growing in the BABE reactor are fed to the main process and in this manner help maintain a stable population of nitrifiers, even at low temperatures. A first BABE reactor was recently installed on the sewage treatment facility in the Netherlands city of 's-Hertogenbosch.

Nereda provides a compact alternative for nitrogen removal by activated sludge processes (de Kreuk and de Bruin 2005). The microorganisms responsible for the removal of carbon, nitrogen, and phosphorus are not growing in flocs, but in granules with excellent settleability. The effect is that large settlers no longer are required, and higher biomass concentrations can be maintained. Calculations predict a reduction of the required surface area by as much as 75% compared with conventional activated sludge processes. A full-scale industrial application of Nereda to treat wastewater from VIKA, a food industry in Ede, the Netherlands, recently began operating.

PHOSPHATE REMOVAL AND RECOVERY

Economically exploitable phosphate rock is becoming increasingly scarce (Driver et al. 1999) and is a nonrenewable resource, posing a serious problem for the future. This also explains the interest in recovering phosphorus from wastewaters, as either a renewable resource for the phosphorus industry or a substance that can be applied as fertilizer. The total amount of phosphorus in Dutch sewage is estimated at 10,000 metric tons per year. This represents approximately 10% of the annual demand of phosphate rock by Thermphos International, one of the largest phosphorus-producing companies in the world. Located in the Netherlands, Thermphos International has stated the objective of replacing 20% of its intake of phosphate rock with renewable resources.

Several full-scale plants in Italy, the Netherlands, Sweden, and Japan have shown that direct phosphorus recovery from raw sewage or effluents of wastewater treatment plants is technically feasible. The most common methods applied are struvite precipitation ($MgNH_4PO_4 \cdot 6H_2O$) or calcium phosphate crystallization in a Crystallactor, developed in the Netherlands (Gaastra et al. 1998). The economic feasibility is low, however, because the costs of phosphorus recovery still are much higher than the price of phosphate rock (Pinnekamp et al. 2003).

In the Netherlands, more than 80% of the phosphorus in sewage is removed, either by chemical precipitation with metal salts or biologically. In both cases, the phosphorus ends up in the excess biological sludge, which is largely incinerated. The high dry mass and phosphorus content of the incineration ashes indicate that phosphorus extraction from these ashes could be a feasible recovery route. Unfortunately, this requires the ashes to be pretreated to remove the heavy metals, which is an uneconomical and nonsustainable process using huge quantities of different chemicals. A more feasible route probably is to extract phosphorus biologically from sludges produced in wastewater treatment plants (Klapwijk and Temmink 2004). In the biological phosphorus removal process, microorganisms take up the phosphorus in the wastewater and store it in their cells as polyphosphate. Under anaerobic conditions, the phosphorus is released into the bulk water, resulting in considerably higher concentrations (50 to 200·mg·l⁻¹) than in the sewage (5 to 15 mg·l⁻¹). Research initiated by the Dutch Foundation for Applied Water Research (STOWA) is currently being carried out to demonstrate that phosphorus precipitation from this concentrate presents an economically feasible recovery process.

Another interesting option may be used where separation at the source is applied for sewage. In household wastewater, 70% to 80% of the phosphorus is associated with feces and urine, which contribute to only 30% of the total volume of produced wastewater, or even as low as 3% when vacuum toilets are used (Kujawa-Roeleveld et al. 2005). When this water can be separately treated, concentrations of 60 to more than 200 mg·l⁻¹ of phosphorus are possible, which could allow efficient phosphorus recovery.

MEMBRANE BIOREACTORS

Wastewater generally is treated by activated sludge processes. Biomass consisting of aggregates (flocs) of microorganisms performs the treatment process, and in large settlers, this biomass is separated from the effluent and recirculated to the biological reactor. In membrane bioreactors (MBR), these settlers are replaced by micro- or ultrafiltration membrane units (fig. 7.2). These units can be applied in a sidestream of the biological reactor or submerged into this reactor.

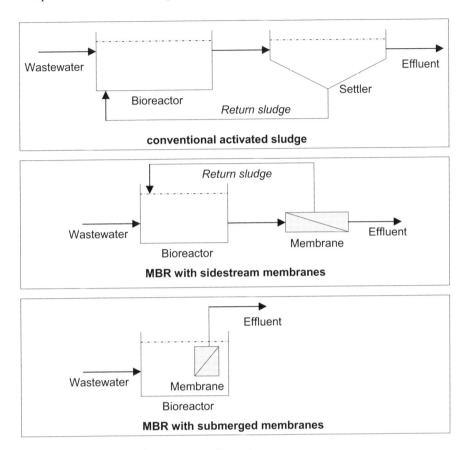

Figure 7.2 *Membrane bioreactor configurations*

For treatment of industrial wastewaters, typically with flow rates below 100 cubic meters per hour ($m^3 \cdot h^{-1}$), many full-scale MBR systems are now being used. This is because MBR systems have two major advantages over conventional activated sludge systems: a smaller footprint, because higher biomass concentrations can be maintained and large settlers no longer are required, and an excellent effluent quality with respect to pathogens and suspended solids. Another potential advantage, which certainly needs to be further developed, is the capability of MBR systems to retain nonaggregating microorganisms. This situation is of particular interest when industrial water loops are closed and extreme conditions arise with respect to pH, salinity, or temperature, or when a particular wastewater requires biological treatment by slow-growing microorganisms. The paper and board industries are some examples of those using treatment with MBR systems at high temperatures, typically 50° to 55°C. This not only permits reuse of the treated wastewater, but also diminishes energy losses due to cooling and reheating of the process water.

More stringent discharge standards for nutrients and micropollutants imposed by the WFD have forced Dutch water boards to reconsider their wastewater treatment systems. Because of this, much research effort has been directed toward the application of MBR systems. Whereas sidestream operation generally is preferred for industrial applications, submerged MBR systems are considered more efficient for sewage treatment because of lower energy consumption. MBR systems already are being used or planned for sewage treatment in the Netherlands in areas with vulnerable receiving waters or that lack space to build conventional wastewater treatment plants. The investment and operational costs still are considerably higher than for conventional treatment, however, and this together with the high complexity of operation explains why MBR systems are not more widely used for sewage treatment. The main reason from a process point of view is fouling of the membranes. This results in a higher installed membrane surface area, more frequent chemical cleaning, and higher energy consumption. Most research therefore has been directed toward possible ways to reduce membrane fouling.

Another important advantage of MBR systems is their ability to remove heavy metals, organic micropollutants, endocrine-disrupting compounds, medicine residues, and other emerging compounds. Many micropollutants are present in the effluent of sewage treatment plants at concentrations above desirable levels. MBR systems remove the micropollutants associated with suspended solids and could be used to provide pretreatment before more advanced physical-chemical removal by other methods such as activated carbon or ozonation. These systems also allow for longer sludge retention times and therefore the possibility of retaining slow-growing microorganisms, which could enhance biological removal of organic micropollutants (e.g., Clara et al. 2005).

BIOELECTROCHEMICAL CONVERSION PROCESSES

Recovery of energy from wastewater is mostly done by anaerobic conversion of COD by methanogenic bacteria into biogas (a mixture of CH_4 and CO_2). This gas is used for heating or in the generation of electricity using combustion engines. For an overview of methane production processes from wastewater and biomass, see Reith et al. (2003). Production of electricity from wastewater involves three main steps: conversion of COD into biogas; purification of biogas; and burning methane in combustion engines, generating electricity.

A new approach toward energy production from wastewater is the application of bioelectrochemical conversion processes, using electrochemically active microorganisms (Logan 2005; Rabaey and Verstraete 2005; Rabaey et al. 2005). These microorganisms convert the biodegradable materials (e.g., fatty acids) in wastewater to carbon dioxide, protons, and electrons. The produced electrons are transferred to an electrode, which is therefore referred to as a biological anode. Because the electrons are released by these microorganisms at a high energy level, almost at the energy level of the electrons in the biodegradable material itself, they can be used for driving bioelectrochemical conversion processes. Within Wetsus, two technologies in this field are currently being investigated: the microbial fuel cell and biocatalyzed electrolysis (see fig. 7.3).

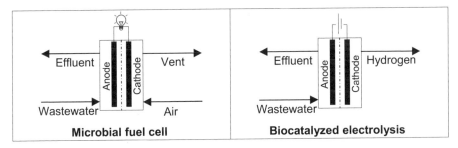

Figure 7.3 *Microbial fuel cell and biocatalyzed electrolysis*

In a microbial fuel cell, the oxidation of biodegradable material at the biological anode is electrochemically coupled to the reduction of oxygen at the cathode. Because oxygen accepts the electrons at a lower energy level than that at which they are produced at the biological anode, a voltage difference is created between anode and cathode, which causes the electrons to flow from anode to cathode. In this way, electricity is produced from wastewater in a single step. Conventional technology, using anaerobic treatment, needs at least three steps to convert the biodegradable material in wastewater to electrical energy: biogas production, biogas treatment, and application of a gas motor. Microbial fuels cells therefore offer an interesting alternative, but the technology is still in the developing stage. The current generation of laboratory microbial fuel cell systems produces up to 100 watts per cubic meter (W/m^3) of reactor volume, whereas anaerobic treatment of wastewater is well established and produces up to 1,000 W/m^3 of reactor volume. Microbial fuel cell technology is evolving rapidly, however, and is expected to reach 1,000 W/m^3 within five years. Furthermore, the conversion efficiency of biodegradable material to electricity can be twice as high with microbial fuel cell technology—60% efficiency for microbial fuel cells versus 30% for conventional anaerobic treatment—which makes this technology an interesting research topic.

Within Wetsus and Wageningen University, a new technology related to the microbial fuel cell, called biocatalyzed electrolysis, has been developed and patented (Rozendal and Buisman 2005). Like the microbial fuel cell, biocatalyzed electrolysis applies electrochemically active microorganisms, but it produces pure hydrogen gas instead of electricity (Rozendal et al. 2006). Renewably produced hydrogen is widely considered as an alternative clean fuel for transportation and a green chemical, and large amounts theoretically can be produced from organic materials using fermentation technology. The hydrogen production efficiency of the currently available technologies, such as dark fermentation, is poor (~15%), however. Biocatalyzed electrolysis is capable of boosting this efficiency to over 90% by investing a small amount of electrical energy. Compared with conventional water electrolysis, biocatalyzed electrolysis requires more than four times less electrical energy (biocatalyzed electrolysis: < 1.0 kWh/Nm^3 H_2; water electrolysis: > 4.5 kWh/Nm^3 H_2). Furthermore, the innovative design of biocatalyzed electrolysis allows for hydrogen production from a much wider variety of wastewaters. This makes biocatalyzed electrolysis a revolutionary breakthrough technology in the field of biological hydrogen production from wastewaters.

As biocatalyzed electrolysis was discovered in 2003, the research has just passed the proof of principle stage. It is now focused on improving the process in order to arrive at a mature technology that is capable of producing over 10 Nm^3 H$_2$/m^3 of reactor volume per day. At that rate, biocatalyzed electrolysis should prove to be useful both as a wastewater treatment and for hydrogen production technology.

CONCLUSIONS

The new technologies and policies described in this chapter show our view on wastewater treatment technology. New technologies are necessary for sustainable wastewater treatment in the future, but government, industry, and consumers play a role in the process too. Separation at the source requires both infrastructure change and consumer commitment. As a consequence of this method, treatment plants receive a different type of wastewater as influent, and treatment procedures are likely to change because of this. It is clear that positive cooperation is necessary among all organizations that deal with the different aspects of this process.

Investment in long-term multidisciplinary research via collaboration with different partners—industry, knowledge institutions, and government—is very important to face the challenges that will arise in the future when the Netherlands has to comply with the strict guidelines of the WFD. Estimates of the costs of implementing these guidelines using existing infrastructure and technologies vary between 5 and 30 billion euros (CPB 2004). New research initiatives, such as TTI Water Technology, may lead to a substantial reduction in these costs by developing innovative technologies for wastewater treatment. Costs may be reduced through reuse of energy and minerals; development of new, more economical treatment technologies; and optimization of existing technologies. In the future, wastewater may be seen not as a waste product to dispose of, but as a valuable source of water, energy, and nutrients that must be harvested and reused.

REFERENCES

Berends, D.H., S. Salem, H. van der Roest, and M.C. van Loosdrecht. 2005. Boosting nitrification with the BABE technology. *Water Science and Technology* 52 (4): 63–70.

Clara, M., B. Strenn, O. Gans, E. Martinez, N. Kreuzinger, and H. Kroiss. 2005. Removal of selected pharmaceuticals, fragrances and endocrine disrupting compounds in a membrane bioreactor and conventional wastewater treatment plants. *Water Research* 39 (19): 4797–4807.

CPB (Centraal Planbureau). 2004. *Kaderrichtlijn Water: enige aandachtspunten* [*Water Framework Directive: Points to consider*]. The Hague: CPB.

de Kreuk, M.K., and L.M.M. de Bruin. 2004. *Aerobic granular reactor technology*. London: IWA Publishing.

Driver, J., D. Lijmbach, and I. Steen. 1999. Why recover phosphorus for recycling, and how? *Environmental Technology* 20:651–62.

EEA (European Environment Agency). 2005. Effectiveness of urban wastewater treatment policies in selected countries: An EEA pilot study. Copenhagen: EEA Report No. 2/2005.

Eriksson E., K. Auffarth, M. Henze, and A. Ledin. 2002. Characteristics of grey wastewater. *Urban Water* 4:85–104.

Gaastra, S., R. Schemen, P. Pakker, and M. Bannink. 1998. Full scale phosphate recovery at sewage treatment plant Geesterambacht, Holland. Paper presented at the International Conference on Phosphorus Recovery from Sewage and Animal Wastes. May 1998, Warwich, UK.

Klapwijk, A., and H. Temmink. 2004. P-recovery from sewage for the elementary P-industry, In *Phosphorus in Environmental technologies*, ed. E. Valsami-Jones, 519–26. London: IWA Publishing.

Kujawa-Roeleveld K., T. Fernandes, Y. Wiryawan, A. Tawfik, M. Visser, and G. Zeeman. 2005. Performance of UASB septic tank for treatment of concentrated black water within DESAR concept. *Water Science and Technology* 52 (1–2): 307–13.

Logan, B.E. 2005. Simultaneous wastewater treatment and biological electricity generation. *Water Science and Technology* 52 (1–2): 31–37.

Mulder, A. 2003. The quest for sustainable nitrogen removal technologies. *Water Science and Technology* 48 (1): 67–75.

Palmquist H., and J. Hanaeus. 2005. Hazardous substances in separately collected grey- and blackwater from ordinary Swedish households. *Science of the Total Environment* 348 (1–3): 151–63.

Pinnekamp, J., P. Baumann, T. Buer, P. Cornel, D. Donnert, U. Göttlicher-Schmidle, U. Heinzmann, N. Jardin, J. Londong, J. Müller, F. von Sothen, and H. Temmink. 2003. Phosphorrückgewinnung [Phosphate recovery]. KA-Abwasser. *Abfall* 50 (6): 805–14.

Rabaey K., P. Clauwaert, P. Aelterman, and W. Verstraete. 2005. Tubular microbial fuel cells for efficient electricity generation. *Environmental Science and Technology* 39 (20): 8077–82.

Rabaey K., and W. Verstraete. 2005. Microbial fuel cells: Novel biotechnology for energy generation. *Trends in Biotechnology* 23 (6): 291–98.

Reis M.A., L.S. Serafim, P.C. Lemos, A.M. Ramos, F.R. Aguiar, and M.C. van Loosdrecht. 2003. Production of polyhydroxyalkanoates by mixed microbial cultures. *Bioprocess and Biosystems Engineering* 25 (6): 377–85.

Reith, J.H., R.H. Wijffels, and H. Barten. 2003. *Bio-methane and Bio-hydrogen: Status and perspectives of biological methane and hydrogen production.* Petten, Netherlands: Dutch Biological Hydrogen Foundation.

Rozendal, R.A., and C.J.N. Buisman. 2005. Process for producing hydrogen. International Patent Number WO-2005-005981.

Rozendal, R.A., H.V.M. Hamelers, G.J.W. Euverink, S.J. Metz, and C.J.N. Buisman. 2006. Principle and perspectives of hydrogen production through biocatalyzed electrolysis. *International Journal of Hydrogen Energy* 31 (12): 1632–40.

Sliekers, A.O., K.A. Third, W. Abma, J.G. Kuenen, and M.S. Jetten. 2003. CANON and Anammox in a gas-lift reactor. *FEMS Microbiology Letters* 218 (2): 339–44.

van Kempen, R., J.W. Mulder, C.A. Uijterlinde, and M.C. van Loosdrecht. 2001. Overview: Full-scale experience of the SHARON process for treatment of rejection water of digested sludge dewatering. *Water Science and Technology* 44 (1): 145–52.

Part III

INSTITUTIONAL, GOVERNANCE, AND MANAGEMENT THEORIES AND PRACTICES

CHAPTER 8

Institutional Evolution of the Dutch Water Board Model

Stefan M.M. Kuks

T HE NETHERLANDS HAS a long history of water management. As early as the 11th and 12th centuries, local communities started to organize to manage water systems and built dikes to protect against flooding from the sea and rivers. At that time, removal of peat for fuel and clay for building material was already causing land subsidence, necessitating additional measures such as building dikes. In the 15th century, land subsidence was so great that agricultural fields remained waterlogged for a large part of the year. More drastic measures were needed, and windmills were introduced to pump the extra water from the land. During the next century, windmills were also used to make new land available by draining the lakes that resulted from peat extraction. In the eighteenth and nineteenth centuries, more windmills were built to pump water out of local collection canals, known as boezems, and into open waters.

The first democratic district water boards, stakeholder organizations consisting of elected representatives from local farming communities, were established in the 13th century. The rulers of the Netherlands soon recognized these boards as competent water authorities, and they remained independent of national developments until the 19th century. The need for central coordination led in 1798 to the establishment of a state water authority, Rijkswaterstaat. This state department became the leading agency for the large-scale construction of a flood protection infrastructure consisting of dikes along the shores and main rivers, as well as for large land reclamation projects. After a period of French domination, the Netherlands became a monarchy in 1813 and received a new constitution the next year.

Today water policy is drawn up and implemented at both the national level and that of the provinces and water boards. From a historical perspective, provinces, water boards, and municipalities have had a quite autonomous jurisdiction. Since World War II, however, their autonomy has been framed increasingly in terms of a model of close collaboration with central government, in which the central government takes the initiative in policymaking, and noncentral authorities cooperate with additional policymaking and implementation within the national policy framework. Provinces and municipalities even depend on subsidies from the national budget. Water boards, on the other hand, do not rely on such subsidies and do not want to; they are authorized to fully recover the costs of their activities through their own taxation.

Water boards are an old and special level of administration. They were primarily responsible, from the Middle Ages until the mid-20th century, for protection against flooding and management of water in the polders in the low-lying regions. After the Second World War, particularly since around 1970, they have acquired wider powers to combat water pollution, including the responsibility for the construction and operation of wastewater treatment facilities. Water boards have a democratic structure, based on a profit-payment-participation principle: those having an interest in water management may participate and have to pay for water services in proportion to their interest. The general council of a water board comprises representatives of several groups: farmers, landowners, building owners, industries, and inhabitants. A water board has regulatory and taxation authority, raising its own taxes separately for quality and quantity management, based on the principles of full cost recovery and polluter pays. Regarding water quality management, municipalities are responsible for planning, building, and operating sewer networks in their areas. Besides water quality management by the water boards, they also have regulatory authority in that they license industrial discharges into the networks. Additionally, the country has about 10 water supply companies for some 16 million inhabitants, which means on average 1,600,000 inhabitants or 500,000 households per company. These are public enterprises, often at the provincial scale or higher, with municipalities and provinces as shareholders, but operating under civil law.

This chapter examines the Dutch water board model. It begins by exploring the evolution of water governance in the Netherlands and how the position of water boards in the Dutch administrative structure evolved. It then looks at important transitions and paradigm changes that have occurred in recent decades, discusses the implications of climate change and the restoration of floodplains, and links water management with urban planning.

CENTRALIZED WATER MANAGEMENT

Our analysis of the Dutch water administration and water board model starts with the period 1798–1814, when the country made its first attempts at a centralized approach to water management. This was the period of French domination in the Netherlands, which resulted in a new administrative order with more centralized power, a new constitution, and a new civil code. With respects to property rights, this period marks the transition from feudal to civil rights.

Centralization as a French Legacy

The history of public water management in the Netherlands started as early as the 13th century, with the recognition of water boards as public authorities by the nation's rulers. As bottom-up organizations of farmers and landowners with an interest in flood protection and water drainage, they operated on a rather small scale. Often labeled "farmer republics," water boards were powerful local organizations that combined legislative, executive, and jurisdictional powers. For many centuries, they have been able to resist pressure from the central state.

In the seventeenth and eighteenth centuries, water management was still under the jurisdiction of these local authorities. The central government could not intervene in the jurisdiction of noncentral authorities, except when the interest of military defense was at stake. Throughout the 18th century, however, various flooding disasters in Dutch river basins demonstrated that the rather small-scale approach of water boards lacked central coordination and a broader scope. At that time, many people were concerned about the devastating impact of these floods, which even threatened the safety and survival of large parts of Dutch territory. It was evident that the rather fragmented water governance system, ruled by provinces and water boards, was losing its grip on the situation. Despite incidental cases of interprovincial coordination in river domains, the water policies of provinces and water boards came under increasing criticism. Nevertheless, in the political culture of that time, the autonomy and mutual independence of public bodies was considered important. Noncentral authorities were not willing to give up even the smallest part of their jurisdiction. Another obstacle was that private landowners in the floodplains could assert their rights by obstructing public intervention.

Despite all this, by the end of the 18th century, the criticism of water managers gave impetus to a movement of state reformists to politicize water management and plead for a more centrally governed unitary state. In 1795, the reformist ideas got a chance when the French invaded the Netherlands, wiped out the existing Republic of the Seven United Provinces, and allowed the reformists to establish a Batavian Republic (1795–1806). In 1798, the new republic adopted legislation that allowed the central government to exercise supervision over all noncentral public authorities with a water governance task. Related to this, the state water authority Rijkswaterstaat was established to take the lead in a nationally coordinated approach to water governance. In practice, this appeared to be a form of extreme centralization, resulting in great tensions between the state and provincial authorities. The establishment of Rijkswaterstaat marks the transition from a solely local, uncoordinated approach to one of tackling water problems in the main water systems based on a nationwide overview. During the subsequent Napoleonic era (1806–1813), the French rulers vigorously pursued their centralization of water governance (Bosch 2001).

Rivalry among the Central Government, Provinces, and Water Boards

In 1813, the Netherlands became sovereign again and changed into a constitutional monarchy. Although the rather conservative rulers of the water boards agitated strongly against centralization as a "French habit" and regarded the earlier legislation as an arrangement of an occupying power, the centralized system of water governance remained in place. Several policies from the French period were continued, such as the Dike Act of 1806, which attributed to the central state all property rights in the river domains up to the dikes. Those who were deprived of their property rights had to be compensated on a fair basis. This act has always been regarded as the first water management legislation in the Netherlands.

The constitution of 1814 even incorporated the supervisory role of the monarch and the central government with respect to water governance. According to this constitution, the water boards could retain their own jurisdiction only insofar as no jurisdiction was defined by the central state. In practice, however, the monarch was aware that successful water governance had to rely on broad support from society and cooperation with water boards and provinces. During the period 1814–1848, he partially restored the jurisdiction of provinces and water boards as it existed before the period of French domination. He even repealed substantial parts of the controversial Dike Act of 1806. Another reason for his actions was that the central government did not have the financial means required for the effectuation of an all-embracing supervisory role. Although the Competences Act (Bevoegdhedenwet) of 1841 deprived the water boards of their administration of justice, which was considered to be no longer compatible with the general administration of justice, the water boards remained strong thanks to their legislative and executive powers.

A revision of the constitution in 1848 put an end to the personal influence of the monarch on water governance (Bosch 2001). It placed the government under parliamentary control and incorporated changed ideas about the form of governance. The new constitution recognized the autonomous position of the water boards within the general administrative structure of the Netherlands. It also proclaimed the need for separate constitutional legislation for each of the lower administrations, which in the second half of the 19th century resulted in a Provinces Act and a Municipalities Act, but not in a separate Water Boards Act.

The evolution of water governance in the 19th century shows an ongoing rivalry among the central government, provinces, and water boards. Although the divide among central, provincial, and local jurisdictions was stabilized in formal terms, the practice of water governance demonstrated a lot of uncertainty on how this divide should be understood (Brainich von Brainich-Felth 1993).

Adoption of a Basic Pattern for Cogovernance

Disastrous river floods in 1876 and 1880 strengthened the central government in its endeavor to centralize flood protection and river management. It wanted to have more control over the main water systems and was willing to invest much larger amounts of money than the noncentral authorities ever could do on their own. During the period 1887–1916, several important items of legislation were adopted to institutionalize the division of responsibilities between the state and regional water authorities. The classical design of the "water state" in the Netherlands dates from that period.

In 1887, an amendment of the constitution recognized the state as main supervisor of the nation's water management. The Act of 1891 provided that the state could construct and operate waterworks with a national interest, allowing it to set up regulations necessary for state water management. The By-Laws Act (Keurenwet) of 1895 allowed the water boards to have their own regulatory authority (by ordinance, called a Keur) but required the central and provincial governments to supervise such ordinances. The Water State Act 1900 (Waterstaatswet 1900) introduced various far-reaching capabilities for the state and the provinces, allowing them to take over waterworks from the lower administrative levels (provinces or water boards) or supervise these works. On the other hand, the same act made it possible to transfer the responsibility for dike fortification programs from the state to provinces and water boards. The Act on Reclamation and Embankment (Wet op de droogmakerijen en indijkingen) of 1904 entitled the state to reclaim land and created a concession system for land reclamation by others. The Rivers Act of 1908 made the state responsible for the various functions of rivers, allowing it to start up waterworks serving these river functions, taking into account procedural and material conditions. Because of the dynamic movements of the rivers, and because river management would have an impact on large parts of the country, state control was considered to be of crucial importance.

In 1916, a flood disaster along the coast of the Zuider Zee, an inland sea in the heart of the country with an open end at the north side, strongly impelled the state water authority to develop a large-scale plan for flood control in that area. The disaster occurred as a result of the poor state of specific dikes and locks along the coast. State supervision of the many small water boards in the area was disputed, and the disaster led to a concentration and scale enlargement of water boards in the flooded area. Another consequence was a state plan for the construction of a series of dike fortifications (see also Chapter 1).

The 1953 flood disaster in the southwest of the country, in the province of Zeeland, shocked the nation, which felt that a modern, post–World War II state should no longer allow this kind of risk. Since then, risk prevention and exclusion have strongly influenced and dominated the management approach adopted by the state water authority. Like earlier disasters, that of 1953 resulted in two typical reactions. First, immediate drastic action was initiated, resulting in the Delta Plan for the construction of dike fortifications and storm barriers along the entire North Sea coast of the Netherlands, with an emphasis on the Zeeland coast. Second, the flooded area's water boards, which in the first half of the 20th century had strongly resisted institutional change, had to fundamentally change their closed, internal-oriented attitude. The resistance of the many small "farmer republics" was broken, and they merged into larger, better equipped organizations (Brainich von Brainich-Felth 1993).

EARLY INTEGRATED MANAGEMENT ATTEMPTS

Until the 1950s, the Dutch national water regime was relatively simple. Water management was mainly a matter of flood prevention, water level control, and sanitation, developing systems for drinking-water supply and sewage removal. During the 1950s and 1960s, the complexity increased. The initial attempts toward integrated water management were made at the end of the 1960s with the adoption of the *First National Policy Memorandum on Water Management* (Rijkswaterstaat 1968) and the adoption of the Surface Water Pollution Act in 1969. The quantity-oriented policy plan focused not only on flood protection and drainage (water security), but also on water scarcity and the competing demands of water supply, agriculture, and navigation. The Surface Water Pollution Act also involved the quantity-oriented water managers in active and passive water quality management. This means that in addition to constructing and operating wastewater treatment plants (active quality management), they also had to work on the prevention of surface water pollution by permitting and charging for wastewater discharges (passive quality management). Water demand control and quality protection thus became additional foci of water managers (Grijns and Wisserhof 1992).

The 1968 transition with respect to water demand control was part of a transformation process that started as early as the 1950s. The years after World War II were a period of use expansion and increasing rivalry between public and private interests. Concerns were raised about how to meet the demands for natural resources—water, space, and nature—needed by a growing economy and population that also demanded a higher standard of living. The Groundwater Act for Water Supply Companies was passed in 1954 to better guarantee a constant and undisturbed public water supply. Landowners had to permit extractions from aquifers under their property to fulfill the increased demand. In 1962, the Physical Planning Act was adopted, allowing expropriation of land for water drainage as a public service and introducing disadvantage compensation for the private property effects of public planning. The next year, the Fisheries Act was introduced to prevent overharvesting and generate a more efficient fisheries branch. This act was an early attempt to prevent exhaustion of natural resources and protect certain species and water- related biodiversity. In addition, the Clearances Act (Ontgrondingwet) of 1965 and Nature Conservation Act of 1967 formed the basis for the protection of nature and landscape resources against rival water and land uses. As a result, the 1950s and 1960s were characterized by controlled use expansion, deliberation of public versus private interests, and redistribution of property rights (van der Heide 1992; van Hall 1992). These issues were reflected in the first national water plan of 1968, which mainly focused on how to meet future demands of an increasing population and prevent rivalries related to water resources. The plan clearly recognized problems of groundwater scarcity and the need for demand-side management (Snijdelaar 1993).

While water management became more integrated in terms of scope during the 1960s, integration in terms of control appeared to be mixed. In particular, the Physical Planning Act of 1962, allowing expropriation for water drainage as a public service, was initially responsible for increased fragmentation. During the 1960s and 1970s, this act enabled a huge expansion of water drainage infrastructure by restructuring and canalization of many watercourses that had previously been quite natural. Natural curves (meanders) were cut off in the context of parceling out agricultural land, to improve productivity. The regional water boards, which at least until the 1980s were dominated by farmers, had a strong hand in the restructuring of rural areas, at the cost of their biodiversity. On the other hand, in 1974, the Physical Planning Act was extended with a set of participatory instruments for large-scale infrastructural works, which allowed use considerations other than flood protection and land reclamation to enter into decisionmaking on water infrastructure. In fact, these new instruments required consultation with interest groups in decisionmaking on large-scale infrastructural waterworks, to better account for rival water values and ecological effects. The extension of the Physical Planning Act was triggered by the democratization and participative tendencies of the 1960s and 1970s, and especially by broad opposition in society to traditional water management, which paid no heed to other water values.

The 1969 transition with respect to water quality protection can also be seen as part of a transformation process that started in the 1950s and represents a change in focus from sanitation to quality protection. Sanitation had already been a focus of water management since the early 20th century, when sewage and supply systems started to be constructed as public services, mainly at municipal scale. After World War II, the infrastructure for sewage and water supply was gradually extended to rural areas. In the 1950s, the Dutch water supply became institutionalized by national legislation to guarantee a supply of good quality, in sufficient amounts, and with affordable prices for all citizens. The Water Supply Act of 1957 introduced quality standards for drinking water.

Meanwhile, awareness was growing that sanitation measures would not be enough. Something needed to be done about the increasing pollution of water resources related to the expansion of economic activities after the Second World War. As early as the 1950s and early 1960s, many water boards and municipalities became active in the preliminary construction of wastewater treatment plants to prevent direct discharge of untreated sewage into surface waters. Water boards and municipalities were insufficiently equipped to handle this in a systematic way, however. Initiatives were mostly restricted to areas with a high concentration of inhabitants and industrial activities.

This changed when, around 1970, many European countries, on the basis of international agreements, adopted legislation to protect surface water quality. The Netherlands did so in 1969, with the passage of the Surface Water Pollution Act. The contents of such legislation varied greatly among countries at that time. The Dutch act included a permitting system to regulate industrial wastewater discharges and a charge system with strong incentives based on the polluter-pays and full cost recovery principles. The costs of construction, operation, and maintenance of wastewater treatment plants were to be fully recovered from the polluters, equivalent to their emitted amount of pollution. The charge system applied to both industrial and domestic polluters (Leemhuis-Stout 1992).

The 1969 transition not only resulted in greater integration in terms of a wider scope, but also contributed to increased control of Dutch water management. The question of which governance level should be responsible for operational water quality management was resolved by allowing the provinces to delegate this responsibility to the regional water boards, which is what most provinces did. Only three provinces—Utrecht, Friesland, and Groningen—carried out these tasks themselves, and two cities, Amsterdam and Tilburg, refused to relinquish their active role in sewage treatment. In 1992, a constitutional act finally determined that water boards should have primacy over regional water management, which meant that provinces and municipalities had to transfer their operational water management tasks to the water boards.

The new responsibility for water quality protection completely changed the water board world as it existed before 1969. In fact, the 1969 transition was an important step toward the creation of so-called all-in water authorities at water basin scale, because the water boards were already involved in quantity management at that scale (IJff 1993; Schorer 1993). Water boards could expand their personnel and expertise in water management. Small water boards merged into larger ones, as the construction and operation of wastewater treatment plants especially required a certain economy of scale. The participatory structure of water boards, which already allowed farmers and landowners to be represented on the board as parties with an interest in water quantity management, now also permitted participation by industrial and domestic polluters as users of the water basin. Their involvement was based on the fact that the Surface Water Pollution Act required that they be fully charged for all costs of water quality management, both active and passive. To facilitate effective implementation of this act, the water boards were granted the taxation authority to charge polluters in order to acquire the resources they needed for their water quality tasks, and water quality planning was done at the national level, prescribing objectives for the water boards in terms of reduction levels for nitrogen and phosphates as main surface water contaminants. The Dutch pollution charge appeared to be very successful in achieving water quality objectives as well as cost-effective, considering the social costs and technological innovations involved (Andersen 1999; Bressers 1983).

Although the institutionalization of water quality management has been an important step toward integrated water management, it did not mean a direct integration between quality and quantity management. Initially, water quality management was settled as a sectoral water policy, including its own separate water planning. In 1975, 1980, and 1985, the Dutch Environmental Department introduced sectoral plans for water quality protection, whereas in 1968 and 1984, the Water Department presented sectoral policy documents for water quantity issues (Snijdelaar 1993). The Ministry for the Environment coordinated water quality issues, but other water issues were controlled by the Ministry of Transport, Public Works and Water Management. So the years from 1969 until at least 1985 could also be characterized as a period of increasing complexity and fragmentation.

NATIONAL POLICY ON INTEGRATED WATER MANAGEMENT

A second important transition occurred around 1985, when the Dutch national water ministry launched a policy view on integrated water management as a new approach for water managers. It advocated considering water as a system in which surface water and groundwater were interconnected. This new approach would not only integrate quantity and quality aspects of the water system, but also take the system's ecology into account. Policymakers thought the natural life in the rivers' banks and soils had been too neglected by water managers and should be respected much more. The policy view on integrated water management also advocated improving the decisionmaking process. It maintained that external functional relations of water systems should be recognized, which meant that water managers should consider the complete variety of use functions of a water system, including the interests of nature, landscape, and the environment. In fact, this second transition has been a crucial step toward implementing a water basin approach that allows ecological considerations to enter water management decisionmaking (Grijns and Wisserhof 1992).

The policy vision of 1985, which had been preceded by the *Second National Policy Memorandum on Water Management* (V&W 1984), became formalized in the *Third National Policy Memorandum on Water Management* (V&W 1989). The second policy memorandum had recognized water depletion due to overdrainage as a major problem for water management. It also advocated integration between surface water and groundwater quantity management but did not include quality aspects (Snijdelaar 1993). Generally speaking, the 1985 transition had been triggered by a general growing environmental and ecological awareness in society, as well as a trend toward deregulation and integration in politics in the early 1980s, resulting in a political demand for more coordination by means of policy planning. The same developments are clearly visible in Dutch environmental politics of the 1980s, which culminated in the National Environmental Policy Plan of 1988, the first Dutch policy plan intended to coordinate all sectoral environmental policies at the national level. Another important change in this decade was the constitutional revision of 1983, which proclaimed that the public domain should be dedicated to the protection and sustainable improvement of the living environment, including the natural water system. The newly added Article 21 of the constitution provided license for expropriation of all property rights that could harm the protection of the living environment. Besides these more general triggers, the 1985 transition was a consequence of several more specific contexts in the water policy field.

First, the ecological transition of 1985 should be considered in the context of an evolutionary change in the water management approach of Rijkswaterstaat. In terms of policy learning at the national level, the experiences with IJsselmeer (former Zuider Zee) and the Delta Plan have been important. Although these have been very prestigious projects for Rijkswaterstaat, they also elicited criticism from various groups in society on the predominant civil engineering orientation of this organization. In fact, these criticisms, which started to find expression in the 1960s and 1970s, changed the approach of Rijkswaterstaat by politicizing water management and initiating a debate in society over water values. The critics placed a greater value on the meaning of "open" water for recreation, nature conservation, water storage, and the experience of unspoiled space in an already crowded and highly planned country. For the land reclamation project, this resulted in the canceling of the last scheduled polder, the Markerwaard. In the early 1980s, the societal debate on water values and the politicization of water management continued, resulting in the introduction of an ecosystem approach. This approach led to a change in the design of the last storm barrier that had to be constructed in the Zeeland area. It was made permeable, allowing salt water to pass through the barrier and leaving the ecosystem of the estuary behind it untouched. The confrontations in the 1970s and 1980s threatened the authority and autonomy of the water engineers and managers in the Netherlands. Recognizing other use functions of water systems and developing an ecosystem approach has been their way to survive and get along with their critics. The same kind of evolution, however delayed, happened at the noncentral level of water boards, where the farmers' dominance of regional water management could no longer be maintained, and rival user groups claimed the right to participate and have their say (Disco 1998; Snijdelaar 1993).

Second, the ecological transition of 1985 should be considered in the context of an increasing attention to groundwater aspects of water systems. After the extension of Dutch water management into quality protection of surface water in the 1960s and 1970s, the 1980s were important years for the institutionalization of groundwater management in the Netherlands. In 1981, the Groundwater Act was adopted to redistribute extraction rights among groundwater users. A provision was also added to have the extractors compensate those who were bearing the negative effects of water extraction and lower groundwater tables. The importance of this act is that it proclaimed that public supply could no longer dominate the deliberation of interests. All interests should be treated equally, which indicated that any specific demand could no longer be met in an unlimited amount. The act also allowed the provinces to charge for groundwater extractions, with the revenues to be used for policy measures to prevent water depletion. With respect to groundwater, regulation of both its quantity and quality aspects started in the 1980s.

Whereas the Groundwater Act of 1981 mainly dealt with water distribution and only in a limited way with water depletion, the Water Management Act was being developed throughout the 1980s (and adopted in 1989) to create more regulatory instruments for control of surface water and groundwater levels. These instruments could be applied to restrict all use rights affecting water tables, not only to prevent water depletion, but also to protect ecosystems. In fact, the Water Management Act has been the basis for the regional water boards to create ordinances for the regulation of water uses, in order to protect the natural and ecological values of water systems. Ecological considerations may be included in decisionmaking on water basins, according to a so-called broad water system approach (IJff 1993; Teeuwen et al. 1993). It has been decided that ecological considerations are in the interest of the general public, and therefore the general public should have seats and representation on the water boards. Because the charging system administered by the water boards is based on a profit-payment-participation principle, the extended approach also implies that citizens should bear a certain share of the total costs of water management. In other words, since the early 1990s, Dutch citizens have been identified as "ecological users" of water resources and charged for that use.

The rising influence of ecological and environmental considerations in Dutch water management during the 1980s indicates that the need for cooperation among those responsible for water, environmental, nature conservation, and agricultural policies increased strongly during that period. The groundwater protection policy, with restrictions on fertilizer applications, for instance, has been the result of active involvement in the early 1980s by the Dutch environmental ministry in other policy sectors as it tried to consult directly with target groups and break through existing "iron triangles," such as the one among the agricultural ministry, farming interest groups, and their representatives in Parliament. Although these were attempts toward greater integration, or at least interpolicy coordination, they started to result in more complexity and even fragmentation. Sectoral policy plans for water, environment, nature, and land use individually became more integrated during the 1980s, but integration among these policy sectors seemed very difficult to achieve. Increased complexity was seen not only at the national level, but also at noncentral levels of administration, where the strategic national plans needed to be implemented as operational plans.

INTEGRATING WATER MANAGEMENT AND LAND USE PLANNING

Triggered by serious river floods in 1993 and 1995, which were ascribed to climate change, a new policy document titled Room for Water was presented in 1995, stressing the need to integrate water management with land use planning. The document advocated better preparation for flooding events triggered by climate change by creating more space along riverbanks for water retention as a means of natural flood protection, in contrast to artificial protection in the form of dike fortifications. This new approach could be combined with the water basin concept of 1985, as retention areas provide the opportunity for natural and ecological restoration of water systems. Moreover, they could help replenish groundwater stocks in order to prevent water depletion during dry periods. Thus the 1995 transition was triggered by international alarm over climate change, the problem of water depletion, as well as the preference to restore the natural flow of rivers and valuable ecosystems along the riverbanks.

Like the 1985 transition, the policy document of 1995 was formalized, introduced as the *Fourth National Policy Memorandum on Water Management* (V&W 1998). In contrast to the previous policy plan of 1989, this plan focused especially on climate change and the restoration of the natural dynamics of water systems. It advocated regarding water and its natural movements as key determining factors in land use decisionmaking and emphasized the value of water in terms of open, unspoiled landscape. In fact, the 1995 and 1998 documents were attempts to achieve the adoption of a principle for the integration between land use decisionmaking and water management: "Where natural water is competing with other claims on the limited remaining space in the Netherlands, space for water should prevail" (Hofstra 1999).

To better understand the 1995 transition, one should consider it in the evolutionary context of river management in the Netherlands going back to the 1950s. The huge flood disaster of 1953 in the province of Zeeland resulted in the Delta Plan (see Chapter 1) for flood prevention, along not only the coasts, but also the main rivers. When the implementation of the Delta Plan started in the 1960s, the extensive and irreversible landscape interventions along the rivers attracted increasing criticism from inhabitants of the river areas. As a consequence, a state commission concluded in 1975 that procedures for gaining support from citizens and allowing their participation should be better incorporated in the decisionmaking process concerning dike enhancement. During the 1980s, however, the recommendations of the state commission remained unimplemented, and ongoing dike fortifications were often debated in court. Valuable pieces of landscape and authentic cultivation along the rivers disappeared, due to the size dimensions applied by the state water authority for strengthening river dikes. In 1993, triggered by political pressure to reconsider the dike fortification program, another state commission recommended incorporating landscape, nature, and cultural heritage values into the decisionmaking process, in addition to safety aspects. Such a broader deliberation of interests was in line with the integrated water system approach adopted in 1985. This state commission was asked again to advise on how to continue dike reinforcement along the Meuse River when this became a question after heavy flooding in 1993. One year later, the commission recommended enlarging and deepening the river basin in combination with the natural development of floodplains and restoration of the river dynamics. In fact, this advice has been the basis for a fundamental rethinking of river management at a national scale (Heegstra 1999).

The threat of dikes bursting in December 1993 and again in January 1995 drew a response at the national level in the form of the Main Rivers Delta Plan in 1995, in addition to the policy document Space for Water. This Delta Plan had several goals. First was to speed up reinforcement of the remaining weak spots in the dike infrastructure along the main rivers, by means of an emergency act called Delta Act Large Rivers (Deltawet Grote Rivieren). This approach was successful, as all dike improvement works were completed within two years. Second, the plan aimed to accelerate the adoption of the Act on Flood Protection (Wet op de Waterkering), which had been delayed since the 1980s because of a political debate over which values should prevail in dike fortification projects. In 1996, this act was adopted, by which Parliament agreed to a system of better safety norms and improved participation rights for citizens. Third, the plan introduced a new approach to river management, which was effectuated that same year with the presentation of the policy document Room for the River (see Chapter 10). This document strongly suggested that the concept of "space for the river" be a guiding principle in land use planning along the riverbanks: construction of housing and other economic activities in floodplains should be avoided in principle (Heegstra 1999; Hofstra 1999).

In the fall of 1998, the Netherlands had to deal with a high amount of rainfall, necessitating the inundation of polders to prevent dike bursts close to cities and villages. High water levels in the IJsselmeer and other estuaries hampered the clearance capacity of the Dutch drainage infrastructure. This situation, which is typical of a delta area such as the Netherlands, brought an acute awareness that a rising sea level in combination with extreme rainfall pressure, both attributed to climate change, would create dangerous inundation risks. It has been the basis for broad political consensus that integrated river management (integrated in the sense of sustainable flood protection) should have high political priority, which has been a definite breakthrough. The state decided to amend both the River Management Act, broadening its jurisdiction with respect to the expropriation of floodplain grounds, and the Physical Planning Decree (Article 10), requiring that local land use plans must always be assessed by the regional water board on water risks before they can be adopted.

Further, a state commission on 21st-century water management was asked to advise on how to institutionalize integrated river management. When this commission reported in 2000, it recommended creating titles to expropriate and limit land use rights in floodplains, as well as dividing the liability for flood damage among the national and regional water authorities and private property owners. Water boards could avoid such liability by developing sufficient areas for water retention, based on a system of safety norms that determined what the storage capacity in a region should be (Commissie WB21).

Despite the many integration attempts, water management is still highly complex and fragmented. This renders decisionmaking rather difficult, especially at the level of the water boards and municipalities: the former consider water as a guiding principle in spatial planning and prefer to leave areas undeveloped if a risk of inundation exists, whereas the latter have an interest in economic and urban expansion within their geographical boundaries and the final say in spatial planning.

CONCLUSIONS

In the evolution of Dutch water governance, three major aspects played a role the entire time. First has been the constant problem the Netherlands faces related to its position at the sea edge in a low-lying area, with large parts of the country below sea level, and also as the delta for four European rivers, the Rhine, Meuse, Scheldt, and Ems. The need to protect the land from high water from the rivers and sea along with the tradition of artificially draining low-lying areas have led the country to develop a complex hydraulic infrastructure. Through the ages, the flow and level of almost every water body in the country have been subject to human control.

The second aspect concerns the water board tradition in the Netherlands. Since 1798, a form of cogovernance between national and regional water authorities has developed. Despite a constant tendency toward centralization, the water boards succeeded in maintaining a position in regional water management. Meanwhile, water management became professionalized not only at the national level, but also at the regional level, where the early small-scale water boards for drainage and flood protection transformed into "all-in" water boards dealing with tributary water basins. The number of water boards decreased from 2,700 in 1900 to 27 in 2007. The flood disasters of 1916 and 1953 provided a powerful impetus for small water boards to merge into larger organizations, as several river floods had done in the 19th century. The professionalization of regional water management, strongly encouraged by the central state from the 1960s on, also resulted in mergers. The transitions of 1968 (introducing water planning), 1969 (introducing water quality management), and 1985 (introducing the ecology-based water system approach) have professionalized the water boards and strengthened their position in water management. Water boards appear to have been effective organizations for the implementation of national water policies, while also successfully shouldering the responsibility for regional water management.

Since the 1980s, the cogoverning position of water boards in the Dutch administrative structure has been recognized by the revised constitution of 1983 and the Water Boards Act of 1992, which both approve the water boards as being of essential interest to a country that is living with flood risks over large parts of its area. The taxation system of water boards has given the Netherlands a tradition of water services based on full cost recovery charges, which corresponds with the idea of the EU Water Framework Directive (WFD) "to get the prices of water services right" (Andersen 1999; Hahn 1995; Kuks 2006). The democratic and participatory structure of water boards corresponds with the idea of the WFD "to get all users involved." A complication that regional water boards increasingly face, however, is that they depend on provinces and municipalities as physical planning authorities. In order to get water visions adopted as a guiding principle for physical planning, a complicated process of mutual consultation and cooperation is required. In other words, a lack of understanding between the administrative organizations of water management and physical planning is complicating water governance.

The third major aspect in the evolution of Dutch water governance has been the public debate on the effects of large waterworks and the need to take rival interests into account. Already in the 19th century, provisions were created to compensate citizens not only in cases of expropriation, but also where private properties were disadvantaged by public waterworks. During the 20h century, more and more legal provisions for compensation were added. Some legal provisions were adopted in the 1960s for a better deliberation of interests in order to prevent the exhaustion of specific types of natural resources. In the 1970s, public protests against the classical water engineering approach by Rijkswaterstaat politicized water management and initiated a debate in society over various water values. Since then, spatial planning has been used as an instrument to deal with rival interests in case of large infrastructural water works. Not only spatial planning was important; the water management sector also developed its own planning instruments. The Netherlands has had a tradition of national water policy plans, which started out being sectoral plans mainly focusing on water quantity issues (1968, 1984) but later became integrated plans (1989, 1998). Planning is used as an instrument for policy coordination between the higher and lower administrative levels (vertical integration), as well as among policy sectors (water, environmental, nature, and spatial planning) at the same administrative level (horizontal integration). The functioning of the Netherlands as a decentralized unitary state is based to a great degree on coordination by planning.

REFERENCES

Andersen, M.S. 1999. Governance by green taxes: Implementing clean water policies in Europe, 1970-1990. *Environmental Economics and Policy Studies* 2:39–63.

Bosch, A. 2001. Politiek-bestuurlijke aspecten van centrale waterstaatszorg 1798–1849 [Political-administrative aspects of central water management 1798–1849]). *Openbaar bestuur [Public administration]* 11:7–10.

Brainich von Brainich-Felth, C.H. 1993. Centralisatie en Waterschapswetgeving [Centralization and waterboard legislation]. In *Waterschappen in Nederland. Een bestuurskundige verkenning van de institutionele ontwikkeling [Water boards in the Netherlands. A public administrative exploration of the institutional development]*, ed. J.C.N. Raadschelders and Th.A.J. Toonen, 107–31. Hilversum, Netherlands: Verloren.

Bressers, J.Th.A. 1983. *Beleidseffectiviteit en waterkwaliteitsbeleid. Een bestuurskundig onderzoek* [*Policy effectiveness and water quality policy. A public administrative study*]. Enschede, Netherlands: University of Twente.

Commissie WB21 (Commissie Waterbeheer 21e eeuw). 2000. *Waterbeleid voor de 21e eeuw: Geef water de ruimte en de aandacht die het verdient* [*Water policy for the 21st century: Give water the space and attention it deserves*]. The Hague: Commissie WB21.

Disco, C. 1998. Waterstaat [Water state]. In *Techniek in Nederland in de Twintigste Eeuw*, Deel I [*Technology in the Netherlands in the Twentieth Century*, Part I], ed. J.W. Schot et al., 52–207. Zutphen, Netherlands: Walburg Pers.

Grijns, L.C., and J. Wisserhof. 1992. *Ontwikkelingen in Integraal Waterbeheer. Verkenning van beleid, beheer en onderzoek* [*Developments in integral water management: Exploration of policy, management and research*]. Delft, Netherlands: Delft University Press.

Hahn, R.W. 1995. Economic prescriptions for environmental problems: Lessons from the United States and Continental Europe. In *Markets, the state and the environment: Towards integration*, ed. R. Eckersley, 129–56. Melbourne, Australia: Macmillan.

Heegstra, H.G. 1999. Verleden, heden en toekomst van het rivierbeheer [Past, present and future of river management]. In *de Staat van Water. Opstellen over juridische, technische, financiele en politiek-bestuurlijke aspecten van waterbeheer* [*The state of water. Essays on judicial, technological, financial and political-administrative aspects of water management*], ed. A. van Hall et al., 55–66. Lelystad, Netherlands: Koninklijke Vermande.

Hofstra, M.A. 1999. De *Vierde nota waterhuishouding* en de *Vijfde nota ruimtelijke ordening*. Verbanden in planvorming en integratie van beleid [The *Fourth National Policy Memorandum on Water Management* and the *Fifth National Policy Memorandum on Spatial Planning*. Relations in planning and policy integration]. In *de Staat van Water. Opstellen over juridische, technische, financiele en politiek-bestuurlijke aspecten van waterbeheer* [*The state of water. Essays on judicial, technological, financial and political-administrative aspects of water management*], ed. A. van Hall et al., 77–89. Lelystad, Netherlands: Koninklijke Vermande.

IJff, J. 1993. Omwentelingen in het waterschapsbestel 1968–1993 [Transitions in the water board sector 1968–1993]. In *Waterschappen in Nederland. Een bestuurskundige verkenning van de institutionele ontwikkeling* [*Water boards in the Netherlands. A public administrative exploration of the institutional development*], ed. J.C.N. Raadschelders and Th.A.J. Toonen, 13–29. Hilversum, Netherlands: Verloren.

Kuks, S.M.M. 2006. The privatization debate on water services in the Netherlands: Public performance of the water sector and the implications of market forces. *Water Policy* 8:147–69.

Leemhuis-Stout, J.M. 1992. Twintig jaren (regionaal) waterkwaliteitsbeheer [Twenty years of (regional) water quality management]. In *Waterstaatswetgeving. Verleden, heden en toekomst. Bundel ter gelegenheid van het honderdjarig bestaan van de Staatscommissie voor de Waterstaatswetgeving* [*Water legislation. Past, present and future. Essays on the occasion of the hundredth anniversary of the State Commission for Water Legislation*], ed. S.B. Boelens, Th.G. Drupsteen, H. van der Linden, P.J. de Loor, and J.J.I. Verburg, 183–96. Zwolle, Netherlands: W.E.J. Tjeenk Willink.

Rijkswaterstaat. 1968. *De Waterhuishouding van Nederland (Eerste nota Waterhuishouding)* [*First National Policy Memorandum on Water Management*]. The Hague: Staatsuitgeverij.

Schorer, K.F.H. 1993. Het waterschapsbestel 1958–1993 [The water board sector 1958–1993]. In *de waterstaatszorg in Nederland. Verankerd in het verleden, flexibel naar de toekomst* [*Watermanagement in the Netherlands. Settled in the past, flexible regarding the future*], ed. M. Snijdelaar et al., 55–72. The Hague: VUGA.

Snijdelaar, M. 1993. Ontwikkelingen in de waterstaatszorg vanaf de jaren vijftig [Developments in water management since the 1950s]. In *de waterstaatszorg in Nederland. Verankerd in het verleden, flexibel naar de toekomst* [*Water management in the Netherlands. Settled in the past, flexible regarding the future*], ed. M. Snijdelaar et al., 9–35. The Hague: VUGA.

Teeuwen, H.H.A., J.H. Dronkers, and J.B. Dijkstra. 1993. Omgaan met de brede kijk door waterschappen [Dealing with the broad scope at water boards]. In *de waterstaatszorg in Nederland. Verankerd in het verleden, flexibel naar de toekomst* [*Water management in the Netherlands. Settled in the past, flexible regarding the future*], ed. M. Snijdelaar et al., 37–54. The Hague: VUGA.

V&W. 1984. *Tweede nota Waterhuishouding* [*Second National Policy Memorandum on Water Management*]. The Hague: Staatsuitgeverij, Ministry of Transport, Public Works and Water Management.

―――. 1989. *Derde nota Waterhuishouding* [*Third National Policy Memorandum on Water Management*]. The Hague: Ministry of Transport, Public Works and Water Management.

―――. 1998. *Vierde nota Waterhuishouding* [*Fourth National Policy Memorandum on Water Management*]. The Hague: Ministry of Transport, Public Works and Water Management.

van der Heide, O. 1992. De bestuurlijke organisatie van de waterstaatszorg [The administrative organization of water management]. In *Waterstaatswetgeving. Verleden, heden en toekomst. Bundel ter gelegenheid van het honderdjarig bestaan van de Staatscommissie voor de Waterstaatswetgeving* [*Water legislation. Past, present and future. Essays on the occasion of the hundredth anniversary of the State Commission for Water Legislation*], ed. S.B. Boelens, Th.G. Drupsteen, H. van der Linden, P.J. de Loor, and J.J.I.Verburg, 93–107. Zwolle, Netherlands: W.E.J. Tjeenk Willink.

van Hall, A. 1992. Naar een samenhangend waterbeheer, bezien vanuit de kwantiteitszorg [Toward more coherent water management, from the perspective of quantity management]. In *Waterstaatswetgeving. Verleden, heden en toekomst. Bundel ter gelegenheid van het honderdjarig bestaan van de Staatscommissie voor de Waterstaatswetgeving* [*Water legislation. Past, present and future. Essays on the occasion of the hundredth anniversary of the State Commission for Water Legislation*], ed. S.B. Boelens, Th.G. Drupsteen, H. van der Linden, P.J. de Loor, and J.J.I.Verburg, 155–82. Zwolle, Netherlands: W.E.J. Tjeenk Willink.

CHAPTER 9

Governance of Water Resources

Wim van Leussen and Kris Lulofs

*W*ATER MANAGEMENT in the Netherlands is highly consensus based, which seems to be rooted in the decisionmaking process associated with water resources in the polders since the Middle Ages. At that time, such decisions were made by the water boards, democratic stakeholder organizations consisting of elected representatives from the local communities (see Chapter 8). This decision-making system has continued for many centuries and still characterizes present-day water resource governance in the Netherlands. The mode of governance has varied depending on the specific situation, and several periods with a characteristic management structure can be distinguished.

During the last few decades, policy planning has played a dominant role in the decisionmaking process. Between 1968 and 1998, four consecutive national water policy plans came into force (see Chapter 1 for details). In the late 1980s, the Dutch system of integrated water management was adopted, taking into account the many functions fulfilled by water systems (see Chapter 1). In the Netherlands today, water management follows the guidelines for water quality given in the EU Water Framework Directive, and those for water quantity in the Netherlands' legislation titled Water Management Policy in the 21st Century. The European dimension is of increasing importance for Dutch water management, in accordance with the so-called "catchment approach." A catchment, also called a drainage basin or watershed, is the hydrological area from which the river receives its water. The "catchment approach" refers to an effective management of all relevant components and interactions within such an area, including both the surface water and groundwater, with all the physical, chemical, and biological components, as well as humans and their anthropological impacts.

This chapter provides an overview of the governance of water resources in the Netherlands. It first presents a theoretical framework of the governance concept, then examines the unique general management structure in the Netherlands and looks at its historical development. Water policy and the institutional organization of water management have been affected over the years by changes in the country's socioeconomic and political circumstances, and they have been transformed dramatically in recent decades as their connections with other policy fields are expanding. The international dimension, particularly European, also has been of increasing importance.

Water resources management is functioning in an ever more complex context, with a greater variety of relevant policy fields, a higher number of stakeholders, and dedicated governance structures at the international, national, regional, and local levels. Switching among these levels and coupling them for adequate results is one of the main challenges in water management today, calling for governance approaches that are multilevel, multiactor, and multiresource. The implementation of water policy in light of so many considerations and sometimes conflicting rules is at the heart of present-day water resources management.

THEORETICAL FRAMEWORK

The term "governance" has taken a central place in contemporary debates in the social sciences. A wide variety of definitions and interpretations of this term exist, however: as a set of institutional arrangements in the form of hierarchies, markets, networks, or communities; as a process directed to the outcome of some fields of politics; or as an analytic framework from which more insight can be obtained into the world of politics and government (see Pierre and Peters 2000). For the purposes of our discussion, we define "governance" as the capability of government to make and implement water resource policy, including the whole cycle of preparation, decisionmaking, implementation, and evaluation. The key point is to create an adequate vision and bring it to pass in the real world. This requires a good knowledge of real problems within society and the ability to evaluate the feasibility of proposed solutions. Because society is dynamic, constantly changing over time, the governance process also requires continual updating and adaptation to current circumstances.

For water resources, governance means giving direction to management so that required conditions are met, such as a certain degree of safety against flooding, a good ecological status of the water systems, sustainable development of river basins, or a particular level of resilience. At present, however, more and more objectives are having to be achieved at the same time, involving a greater number of policy fields and stakeholders. These developments make public policy, especially the governance elements, of increasing importance within modern integrated water management (van Leussen 2004), resulting in more complex approaches (Kuks 2004) and many interdependent relationships. The increased complexity is principally caused by the strong linkages between water management and spatial planning, particularly as a consequence of the catchment approach.

More and more, the decisionmaking power of the government, which has the primary responsibility for water resource management, is limited and must be shared with many other important actors in the same policy fields or related ones such as nature conservancy, rural and urban planning, or agriculture. In addition, the boundaries of the catchments often do not coincide with political boundaries, which makes decisionmaking regarding measures and activities in the catchment still more difficult— all the more so when river basins or catchments cross international boundaries.

After making decisions in such a complex policy field, often the process starts again, involving some new actors, further decisions, and discussions of additional opportunities (Teisman 2005). This seems to be characteristic of present-day water resource management on a river basin scale. Effective governance, trying to reach agreed targets, requires novel concepts of leadership that are not tied to power and position, but are centered on collaboration among many actors. It represents a shift from the more rigid and controlling image associated with traditional leadership to a new paradigm based on autonomy, flexibility, creativity, and responsibility (Denhardt 1993). This type of leadership is an art amid a complex field involving many stakeholders and preferences, various actors with more or less power, consideration of socioeconomic balances, and existing laws and regulations.

Kooiman (2002) attributed the increasing interest for governance to a growing awareness that governments are not the only crucial actors in addressing major societal problems, traditional and new modes of government-society interactions are needed to tackle these issues, governing arrangements and mechanisms will differ among levels of society and vary by sector, and concomitantly, many governance issues are interdependent or become linked. To analyze the governing interactions, Kooiman (2000) distinguished three modes of governance:

- *Hierarchical governance* is characterized by command and control. Rights and duties are organized according to superordinate and subordinate responsibilities and tasks. Sociopolitical interventions are generally performed by means of laws, regulations, and policies. Developments in a specific policy field and the activities of the actors are goal-directed, influenced by one central governing organization.
- *Cogovernance* involves the cooperation, coordination, and communication of the various actors. Usually, some kind of formal organizational arrangement exists. The actors are aware of the need to reach some objective and generally know that it can be met effectively through the cooperation of all involved. Governance is done by complex networks of various actors, such as governmental agencies, nongovernmental organizations, and private groups. Kickert et al. (1997) defined such networks as more or less stable patterns of social relations among interdependent actors, which take shape around policy problems or programs.
- *Self-governance* refers to the capacity of the engaged actors to govern themselves with a high degree of autonomy.

Water governance occurs within the political-administrative system of the Netherlands, which is a decentralized unitary state combining centralized, hierarchical control by the central government with delegation of authority to the regional and local governments of provinces and municipalities. The water boards fulfill a special role as a "functional government" (see Chapter 8). They are responsible for the management of both the quantity and quality of the surface waters in their regions. Currently, 27 water boards are active in the Netherlands. They have a democratic structure with their own elections and taxation authority. The general council of a water board comprises representatives of several groups: farmers, landowners, owners of buildings, industries, and inhabitants.

At the level of the central government, water policies are coordinated by the Ministry of Transport, Public Works and Water Management, but the policies for drinking water and standards for water quality are in the hands of the Ministry of Housing, Spatial Planning and the Environment. For aspects of water management related to agriculture and nature conservation, the Ministry of Agriculture, Nature Management and Food Safety has special responsibility. This means that integrated water management requires an increased cooperation among a number of ministries. The overall coordination of water management is the duty of the Ministry of Transport, Public Works and Water Management.

The Netherlands has a tradition of government consultation with various groups in society. The national water policy generally results from intensive deliberations among the responsible ministry, related ministries, and representative organizations of the subnational authorities: the Association of the Provinces of the Netherlands (IPO), Association of Water Boards (UvW), and Association of Netherlands Municipalities (VNG). Each of these organizations has its own bureaucracies. The decisionmaking process is strongly consensus based, which means that decisions are negotiated among the leaders of the authorities. In this approach, the decisionmaking process is more an example of governance than government. The move from government to governance that is now observed in many other countries has a long history in the Netherlands (Andeweg and Irwin 2005).

THE NETHERLANDS

The very existence of the Netherlands has been based on a continuous struggle to manage water over the centuries (see Chapter 1), and the country therefore sometimes is called "Waterland." In *Searching for the Fundamentals in Dutch History*, Verwey (1980) shows how Dutch culture is interwoven with water. From the point of view of water resource governance, three main periods can be distinguished:

* Local and regional water management (1200–1798)
* Centrally guided water management (1798–2000)
* EU-directed water management (2000–present)

Each of these main periods saw a variety of institutional developments. Before 1200, most people lived in small settlements in rural areas. Such a community grouped around a chief farm or court owned by nobility or the church. For defense against floods, primitive dikes with hydraulic structures were built, or people lived on higher ground. The landowners had to maintain the hydraulic structures, and local administration supervises the maintenance.

Local and Regional Water Management, 1200–1798

This period was characterized by intense battles with flooding from both the sea and the major rivers. Dikes were built, and large areas of land were reclaimed from the water and transformed into productive agricultural regions. In the 13th century, the first democratic district water boards were established, consisting of elected representatives from local farming communities. (See Chapter 8 for an overview of the institutional evolution of water boards.) The *water boards* had the task of caring for the dikes, locks, sluices, and dams, as well as the management of water in specific areas. In the 15th century, the creation of polders expanded enormously, when windmills were used to drain off the surplus water from hundreds of hectares of land into higher drainage canals and river stretches. *Polder boards* were established, with the responsibility for the maintenance of the windmills, the access watercourses to these windmills, and the low embankments surrounding the polders. The boundaries of a mill polder did not always correspond with those of the local territories; some polders consisted of several local communities, others of only part of one.

Centrally Guided Water Management, 1798–2000

The Batavian-French period (1795–1813) marked the beginning of modern times in the Netherlands in a number of respects. Freedom of religion, equity of the law, land registry, and other foundations of modern society are rooted in this period. An important achievement was the development of a national administration. This service not only had a role in the field of water management, but also was responsible for the national roads. In 1798, a bureau was set up for these tasks: the *Rijkswaterstaat* (Bosch and van der Ham 1998). This state department became the leading agency for the large-scale construction of a flood protection infrastructure, consisting of dikes along the shores and main rivers, as well as for extensive land reclamation projects. The result was a high degree of safety against flooding, and new aspects of water management were also introduced, including water quality, ecological aspects, nature conservation, and landscape development. Over this period, water management became increasingly connected to other policy fields, such as spatial planning, agriculture, and recreation, and the public policy aspects grew in importance.

EU-Directed Water Management, 21st Century

Water management in the 21st century is strongly influenced by European water policy and law, which began in the 20th century as part of the European policy for the environment. Water legislation was one of the first sectors to be covered by EU environmental policy. Since the early 1970s, water protection has been a subject of rising concern. The period 1973–1990 focused on the protection of water used for human activities. Environmental quality standards (EQS) were specified in a number of directives, such as the Surface Water Directive (1975), Dangerous Substances Directive (1976), and Drinking Water Directive (1980). The next period, 1991–1998, focused more on limiting certain diffuse and point-source emissions. The eutrophication of waters, caused by an abundance of nitrates and phosphates, received particular attention. One of the biggest problems for future water protection, however, is that no directive has been completely implemented and applied by the member states. An example is the Nitrate Directive, which most European countries had problems implementing. The reduction of diffuse pollution and required changes in agricultural production created far more difficulties than the control of the easily identifiable sources of urban wastewater pollution.

Pressure for a fundamental rethinking of EU water policy came to a head in mid-1995. The European Commission, which had already been considering the need for a more global approach to water policy, accepted requests from the European Parliament's Environmental Committee and the Council of Environmental Ministers. The commission agreed to produce a framework for water policy and, if appropriate, make a legislative proposal to ensure the overall consistency of water policy. Draft legislation was circulated in 1996, and amendments were processed in 1997 and 1998. The final text was adopted in October 2000, and the Water Framework Directive (WFD) came into force in December of that year. The directive's overriding requirement is that the member states ensure that a good chemical and ecological status is achieved in all European waters by the end of 2015 (see Chapter 11 for more details on the WFD).

Historical Governance Structure

The modes of water resource governance were quite different in these periods. During the period 1200–1798, the water and polder boards had a form of self-governance, being responsible for defense against flooding for local areas, surrounded by dikes. In the period 1798–2000, the water resource governance could be characterized as hierarchical, where national administrations became more and more powerful. At present, especially because of the catchment approach, water resource governance is shifting to a form of cogovernance, in which an increasing number of relevant stakeholders must cooperate to define and reach the agreed objectives. In actual practice, governance often has been more a mix of the theoretical modes. One could conclude that each period needed and received its own specific governance structure.

THE EUROPEAN DIMENSION

The Netherlands is situated in the delta of four major rivers, with the larger part of all their catchments outside the country. The rivers' quantity (discharge and water levels), quality (pollution), and ecological functioning (biodiversity) within the Netherlands is strongly dependent on what is happening in the neighboring countries, and thus the European, or international, dimension has been of eminent importance in Dutch water management for a long time. Cooperation across borders operates at three levels: EU-directed water management; international cooperation on border-crossing rivers; and bilateral cooperation at the local and regional scales.

EU-Directed Water Management

The European countries' water management policies are more and more directed by EU policy frameworks and guidelines. During recent decades, a number of EU directives in relation to water policy came into force, all with the intention of improving water quality and preventing further deterioration. Although these directives are important milestones in the development of a European water policy, and considerable progress has been made on specific issues, in the mid-1990s it was agreed that this approach was too fragmented. Europe needed a more coherent water policy and greater involvement of its citizens.

The Water Framework Directive came into force in December 2000 (EC 2000). In January 2006, the European Commission proposed a directive on the assessment and management of floods (EC 2006), which came into force in December 2007. The objective of this EU Floods Directive is to reduce and manage the risks of floods pose to human health, the environment, infrastructure, and property. The background is that between 1998 and 2004, Europe suffered more than 100 major damaging floods, including catastrophic ones along the Danube and Elbe rivers in the summer of 2002. Severe floods in 2005 further reinforced the need for concerted action. The directive provides for flood mapping in all areas with significant risk. It calls for flood risk management plans to be produced for these regions, with appropriate levels of protection specified, focusing on the reduction of the probability of flooding and the potential consequences to human health, the environment, and economic activity, and taking into account relevant aspects: water management, soil management, spatial planning, land use, and nature conservation. Although the Floods Directive is not as far-reaching as the WFD and gives the member states considerable flexibility in determining the level of protection required, it is an important step toward solving the flood problems on the river basin scale.

International Cooperation on Border-Crossing Rivers

Transboundary cooperation related to international border-crossing rivers has already existed for some time. This is the case for all four major Netherlands rivers—the Rhine, Meuse, Scheldt, and Ems—although the most progress in jointly solving problems has been made for the Rhine. The first international contacts regarding the water quality of the Rhine date from the 19th century. The earliest mutually experienced problems were navigational and shipping issues and a decline in the salmon population. Environmental problems followed and, more recently, the need for collaboration on the protection against floods (see Chapter 1 and Dieperink and Glasbergen 1999 for examples). The International Rhine Commission (IRC) and International Meuse Commission (IMC) have been actively working for improvement of water quality and reduction of flooding frequency. Although the most important progress has been made after emergency situations caused by an extreme flood or dangerous pollution event, these river commissions have been effective organizations through which important improvements were achieved.

Bilateral Cooperation at the Local and Regional Scales

Transboundary water management also occurs at the smaller regional and local scales, where the cooperation and exchange of information mainly take place in border-crossing catchment or subcatchment committees. For cooperation between the Netherlands and Germany, the Permanent Dutch-German Boundary Waters Committee (PGC) was created, under which seven subcommittees are active. They were installed in 1963 and exchange information on river discharges, flood prevention, protection against pollution, and ecological developments. At the boundary between the Netherlands and Flanders, Belgium, four subcommittees are active: Thornerbeek-Jeker-Voer, Dommel, Mark and Merkske, and Kreken and Polders. At the boundary with Walloon, Belgium, a subcommittee for the Geul River was installed in 1996.

Bilateral cooperation for the implementation of the EU Water Framework Directive on these smaller scales generally occurs in ad hoc working groups. At the working level, this functions well. At the political level, however, an essential governance problem arises out of differences in the countries' institutional structures, particularly when one is a unitary state and the other a federal state. Often competent authorities from one country do not have counterparts at the same hierarchical level in another. Because of these differences, the discussions on coordination, problems to be solved, or potential future conflicts become more complex. Nevertheless, the Netherlands and the federal states Nordrhine-Westphalia and Lower Saxony in Germany have made progress in implementing the WFD for the river basin district Rhinedelta, the most downstream region of the Rhine basin, through intense bilateral cooperation, showing that this form of transboundary water management can be successful (van Leussen et al. 2007).

INSTITUTIONAL STRUCTURE

Up to present, the governance system of water management in the Netherlands can be defined as multilevel governance system with a relatively high degree of decentralization. Ministries operate at the national level, provinces (a total of 12) and water boards (27) at the regional level, and municipalities (443) at the local level. From a historical perspective, provinces, water boards, and municipalities have had a rather autonomous jurisdiction. Since World War II, however, their autonomy has been increasingly framed by a model of close cooperation with the central government, in which the central government takes the initiative in policymaking, and noncentral authorities cooperate by additional policymaking and implementation within the national policy frames. Provinces and municipalities even depend on subsidies from the national budget. Water boards, on the other hand, cannot rely on such subsidies and have to fully finance their activities by their own taxation. A typical Dutch feature is the long tradition of government consultation with various groups in society, known as the polder model. Table 9-1 shows schematically the institutional structure of water management in the Netherlands.

Working according to the catchment or river basin approach on the basis of European directives with strict deadlines has added new dimensions to the existing institutional structure. The national, regional, and local water policies now need to adhere to European regulations and thus be developed within the guidelines of this set of legislative rules. The complexity of this process increases all the more

Table 9-1 *Multilevel governance structure for water management in the Netherlands*

Governance level	Authority	Planning documents
International	European Union (EU)	Water Framework Directive Bathing Water Directive Drinking Water Directive Several other directives dealing with water, air, waste, and nature protection
	River Basin Commissions (IRC, IMC, and others)	Rhine Action Plan Meuse Action Plan Other plans
National	Ministry of Transport, Public Works and Water Management	National Policy Document on Water Management
	Ministry of Housing, Physical Planning and Environment	National Environmental Policy Plan
	Ministry of Agriculture, Nature and Food Safety	Policy Plans for Agricultural Development (e.g., Nitrate Policy) National Policy Plan for Nature Development
Regional	Provinces	Provincial Environmental Policy Plan Provincial Water Management plan
	Water boards	Water Management Plan of Water Board (quantitative and qualitative)
Local	Municipalities	Municipal Development Plan Municipal Sewerage Plan

when catchment boundaries are not the same as the political boundaries, which is almost always the case. In the Netherlands, this problem has been solved by dividing the country into four river basin districts—the Rhine, Meuse, Scheldt, and Ems—and further splitting up the Rhine area into four subcatchments. This created seven river subbasins, for each of which consultative committees were installed at the political, professional, and working levels. An analogous structure has been established at the national level. In this way, the institutional organization for the implementation of the WFD has been split up into national and regional hierarchies, as summarized in table 9-2.

Good communication between these hierarchies is critical for effective and efficient implementation of the WFD. River basin coordinators have an intermediary task in each of their districts. The final national decisions are made by the National Committee of Governors (LBOW), although the ultimate responsibility rests with the minister of Transport, Public Works and Water Management, who is also the chairman of the LBOW. Each of the seven Regional Committees of Governors (RBOs) engages in collaborative decisionmaking at the regional scale, although the final responsibility remains with the regional governments and boards of governors: the provinces and water boards, and the municipalities for local decisions.

Table 9-2 *Collaborative governance structure for the implementation of the WFD*

	National hierarchy		Regional hierarchy	
Political level	National Committee of Governors (LBOW)	Agreements on national policy and guidelines	Regional Committee of Governors (RBO)	Agreements on regional management plans for the river basin district
Professional level	Strategy Group (RG)	Framing the national guidelines	Regional Committee of Water Professionals (RAO)	Preparing regional river basin management plans
Working level	Working Group (WG)	Proposals for typology, reference conditions, economic analysis, and so on	Regional Working Groups (RWGs)	Regional determinations of pressures, characteristics of water bodies, economic analysis, monitoring, and so on

Thus the basic responsibilities of the governing institutions did not change, but the interdependency and collaboration among them increased significantly.

Another result of the implementation of the WFD is that because of the European legislation, public participation has a larger role in determining the water agenda. At the national level, representatives of nongovernmental groups are consulted in a deliberative platform called the Consultative Committee for Water Management and North Sea Affairs (OWN). Much attention is given by the national government to supplying information to the general public in a campaign called *Nederland leeft met water* (The Netherlands is living with water), with its own website (www.nederlandleeftmetwater.nl). At the regional scale, comparable deliberative platforms are active, giving their input to the RBOs. To prepare the real implementation at the regional and local scale, discussions on objectives and measures happen in more or less informal groups in smaller areas, for example water bodies or groups of water bodies, in which water boards, municipalities, and representatives of local target groups consider the alternatives and look for optimal solutions. An example is the regional water management plans for subbasins of the river basin district Eems in the northeastern part of the Netherlands. As part of the project Water Carrier (Waterdrager), all relevant stakeholders work out the regional catchment and subcatchment plans jointly on the basis of a regional water covenant. These integrated water management plans include flood management, water quality in accordance with the WFD, water scarcity management, anticipation of climate change, and bottom subsidence. (Meijer 2004; Meijer and Hartman 2006; PWW 2006; also see Chapter 12 for more information on public participation).

FINANCING MECHANISMS

The Netherlands spends about 5 billion euros each year on water resource management. This includes maintaining state and nonstate waterways, harbors, dikes and seawalls, and dunes; managing surface water and groundwater quality and quantity; and operating water treatment plants and sewage systems. Roughly half of the money is spent by water boards, about a quarter each by the state and municipalities, and a tiny fraction by provinces.

At the national level, almost all spending of the state Directorate General for Public Works and Water Management (DG Water) comes out of the general state budget. A small part, about 3%, is covered by collecting pollution fees from companies and water boards for emitting polluted water into state waters, according to the "polluter pays" principle. (Water boards normally pay for the effluents from waste water treatment plants into state waters.)

Because the 12 provinces take care of the interpretation and application of national water policies in their regional context, creation and termination of water boards, and supervision of policy implementation by water boards, almost all water activities of the provinces are paid out of the state budget. Technically, this is done by adding money to the Province Fund (Huisman 2002). The autonomous provincial tax base includes a levy on the extraction of groundwater, but this brings in little money—on average, about 1 million euros annually per province. The general state budget is charged for about 92% of the water management spending of the provinces; only about 8% is covered by the groundwater tax.

Water boards usually are responsible for local and regional water management, which in most cases includes flood protection and wastewater treatment. They have a substantial autonomous tax base. Citizens and companies normally have to pay two taxes to finance quantitative and qualitative water management. The tax for quantitative water management is subdivided into an inhabitant's tax, paid by every main tenant within the working area of the water board; and a property tax, paid by owners of land and estates, and calculated on the basis of the land's surface area and the economic value of any buildings. The tax for qualitative water management is paid by households, farms, and businesses that contribute to wastewater pollution by discharging oxygen-consuming substances, heavy metals, chlorides, sulfates, or phosphates. For practical reasons, measurement is not mandatory unless maximum amounts of pollution per category are exceeded; otherwise, standard categories apply (Bressers and Lulofs 2004; Huisman 2002). The pollution fee covers about two-thirds of the total expenditures of the water boards, and the inhabitant's and property taxes about one-third.

The final level of regional water management is the municipalities, which are responsible for collecting wastewater—in other words, managing the sewage system. In urban areas, this includes management of rainwater that enters the sewage system. Roughly 90% of the municipalities' expenditures are covered by a sewage tax. A few municipalities choose to raise their revenue differently, charging a local real estate tax. Most municipalities use the sewage tax, however, because of the desire for a close, clear, and transparent relationship between taxing and spending.

In addition to all these structural financing mechanisms, sometimes the state makes special one-time disbursements. For instance, for the implementation of the Water Policy for the 21st Century (Commissie WB21 2000), DG Water contributed 100 million euros to the regional water managers to expedite the negotiation process between central and noncentral governments for 310 flooding projects by 43 municipalities and 23 water boards. These projects started in 2004 and will end in 2010 (TK 2005–2006, *20*).

Total expenditures for water resource management have steadily risen from about 3.2 billion euros in 1998 to 4.8 billion in 2005 (Huisman 2002; LBOW 2006). Table 9-3 shows the breakdown of expenditures for water resource management tasks in 2005 in million euros.

For a Dutch household, the price of water can be calculated. In 2005, a household paid an average of 700 euros for all indicated water resource management costs. This total expenditure consisted of 124 euros for the municipal sewage tax, 193 euros for the two taxes paid to the water board, 210 euros collected by the general national tax system, and 173 euros to the drinking-water companies (LOBW 2006).

CONCLUSIONS

Water resource management in the Netherlands dates back to about 1200, with a long period of self-governance. This was followed by a period of hierarchical governance, or centrally guided water management, with different governance structures at the various political levels. The Dutch decentralized unitary state combined centralized hierarchical control with delegation of authority to regional and local governments. Ministries operate at the national level, provinces and water boards at the regional level, and municipalities at the local level. The national government takes the initiative in policymaking, and noncentral authorities cooperate by additional policymaking and implementation within the national policy frames. A typical Dutch feature is the long tradition of governance in consultation with various stakeholder groups in society, known as the polder model.

In the 21st century, the Netherlands' water management policies are increasingly directed by EU policy and guidelines. One aspect that has received more attention is the catchment approach. This was already an essential element in the

Table **9-3** *Public water management expenditures in 2005 (in million euros)*

	Flood protection	Water management		Total	%
		Quantity	Quality		
State	397	823		1,220	26.5
Province	113	37		150	3.1
Water boards	190	700	1,425	2,315	48.4
Municipalities		1,100		1,100	23.0
Total	700	4,085		4,785	100.0

Source: Calculations based on LBOW 2006.

Fourth National Policy Memorandum on Water Management (1998). Because the greater part of the catchments of all major rivers in the Netherlands are situated in other countries, however, Dutch water management was directed primarily toward the delta. Today, however, problem solving on the scale of the whole catchment has a high priority. This means increasing collaboration with other countries as well as other policy fields such as spatial planning, agriculture, nature development, and recreation. This period of water resource management can be characterized as one of cogovernance, but within the typical Dutch institutional structure, where decisionmaking is based on consensus. All relevant stakeholders are actively involved at the local level and relatively small regional scales. At the national level, enabling public participation takes the form of providing information and meeting for consultations at prescribed times.

The big challenge for the Netherlands in the coming years, from a governance point of view, will be to bridge the gap between the formal institutional structure (table 9-1) and informal collaborative structure (table 9-2). Fairly soon, in order to meet the criteria of the EU directives, integrated water management (water quality *and* flood management) will be on the agenda of all informal committees of governors, whereas the governments at the national (state), regional (provinces and water boards), and local (municipalities) levels will still be responsible for the official legal decisionmaking. Dealing with this governance problem will be particularly essential in the implementation stage, when measures must be agreed on and carried out before stringent deadlines.

REFERENCES

Andeweg, R.B., and G.A. Irwin. 2005. *Governance and politics of the Netherlands.* 2nd ed. New York: Palgrave Macmillan.

Bosch, A., and W. van der Ham. 1998. *Twee eeuwen Rijkswaterstaat 1798–1998* [*Two centuries Rijkswaterstaat 1798–1998*]. Zaltbommel, Netherlands: Europese Bibliotheek.

Bressers, J.Th.A., and K.R.D. Lulofs. 2004. Industrial water pollution in the Netherlands: A fee-based approach. In *Choosing environmental policy: Comparing instruments and outcomes in the United States and Europe,* ed. W. Harrington, R.D. Morgenstern, and T. Sterner, 91–116. Washington, DC: Resources for the Future Press.

Commissie WB21 (Commissie Waterbeheer 21e eeuw). 2000. *Waterbeleid voor de 21e eeuw: Geef water de ruimte en de aandacht die het verdient.* [Water policy for the 21st century: Give water the space and attention it deserves]. The Hague, Netherlands: Commissie WB21.

Denhardt, R.B. 1993. *The pursuit of significance: Strategies for managerial success in public organizations.* Prospect Heights, IL: Waveland Press.

Dieperink, C., and P. Glasbergen. 1999. Het beheer van onze internationale rivieren: lessen uit de ontwikkeling van de Rijn-, Maas- en Scheldecommissie [The management of our international rivers: Lessons from the development of the international Rhine, Meuse and Scheldt Commissions]. In *de staat van water. Opstellen over juridische, technische, financiële en politiek-bestuurlijke aspecten van waterbeheer,* ed. by A. van Hall, Th.G. Drupsteen, and H.J.M. Havekes, 43–54. Lelystad, Netherlands: Koninklijke Vermande.

EC (European Commission). 2000. Directive 2000/60/EC of the European Parliament and of the Council of 23 October 2000 establishing a framework for Community action in the field of water policy. *Official Journal of the European Communities* L 327:1–72.

———. 2006. Proposal for a directive of the European Parliament and of the Council on the Assessment and Management of Floods. SEC(2006)66.

Huisman, P. 2002. How the Netherlands finance public water management. *European Water Management Online*, official publication of the European Water Association (EWA), 2002 3. www.ewaonline.de/journal/2002_03.pdf (accessed October 17, 2008).

———. 2004. *Water in the Netherlands: Managing checks and balances.* Delft: Netherlands Hydrographical Society.

Kickert, W.J.M., E-H. Klijn, and J.F.M. Koppenjan. 1997. *Managing complex networks.* London: Sage.

Kooiman, J. 2000. Societal governance: Levels, modes, and orders of social-political interaction. In *Debating governance, authority, steering, and democracy,* ed. J. Pierre, 138–64. Oxford: Oxford University Press.

———. 2002. Governance: A social-political perspective. In *Participatory governance: Political and societal implications,* ed. J.R. Grote and D. Gbikpi, 71–96. Opladen, Germany: Beske and Budrich.

Kuks, S.M.M. 2004. Water governance and institutional change. PhD thesis, University of Twente.

LBOW (Landelijk Bestuurlijk Overleg Water). 2006. *Water in Beeld 2006: Voortgangsrapportage over het waterbeheer in Nederland* [*Water in focus 2006: Annual report on water management in the Netherlands*]. www.waterinbeeld.nl (accessed September 9, 2008).

Meijer, M. 2004. *Waterdrager, Projectplan op hoofdlijnen* [*Water Carrier, outline project plan*]. Veendam, Netherlands: Waterschap Hunze en Aas.

Meijer, M., and A. Hartman. 2006. *Regionaal Waterplan Westerwolde. Strategie en Maatregelenplan* [*Regional water plan Westerwolde. Strategy and plan of measures*]. Veendam, Netherlands: Waterschap Hunze en Aas.

Pierre, J., and B.G. Peters. 2000. *Governance, politics and the state.* New York: St. Martin's Press.

Projectgroep Waterdrager Westerwolde. 2006. *Regionaal waterplan Westerwolde. Probleemanalyse* [*Regional water plan Westerwolde. Problem analysis*]. Veendam, Netherlands: Waterschap Hunze en Aas.

Teisman, G.R. 2005. *Publiek Management op de Grens van Chaos en Orde. Over leidinggeven en organiseren in complexiteit* [*Public management at the edge of chaos and order. On managing and organizing in complexity*]. The Hague: SDU.

TK (Tweede Kamer). 2005–2006. *Second Chamber of Parliament, Appointment Budget Ministry of Transport, Public Works and Water Management.* 30300 chap. 12, no. 2. The Hague: SDU.

van Leussen, W. 2004. The increasing role of public policy in integrated water management. In *Managing water scarcity: Experiences and prospects,* ed. A. Vaidyanathan and H. Oudshoorn, 315–35. New Delhi, India: Manohar.

van Leussen, W., E. van Slobbe, and H.G. Meiners. 2007. Transboundary governance and the problem of scale for the implementation of the European Water Framework Directive at the Dutch-German border. In *Adaptive and Integrated Water Management. Coping with Complexity and Uncertainty,* ed. C. Pahl-Wostl, P. Kabat, and J. Möltgen. CD-ROM, session D4, "multilevel governance." Proceedings CAIWA 2007, Basel, Switzerland.

Verwey, G. 1980. *Op zoek naar het wezenlijke in de Nederlandse geschiedenis* [*Searching for the fundamentals in Dutch history*]. Amsterdam: Elsevier.

CHAPTER 10

Water Policy and Spatial Planning
Linkages between Water and Land Use

Henk Voogd and Johan Woltjer

WIDESPREAD FLOODING in 2005, both in Central Europe and as a result of Hurricane Katrina in New Orleans, Louisiana, focused worldwide attention on the importance of thoughtful and adequate water management (see Chapter 4 on flood risk). These are usually called natural disasters, but how "natural" are these events? It can be argued that they are to some extent "human-made" if preventive measures were inadequate or lacking (Voogd 2004). This is important if adequate protective measures are not taken despite a considerable probability of flooding, such as in the case of New Orleans (Maimone 2006).

Past disasters as well as expected climatic changes indicate that flooding will remain a problem in the years to come. Estimates by the European Environment Agency (EEA 2004), for example, indicate that more than 10 million people live in areas at risk of extreme floods along the Rhine River. EEA further estimates that the total value of economic assets in coastal areas at risk of substantial flooding ranges between 500 and 1,000 billion euros. Hence water management must be given more consideration in planning, particularly regarding quantity regulation in river basins, the geographical areas drained by rivers and their tributaries.

Especially with respect to water protection, much can be learned from the Dutch experience, in both a negative and a positive sense. The Netherlands has centuries of experience in combating flooding (see Chapter 1). By discussing Dutch experiences, we will show in this chapter that land use planning has a significant role to play in preventing and coping with such disasters. The general slogan of modern water policy in the Netherlands is that "water should get room before it takes it!"

In Dutch practice in the past, land use and water management policies often conflicted (Schwartz 2004). The planning and implementation of widespread housing development throughout the Netherlands during the 1990s, for example, occurred without considering local and regional water system characteristics. Politicians and planners generally selected building locations based on criteria such as accessibility, proximity, and availability. Even key government agencies such as the national Directorate General for Public Works and Water Management (Rijkswaterstaat) and the water boards, whose central task is to manage water systems, overlooked the potential dangers of major housing development in areas prone to flooding. Thus large-scale housing sites such as the Vinex districts were implemented in flood-prone areas such as river headlands, polders, and wetlands, with relatively little discussion (Rathenau 2000).

Two lines of argument, concerning safety and resources, illustrate the need for more effective integration of land use and water planning. In the Low Countries, the *safety argument* (i.e., being protected from flooding and other kinds of threats from rivers and the sea) has prevailed for many centuries because a considerable part of the land is under direct threat of overflow by the sea or larger rivers. Although the risk of flooding has decreased as a result of technical measures such as increasing the height of dikes, climate change and soil subsidence are continual stimuli for additional measures (see also Chapter 4 on flood safety policy). The *resources argument* is another reason for improving linkages between water and land use policies. Spatial development is facilitated by the physical resources of land and water. In the past, the availability of water for drinking, farming, production, and navigation has been a precondition for spatial development. At the same time, spatial development can affect water resources in many ways. Groundwater levels may drop because of overexploitation; water may be polluted by industrial, residential, and farming activities; flow direction and speed may be altered by the construction of infrastructure and built-up areas. All these can affect the resources used by humans and ecosystems. In order to protect water resources, the impact of spatial development must be assessed.

Water management and spatial planning are inherently connected (see also Woltjer and Al 2007). Urban development is often motivated by the presence of water or restricted by its lack. Water problems such as pollution and flooding often have their root causes on land. Some kinds of land uses, such as dense urban development, can actually be a cause of flooding. Others, such as agriculture or industry, may lead to deterioration of water quality, depletion of adequate groundwater, dehydration of nature areas, and other related problems.

Consequently, this chapter discusses various kinds of linkage strategies between water management and spatial planning. A key move involved a shift from regulatory practice to strategic thinking. Among other things, water policy has changed from a separated undertaking by specialists to one of an assortment of interests associated with spatial planning and land use. These linkage approaches raise pivotal questions, such as what the possible policy approaches might be, given a closer relationship between water management and spatial planning. Considering the Netherlands' long history and accrued experience of dealing with these issues, we examine principally the Dutch case to explore this important question.

After a discussion of the basics of policymaking for Dutch water management and spatial planning, this chapter describes some paramount developments in the gradually closer mutual relationship between the fields, then introduces two prevailing approaches to furthering linkages: improving regulatory practice and introducing strategic thinking. Some recent policy proposals, tools, and experiments will be touched upon, such as "room for water," water storage, the water assessment test, water regimes, the water opportunity map, the river basin approach, and cases such as New Arcanie and the Blue City.

DUTCH WATER MANAGEMENT
AND SPATIAL PLANNING

In order to understand Dutch water management and spatial planning, one must be aware of the Netherlands' administrative structure (see chapter 8 for more details). Based on the conventional government roles, water management in the Netherlands is the shared responsibility of the central government, 12 provinces, and 27 water boards, with the tasks divided among the various agencies and levels (e.g., Bressers et al. 1995; Perdok and Wessel 1998; see also Chapters 8 and 9). Water policy is drawn up and implemented at both the national and the provincial and water board levels.

The main water system of the Netherlands includes the coastal zone and the major rivers, and the Ministry of Transport, Public Works and Water Management controls this area nationally. The regional water systems include polder water (as explained in the Introduction) and the surrounding outlet and drainage waters. These are controlled by water boards, which play an essential role within regional water systems. Water boards are responsible for the tasks of flood defense and water quantity and quality management (see Chapter 9 on governance). Flood defense refers to the protection of land against flooding by ensuring that dikes, dams, and dunes are in good condition. Issues of groundwater lie with the provinces, sewage and local surface water with municipalities, and drinking water with privatized supply companies. Several ministries and provinces have strategic tasks related to standards, designation of water protection, transportation, and safety. Clearly, many government actors are involved, which results in the responsibilities being very fragmented.

The challenge to establish closer links between water and land use is great, as spatial planning has a separate decisionmaking system that recently was fundamentally renewed. Figure 10.1 provides an overview of Dutch water management as well as the spatial planning system introduced in 2007 by the new Act on Spatial Planning. This act made a distinction between strategic plans that are legally only self-binding and planning decrees that are binding for lower governments. Overall, for spatial planning, the state sets broad guidelines by means of a strategic plan regarding chief land use patterns and necessary long-term changes, which is then self-binding for the national government. Provinces may translate these guidelines into specific regional strategic plans (self-binding for the province) and operational planning decrees (binding for local governments within the jurisdiction of the province). Municipalities must prepare detailed plans for land use in accordance with provincial planning decrees. The local land use plans allocate functions, such as housing, industry, and public services, as well as room for building infrastructure such as roads, canals, railway lines, and parks. According to the Act on Spatial Planning, the

Water management		Spatial planning

National level
 Ministry of Transport, Public Works and Water Management
    ▪ Management of main water system
    ▪ Development of national water policy and legislation
    ▪ Implementation of European Guidelines for Water
		National level
		 Ministry of Spatial Planning and Environment
		    ▪ Broad strategic lines of spatial policy (self-binding)
		    ▪ Implementation of European Guidelines for the Environment (binding for other governments)

Provincial level
 Provinces (12)
    ▪ Development of groundwater plans, and regulation
    ▪ Supervision of water boards
		Provincial level
		 Provinces (12)
		    ▪ Regional strategic plan (self-binding)
		    ▪ Planning decrees (binding for local governments)

Local and regional level
 Water boards (27)
    ▪ Management of regional water system (flood defense, water levels)
    ▪ Treatment of urban wastewater and water quality (licenses)
	Local level
	 Municipalities (443)
	    ▪ Sewage system
	    ▪ Drainage system
	    ▪ Urban water policy
		Local level
		 Municipalities (443)
		    ▪ Local land use plans
		    ▪ Allocating and regulating local usage of land
		    ▪ Municipal structure plan (optional)

Figure 10.1 *An overview of the Dutch water management and spatial-planning systems*

provinces (and even the state) are also entitled to make local land use plans. This is relevant if land uses need to be planned that are not supported by the municipality, such as major infrastructure projects or national sea defense works. Provinces aim at policy integration and have planning duties in various fields. These duties include achieving accord among the diverse interests related to housing, transport, industry, nature, and agriculture. Water plays a fairly subordinate role in these responsibilities.

Although water management and land use are strongly interdependent, the problem remains that the two fields of policymaking are essentially separate. In the Dutch case, water management tasks are principally the domain of technical engineers, who have their own system of regulation and plans and operate within well-established water agencies with exclusive taxation power and well-defined geographical areas of operation (see, e.g., Wolsink 2006). Today, however, the prevailing issues of climate change and European coordination call for intensified integration. For this reason, Dutch water managers and planners alike are now seeking ways to connect water management and spatial planning. These issues are central to the following section, followed by a discussion of some prevailing linkage strategies in the Dutch situation.

RECENT DEVELOPMENTS

In the last few decades, heightened flood risks throughout Europe have been the starting point for the construction of major flood control works (EEA 2004). Several flooding incidents around the Thames River instigated a plan for a barrier to regulate tidal waters from the North Sea. A destructive flood in Venice in 1966 led to the construction of large gates in the Adriatic Sea. After the 1953 flooding, in which about 1,835 people were killed, the Delta Plan was developed and executed (see Chapter 1). These examples illustrate the dominant approach toward water management, a technical one aimed at ensuring safety and protecting land by blocking out water.

Technical measures such as dikes, dams, canals, ditches, and pumping stations have been paramount for the existence of the Netherlands as a country. They no longer are sufficient, however, for impending problems related to climate change, such as a higher seawater level or increasing rainfall. Current climate predictions for the Netherlands in particular, such as those in table 10-1, are close to disastrous. In essence, key urban centers are directly threatened by more intense rain during the winter, rising seawater, and major flooding (EEA 2004; also see Chapter 4). Thus a clear sense of urgency has arisen to produce new policy strategies aimed at integrating issues of urban and regional planning and water management (e.g., Kabat et al. 2005).

Another important development has been the emergence of a European water policy (see Chapter 9). Since the end of the Second World War, a move toward integration led to the gradual development of the European Union (EU) as a governing authority, with a subsequent shift from nation-state controlled management to decisionmaking within European regions (e.g., Kaika 2003). A major milestone was set in 2000, when the EU Water Framework Directive (WFD) was signed by the member states (see EC 2000 and Chapter 11).

The requirements set forth by the WFD elucidate the challenge for water managers and spatial planners in bridging the gap between aquatic issues and spatial developments. A finer attunement between water and spatial planning is essential. The WFD also implies that close collaboration between water managers and spatial planners during the strategic phases of planning and decisionmaking is vital. Two main general approaches to establishing further linkages between water management and spatial planning have emerged: improving regulatory practice and introducing strategic thinking.

IMPROVING REGULATORY PRACTICE

This first approach, improving regulatory practice (e.g., Schwartz 2004), relates to a more conventional way to deal with the challenge of linking water and land use. Regulatory practice refers to any action by public agencies, taking general rules or

Table 10-1 *Climate predictions for the Netherlands in 2100*

Climate variable	Low-impact predictions	Mid-impact predictions	High-impact predictions
Temperature	+1°C	+2°C	+4–6°C
Average summer precipitation	+1%	+2%	+4%
Average winter precipitation	+6%	+12%	+25%
Sea level rise	+20 cm	+60 cm	+110 cm

Source: KNMI 2001.

regulations as a standard for policymaking. To improve the relation between water and land use in the Netherlands, the main emphasis actually has been on improving regulatory practice. We will first discuss the focus on designating space for water in statutory spatial plans, then examine one of the most clearly elaborated instruments: the water assessment test, which is compulsory for spatial plans such as those for municipal land use.

Establishing Room for Water in Spatial Plans

Flooding threats in the Netherlands in 1993, 1995, and 1998 led to the realization that conventional water management would no longer be adequate to deal with issues such as climate change, rising sea levels, local land subsidence, and urbanization pressures. A national committee (see Commissie WB21 2000) therefore suggested a shift toward allowing water to occupy more space (see Chapter 5 for the economic aspects). In anticipation of the changing climate and rising sea level, the committee recommended retaining water rather than draining it away. Spatial measures would include the construction of water retention and storage areas near cities and rivers. The key guiding principle now featured a three-step strategy: first, holding water in aquifers and higher parts of the water system; next, storing it in lower parts of the water system, designed for emergencies; and finally, discharging it into a downstream water system (see, e.g., Schwartz and Voogd 2004). The sequence of these measures—in short, retain-store-discharge—indicates their priority. The basis of this principle is its emphasis on spatial measures, for example, to change land use in order to (a) prevent fast runoff from surface areas, (b) enable and safeguard the storage and discharge capacity of the water system, and (c) prevent damage to built-up areas downstream.

This strategy was soon elaborated in new water policy documents such as *A Different Approach to Water* (V&W 2000) and was subsequently adopted in regulatory spatial plans such as the recent *Spatial Planning Memorandum* (VROM 2005) and provincial regional plans. Water managers experimented with various forms of regulation. In one region, urban land use plans included small-scale zoned locations where water could be retained temporarily during times of extreme rainfall (the water storage stage). Surplus water would flow into ponds, parks, or separate reservoirs in the vicinity of houses, alleviating the immediate threat of flooding. Another example is dynamic coastal management, an approach in which regional plans assigned certain areas of coastal land to tolerate the natural process of flooding (e.g., Goosen et al. 1998).

A more appealing example, perhaps, was a policy initiative aimed at improved river management titled Room for the River. Because large rivers such as the Rhine have to deal with increasing amounts of water (up to 18,000 cubic meters per second), deliberate efforts have been made to enlarge the area through which their waters run. A conversion of dominant land uses in the environs of these main rivers from urban and agricultural to water was considered a practical policy intervention to deal with flood risks. One idea was to enlarge total river areas via the construction of ecological side channels (van der Brugge et al. 2005). Another, as suggested in national planning documents, was the inclusion of some zones for emergency flooding adjacent to larger rivers.

The background to the Room for the River initiative was set in February 1995, when large areas around the Rhine and Meuse rivers were inundated, and floods threatened many major towns, forcing a large-scale evacuation. This event stimulated public and political pressure to take preventive measures as far as possible. One of the spatial measures was enlarging the capacity of the river basins, among other methods by designating special overflow or retention areas. The intention basically was to clear holes in some dikes during emergencies to flood sparsely populated farmland and lessen dangers elsewhere (Commissie Noodoverloopgebieden 2002). A surrounding dike would protect villages and hamlets in designated retention areas. Figure 10.2 provides an overview of the retention areas suggested for a specific part of the Rhine and Meuse area in the east of the Netherlands. The map displays the key waterways involved—the Maas, Waal, IJssel, and Nederrijn—and presents suggested overflow areas, including the names of local villages in those areas.

The idea behind the overflow areas was that emergency flooding situations could be alleviated by controlled "harmless inundations" of regions with "minor economic value," such as natural areas and grasslands. This idea met with opposition, however, from inhabitants of the designated overflow areas, the provincial authorities, and the national Parliament. The proposed size of the retention areas shocked many people, and engineers maintained that overflow areas could never

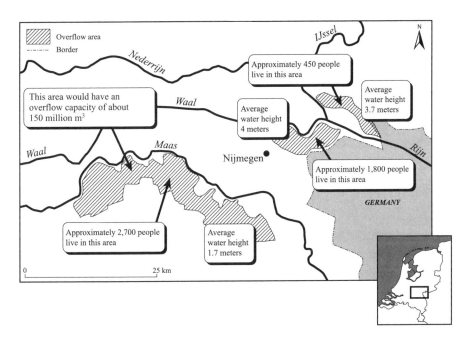

Figure 10.2 *Overflow areas suggested by a national advisory committee as a response to the flooding threats in 1993 and 1995 from the Rhine and Meuse rivers*

Source: Adapted from Luteijn 2002.

substitute for "old-fashioned" engineering solutions such as increasing the height of river dikes and deepening riverbeds. It could be said that the controversy was between "space for the river" and "speed for the river," in other words, getting rid of the abundance of water as quickly as possible. Although it may be tempting to drain water away rapidly during periods of excess, this generally means that the problem is simply displaced to an area situated downstream. Therefore, "speed for the river" is not considered a proper solution by either local communities downstream or the national government (e.g., V&W 2004). In the report *Room for the River* (V&W 2004), the government drastically reduced the size of the retention areas compared with the proposal as shown in the figure. It chose to create overflow capacity near the rivers, such as by linking retention areas to clay and gravel extraction and repositioning dikes.

Water Assessment Test

The water assessment test (WAT), which was introduced in 2002 (V&W 2001), was another attempt to establish an improved regulatory instrument for handling water considerations lacking in spatial plans. Until recently, Dutch water boards focused heavily on the technical aspects of water management, but a broader perspective is required that also involves land use measures. The legal situation in the Netherlands, however, is such that water boards are unable to manage spatial measures independently from other public authorities and private stakeholders. Water authorities can make their wishes clear to urban planners, who may then incorporate them into their spatial policies, but this simplistic view neglects the reality—or rather, the complexity—of spatial planning. Spatial planners have to deal with many interests apart from those relating to water. It is therefore important that the water boards be formally involved in land use planning. This is realized by means of the WAT.

The WAT is a general framework for assessing land use proposals. Its goal is to guarantee that water interests are taken into account in spatial and land use planning, so that a negative effect on the water system is prevented or compensated for elsewhere (RIZA 2003). This process involves a somewhat closer collaboration between the engineers of the water boards and planners at municipalities with regard to issues of water management. The result of this assessment implies a considerable amount of concrete "water text" in municipal land use plans, describing how the consequences of these plans will affect present quantities and qualities of water.

The WAT framework consists of a checklist and a clarification of the roles of the actors involved. It includes all relevant water management aspects: flood protection, water quality, and depletion. Depending on the location, all aspects must be considered by the authority responsible for land use planning. It is therefore embedded in a land use planning process that provides for early consultation, advice, consideration, and final judgments regarding water management aspects in spatial plans and decisions.

All government authorities are required to use the WAT. It is an obligatory assessment of spatial plans that determines the consequences for water management. If water management priorities, such as the preference for collecting and storing water over discharging it, cannot be realized, explanations must be provided and compensating measures taken. Compensation and mitigation measures are part of the land use decisions relating to the spatial plan. The cost must, in principle, be borne by the initiator.

The WAT distinguishes three types of actors: the initiator, advisor, and reviewer (table 10-2). The initiator is the authority that wishes to implement a land use change, such as the development of an urban area, infrastructure, or natural environment. This can be a local, regional, or national authority or a private organization. In the latter case, the responsible public authority—municipal, provincial, or national—performs the WAT. The advisor is the water authority with jurisdiction: the water board, groundwater authority, or national Rijkswaterstaat. The reviewer is the authority that, according to urban and regional planning legislation, should review land use decisions. For example, the provincial authority reviews land use decisions made by municipal authorities.

Most types of land use plans and decisions (e.g., zoning, regional, and infrastructure plans) can include a WAT. The test can be used to review not only new plans, but also revisions and dispensations. The determining factor is the relevance of the plan or decision in terms of water resources. The exact meaning of "relevance" is the decision of the advisor: the water authority. The advisor bases this judgment on the specific circumstances in the water system. This implies that (a) advisors must clarify the vision of the plan regarding aspects within their jurisdiction that

Table 10-2 *The roles of initiators, advisors, and reviewers in the WAT*

Initiator	Advisor	Reviewer
1. Prepares land use development initiative		
2. Reviews and determines relevance for water		
3. Presents the initiative to the advisor		
	4. Assesses all aspects relating to water	
	5. Proposes mitigation and compensation measures	
	6. Advises the initiator	
7. Considers advice		
8. Decides on initiative for land use development		
9. Draws up land use decision, water clause		
		10. Reviews and decides on procedure and contents of land use decision
11. Implements decision: review and modification, licensing, and construction		

Note: Adapted from Schwartz and Voogd 2004.

relate to water, and (b) initiators must be aware of these aspects and decide whether they should be applied to the land use plan or decision. A result might be that initiators, to be on the safe side, send *all* land use plans and decisions to the advisor.

If we look at the intentions behind WAT, it would be fair to say that it is part of an effort to improve regulatory instruments aimed at institutionalizing linkages between water management and land use planning. The role of the WAT resembles that of the environmental impact assessment. Its regulatory implications include a stronger role for water considerations in land use plans, reflected by some descriptions as providing water impact assessment, and prescribed consultation between municipality and water board.

The delegation of roles and responsibilities among the various authorities is a key element of the WAT. It is basically the responsibility of the land use authority with regard to decisionmaking on land use, as laid down in the legislation on urban and regional planning. The water authorities are responsible for protecting and managing water resources. Because the water board is seen to have an advisory role, and is not regarded as an assessor with final decisionmaking powers, the implication is that land use authorities can decide to give their own responsibilities priority over those of the water authorities.

A WAT emphasizes the interdependence between water authorities and land use authorities and is designed to encourage cooperation by clarifying the different roles in decisionmaking related to land use. In addition, the WAT provides a checklist of water themes for incorporation in actual processes. The advantage of this approach is that responsibilities are clearly separate. Land use authorities make the final decision on whether to incorporate aspects related to water management. Water managers advise on how these aspects can be incorporated, using the WAT checklist as a guideline. If the aspects are not incorporated, and water managers are held accountable for shortcomings, they can point to the responsibility of the land use authorities. In doing so, water management is subordinated to land use management, although this must be explicitly justified. The water authorities thus are faced with the problem that *they* may be held accountable for inadequate protection and management of resources.

A disadvantage might be that focusing on responsibilities is not conducive to cooperation, but rather stimulates opponents to adopt a "wait-and-see" approach. Nor does the fact that initiators have to finance mitigation and compensation measures encourage to a cooperative approach. This is an undesirable situation for water authorities, which are responsible yet also dependent.

Desired Ground and Surface Water Regimes

Another attempt to improve regulatory practice is the recent effort by provinces and water boards to establish "desired" ground and surface water regimes (GGORs) for their areas. The central idea behind this instrument is that the provincial government, after close dialogue with water boards and municipalities, includes in its spatial plans a preferential groundwater regime for certain land uses. These regimes then provide an indication of the type of surface water management and its link to a variety of land uses, such as housing, nature, and agriculture. The GGOR specifies the preferred variations in groundwater levels, based on an assessment of all relevant land use interests involved (CIW 2003).

By determining a water regime, some water management objectives essentially are linked to an area. The regime is thought to reflect the prevailing usage of this particular area. The idea is that local water management efforts, such as the safeguarding of certain groundwater levels through a system of dams, pumps, and ditches, will correspond to principal land uses. The water board will have a responsibility to adjust its activities to any GGOR at hand.

INTRODUCING STRATEGIC THINKING

The second approach introduces a stronger role for strategic thinking in preparing decisions about water. A strategic policy approach refers to an emphasis on influencing the social and political circumstances under which policy implementation becomes more likely in the long term. Strategic planners, for example, actively seek opportunities to strengthen their claims politically and socially and connect them to other policy arenas. The strategic approach assumes that it is paramount for any water decision to invest in political, intellectual, and social capacities and relate water considerations to other topics in regional governance (e.g., economy, health, city marketing). This section examines the water opportunity map and the river basin approach, highlighting to a certain extent an increased reliance on strategy making. It also gives some examples of recent innovative projects, proposals, and strategies.

The Water Opportunity Map

Water boards are traditionally inclined to focus on technical aspects of water management. The growing awareness of the relevance of spatial measures, however, has led to a more proactive approach by water boards with respect to land use planning. The water opportunity map (WOM) is part of this development. Fopma (2001) defines a WOM as "an information and communication instrument for land use planning that visualises land use possibilities and impossibilities regarding sustainable water management." Its purpose is to strategically influence spatial policymaking. Because no general framework has been drawn up by national or regional authorities, a wide variety of approaches exist; in fact, there is no such thing as *the* WOM. Several types of WOMs can be distinguished (van Dijk 2001; van der Vlist and Schouffoer 2001). Some indicate the suitability *for a given land use*, with a subtype that focuses exclusively on urban land use, water storage, or combined land use; others present a vision of the *future*; and still others combine *suitability* and *a vision*.

A WOM consists of a set of maps and explanatory notes, and visualization is an important aspect of all WOMs. A geographical information system (GIS) is often used for this purpose. The maps are based on water system information: hydrology, groundwater and surface water flow and direction, and soil conditions, including unprotected aquifers and soil material. This information is linked to types of land use, each of which has specific preconditions for levels, volumes, and quality of groundwater and surface water. By combining the water system conditions and preconditions for land use, different types of land use can be combined and allocated to given areas. Based on the water system conditions and current land use, views on preferred land use for the future can be developed. The explanatory notes relating to a WOM include background details on how it was made and information about its relevance for decisionmaking and further procedures relating to land use. For example, a WOM may indicate the suitability of a given area for urban development. Spatial reservations, such as buffer areas for storm water to be used during periods of heavy rainfall, appear on the map. A WOM may also show nature development areas and the lowest regions.

Soon after their introduction in 2000, WOM initiatives spread throughout the Netherlands. The popularity of this new instrument illustrates that the water authorities needed a tool to deal with land use processes. WOMs are usually drawn up by one or more water boards, often in cooperation with water specialists from other authorities such as the provincial government, municipalities, and regional branches of the national government. In almost all applications, private consultants have supported the WOM (van Dijk 2001).

Currently, a WOM has no legal status. Ideas vary as to whether it should take the form of legislation, be incorporated in regional plans, become part of water authority decisionmaking, or be left to civil servants. It now serves what potentially is a highly strategic role, but a more regulatory position is being discussed. The question of whether and how authorities should be involved, for example, is a relevant one for the WOM process. WOMs produced jointly with municipalities probably will be used as input for municipal spatial planning more frequently than ones that involved no cooperation. The extra effort invested in preparing this kind of WOM could well be beneficial later in the planning process.

The River Basin Approach

EU efforts to establish a river basin approach throughout the continent reflect another aspect of strategic action (e.g., Howe and White 2002). The 2000 Water Framework Directive (WFD) echoes this approach (see EC 2000). At first sight, the WFD appears to rely on regulatory government. Its main aim is to deliver improved water quality by using only water-related environmental criteria and breaking the country down into regions based on hydrological criteria (i.e., river basins), which makes the directive strictly regulatory in nature. At the same time, however, the river basin approach also introduces a new strategic perspective toward integration, especially the long-term union of ecological, economic, and land use related features of water policy (e.g., Page and Kaika 2003).

Implementation of the European WFD, with its emphasis on river basins, implies a particularly strong link between land use issues and spatial development. Under the WFD, every river basin management plan has to incorporate not only an analysis of the characteristics of each water body, such as the presence of diffuse and point-source pollution, but also a review of the impact of human activity on the status of surface water and groundwater. This would entail a spatial investigation of pressures and impacts resulting from growth and urbanization and an examination of associated land uses that might affect water in some way, such as agriculture, industry, public works, nature protection, transport, and housing. Furthermore, many water problems, such as pollution, are created on land and follow a downstream pattern. A fundamental point to the river basin approach in the WFD, therefore, is that land and water have to be viewed in mutual coherence.

The river basin approach also implies that the directive is likely to influence spatial planning and prevailing land uses in the various EU member states (White and Howe 2003). The specific results, however, remain unclear. Exploratory studies in the Netherlands suggest some major consequences for the agricultural sector (van der Bolt et al. 2003). Although there is no official European spatial plan, the EU has been gradually gaining more authority over land use in its member states via directives such as the WFD. In line with EU policy embedded in the Birds and Habitats Directives and the clean air strategy, for example, the WFD will leave a clear mark on spatial planning efforts throughout the member states. European water policy is generally focused on ensuring good water quality by setting legally based ecological standards. With these strict environmental criteria, extensive areas will no longer be available for autonomous urban development by the member states. In this sense, the WFD denotes a "Europeanization of planning" (Howe and White 2002). Given the emphasis on generalized standards, European environmental policy such as that set forth in the WFD is characterized by a regulatory approach (Lenschow 2002).

The emphasis on creating new administrative units within cross-boundary river basins and, following from this, the integrated long-term management of rivers and lakes in new social units of coordination mean, however, that responsibilities related to land use are strengthened and the creation of coherent policy visions becomes desirable. Thus a strategic approach comes to the fore. Accordingly, the WFD reflects an enormous rescaling of decisions related to waters—ground, surface, and coastal—at a number of decisionmaking levels, with a "spiralling proliferation of new water-related institutions, bodies, and actors that are involved in policymaking and strategic planning at a variety of geographical scales" (Swyngedouw et al. 2002, 26). This also implies a colossal institutional change in countries that share large rivers with many neighboring countries, as is the case for the Netherlands with the Rhine, Meuse, and Scheldt.

Innovative Solutions and Strategic Capacities

An illustrative example of a recent innovative and more strategic effort to merge water management and spatial planning considerations is a multifunctional project called Wieringerrandmeer (Wieringen Border Lake). It involved an initiative to create a lake between the former coast and empoldered land (reclaimed from the sea) in the province of North Holland and simultaneously provide housing, new economic activity, recreational facilities, improved ecological conditions, and enhanced water management. The project's relatively independent team of planners, headed by the provincial government, displayed a remarkable ability to set up institutional capacity, principally in cooperation with private parties. A key strategic move was the enlargement of the project from simply the construction of a lake to a truly regional enterprise that would contribute in terms of housing and business activity to the entire northern part of the province. Numerous meetings and conferences were held in an effort to give the project and its potential as much exposure as possible and link it to a new strategic style of planning (Woltjer and Al 2007).

A somewhat similar undertaking is the Blue City project, in the province of Groningen, where, in an effort to improve the local economy, an 800-hectare lake and related recreational and housing facilities were constructed (Dammers et al. 2004).

Another interesting innovative solution to increased flooding risks was a creative response to diminishing opportunities to build in riverbed areas. After the near flooding crisis in the late 1990s, the Dutch national government prohibited building new developments in riverbeds. This led to opposition from local governments near the rivers, which feared that they would have hardly any opportunities left for urban expansion, or at least for attractive new housing along the riverside. Another pressure against this decision came from private development corporations that were challenged by the idea of designing waterproof buildings or, in marketing terms, "amphibious living." Already in the early 1980s, the first example of a "floating hamlet" was created near the town of Roermond. This project was stimulated by a sand and gravel production company called Smals BV, which wanted to show that housing on the water of a former gravel pit was quite possible.

In recent years, many more innovative proposals have been made, such as the New Arcanie design of a city on water. So far, none of these ideas has been realized, but this may change. In September 2005, the national government suddenly rescinded the ban on building in the riverbed at 15 places, provided that the developer would create at least a similar amount of overflow space for the river elsewhere as a kind of compensation. This new development will evolve further, perhaps even into new forms of "amphibious living."

Cases such as these show that a strategic approach toward water planning is emerging, one that attempts to "frame mindsets" and "organize attention" of actors such as users, politicians, and investors, and to transform a culture formerly focused on setting restrictions based on government control to one that anticipates emerging opportunities. It is an approach emphasizing more strategic processes of adapting to threats and opportunities (e.g., Hamel and Prahalad 1994), along with investment in capacity building or the quality of relational networks in a place (Healey et al. 1999). Water managers and planners are dealing with contextual factors such as economic and political developments, strategies by private actors and colleague government agencies, and changing regulations and techniques. An analysis of these developments will clarify associated opportunities and threats, such as those related to possibility of building cities on water.

Generally, regulatory practice is changing. A move is on to establish legislation aimed at strengthening the role of water considerations within land use projects. This initial move is strong in countries such as the Netherlands and the United Kingdom, where agencies such as the Dutch water board and the British regional water authorities (White and Howe 2003) fulfill a strictly functional role toward water management, largely separated from spatial planning. The main challenge in this context is to introduce some legal connections between land use planning and issues such as water pollution and flooding.

Another transformation is that from appointing areas in which a certain sectoral protection regime dominates (e.g., groundwater protection zones, wetlands, or environmental protection zones) to more regionally and locally based integrated approaches to solve economic, environmental, social, agricultural, and water problems simultaneously. Water becomes related to other policy fields as well, organized in broader units (regions) of policy coordination. It thus plays a key role in regional planning, as water can provide a regional identity, create a pleasing living environment, attract investment, and serve as a binding social element. The challenge here also is to depart from water management as exclusively a technical exercise, involving specifications of parameters, possible measures, and detailed instructions on preparing management plans (Heimerl and Kohler 2003). A more strategic approach comes to the fore, such as in the French river basin management, which features integrated master plans and the participation of a large number of stakeholders, including representatives of water distribution companies, nature conservation organizations, and local government. Some underlying intentions are to create a collective water awareness within cities, regions, and river basins while leaving space for sociopolitical networking and negotiated solutions (Bongaerts 2002; Piégay et al. 2002).

CONCLUSIONS

This chapter has investigated options for establishing further the relationship between water management and spatial planning. This relationship is articulated in a variety of ways. Housing on water, for example, may need specific efforts aimed at avoiding phosphate content in the water or providing options for recreational usage. Nature development may necessitate specific water levels. City planners may require investment capacities and aesthetic qualities. Conversely, water quality standards may call for restrictions on possible land uses. The link with spatial planning therefore is very strong.

In the Dutch case, however, water management often still focuses to a large extent on regulatory action, emphasizing measures, norms, and standards to ensure water quality protection and flood control. Water is not yet a fully integrated element of spatial-planning considerations, let alone a factor of social coherence and participation emphasizing issues such as regional identity, quality of life, health, taste, and attractiveness.

The WAT and WOM can be very meaningful tools for facilitating the integration between land use planning and water management. A water opportunity map (WOM) is a potential strategic starting point for influencing decisionmaking on land use from a water perspective. It can be a basis for negotiations with land use authorities, such as during the assessment of a land use decision by means of a water assessment test (WAT). Both the WOM and WAT, as well as the GGOR water regime tool, can play a leading role in providing adequate water information for longer-term decisionmaking in land use planning.

The Dutch policy regarding flood protection is also clear: in addition to river-widening measures, retention areas are required in the event of a potential flooding.

To put it in other words, "room for the river" takes precedence over "speed for the river." Land use planning practice in the Netherlands has shown, however, that this is not a simple task. When grasslands are appointed as flood storage areas, farmers will present huge emotional barriers, and improving regulatory instruments, such as the adoption of retention areas in regional plans or the usage of the water assessment test, will not be sufficient to placate them. Further strategic efforts, perhaps aimed at building trust and providing options for compensation, will be required.

This kind of observation is exemplary for current Dutch efforts to synchronize water management and spatial planning, which have taken two kinds of approaches. One is to improve regulatory practice. In the broader field of spatial planning, regulatory practice already features many references to water, such as location requirements for harbors, sewage systems, permit conditions for mineral excavation, and nature restoration. In the Dutch context, the regulatory level has shown various successful attempts at integrating water management considerations into land use planning practice, emphasizing a formally established role for water in regional and local spatial plans.

At the same time, a second, more strategic approach has emerged that can be seen as a supplement to regulatory practice. This approach is used, for example, when water managers actively seek opportunities to politically and socially strengthen their claims, and embed them in policy processes elsewhere. Although water management is still based largely on decisionmaking in separate functional regions, emphasizing sectoral claims related to ensuring sufficient space for water and quality that meets environmental standards, it increasingly attempts to work in conjunction with spatial planning, encouraging land use planners to take water into account when making decisions for a certain location (Vlist and Wagemaker 2003; Wolsink 2006).

The strategic approach is anchored in the idea that a need exists for investment in institutional capacities related to integrating water considerations into regional planning, and vice versa. This is a challenging mode of policymaking, as there are impeding institutional conditions, as shown above for the Netherlands, with regard to assuming principally a strategic water planning style. Attention to building social relations and informal networks and arenas in which water can serve as a vehicle for creating and ensuring some qualities related to attractive living and working conditions, then, becomes crucial. As the examples of the Blue City and Wieringen Border Lake projects illustrate, spatial planners have a particular interest in such an approach. Water managers, above all those in the water boards, are more inclined toward government control and a regulatory approach.

A significant challenge in this strategic approach is to deal with tensions between water managers and spatial planners related to a fundamentally rooted institutional heritage: both water and planning actors have developed their own institutional structures, ways of action, and geographical divisions, based on a situation in which water and land use were separated. Cultures, knowledge, planning, and procedures differ. Water agencies, for example, often have a more profound technical orientation, emerging from a responsibility to maintain the regional water system and ensure certain water levels, whereas spatial planners are more likely to think in terms of visions and concepts that might support political positions or private investment packages.

A move toward further strategic water planning would focus on defining platforms for strategy building related to water. A key requirement would be that policymakers aim to encourage the identification of interesting possibilities for multiple land use, aesthetic appeal, and innovative solutions (Al 2004). In line with French efforts to link water and land use issues within river basins via regional institutional capacity and water culture, the establishment of new platforms would then be a necessary and essential challenge. A further association of water management and spatial planning would highlight informal coordination platforms in the region performing strategic scans of emerging societal developments and associated opportunities and threats, looking at ways to "live with water," and building a politically and socially strengthened role for water management claims and water as a catalyst for innovative living and working conditions. In the Dutch case, however, the approach to furthering linkages between water management and spatial planning currently is one of improving legal instruments to include "space for water" and water regimes in statutory land use plans, provide impact assessment, and improve the exchange of knowledge and information between water managers and spatial planners. A more strategic approach is only beginning to take shape.

REFERENCES

Al, N.M. 2004. Water schept kansen [Water offers opportunities]. *Rooilijn* 10:504–9.

Bongaerts, J.C. 2002. European water law: Water policy and water resources management in France, the projet de loi sur l'eau. *European Environmental Law Review* 11 (8–9): 239–44.

Bressers, J.T.A., D. Huitema, and S.M.M. Kuks. 1995. Policy networks in Dutch water policy. In *Networks for water policy: A comparative perspective*, ed. J.T.A. Bressers, L.J. O'Toole, and J.J. Richardson, 24–51. London: Frank Cass.

CIW (Commissie Integraal Waterbeheer). 2003. *Werken met GGOR, een hulpmiddel voor maatwerk bij de afstemming van integraal waterbeheer en ruimtelijk beleid* [*Working with GGOR, an aid to a tailor-made attunement between water management and spatial policy*]. The Hague: CIW.

Commissie Noodoverloopgebieden. 2002. *Eindrapport van de Commissie Noodoverloopgebieden* [*Final report of the Emergency Flooding Areas Committee*]. The Hague: Commissie Noodoverloopgebieden.

Commissie WB21 (Commissie Waterbeheer 21e eeuw). 2000. *Waterbeleid voor de 21e eeuw: Geef water de ruimte en de aandacht die het verdient* [*Water policy for the 21st century: Give water the space and attention it deserves*]. The Hague: Commissie WB21.

Dammers, E., F. Verwest, B. Staffhorst, and W. Verschoor. 2004. *Ontwikkelingsplanologie. Lessen uit en voor de praktijk* [*Development-oriented planning. Lessons from and for Practice*]. Rotterdam: NAi Uitgevers.

EC (European Commission). 2000. Directive 2000/60/EC of the European Parliament and of the Council of 23 October 2000 establishing a framework for Community action in the field of water policy. *Official Journal of the European Communities* L 327:1–72.

EEA (European Environment Agency). 2004. *Mapping the impacts of recent natural disasters and technological accidents in Europe*. Environmental Issue Report no. 35. Brussels: EEA.

Fopma, M. 2001. Wijs bouwen met de waterkansenkaart [Smart building using the water opportunity map]. *Rooilijn* 34 (9): 459–65.

Goosen, H., C.H. Hulsbergen, R.J.T. Klein, and M.J. Smit. 1998. Resilience and vulnerability: Coastal dynamics or Dutch dikes? *Geographical Journal* 164:120–32.

Hamel, G., and C.K. Prahalad. 1994. *Competing for the future*. Boston: Harvard Business School Press.

Harvey, D. 1989. From managerialism to entrepreneurialism: The transformation in urban governance in late capitalism. *Geographiska Annaler* 71B (1): 3–18.

Healey, P., A. Khakee, A. Motte, and B.Needham. 1999. European Developments in Strategic Spatial Planning. *European Planning Studies* 7 (3): 339–356.

Heimerl, S., and B. Kohler. 2003. Implementation of the EU Water Framework Directive in Germany. *International Journal on Hydropower and Dams* 10 (5): 88–93.

Howe, J., and I. White. 2002. The potential implications of the European Union Water Framework Directive on domestic planning systems: A UK case study. *European Planning Studies* 10 (8): 1027–38.

Kabat, P., W. van Vierssen, J. Veraart, P. Vellinga, and J. Aerts. 2005. Climate proofing the Netherlands. *Nature* 438:283–84.

Kaika, M. 2003. The Water Framework Directive: A new directive for a changing social, political and economic European framework. *European Planning Studies* 11 (3): 299–316.

KNMI (Koninklijk Nederlands Meteorologisch Instituut). 2001. *Climate scenarios for impact studies in the Netherlands.* De Bilt, Netherlands: KNMI.

Lenschow, A. 2002. New regulatory approaches in "greening" EU policies. *European Law Journal* 8 (1): 19–37.

Maimone, M. 2006. *Water resource planning, from theory to practice.* Groningen, Netherlands: Geo Press.

Page, B., and M. Kaika. 2003. The EU Water Framework Directive. Part 2, Policy innovation and the shifting choreography of governance. *European Environment* 13:328–43.

Perdok, P.J., and J. Wessel. 1998. Netherlands. In *Institutions for water resources management in Europe*, ed. F. Nunes Correira, 327–448. Rotterdam: Balkema.

Piégay, H., P. Dupont, and J.A. Faby. 2002. Questions of water resources management: Feedback on the implementation of the French SAGE and SDAGE plans (1992–2001). *Water Policy* 4:239–62.

Rathenau. 2000. *Het blauwe goud verzilveren: integraal waterbeheer en het belang van omdenken* [*Make the most of the blue gold: Integrated water management and the importance of thinking differently*]. The Hague: Rathenau Institute.

RIZA (Rijksinstituut voor Integraal Zoetwaterbeheer en Afvalwaterbehandeling). 2003. *Handleiding Watertoets* [*Water assessment manual*]. Lelystad, Netherlands: RIZA.

Schwartz, M. 2004 *Water en ruimtelijke besluitvorming* [*Water and spatial decisionmaking*]. Groningen, Netherlands: Geo Press.

Schwartz, M., and H. Voogd. 2004. Safeguarding water interests in Dutch land use planning. In *Environmental and Infrastructure Planning*, ed. G. Linden and H. Voogd, 81–91. Groningen, Netherlands: Geo Press.

Swyngedouw, E., B. Page, and M. Kaika. 2002. Sustainability and policy innovation in multi-level context: Cross cutting issues in the water sector. In *participatory governance in multi-level context: Concepts and experience*, ed. H. Heinalt, P. Getimis, G. Kafkalis, R. Smith, and E. Swyngedouw, 107–31. Opladen: Leske and Budritch.

V&W (Ministerie van Verkeer en Waterstaat). 2000. *Een andere benadering van water: Waterbeleid in de 21e eeuw* [*A different approach to water: Water policy in the 21st century*]. The Hague: V&W.

———. 2001. *De borging van wateraspecten in ruimtelijke plannen* [*On the safeguarding of water in spatial plans and decisions*]. The Hague: V&W.

———. 2004. *Ruimte voor de Rivier, planologische kernbeslissing, deel 1* [*Room for the river: Key planning decision, part 1*]. The Hague: V&W.

van der Bolt, F.J.E., H. van den Bosch, Th.C.M. Brock, P.J.G.J. Hellegers, C. Kwakernaak, T.P. Leenders, O.F. Schoumans, and P.F.M. Verdonschot. 2003. *AQUAREIN: Gevolgen van de Europese Kaderrichtlijn Water voor landbouw, natuur, recreatie en visserij* [*AQUAREIN: Consequences of the European Water Framework Directive for agriculture, nature, recreation, and fisheries*]. Report no. 835. Wageningen, Netherlands: Alterra.

van der Brugge, R., J. Rotmans, and D. Loorbach. 2005. The transition in Dutch water management. *Regional Environmental Change* 5:164–76.

van der Vlist, M.J., and H. Schouffoer. 2001. Waterkansenkaart [Water opportunity map]. *Stedebouw & Ruimtelijke Ordening* 82 (2): 18–22.

van der Vlist, M., and F. Wagemaker. 2003. De Watertoets [The water assessment]. In *Ruimte en Water* [*Space and water*], ed. M. Hidding and M. van der Vlist, 99–113. The Hague: Sdu.

van Dijk, J.M. 2001. *Waterkansenkaarten, inventarisatie en analyse van waterkansenkaarten in Nederland [Water opportunity maps, inventory and analyses of water opportunity maps in the Netherlands].* Lelystad, Netherlands: RIZA.

Voogd, H. 2004. Disaster prevention in urban environments. *European Journal of Spatial Development.* www.nordregio.se /EJSD/ -Refereed Articles Sept., no. 12.

VROM (Ministerie van Volkshuisvesting, Ruimtelijke Ordening en Milieu). 2005. *Nota Ruimte [Spatial planning memorandum].* The Hague: VROM.

White, I., and J. Howe. 2003. Planning and the European Union Water Framework Directive. *Journal of Environmental Planning and Management* 46 (4): 621–31.

Wolsink, M. 2006. River basin approach and integrated water management: Governance pitfalls for the Dutch space-water-adjustment management principle. *Geoforum* 37 (4): 473–87.

Woltjer, J., and N. Al. 2007. The integration of water management and spatial planning. *Journal of the American Planning Association* 73: 211–22.

CHAPTER II

Interaction between European and Dutch Water Law

Marleen (H.F.M.W.) van Rijswick

T HE DUTCH ARE FAMOUS for their water management. Living for many centuries with a large part of their country below sea level, they have had to find ways to protect residents and property against flooding. From the beginning, it was clear that the only way to manage water problems was to work together, sharing responsibilities, money, and efforts (van de Ven 2004). The Dutch eventually came up with the polder model (see Chapter 9), and water management in the Netherlands is still organized around this model, although this may change in the future because of the influence of European Union (EU) environmental and water law. The Dutch are renowned not only for their cooperation-based methods, but also for their technical knowledge. They have successfully developed the technology to live in a delta below sea level, construct polders, and build dikes.

The legal arrangements necessary for this cooperative and innovative way of working are not so well known, however, although they have been of great importance for the successful struggle against water. In this context, the water boards have played a crucial role, with the task of local water management in designated regions (Havekes et al. 2003; see also Chapter 8). The fact that water boards are financially self-supporting has been an important reason for the success of water management in the Netherlands (Uijterlinde et al. 2003; see also Chapter 9), as has the fact that the Dutch realized early on that they had to invest in safety. Cooperative arrangements work best if all participants see their benefits (van Rijswick 2008; van Rijswick and Driessen 2006). Members of the water boards are elected from among the residents of an area, who benefit from the work of the local board and pay for water management in their area.

This chapter focuses on the interaction between European and Dutch water legislation, which together form one legal order. To understand Dutch water law, one needs to be knowledgeable about European water law, which takes precedence if any legal disputes arise. Several recent developments in both Dutch and European water law have had a great influence on existing legal arrangements. Dutch water law has inspired some of the European legislation, yet at the same time, it is being thoroughly revised because of European water law, especially the Water Framework Directive (WFD). The new Dutch Water Act has already taken into account new European developments, such as the Directive on Flood Protection and the Framework Directive on Marine Strategy.[1]

It is not only the legislation that is being altered. The Netherlands is developing a new vision on water management in anticipation of expected climate changes, among other factors. Up until 1985, water management was based on a sector approach, with different policies and legislation concerning the quality and quantity of surface water, groundwater, and marine waters individually. Protection against flooding was also a separate part of water management, with its own instruments and legislation. Another change has been from the use of technical solutions, such as dikes and storm surge barriers, to a new approach from about 2000 onward, which holds that water should be given more space and stored in the system as long as possible for times of drought.

Yet another development that has been receiving increasing attention is a move from government to governance (see Chapter 9). The WFD is a good example of this development, which has led from directives with concrete norms, standards, and uniformity to ones where norms and standards are made by many actors and on many levels, with a lack of democratic control because of the Common Implementation Strategy and soft law documents, and with the possibility to differentiate among regions.

The legal system of EU environmental and water law could be defined as a right-based approach. Directives make clear what level of protection is guaranteed. New EU legislation is characterized by more attention to procedures, multilevel governance, adaptive governance, transition management, cooperation, and flexibility. When it comes to safeguarding water rights, legal protection and enforcement are important. Governance does not fit well into this protective role of law or in concepts such as the rule of law and the legitimacy of norms and standards that should be created in a democratic decisionmaking process (Scott 2000; Scott and Trubeck 2002). The role of the Common Implementation Strategy for the WFD and the use of soft law to subsequently elucidate the scope and meaning of a directive's obligations are steadily increasing. The guidances for the implementation of the WFD are an example of this. There is no doubt that it is good to know the meaning of the obligations arising from the directive and to work together to improve the aquatic environment in a multilevel framework with a great deal of room for flexibility, decentralized decisionmaking within networks with a focus on effective problem solutions and the development of knowledge, but it is better to know what the consequences of legal obligations following from environmental directives would be before making a commitment. The issue with soft law such as the WFD guidances is the lack of democratic legitimacy. It is not clear who establishes a guidance, and the powers of the democratically elected bodies—the national and European Parliament—are negligent while the impact of a guidance on the implementation and final execution may be substantive, particularly when the European Commission was involved in its wording.

Part of the political balance of the scope of water rights, however, must be that the lower limit of each water right is monitored. The lower limit is formed by the minimal water rights, without which a decent existence would not be possible. These minimal water rights, laid down in norms, concern safety, drinking water, clean water, and scarce water. For this minimum, effective enforcement by the courts is necessary, and public and political responsibilities must be clear. New governance could be used for all water ambitions that go farther than these minimal rights.

The rule of law requires that legislation be properly legitimized, and this should be observed in water management too. It is imperative that the rights of interested parties to be properly informed, be involved in the decisionmaking process, and have access to the courts when their interests are wrongfully damaged or their rights violated not be eroded.

One could argue that a development toward governance is not completely new in Dutch water law. Still, the Netherlands does have to deal with the increasing problem of how to combine the protective and normative aspects of water law—with its strong focus on the rule of law, the legitimacy of norms and standards created in a democratic decisionmaking process, legal certainty, and enforceability—with the concepts of new approaches such as multiactor and multilevel governance, transition management, and adaptive governance (van Rijswick 2008).

International cooperation in river basin districts seems necessary to deal with new problems (Hey and van Rijswick in press) concerning the poor quality of surface water, as well as an overabundance or shortage. For the Netherlands, located downstream of four river basins, this new approach is crucial for the success of future water management. Cooperation is therefore necessary not only on the local and regional levels, but also on an international level. The WFD has given new impetus to transboundary water management.

Cooperation and the polder model have been typical of the Dutch approach to water management. In the Middle Ages, water management was based on cooperation among several owners and users of land, who all benefited from protection against water. Later, cooperation was necessary among several policy areas, such as spatial planning, agriculture, and industries, in order to realize the general desire to have sufficient economic activities combined with sustainable water management. Cooperation and the polder model formerly worked in a fairly diffuse way, aiming to meet shared goals such as protecting the water system combined with more intensely using land for agricultural purposes, building new housing developments while reducing water problems, or increasing the amount of emissions from industry yet still improving the water quality. This form of cooperation is a search for the best compromise, and for water management, it has been very successful with regard to safety, flood defenses, and water quantity and quality.

Under the influence of European law, with its strict binding rules and obligations to guarantee certain results, especially concerning environmental quality standards, Dutch management is also changing in this area. Until recent years, the Dutch were not too concerned about the strict obligations of the European water directives, although the European Court of Justice declared many years ago that environmental quality standards are "an obligation to guarantee a certain result." Now that the WFD has come into force, a certain sense of resistance exists in the Netherlands regarding these strictly binding obligations. What will they mean for the tradition of cooperation, poldering, and striving for common goals without legally binding obligations? Do the Dutch have to change their way of working?

Any fear of these binding obligations, which aim to achieve good status of all waters, is counterproductive. Some local and regional authorities want to take these measures and formulate these goals, which are certain to achieve the desired results, only because they fear the consequences of neglecting to implement the directive. Dutch resistance seems to be stronger with regard to the ecological norms and standards that have to be created at the national level than to the binding European standards concerning the chemical status of the priority substances. It can be argued that all parties would benefit from clear goals and standards (Smit et al. 2008). This fear can be diminished by gaining knowledge of the WFD and starting to work with it in the proactive and innovative way the Dutch are accustomed to when solving water problems. The binding obligations of the ambitious directive can help the Netherlands attain the goals for modern water management in cooperation other with policy areas such as spatial planning, the environment, nature conservation, agriculture, and industry. The threat of paying high fines or losing an advantageous position in negotiations in other policy areas of the EU (which in the end could cost a lot more money) can help motivate the authorities to take the necessary measures. To avoid condemnations by the European Court of Justice, it is necessary to have strong legal instruments at state level to influence the decisions of decentralized administrative bodies. This will seriously change the Dutch way of working. Decisionmaking at a decentralized level still will be possible in the future, but with clear limits on negotiation when setting specific goals and measures, as the European directives are binding.

This chapter describes Dutch water legislation with respect to the development toward integrated water management in the Netherlands as well as the EU. It begins with a focus on the integration of water legislation in general, including the changes in Dutch legislation up until the autumn of 2008 and the situation of water legislation in the EU until the WFD came into force. The recent changes—an integrated approach to water systems within river basin districts, a new vision of water management because of climate changes, and the influence of the legal system of European law on Dutch water legislation and management—are the main topics of the chapter. It provides an overview of Dutch and European water legislation, the WFD and its implementation in Dutch law, other relevant European water directives, and recent developments regarding integrated water legislation in the Netherlands.

DEVELOPMENTS IN DUTCH WATER MANAGEMENT

In 2000, the Dutch government came out with Water Policy for the 21st Century (WB21), as well as the Fifth Note on Spatial Planning.[2] Both call for a more prominent role for water management in relation to spatial planning. The Committee for Water Management for the 21st Century examined the possibilities for maximum water storage. This committee not only introduced a legal instrument to create an interaction between decisionmaking in the fields of water management and spatial planning (see Chapter 10), but also drew attention to the fact that water needs more room and should be kept in the water system as long as possible, released into the sea only as a final option.

In February 2001, in response to WB21, the central authorities, Interprovincial Consultations, Association of Water Boards, and Association of Netherlands Municipalities concluded the Preliminary Agreement concerning Water Policy for the 21st Century, which was a first step toward a joint approach to modern water problems. The agreement focuses on cooperation among competent authorities in several fields, including water management, the environment, spatial planning, and nature conservation. The Room for the River policy (introduced in the *Beleidslijn Ruimte voor de Rivier*, Stcrt. 1997, no. 87) aims to avoid any further building in the winter beds of the Dutch rivers, so that no more space to hold water will be lost. This key planning decision brings with it a large number of concrete measures that should result in greater protection against flooding because of climate change. On July 2, 2003 the National Administrative Agreement on Water was concluded by the same parties that were involved in the preliminary agreement mentioned above. In June 2008, this agreement was actualized.

The objective of the National Administrative Agreement on Water is "to get the water system in order and to keep it in order" by 2015, so as to anticipate changing conditions such as the expected climate change, rising sea levels, lowering of the soil surface, and an increase in hard surfaces such as streets as well as housing developments. In preparation, agreements have been concluded regarding such matters as safety, flooding, water quality, freshwater and groundwater deficits, and aquatic sediment.

The approach and implementation take place in stages, with the aid of an integrated working method. Implementation could be combined with plans in other policy areas, such as the reconstruction of rural areas, establishment of the National Ecological Network (the main ecological network of connected areas throughout the Netherlands, similar to the European Natura 2000 network), mining of surface minerals, rural development, cultural history, residential construction, and the building of industrial parks and infrastructure, all while taking account of the Birds and Habitats Directives. Tasks have been divided among the central authorities, provinces, water boards, and municipalities. The agreements establishing duties for the bodies involved must be laid down in the river basin management plans by 2009 at the latest. This ensures conformity with the structure and obligations of the WFD. Although there can be discussion over whether groundwater management should be regulated at the European level because of the principle of subsidiary, the Nitrates, Nature Conservation, and Groundwater Directives have regulated groundwater issues for a long time. With the implementation of the Water Framework Directive, groundwater management increasingly will be regulated on the European level. Because groundwater pollution is strongly connected with soil pollution, and soil pollution is caused by industrial and agricultural activities with a strong influence on the internal market, it is logical that the EU will also focus on groundwater management.

DUTCH WATER LAW

Dutch water legislation still includes acts dating from the nineteenth and early twentieth centuries, such as the Water Management Act 1900, along with the modern water management legislation. It originally was based on a sector approach but in recent decades has been moving increasingly toward integrated management.

The Sector Approach

Traditionally, for every new water problem the country faced, it enacted new legislation, such as the Pollution of Surface Waters Act after severe water quality problems, the Marine Pollution Act to protect the quality of seawater, and the Groundwater Act to regulate the distribution of scarce groundwater resources after a period of extreme drought. Groundwater quality is partly regulated by the Soil Protection Act and partly (as far as licenses for industrial activities are concerned) by the Environmental Management Act. Also within the scope of the Environmental Management Act are sewage management, most discharges into the sewage system, and water quality requirements. Unlike other EU member states, the Netherlands does not regulate authorization to discharge in environmental legislation, but in a true water act—the Pollution of Surface Waters Act, with the regional water boards and the minister of Water Management as competent authorities.

Besides water quality legislation, the Netherlands has several acts concerning flood protection and water quantity management, including the Land Reclamation and Dykes Act, Flood Defences Act, Public Works (Management of Water Control Works) Act, Water Management Act 1900, and Earth Removal Act. Management of surface water quantity has been regulated since 1986 under the Water Management Act; before then, it was governed by local regulations from the water boards. Local and provincial regulations guided flood protection until the Flood Defences Act came into force. Special legislation known as the Delta Act was enacted after severe flooding in Zeeland in 1953.[3]

Dutch Integrated Water Management

It eventually became clear that the sector approach on which water management and the accompanying legislation was based was no longer sufficient, and the Netherlands turned to a new, more integrated approach based on water systems in 1985 (see Chapters 1 and 8). For several years, flood protection was also assumed to be part of integrated water system management. The legal system, however, did not follow this integrated approach, and the Netherlands still has an overabundance of water legislation that is difficult to understand and should be thoroughly revised in order to make integrated water system management and proper implementation of new European legislation possible. In Dutch administrative law, the principles of legality and specialty play important roles. The principle of legality means that the actions of administrative bodies should be based directly or indirectly on legal regulations (acts). The principle of specialty means that the powers of administrative bodies may be used only for the purpose for which they are intended. In other words, the authority to request a license based on the Pollution of Surface Waters Act may be used only to protect the quality of surface water. Permits with regulations that also see to the protection of water quantity or that may be useful in attaining good ecological status are not allowed and will be qualified by the court as an abuse of power. Thus it is apparent that this legal system can cause difficulties for integrated water system management.

Because of these problems with the Dutch system of water legislation, and in order to provide a proper legal framework within which to implement the WFD in an adequate way, the Netherlands is preparing new integrated water legislation in the form of the Dutch Water Act. This act is now being discussed in the First Chamber of Parliament and will probably come into force in the autumn of 2009. This legislation will also make room for new solutions concerning safety and flood protection, given the new Dutch approach to protecting people and property against these risks. The Room for the River approach will have a great effect on possible developments and spatial planning, because the Netherlands is such a small and densely populated country.

European Integrated Water Management

At the European level, as well as the international level, a similar development took place, although not in the same order. European water law started as part of European environmental law, with a focus on water quality. In the last century, directives came into force concerning the quality of drinking water, bathing water, and fresh fish water, along with others regulating the discharges of polluting substances into surface waters and groundwater. Special directives protected waters from pollution with nitrates from agriculture and introduced a proper level of wastewater treatment into the EU. All these directives had their focus on a special aspect of water protection, the sector approach, and the focus was merely on national measures and regulation.

The Helsinki Treaty and some bilateral and multilateral treaties, such as the Rhine Treaties, introduced the concept of *transnational water management* in 1992. Water quantity and protection against flooding were not part of European water legislation, however, perhaps because the solutions always are implemented in a national context, by spatial planning and practical or technical measures. This was not something the EU dealt with, because of the principle of subsidiarity and because these aspects did not seem to have much to do with the internal market, one of the main reasons for creating the EU.

On the European level, things changed with the implementation in 2000 of the WFD, which calls for integrated water management based on a river basin approach. Safety and protection against flooding are not part of its scope, but the Floods Directive, which regulates their assessment and management, is strongly connected with the WFD. There are initial plans for a separate EU Water Quantity Directive, following from policy concerning water scarcity in case of droughts. A new Groundwater Directive has also come into force, and a directive on environmental quality standards for priority substances is being prepared, both as daughter directives of the WFD.

Interaction between European and Dutch Water Law and Management

Looking at these developments, both Dutch and the European, one can see that Dutch experiences with integrated water management have had an influence on European water law. During preparation of the WFD, consultation took place among with the member states, and the Dutch government gave input with regard to the Netherlands' water legislation over the past centuries, including its positive experiences with integrated water system management.

On the other hand, European water law also has had its effects on Dutch law. Although the Netherlands has had water legislation for a long time, the Dutch system had to change, although in some aspects only slightly, with the implementation of the European water directives. This is because strict obligations exist concerning the implementation of European law. It is not enough to have an effective system of water legislation on a national level; the national legislation has to comply with the obligations in the European directives. Dutch water legislation did not always meet these obligations, however, and this led to several decisions by the European Court of Justice condemning the Netherlands for not complying with obligations emanating from the EU water directives. After the implementation of the WFD, it became necessary to think about a complete renewal and integration of Dutch water legislation. The ways these effects have been translated into legislation will be the main issue below.

TOWARD INTEGRATION IN WATER LEGISLATION

This section examines the move toward integrated water management in the legislation of both the Netherlands and the EU, as well as the broader international picture. River basin management plans and the recovery of costs for water services are discussed, as well as the instruments that are necessary to achieve the environmental objectives of the WFD.

Integrated Legislation in the Netherlands

In the mid-1980s, the Water Management Act was initiated, legislation that was meant to eventually lead to an Integrated Water Act. Things never reached that stage, however. The Water Management Act was intended to introduce the initial means for integrated water management in accordance with the water system approach, although in essence, these means consisted only of an integrated planning system. Water management plans are established at the national, provincial, and water board levels and comprise the strategic government note on water management, management plans for national waters (the larger waters), provincial water management plans, and water board management plans for regional waters.

Integrated has a double meaning. First, it refers to internal integration within water management. It means that the water management plans concern both the quality and quantity of groundwater and surface water. Harmonization has been achieved by means of consultation among the different competent authorities in the formulation of those plans; the approval of local authorities' plans by central authorities; the obligation that authorities, in their decisionmaking, take account of their own policy plans; and the requirement to consider higher-level plans in the establishment of lower-level plans. In this way, an integrated approach is achieved concerning the policy regulating the quality and quantity of surface water, and this integrated policy plays a significant role in the final decisionmaking by the water authorities.

Second, the term may refer to external integration among water management and related policy areas. A mechanism to ensure this, known as the "leapfrog arrangement," has been applied to plans made in the fields of water, the environment, spatial planning, traffic and transport, and more recently, with the implementation of the Habitats Directive, nature conservation. This leapfrog arrangement never worked very well, and a different mechanism for external integration has been chosen for the new Dutch Water Act.

Integrated Legislation in the EU

On December 22, 2000, the Water Framework Directive entered into force. Current European water legislation was a mixture of different kinds of directives, and the WFD was implemented to provide a transparent, effective, and coherent legislative framework. It was intended to coordinate, integrate, and from a long-term perspective, further develop the overall principles and structures for protection and sustainable use of water in the EU in accordance with the principles of subsidiarity (van Rijswick 2003). The directive also makes a contribution toward enabling the EU and the member states to meet obligations arising from various international agreements on the protection of marine waters from pollution and on water protection and management, notably the UN Convention on the Protection and Use of Transboundary Watercourses and International Lakes, adopted on March 17, 1992, in Helsinki.[4] The WFD, like the Helsinki Convention, opts for a river basin approach to water management. The directive has broad objectives and interacts with other policy areas and directives. The choice of a river basin management approach has implications for competent national authorities, regulation, planning, and the use of executive instruments.

International Developments in Integrated Legislation

Over the last few years, initiatives have been taken to develop a more coherent and integrated water policy internationally. An important organization in this field is the International Rhine Committee, functioning since 1950. In 1976, the Rhine chemical and chloride treaties came into force.[5] After the disaster near Sandoz in 1986, when the water of the Rhine River was heavily polluted by dangerous chemical substances after a fire in an industrial plant, an integrated approach was pursued by the riparian states.

The Helsinki Convention, drafted within the framework of the UN's European Economic Committee, concerns the protection and use of transboundary watercourses and international lakes, and aims to prevent, control, and reduce serious adverse impacts on the environment in the broadest sense of the term. The convention includes provisions on the protection of groundwater. It contains a number of principles and proceeds from the combined approach of emission limit values and quality objectives. The treaty is based on cooperation agreements among riparian states of transboundary watercourses, with equality and reciprocity as its fundamental principles, which means that the interests of each member have the same importance, and all member states have to respect the interests of the others. Acts of one state may not significantly harm other member states.

As a corollary of the Helsinki Convention, international committees were set up for the protection of the Maas and Scheldt rivers. These international developments have been important for European water law, especially the WFD. In light of the developments, the Council of Europe and the European Parliament invited the European Commission to develop a more coherent water policy through which international agreements could be fulfilled. The WFD was its response to this request.

THE WATER FRAMEWORK DIRECTIVE

The aim of the WFD is to effect an integrated and coherent water policy within the EU. Its purpose is the protection and improvement of all waters within the EU, including surface, ground, transitional, and coastal waters. This protection takes place by managing the entire water system, specifically for each *river basin*. Because river basins often extend over several countries, modern water management needs to have a strongly international transboundary dimension, which calls for a greater role for international cooperation (Keessen et al. 2008). As the approach chosen is based on river basins and the protection of surface waters as well as groundwater, the protection of the soil and ground also fall within the scope of the directive.

Another important feature of the WFD is that it is strongly purpose oriented, in the sense that achieving the aims of the directive takes priority, and this also includes its further legal elaboration. The goals are defined more concretely in the *environmental objectives* of Article 4 in the WFD. The final objective is to achieve a "good status" of the European waters by 2015. The legally vague concept of "good status" is defined further in the annexes to the directive. A distinction is made between the good status of groundwater and that of surface waters. The good status can be divided into a chemical component, which applies for both groundwater and surface waters, and an ecological component, which refers to just surface waters. Protected areas are listed separately in the environmental objectives. Such areas are not designated under the WFD, but on the basis of other EU regulations, such as the Nitrates or Habitats Directive. The WFD requires solely that all these areas be listed in a register and further stipulates that the most stringent protection regime is applicable.

The good status is the ultimate goal of the WFD and is further defined by way of *environmental quality standards*. The elaboration of good status must be laid down in the form of quality standards in statutory provisions. These standards are nothing new in water law; older directives have already set forth many of the quality requirements, both for waters with a specific function (drinking, bathing, fishing, or shellfish) and for certain substances.[6] It may be inferred from case law from the

European Court of Justice that quality requirements must be regarded as obligations to achieve a particular result, which member states have to meet under all circumstances, except when the directive makes exemptions possible. This does not detract from the fact that quality requirements may be formulated as both limit and guidance values. If legal measures such as permit procedures are not effective, then additional actual measures must be taken.[7] As environmental quality requirements have already been in existence in European water law and law in general for some time, it is surprising that this aspect of the WFD in particular has caused much ado in the Netherlands (LBOW 2004).

The chemical quality requirements are familiar to the member states, as they also existed in older water directives, but they refer only to priority substances under the WFD; a directive on priority substances is prepared to establish these chemical quality standards. The ecological quality standards relate to the former "grey list" of *substances* (List II) from Directive 76/464/EEC but are to some extent new insofar as they actually refer to ecological requirements such as *hydromorphology* and the *status of fish and water fauna* and have to be formulated by the member states. The fact that the protection level may not be lower under the WFD than under the protection regime that was provided by the older water directives implies that all existing quality requirements continue to hold.

The requirement of a good status for all waters by 2015 applies to "natural" waters, those that the member states have not designated as "artificial" or "heavily modified." For these latter water bodies, the protection regime is slightly less restrictive: they need to have a good chemical status, but no more than a good potential regarding their ecological status. The WFD also contains a number of possibilities for setting less stringent objectives or postponing the deadline by which they have to be achieved, albeit under strict conditions.[8]

The *instruments* by which the objectives must be realized include both integrated river basin management plans, preferably for the entire transboundary river basin, and programs setting out the steps and measures the member states intend to take to achieve the aims. These measures should include all those necessitated by a number of existing directives.[9] The WFD distinguishes between the measures for diffuse and point-source pollution.

Measures and instruments need to be derived not only from water legislation, but also from other fields of policy. Here again, intensive international cooperation is necessary because of the transboundary river basins. The WFD also contains the obligation to recover the costs of *water services* in accordance with the "polluter pays" principle. Finally, the directive pays a great deal of attention to *public participation* and has opted for a combination of source- and effect-oriented policy. The effect-oriented policy will eventually determine whether the requirements of the WFD have been met.

DUTCH IMPLEMENTATION OF THE WFD

Although the Netherlands was closely involved in the preparations for the WFD, its implementation in this country was not always straightforward (Gilhuis and van

Rijswick 2005; van Rijswick 2004). At the government level, arrangements to start the program of implementation were made at an early stage, as a timely implementation of the directive is required under EU law. The final discussion of the bill to implement the directive was delayed considerably, however, partly because of a report by Alterra that sketched a worst-case scenario for Dutch agriculture as a consequence of the WFD. The Dutch House of Representatives refused to discuss the bill until clarity was given on how the directive would be implemented in the Netherlands; this was prompted by the fear that the country was being far too ambitious in its plans to meet the requirements of the directive. Experiences with the Habitats Directive, whose strong protection regime resulted in many delays in economic investments and public works, were still fresh in people's memories. In addition, the requirements following from the EU air quality directives also caused enormous problems in the Netherlands, as the requirements are hard to fulfill in such a highly populated country, and because of the way the EU directive was legally implemented into Dutch law. The agricultural sector had already been finding it extremely hard to comply with the earlier Nitrate Directive, and a judgment of the European Court of Justice against the Netherlands for noncompliance with the Nitrate Directive made things no easier. It was only after the state secretary presented a memorandum on the pragmatic implementation of the WFD to the House of Parliament that the bill was piloted through without too much further discussion of its contents.[10] In the meantime, the European Court of Justice ruled against various member states because they had not yet implemented the WFD.[11] Proceedings were also pending against the Netherlands, but these were withdrawn after the Water Framework Implementation Act came into force.[12]

The Water Framework Implementation Act includes amendments to the Water Management Act (Wet op de waterhuishouding) and Environmental Management Act (Wet milieubeheer). The Water Management Act has been amended in the sense that the obligatory river basin management plans have been included in the existing National Policy Document on Water Management. The Dutch minister for Transport, Public Works and Water Management is the competent authority for the four Dutch river basins: the Rhine, Maas, Ems, and Scheldt. Provisions have now been added for international consultation, which fulfills the obligation to work on transboundary river basin management plans, and for the implementation of public participation. Amendments in the Environmental Management Act include environmental quality standards for the chemical and ecological status of waters; a sharpening of the standstill principle, or no deterioration principle, which protects the actual water quality from further deterioration; and the implementation of monitoring obligations.

The member states had to comply with a number of obligations in the WFD before the end of 2004. First, they had to compile a description of the river basin districts (Article 3). Second, they had to draw up reports containing a review of the impact of human activity on the status of surface waters and groundwater (Article 5). Third, they had to establish a Register of Protected Areas (Article 6).[13] This register has been completed, although some modifications will probably be needed in the Netherlands, partly because of areas that still have to be designated as protected because they include the location of intake points for drinking-water supplies.[14]

The member states have to qualify their waters in categories such as rivers, lakes, transitional, and coastal, and each has different criteria for good status. Reference conditions determine the status of a particular water body as high, good, moderate, poor, or bad. A great deal of work has gone into formulating this system.[15] Next, the member states must specify the ecological objectives of the various waters, then lay down these objectives in statutory environmental quality standards. In the Netherlands, these are based on the Environmental Management Act and will be discussed in Parliament at the beginning of 2009 before coming into force. After this, the measures needed to bring the waters into the required good status will be determined. The quality requirements for priority substances will take the form of limit values, whereas for other pollutants, the choice may be for guidance values. In cases concerning licenses for plants falling within the scope of the Integrated Pollution and Prevention Control Directive (IPPC), the WFD requires that all quality requirements be included as limit values in the granting of permits.

The need to meet these quality requirements raises the question of the impact they will have on decisions in other policy fields, such as spatial planning, agriculture, or industry. Must every government body take water quality standards into account or even observe them? Do they apply to every decision or only certain ones? On the one hand, the quality requirements have to be designed in such a way that they comply with European obligations; on the other hand, the Dutch as well as the other member states have a strong desire for a certain amount of flexibility. As it appears now, in the Netherlands, the environmental quality standards will have to be taken into account only when making water plans. In other member states, all governmental bodies have to take the WFD goals and standards into account. Achieving a good ecological situation likely will cause some headaches, because the mere adoption of certain measures is by no means guaranteed to bring about particular results.

This then raises the question whether the environmental objectives of the WFD should be regarded as obligations to achieve particular results or merely to make a "best effort." A concern has arisen that these environmental objectives will become obligations to achieve particular results that will be difficult to fulfill. Most member states see these as obligations of results, all though the Dutch legislators still see them as obligations of best effort. To define the ecological goals, in the common implementation strategy, a more pragmatic approach (the so-called Prague method) is developed, in hopes that it will be possible to comply with the WFD simply by implementing the intended measures. Not only has this Prague method been adopted in the Netherlands, but it is a joint development of the member states. Whether this approach will be accepted by the European Court of Justice will not be known until the court gives its final ruling on this matter.

Speaking more generally, it could be argued that the member states may be placed in a difficult position because of the focus on an effect-oriented approach through obligations that are laid down as environmental objectives and quality standards. Although assessments will take place as to whether the required quality has been achieved, member states do not always possess all the instruments necessary to fulfill this responsibility. Causes may be natural factors (e.g., climate change, flowing water, the marine environment, ecological reactions, or unforeseen developments) or a lack of jurisdictional competences (for certain areas of policy, such as the registration and admission of veterinary medicines and plant protection products, more than one member state will be involved). Another problem is that international cooperation is often necessary in water regulation in order to achieve the desired results, and such cooperation will not always be equally successful. To some extent, the old-fashioned source-oriented approach of previous environmental directives posed fewer problems for member states, because each individual member state had control over the obligatory regulation of activities.

Preparation of the management plans for river basins and subbasins is currently taking place in the Netherlands; these have to be determined by the end of 2009 Public participation on these plans started at the end of 2008 (NWP 2009). Various pilot projects are being carried out, as the best structure for these plans is not yet completely clear. These projects explore what measures are needed to achieve certain objectives, and how and in what sequence they will best be applied to obtain the greatest results at the lowest possible cost. The river basin management plans also need to contain an overview of the program of measures by which the member states aim to comply with the objectives. A cost–benefit study will be an important factor in this respect. The actual program of measures in the Netherlands must be sought in various, possibly decentralized, plans.

In 2009, the river basin management plans will be finished, and the determination of quality standards for substances (by the EU) and ecology (by the member states) should be finished by the end of the year. The programs of measures have to be operational in 2012. By 2015, the member states must have complied with the objectives, apart from justifiable exceptions. At this point, we not only will have a clearer picture of the relationships within water management (for protection against pollution, inundation, and flooding), but also the relationships with other policy fields will be worked out in greater detail.

A NEW INTEGRATED DUTCH WATER ACT

In a letter dated July 6, 2004, the state secretary of Transport, Public Works and Water Management informed the lower house of her intention to integrate the heavily fragmented, sectoral water management legislation.[16] To this end, the Outline Note Concerning the Integration of Water Legislation was drafted. A number of reasons lay behind this wish to integrate the legislation on water management. For one, the cabinet's outline coalition agreement titled "Join In, More Work, Fewer Rules" had opted to reduce the burden of regulation. Developments concerning the review of the financing of regional water management were another consideration. Yet another motivation was the desire to review the relationships among the different authorities in charge of water management, as well as between citizens and the authorities, to clarify and modernize the responsibilities (e.g., duties of care and supervisory relationships).

An important substantive reason for a review of the legislation was the policy-inspired change from the sectoral, object-focused management of water control works to a more integrated, function-based management of water systems. This change had occurred over the past 30 years, and the legislation was no longer equipped for these policy and management developments. This had become all the more pressing in light of the European regulations, especially the WFD. The Netherlands thus decided to introduce integrated management of water systems and river basins, in which both the quality and quantity aspects will play a role, in new legislation called the Water Act, which should enter into force in the autumn of 2009. Recent and anticipated EU directives will also be implemented in the act. Achieving the objectives of the EU water directives requires more legislation than that contained in the Water Framework Directive Implementation Act, and it is expected that the Water Act will be better able to make this possible (CAW 2002 and 2005; de Heer et al. 2004).

The Outline Note Concerning the Integration of Water Legislation laid the necessary foundation for the Water Act, which is directed at water system management in the broadest sense of the term and will also regulate the accompanying infrastructure. The act aims to integrate a multitude of statutory regulations in the field of water management law. To this end, connections are being sought with the concept of water system management.

In the summer of 2005, a preliminary draft of the integrated Water Act was made public so that all interested parties, including provinces, municipalities, water boards, drinking-water companies, and environmental organizations, could give feedback. Advice also was sought from some state advisory boards, such as the advisory commission, regarding the water legislation. All these interested parties used this opportunity to provide their comments, which led to certain changes to the proposal. The proposal for this Water Act has been discussed in the legal literature as well.

Purpose and Scope

The Water Act will not result in a complete integration of water legislation, as it concerns only water system management. Water chain management (drinking water and wastewater collection) will not be part of this act, but will be regulated under the Drinking Water Act and the Environmental Management Act. The Water Act aims to combine and integrate the Water Management Act, Pollution of Surface Waters Act, Pollution of Sea Water Act, Groundwater Act, Land Reclamation and Dykes Act, Flood Defences Act, Public Works (Management of Water Control Works) Act, and Water Management Act 1900. Later, parts of the Soil Protection Act (covering aquatic soils) will be included in the act, insofar as it concerns water system management.

The purpose and thus the scope of the Water Act will be, in particular, the protection, improvement, and management of water systems, as regards the following:

• Safety (in relation to flooding)
• Quality (in particular, the good status of all waters)
• Quantity (emergency overflow and water storage)
• Effective and safe use of water systems

Not only will this make the scope of the act wider than that of the WFD, but it will also be more in line with developments within Dutch water management

(WB21). In this way, new European developments in the areas of safety and quantity management may also be anticipated. On the other hand, one could argue that water chain management and water system management have such close connections that it would be preferable to integrate both parts of water management.

Legal Standards

Based on the Water Act, legal standards will be set in place related to several of its goals: quality, quantity, and flood protection. The legal standards for the quality of water directly refer to Article 4 of the WFD—good ecological and chemical status—and will be laid down in a regulation based on the Environmental Management Act as environmental quality standards (AMvB Kwaliteitseisen en monitoring water). Legal standards for flood protection currently are based on the Flood Defences Act but in the future will be based on the Water Act. At present, no legal standards exist for surface water quantity (emergency overflow and water storage), but they too will be based on the Water Act.

Legal standards can play a crucial role in achieving water management goals and thus must have a certain legally binding nature. Concerning internal integration within water system management, the Water Act will give a legally binding role to water standards in decisions based on the act. The act will call for very little external integration, however, other than with spatial planning. Here the water management plans will be based on the Water Act as well as the Spatial Planning Act. With this planning system, which replaces the former leapfrog construction, external integration with spatial planning will be regulated, although not legally binding.

The Dutch government did not make the environmental quality standards based on the Environmental Management Act binding for decisions in other policy areas and based on other acts in the fields of the environment, nature conservation, spatial planning, and products. Serious discussions are ongoing in the Netherlands over whether EU law obliges that environmental quality standards play a binding role in decisionmaking in other policy areas. This question will also be very important for environmental quality standards based on the WFD. Currently, no EU legislation exists in the fields of flood protection or emergency overflow and water storage that gives legal norms or standards for the assumed protection level. This means that the discussion on the external integration of these standards into other policy areas is relevant only at the national level.

External integration *will* take place in a general way, however. National water plans will be signed by several ministers, responsible for the environment, spatial planning, water management, agriculture, and nature conservation. That should lead to responsibility in all these policy fields to achieve the goals of both the WFD and the Dutch Water Act.

Other Regulations and Provisions

Besides integrated goals, another great step forward in the Water Act is the system of one water license for all aspects that may affect the water system. Every individual, industry, or governmental body that undertakes activities that may influence the goals of the Water Act (safety, flood protection, water quality, or water quantity) needs a permit for these activities. Because of the broad goals of the act, no problems should arise concerning the legal principle of specialty. A real integrated approach is thereby made possible.

The competent authorities in the field of water system management will not change to any great extent under the new act. As far as strategic policymaking and supervision are concerned, the Ministry of Traffic, Public Works and Water Management and the provinces are competent. The act calls for only two operational water managers: the state (the minister of Traffic, Public Works and Water Management) for the larger surface waters; and the water boards for all regional waters, both surface water and groundwater.

The planning system under the new Water Act will be very similar to that in the Water Management Act, as described above, with water management plans at the central, provincial, and water board levels, as well as strategic and operational plans. The main change is that the water plans at the central and provincial levels will also be based on the Spatial Planning Act. Besides these other important aspects, the Water Act also will include regulations for the storage of surface water, financial provisions, specifications concerning legal protection, and public participation arrangements.

Relationship with EU Water Law

One of the reasons for establishing the Water Act was the implementation of EU water law, not only the WFD, but also the other water directives mentioned above. One of the main problems in the integration of legislation is where it should stop. Looking at European water law, it is clear that the WFD is not the final piece of legislation to be incorporated. Many other water directives exist, and new ones are being prepared. At both the European and national levels, the integration of legislation is not an easy task. And the fact that external integration with other policy areas lacks proper regulation will make it all the more difficult to attain the ambitious goals of European and Dutch water policy.

Regarding the legal system of EU law, the new Dutch Water Act has proper supervision arrangements, in the form of regulations and individual instructions, for the central government to ensure that decentralized administrative bodies attain the prescribed European and national goals, although only when they fail to attain those goals using traditional methods such as cooperation within the polder model. As far as future European water legislation is concerned, the Water Act is intended for the future. New forthcoming legislation such as the Bathing Water, Flood Protection, and Groundwater Directives will be implemented in the Water Act without serious problems. In this way, the Water Act will both follow European developments such as the WFD and inspire new European water legislation (just as the EU Directive on Flood Protection was based on Dutch water policy concerning flood protection, emergency overflow, and water storage), not only because the Netherlands has ample experience in such aspects, but also because the proposal for the directive on flood protection and management leaves a great deal of room for regional arrangements and contains few binding rules or standards.

CONCLUSIONS

This chapter has provided a general overview of the ways the Water Framework Directive is being implemented in Dutch law. Three important recent transformations are the conversion of water management from a sector approach to an integrated approach to water systems, with changes in legislation coming decades after changes in policy; alterations in water management because of new water problems such as climate change, which will lead to the necessity to provide more room for natural waters alongside the old technical measures; and finally, shifts in attitudes and legal arrangements because of the influence of strictly binding EU law. In all these arenas, one can see the mutual effects on European and Dutch water legislation and water policy.

As to the existing Dutch water legislation, the Netherlands has already, for the most part, based its water policy and management on an integrated approach, but they still have to be translated into legislation. The planning system based on the Water Management Act, in particular, served as the instrument for integrated water management, although this is not sufficient for the genuine and clear fulfillment of the obligations set out in the WFD. This is crucial from the point of view of legal certainty, so as to provide clarity for all parties involved concerning their obligations that follow from EU directives.

After all, the WFD is especially ambitious in its aims and, despite its name, is directed at many more policy areas than just water. This is the result of the objective of achieving good status for all waters and the decision to opt for the river basin approach. The WFD therefore will also require great effort in other fields, such as the environment, spatial planning, agriculture, traffic, and transport. The pursuit of the good ecological status of waters may also give a positive boost to nature conservation. External integration with other policy areas lacks proper regulation, however, on both the European and national levels.

On the implementation of the directive in the Netherlands, it was decided not to review the sector approach and the highly fragmented Dutch water legislation. That was regrettable and a missed opportunity. The legislative process is very slow in the Netherlands, however, and the implementation of the not exactly crystal clear WFD gives rise to many questions that require further study, while remembering that European law demands that directives be implemented on time. Given all this, the decision of the legislators to begin by fulfilling only those obligations that are absolutely necessary is understandable. It has already become clear from the Explanatory Memorandum to the Implementation Act that an integrated Water Act will be prepared. Dutch water legislation will benefit greatly from the thorough review taking place in conjunction with this new act. And it appears from the most recent draft that the Water Act will be able to apply the EU water directives properly.

At this point, it is doubtful that the obligations and objectives of the WFD can be fulfilled with instruments and powers spread out over so many different administrative bodies, water authorities, and those with responsibilities in other policy fields. The authorities in the Netherlands have a strong desire, however, to leave unchanged the existing administrative structures and powers, as well as hold on to the Dutch way of working in water management, based on cooperation, consultation, and common goals. The polder model is highly appreciated here, and it fits well within the new governance approach.

Some countries regarded the WFD as a good opportunity to review their water legislation, and as a result, they have already become equipped with all the right instruments for obtaining good water status. Although the Netherlands may have lagged behind in this respect, it too is working to achieve integration in its water legislation and is now closely conforming with the WFD obligations. The positive elements in the Dutch implementation are the quality standards, which have now been laid down in statutory rules; the tightening of the standstill principle; and increased attention to the relationship between emission control and the quality approach. In these matters, the old water directives in the Netherlands fell short of the mark, and it is a sign of progress that remedies for these defects have been found.

The Dutch Water Act was drafted with an eye to the future, with a great deal of attention paid to national as well as European developments in flood protection, emergency overflow, and water storage. The new directive on flood protection seems to be inspired by developments in the Netherlands regarding more room for water and the fact that water problems should not simply be shifted downstream.

NOTES

1. Directives 2007/60/EC and 2008/56/EC.

2. Directorate General for Public Works and Water Management, the Hague, December 2000. The government position was published after the recommendations of the Committee for Water Management for the 21st Century (Commissie WB21 2000).

3. After the damage to New Orleans, Louisiana, in the wake of Hurricane Katrina, people came from the United States to the Netherlands to learn about the Delta Works and the Dutch system of water management. A new Delta Plan and Delta Act have been proposed recently because of the need to adapt to the effects of climate change.

4. Approved by Council Decision 95/308/EC, OJ L186/42.

5. Agreement Concerning the International Commission for the Protection of the Rhine, Bern 1963; Convention on the Protection of the Rhine against Chemical Pollution, Bonn 1976; Convention on the Protection of the Rhine against Pollution by Chlorides, Bonn 1976.

6. Based on the Drinking Water Directive (75/440/EEC), amended by Directive 79/869/EEC; the Bathing Water Directive (76/160/EEC); the Fishing Waters Directive (2006/44/EC); the Shellfish Water Directive (2006/113/EC); and Directive 76/464/EEC, republished as Directive 2006/11/EC.

7. ECJ 18 June 2002, C-60/01; ECJ 8 March 2001, case C-266/99; ECJ 14 July 1993, case C-56/90; ECJ 12 February 1998, case C-92/96; ECJ 25 November 1992, case C-337/89; ECJ 14 November 2002, case C-316/00. Where water directives are involved, the case law often concerns those that have the protection of public health as an objective.

8. See Syncera Water, Arcadis, Institute for Environmental Studies (VU) and Centre for Environmental Law (UvA), *Verkenning argumentatielijnen fasering en doelverlaging (derogaties) Kaderrichtlijn Water* [*Argumentation to use the exemptions of the WFD*], commissioned by RIZA, April 14, 2005, and Stichting Reinwater, *Kansen uit de Kaderrichtlijn water* [*New chances of the WFD*], 2004.

9. Article 10 WFD and Part A of Annex VI; at least the measures from the Bathing Water Directives (76/160/EEC and 2006/7/EC), Birds Directive (79/409/EEC), Drinking Water

Directive (80/778), Seveso Directive, EIA Directive (85/337/EEC), Sewage Sludge Directive, Urban Waste Water Treatment Directive (91/271/EEC), IPPC Directive (96/61/EEC), Nitrate Directive (91/676/EEC), and Habitats Directive (92/43/EEC).

10. *Pragmatische Implementatie Europese Kaderrichtlijn Water in Nederland; van beelden naar betekenis* [*Pragmatic implementation of the European water framework directive in the Netherlands, from images to meanings*], TK 2003–2004, 28 808, no. 12.

11. ECJ 15 December 2005, C-67/05, *Commission v. German Federal Republic*; ECJ 15 December 2005, C-33/05, *Commission v. Belgium*; ECJ 12 January 2006, C-60/22, *Commission v. Portugal*; ECJ 12 January 2006, C-60/19, *Commission v. Italy*; and most important, ECJ 30 November 2006, Case C-32/05, *Commission v. Luxembourg*.

12. Case C-147/05.

13. For the Article 5 and Article 6 reports, see www.kaderrichtlijnwater.nl.

14. Initially the decision was made to designate the intake points with regard to surface waters. This does not appear to be in line with the requirements of the WFD, however, because the directive talks of the designation of water bodies. The protection areas have been provisionally included in the register in the case of groundwater. The European Commission has since ruled that inclusion in the register must relate to entire groundwater bodies. If the same methodology is applied for surface waters, it may be assumed that the entire water bodies must be included, and not just the intake points.

15. Three reports were presented in October 2004 in Utrecht: References and Draft Measuring Standards for Lakes in the Water Framework Directive, STOWA Report 2004-42; References and Draft Measuring Standards for Rivers in the Water Framework Directive, STOWA Report 2004-43; References and Draft Measuring Standards for Lakes in the Water Framework Directive, *Transitional and Coastal Waters*, STOWA Report 2004-44.

16. TK 2003–2004, 29 694, no. 1.

REFERENCES

CAW (Commissie van Advies inzake de Waterstaatswetgeving [Advisory Committee on Water Legislation]). 2002. *Die op water is, moet varen … Naar integratie van waterwetgeving* [*Those on water have to sail … towards integration of water legislation*]. The Hague: CAW. www.cawsw.nl.
———. 2005. *Voorontwerp Waterwet: voldoende waarborgen voor een duurzaam en samenhangend watersysteembeheer?* [*Preliminary draft Water Law: Sufficient guarantees for a sustainable and coherent water system management?*]. The Hague: CAW.
Commissie WB21 (Commissie Waterbeheer 21e eeuw). 2000. *Waterbeleid voor de 21e eeuw: Geef water de ruimte en de aandacht die het verdient* [*Water policy for the 21st century: Give water the space and attention it deserves*]. The Hague: Commissie WB21.
de Heer, J., S. Nijwening, S. de Vuyst, T. Smit, J. Groenendijk, and H.F.M.W. van Rijswick. 2004. *Towards Integrated Water Legislation in the Netherlands: Lessons from other countries: Case study reports.* The Hague: Ministerie van Verkeer en Waterstaat/RIZA.
Gilhuis, P.C., and H.F.M.W. van Rijswick. 2005. Auswirkungen der Wasserrahmenrichtlinie auf das Wasserrecht und das Umweltmanagementgesetz in den Niederlanden [Consequences of the Water Framework Directive on the water legislation and the environment management law in the Netherlands]. In *Tagungsband Ansätze zur Kodification des Umweltrechts in der Europäschen Union: Die Wasserrahmenrichtlinie und ihre Umsetzung in nationales recht* [*The Water Framework Directive and its conversion into national legislation*], Schriftenreihe der Hochschule Speyer, ed. E. Bohne, 69–83. Band 169. Berlin: Duncker & Humblot.
Havekes, H., F. Koemans, R. Lazaroms, D. Poos, and R. Uijterlinde. 2003. *Water governance: The Dutch water board model.* The Hague: Dutch Association of Water Boards and the Nederlandse Waterschapsbank N.V.

Hey, E., and H.F.M.W. van Rijswick. In press. Transnational water management. In *The European composite administration*, ed. O. Jansen and B. Schöndorf-Haubold. Mortsel, Belgium: Intersentia.

Keessen, A.M., J.J.H. van Kempen, and H.F.M.W. van Rijswick. 2008. Transnational river basin management in Europe. *Utrecht Law Review* 4:35–56. www.utrechtlawreview.org.

LBOW (Landelijk Bestuurlijk Overleg Water). 2004. Notitie inspannings- en resultaatsverplichting [Note concerning obligations of result or obligations on best efforts]. www.kaderrichtlijnwater .nl/aspx/download.aspx?PagIdt=14068&File=notitieinspannings-versusresultaatsverplicht-ingkrw1.doc (accessed February 12, 2009).

NWP (Nationaal Water Plan). 2009. www.nationaalwaterplan.nl (accessed February 11, 2009).

Scott, J. 2000. Flexibility, "proceduralization", and environmental governance in the EU. In *Constitutional change in the EU. From uniformity to flexibility?* ed. G. de Búrca and J. Scott, 259–80. Oxford and Portland, OR: Hart Publishing.

Scott, J., and D.M. Trubeck. 2002. Mind the gap: Law and new approaches to governance in the European Union. *European Law Journal* 8:1–18.

Smit, A.A.H., C. Dieperink, P. Driessen, and H.F.M.W. van Rijswick. 2008. Een onmogelijke opgave? Een onderzoek naar de wijze waarop waterschappen invulling geven aan de wateropgaven en de spanningen die zich daarbij voordoen, Kaderrichtlijn water en Natura 2000 [A mission impossible? Research after the way water boards implement the water assignment and the related tensions, Water Framework Directive and Natura 2000]. Research report, Utrecht University, Utrecht, Netherlands.

Uijterlinde, R.W., A. Janssen, and C. Figuères. 2003. *Success factors in self-financing local water management: A contribution to the Third World Water Forum in Japan 2003.* The Hague: NWB/UNESCO–IHE Institute for Water Education.

van de Ven, G.P. 2004. *Man-made lowlands.* Utrecht, Netherlands: Nederlands Nationaal Comite of the International Commission on Irrigation and Drainage (ICDI)/Stichting Matrijs.

van Rijswick, H.F.M.W. 2003. EC water law in transition: The challenge of integration. In *Yearbook of European environmental law*, ed. H. Somsen. Oxford: Oxford University Press, 249–304.

———. 2004. The implementation of the WFD in Dutch law: A slow but steady improvement. *Journal for European Environmental and Planning Law* 3:218–27.

———. 2008. *Moving water and the law: On the distribution of water rights and water duties within river basins in European and Dutch water law.* Groningen, Netherlands: Europa Law Publishing.

van Rijswick, H.F.M.W., and P.P.J. Driessen. 2006. *Juridisch bestuurlijke capaciteit in het waterbeleid* [Legal-governmental capacity in water policy]. Utrecht, Netherlands: Utrecht University.

CHAPTER 12

Innovative Approaches to Public Participation in Water Management

Dave Huitema, Marleen van de Kerkhof, Erna Ovaa, and Leontien Bos-Gorter

THIS CHAPTER FOCUSES on the issue of public participation in the context of Dutch water management. It presents a wide range of possible methods for involving the public in water management, sketches differences in their design and effectiveness, and shows how they could be evaluated from the perspective of a water manager. By demonstrating the design and performance of the more innovative methods, we hope to provide an impetus for the continued development of this field.

The definition of public participation is quite varied; here it is defined as the taking part, by ordinary citizens or their collectives, in the process by which policies are shaped and implemented (cf. Birch 1993, *80*). Specific interest is in the aspects of public participation that relate to the policymaking processes of water managers (see also Chapter 9). Examples include the development of water management plans and the decisionmaking process for water management infrastructure.

Public participation is increasingly being regarded as an important element of a well-functioning and legitimate democracy; the fact that citizens vote periodically is merely a minimum requirement for a government to be deemed democratic. Citizens involved in policymaking processes are here called participants. A distinction can be made between citizens operating individually (e.g., because a citizen wants to defend the value of his or her house in an area where water managers are changing protection levels) and those operating in a collective. Such collectives are often referred to as nongovernmental organizations (NGOs) or interest groups. These are umbrella terms that apply to a range of groups that act collectively to promote their political agendas. The work of both individual citizens and their collectives is addressed in this chapter, although the emphasis may shift from paragraph to paragraph.

The reader may wonder why public participation is an item for discussion in the Netherlands at all. Some publications (e.g., Kaijser 2002) have described Dutch water management as "self-government," implying that the typical distance between government and the public in ordinary government organizations should perhaps not be an issue. In our opinion, it is an error to describe Dutch water management as being in a state of self-government. Granted, the water boards have always operated in a cooperative fashion and on a local scale that stood out against the more feudal government systems found in the rest of Europe (see, e.g., Noordegraaf et al. 2006; Vandersmissen and den Hengst 1998; and Chapter 9 of this book). Although water boards in the past were democratic, however, this democracy extended only to those who were paying for the works of the water boards, namely farmers. In addition, the trend for centralization of Dutch water management has continued since the Napoleonic period (early 19th century) with the foundation of Rijkswaterstaat and the ever-increasing scale of water boards, from thousands of boards to just 27. In fact, a more current analysis of affairs would contend that Dutch water management is a relatively technocratic and closed policy sector (Bressers et al. 1995). The sector has had its share of confrontations with the environmental movement and has been accused at times of pushing forward megalomaniac projects (see, e.g., Huitema and Kuks 2004).

As in other countries, the relevance and salience of public participation in Dutch water management have increased in the past decades.[1] A number of factors are behind this. Some are on what may be called the "demand side" of public participation. As societal attention to environmental goods such as clean water and landscape has grown, so has the desire to participate in the decisions going into managing these goods. Similarly, water management has been increasingly touching on politically sensitive issues such as land use planning. On the "supply side," the number of institutional venues for public participation has increased, especially during the 1970s, when water management activities became subject to land use planning and planning law required that water managers begin experimenting with public participation (see also Chapter 10 on spatial planning).

Interestingly, many new public interest groups used the land use planning arena as an entry point into the world of water management. During the 1980s and 1990s, water managers were faced with increased public opposition to water infrastructure projects. As a means of offsetting this public opposition and avoiding possible legal action further down the road, they began to solicit public opinion in the early stages of project development. Nevertheless, the growth of public participation in water management was not wholly inspired by the need to avoid confrontation. Water managers also understood that they could derive benefits from cooperating with land users in carrying out interrelated water and land use measures. Moreover, they realized much could be learned from the public, whether organized in groups such as NGOs or individual citizens. Even when individuals lack formal education, they often possess local or ordinary knowledge that water managers might find useful in making informed decisions.

In this chapter, we first focus on the methodology for evaluating public participatory processes and give five possible goals that can be used as a yardstick for evaluation. Next, we provide an overview of available and popular participatory methods, detail the design choices water managers face when setting up a process, and describe the current legal requirements for public participation in the Netherlands. Finally, we examine several case studies involving focus groups and a citizens' jury in the IJsselmeer basin and evaluate some of the more innovative public participation methods undertaken.

GOALS AND EFFECTIVENESS OF PUBLIC PARTICIPATION

Public participation is what social scientists call an "essentially contested" concept, as its meaning is approached from many different perspectives. In political science, for instance, two perspectives exist on how public participation can help rectify shortcomings of representative democracy. According to the deliberative perspective, citizens need to participate in the political system and decide on a common course by means of deliberation and shared meanings (see, e.g., Smith and Wales 2000), whereas the pluralist perspective (see, e.g., Rorty 1999) views public participation as a negotiation process in which people promote their individual interests. From that perspective, a decision is based not on shared meanings, but on the aggregation of the interests of the different individuals in a social collective.

In this section, we adopt a functional perspective, assessing whether public participation achieves certain preset goals; we do not argue for increased participation for the sake of participation itself (Coenen et al. 1998). We also include the limitations, or disadvantages, of participation with regard to its effectiveness in reaching these goals. We do take into account the goals of others, such as the participants, but our main focus is on the usefulness of public participation from the perspective of the water manager. Five goals exist for public participation in water management (van de Kerkhof and Huitema 2004): raised awareness; improved decisions; increased legitimacy of decisionmaking; better accountability of decisionmaking; and collective learning.

Raised Awareness

An invitation to discuss an issue can generally contribute to raising awareness of that issue in the mind of the invitee, if only because it is a signal that somebody else considers the topic sufficiently important for public deliberation and the invitee needs to decide whether to participate. Raising awareness is a prominent task for water managers, as water management issues can be thought to follow the "issue attention cycle" (Downs 1972), meaning that public attention to the issues will be cyclical in nature, probably peaking at times of floods or other incidents and waning when issues seem to be under control. Studies of water awareness in the Netherlands (de Boer et al. 2003) show very little realization of the risks associated with living next to massive bodies of water. The collective memory of flooding faded rapidly after 1953 but was heightened somewhat in the 1990s with several floods and near floods. This peaking and waning of attention is dangerous in water management, as long-term risks require constant attention.

Although public participation can contribute to raising awareness, it also has its limitations. One of these relates to the relationship between group size and the degree of participation (Huitema et al. 2005). On the one hand, to have an impact on a large number of people, a participatory process should reach out to as many as possible, preferably an entire community. Large groups do not allow for intensive discussions and interactions, however, so other, "lighter" approaches have to be used, such as sending brochures or leaflets or organizing a public hearing. On the other hand, intensive participation, in which individuals discuss the issues and debate with one another and with external groups, is more likely to be effective in raising awareness but necessarily will involve only a small number of people. If a manager decides to involve only a small group of people, he or she needs to take into account the matter of translation and dissemination to a larger audience, which in practice appears to be difficult. Also, the criteria used to decide who should participate becomes an issue.

Improved Decisions

A second goal of participation is to reach better decisions that take into account the context in which these decisions take place and are implemented. Participation provides a capacity to enrich the decisionmaking process with information about the intended measures and possible consequences and helps the water manager find solutions that are both workable and acceptable. If the manager succeeds in creating a comfortable, cooperative environment for the participants, they may share new information that can be beneficial in the decisionmaking process. For example, farmers in the Canadian province of Manitoba knew the flood pattern of the Red River in detail because of their decades-long connection to the land. When engaged by authorities to share their knowledge, they were able to help pinpoint safe areas during times of flooding that were missing on the provincial experts' maps (Huitema 2002). Participatory exercises also can be expected to show what the citizens believe should be the priorities of water management and what choices should be made. This can be beneficial for water managers.

In the literature, arguments have been made against the idea that the public can contribute to making better decisions. One such contention goes back to the political theories of the early 20th century, in which Schumpeter (1942) maintained that the "average" citizen is not capable of a rational judgment on complex matters that go beyond the experience of his or her daily life. Especially in matters that involve norms and values, such as politics and many environmental problems, Schumpeter regarded the policy preferences of citizens as merely manipulable opinions that change with the issues of the day. As such, these opinions should not be allowed to have much of an impact on the actual decisionmaking process.

Another argument against participation is the notion that citizens are most likely to defend their own short-term interests and free ride on collective goods. Social scientists have developed several concepts for this; one is termed the NIMBY ("not in my back yard") syndrome, which refers to citizens' fervent opposition to siting proposals or land use activities with potential adverse impacts in the areas where they live or have businesses (Huitema 2002; Rosa 1988, referred to in Webler and

Renn 1995, 27). According to this line of reasoning, the emphasis on citizens' own short-term interests makes it complicated and undesirable for government officials to include the citizens' perspectives in their decisionmaking process, as governments need to address collective goods while keeping a long-term perspective.

Increased Legitimacy of Decisionmaking

The third goal of participation is to increase the legitimacy of decisionmaking. Policies and measures produced with the cooperation of citizens, and for which they feel a level of control, will increase public acceptance and support. In addition, it is a well-known phenomenon that involvement breeds further involvement, thereby reducing the perceived distance from decisionmakers.

Again, the extent to which public participation can increase the legitimacy of decisionmaking also has limitations. One is that the outcomes of a participatory exercise run the risk of being used as a justification for decisions that have been made elsewhere by political means. This can devaluate participatory exercises to the level of what Arnstein (1969) calls "tokenism," in which citizens get the chance to voice their opinion but lack the power to ensure that those with decisionmaking authority properly take their views into account. Others even argue that public participation threatens the legitimacy of decisionmaking, as it may override existing legitimate processes and undermine the position of Parliament (Cooke and Kothari 2001). In a representative democracy such as the Netherlands, the citizens elect the members of Parliament or other governing body, who are supposed to represent the voices and interests of the people. Bypassing Parliament by involving a nonelected group of people in the decisionmaking process can be perceived as an unjust allocation of power that decreases the legitimacy of that process.

Better Accountability of Decisionmaking

A fourth goal of public participation is to increase the accountability of decisionmaking. This is grounded in the government being more responsive to the concerns of the public, creating transparency, and granting access to the decisionmaking process. Government actions and decisions need to be motivated (preferably) by referring to arguments that strike a chord with the public and address issues and concerns they may have. Citizen participation is one way of gaining access to the public mind and discovering what concerns people have; this is the responsiveness aspect. At the same time, public participation can fulfill a function in showing the people what the bureaucracy and politicians are doing and why they are doing it. Arguments about political and bureaucratic rationality are plenty. Public participation can help solve certain misconceptions in this field. Open access of the people to public institutions is needed to give them a share of ownership ("this is my water manager") and create a sense of trustworthiness ("the management has nothing to hide").

Although public participation can contribute to increased accountability for decisionmaking, it has limitations here as well. An important one is that government cannot be responsive to the concerns of every single person. What might occur then can also be referred to as the "participation paradox" (Seley 1983), leading to a reinforcement of the interests of those who are already powerful (Cooke and Kothari 2001). The participation paradox means that in order to participate effectively, one needs power resources that are not equally distributed over the affected population. Such resources include, among others, access to relevant information and a voice loud enough to be heard by the decisionmakers. Weaker interests are in a marginal position, so participation facilities will not be of great help for them. As a result, government will mainly become more responsive to the concerns of the "powerful."

Collective Learning

Finally, participation may result in a process of collective learning, in which stakeholders, government, and scientific experts enter into a dialogue and, by interaction and debate, learn how to collectively manage a river basin and deal with conflicting views and interests (see, e.g., Pahl-Wostl 2002; van de Kerkhof 2006). If this succeeds, one could say that a collective vision has been created, which can guide societal action from then on. The scope of such a learning process may differ; perhaps it is more likely that collective learning will occur within the group of participants or between participants and experts, rather than among the entire community.

A limitation to public participation as collective learning is the pessimistic view that a participatory process tends to aggravate conflict and result in deadlock, rather than increase understanding. Highly emotional conflicts may be especially difficult to handle and could even mean participation by a certain group or individual will be at the expense of that of another group or individual.

Table 12-1 summarizes the five goals of public participation discussed so far. In the next section, various methods for public participation are discussed as well as their associated legal aspects.

SETTING UP PARTICIPATORY PROCESSES

Participatory methods can be understood as a collection of procedures designed to involve, consult, and inform citizens so that they can have an input in public decisions. The literature on participation presents a wide variety of methods and techniques that stem from a broad range of disciplines.[2] Water management literature, such as the Guidance Document on Public Participation in Relation to the Water Framework Directive (Drafting Group 2002), also suggests participatory methods. The methods range from those that seek input in the form of opinions (e.g., opinion surveys) to those that elicit judgments and decisions from which actual policy might be derived (e.g., citizens' jury). The majority of participatory methods regarding water management are used to gain public input into value-laden and policy-oriented, rather than technical, aspects.

The degree to which the outcomes of participatory processes are binding has garnered quite a lot of attention from academics and practitioners alike, perhaps as a result of the debate over the relationship between public participation and representative democracy. Almost without exception, writings on public participation

Table 12-1 *Five goals of public participation*

Goal	Aspects
Raised awareness	Among participants Among the wider public
Better decisions	Better insights into facts and consequences of measures Better insights into feasibility
Increased legitimacy	Reduction of the distance between water manager and public Support for measures to be taken
Accountability	Responsiveness Transparency and access
Collective learning	New perspectives for participants New perspectives for water managers Development of a collective vision among participants Emergence of a collective vision in the community

refer to Arnstein (1969), who was dissatisfied with the currently existing methods and proposed a normative "ladder of participation." She distinguished eight "rungs," including "manipulation," "therapy," and "placation," but also "partnership," "delegated power," and "citizen control." For Arnstein, only the last three terms constitute actual public participation. The other rungs are "no participation" and "degrees of tokenism." Arnstein's implicit view was that public participation is "real" only when the participants are able to make binding decisions—in other words, they have power.

Positioning public participation so directly against representative democracy (or the bureaucracy for that matter) is unlikely to increase enthusiasm for public participation among politicians and bureaucrats, as they may see it as a threat to their own power. Moreover, a focus on decisionmaking power may not be enough to facilitate "real" participation. Imagine a participatory process where the public has full authority to decide on a range of water management issues, but with no information whatsoever. Even in a situation where the participants were formally very powerful, a lack of information would cause them to have great difficulty in preparing joint decisions. Thus decisionmaking authority should not be the only design parameter for public participation methods. Water managers should focus on an alternative set of parameters while setting up a participatory process, considering the following:

- *The competences and power assigned to the participants.* Will the participants' advice be binding? Are they permitted to determine which issues they will address? To what extent must they take into account and be bound by existing policy choices? The more power allotted to the participants, the more the process will be participatory in nature.
- *The conditions of access to the process.* Who is in and who is out? It matters a great deal whether participation rights are allotted only to landowners, taxpayers, organized interests, or anyone having or showing an interest. The more liberal the rights of access, the better the conditions for a participatory process.

- *The flow of information to and from the process and the participants.* This is a matter of the participants getting access to all information they may need. The more openness, the more participatory the process. It is also a matter of defining the types of arguments that do and do not count. The stronger the emphasis on arguments related to technical and cost-effectiveness issues, rather than values and goals, the less participatory the process becomes.
- *The costs of the process.* Do participants have to pay their own way to attend events? Must they use their own financial resources for organizing events and hiring experts? Costs associated with participation also include the giving up of free time. The more the costs are borne by a public authority (such as in the form of intervener funding, as is available in Canada; see Huitema 2002), the better the conditions are for a more participatory process.

Each design aspect has the ability to influence the others. Greater access to information tends to be associated with more restrictions on the number and type of participants.[3] An emphasis on technical and economic factors effectively rules out many potential participants. Paying the costs of participants may have an inviting effect. Table 12-2 is a "menu" of participatory methods available to water managers, with different options for each of these parameters. It presents a selection of methods that differ distinctively with regard to authorities assigned to the participants, conditions of access, flows of information, and costs. The methods included are referendum, public hearing, opinion survey, negotiated rulemaking, web panel, citizens' jury, focus group, and social learning group.

The table clearly shows the differences among the methods. With regard to conditions of access, a number of methods involve only a small, selected group of participants (citizens' jury, negotiated rulemaking, focus group, social learning groups), whereas others allow for a potentially large number (referendum, public hearing, opinion survey, web panel).

Concerning information flows, the referendum and opinion survey do not facilitate multiple flows to and from the participants, whereas most of the other methods do. Some of the methods, such as the citizens' jury and social learning group, explicitly focus on facilitating multiple flows of information between the scientific experts and the public or stakeholders. In a focus group, the flow of information from outside is rather low. This is because the focus group aims to elicit the viewpoints and opinions of the participants in that particular group. The process should therefore not be influenced by information from outside the group.

With respect to the costs, in most of the methods the organizers bear the expenses for organizing the participatory exercise, while in many cases the participants have to pay for their own traveling expenses. In some methods, such as the citizens' jury, the participants sometimes receive compensation for giving up free time, although there have been several cases in which they have not. For a number of methods, such as referendum and opinion survey, hardly any expenses are involved for the public to participate.

Regarding the authority afforded to the participants, the methods are rather distinctive. In a referendum or opinion survey, the participants do not have the authority to determine which issues they want to address; these are predetermined by the organizers. In the other methods, the organizers usually define a theme or question

Table 12-2 *Methods for public participation*

Method name	Authorities and competencies	Conditions of access	Information flows	Costs to participate
Referendum	Voting mechanism, all participants have equal influence, outcome often binding	Potentially all members of a population, realistically a significant proportion	Information supply through the media, method does not allow for interaction and debate	Costs borne by organizer, in general no or very low costs for participants, except for travel expenses and the like
Public hearing	Topic is often predetermined, outcome not binding	Interested citizens, limited number because of venue size	Presentation of plans in open forums, public may voice opinions, low level of interaction	Costs borne by organizer, in general no or very low costs for participants, such as travel expenses, giving up free time, and the like
Opinion survey	Topics are predetermined, outcomes of survey not binding	Large samples, usually representative	Written questionnaire or telephone survey, used for information gathering, one-way flow of information and opinions, no interaction among participants	Costs borne by organizer, in general no or very low costs for participants
Negotiated rulemaking	General topic predetermined, information supply on participants' request, independent facilitator moderates discussion, outcomes most of the time not binding but serve to advise policymakers	Small number of representatives of stakeholder groups	Working committee of stakeholder representatives, high degree of interaction and flow of information among stakeholder groups, consensus required on a certain matter	Costs borne by organizer, in general no or very low costs for participants, such as travel expenses, giving up free time, and the like
Web panel	General topic predetermined, participants may determine subtopics, outcomes not binding	Open forum, potentially all members of a population, realistically a significant proportion of interested citizens	Public may voice opinions and discuss electronically, flow of information to the participants often rather low	Costs borne by organizer, in general no or very low costs for the participants

(Continued)

Table 12-2 *Methods for public participation*

Method name	Authorities and competencies	Conditions of access	Information flows	Costs to participate
Citizens' jury	General topic predetermined, information supply on participants' request, independent facilitator moderates discussion, outcomes most of the time not binding but serve to advise policymakers	Jury of 12 to 24 members of the public, to serve as an approximate microcosm of the population	High degree of interaction and flow of information between citizens and experts, consensus not required	Costs often borne by organizer, but sometimes participants have to give up free time and travel without compensation
Focus group	General topic predetermined, participants decide on subtopics they want to discuss, little input from facilitator, outcomes not binding	Small groups of 6 to 10 people, usually from similar backgrounds	Free discussion on general topic, which is recorded, used to assess opinions and attitudes, high degree of interaction between participants, flow of information often rather low	Costs often borne by organizer, but sometimes participants have to give up free time and travel without compensation
Social learning group	Participants set up experiments, measure results, and conduct analyses, supported by scientists, outcomes not binding but serve to advise policymakers	Small number of representatives of stakeholder groups, accompanied by researchers	High degree of interaction and flow of information between stakeholders and scientific experts, consensus not required	Costs borne by organizer, in general no or very low costs for participants, such as travel expenses, giving up free time, and the like

(a charge, in the case of a citizens' jury), within the boundaries of which the participants are free to choose the topics they want to discuss. As to the authority to make actual decisions, in the case of almost all the methods, the outcomes are not binding for policy but serve to advise a public authority. A notable exception is the referendum, which can be binding for policy.

CURRENT DUTCH METHODS

To examine the methods commonly used in Dutch water management in light of the above descriptions, we need to distinguish between what is legally prescribed and what has emerged on top of or outside the legal prescriptions, often referred to as interactive policymaking. This section first describes the former, then addresses the latter, paying special attention to the Dutch implementation of the EU Water Framework Directive (WFD), which requires a renewed interpretation of the legal obligations with regard to participation and also acts as a catalyst for the development of more innovative participatory methods in practice.

Legal Prescriptions for Public Participation

The legal format for public participation can be found in the General Act on Administrative Law.[4] This act lists a number of general procedures for public decisionmaking that could be useful in almost all dealings between citizens and the state. At the same time, the act is specific in that it tailors appropriate procedures to the status of the decision at hand. Water management and land use planning legislation refer to the act by stating what type of procedure applies to each particular type of decision. Licensing procedures (e.g., obtaining a license for discharging wastewater into surface water) are different from those for establishing a water management plan. Although much more could be said about the act's prescriptions for public participation, the essence is that *public hearings* are the favored method. If citizens are not satisfied with the responses of officials at such hearings, they can send written remarks; if they do not receive satisfactory replies, they can go to court. Dutch legislation contains several guarantees for open access to information (with the exception of company secrets), access to hearings is open, and recourse to the courts is a very accessible venue. Testing of government decisions by the courts tends to be relatively in-depth, as the courts can ask for expert advice and generally feel free to replace the administration's decisions with their own. During court cases, the parties rarely meet, except during a brief public hearing, which is basically intended to summarize and check the paper record of the case (Huitema 2002).

Stakeholders with an insider status (e.g., large NGOs, industries, or acknowledged experts) tend to have representatives on various legally prescribed *advisory boards*, such as the Council for Traffic and Water Management. Such boards are a venue for idea formation and occasionally policy negotiation. At a more concrete level, the same groups tend to have representation in the process of standard setting. Much water legislation contains vague and ambiguous language (e.g., calling for emission levels that are as low as reasonably achievable), and in order for the legislation to be implemented, this language must be clarified. Such a task often falls on advisory groups that consist of regulators, experts, NGOs, and industry representatives and have a semiformal status. An example is the Committee for the Implementation of Pollution of Surface Water Act (CUWVO, later CIW), which had an important role in setting actual water treatment standards (Bressers et al. 1995). Such boards and committees are best classified as forms of *regulatory negotiation*.

The WFD, which overrides and overhauls much of the current Dutch approach to water quality management, may bring more variation to the menu of participatory methods. The directive demands that the responsible authorities inform and consult with the public, but also encourage the active involvement of "all interested parties" in the formation of river basin management plans. Because of the WFD "information" obligation to publish even the first versions of the river basin management plans, citizens and organized stakeholders have the opportunity to submit their viewpoints at a much earlier stage of the policymaking process than formerly was the case. This has the potential to increase the influence of these viewpoints in the end products.

The WFD is accompanied by a guidance document on public participation (Drafting Group 2002), which is quite progressive from a methodological perspective, as it describes several highly innovative methods that are not part of the legal fabric in most member states of the Union. Another piece of Dutch legislation is the Implementation Law for the WFD.[5] This provides for all three elements of participation—information, consultation, and involvement—with increased possibilities regarding the general regime of Section 3.4 of the General Act on Administrative Law.

In the first years after the WFD came into force, implementation efforts were concentrated mainly at the national level. In order to encourage the active involvement of all interested parties, nine different "modes for active involvement" were developed, and these have recently been evaluated (Ovaa and Ottow 2006). At the national level, the category of "interested parties" mainly consists of NGOs and organized interest groups. Over the next years of implementation of the WFD, this is likely to change, as more concrete programs and measures developed within the river basins will allow for a greater number of individual farmers and citizens to participate. This can already be seen in the WFD territorial groups (gebiedsgroepen) recently begun in the north of the Netherlands.

By the end of 2008, the draft river basin management plans were made available for public inspection, but as they were implemented through the existing legal planning system for water management and land use planning, the "normal" public participation methods were used. The actual places where decisions could be found were not as obvious as they could have been, as the decisions were spread across municipal, provincial, and national plans. Ordinary citizens could read about these plans online, find out exactly where the decisions on which they wanted to comment appeared, and then express their opinions at public hearings or in writing, whereas interest groups and NGOs were being consulted by means of "sounding board groups," which had already started operating when the plans were being prepared. This means that most of the more innovative methods for involving the public suggested by European guidance were not being used as of 2009.

Extralegal Participation Methods

Several extralegal public participation programs have been used in the Netherlands in the past two decades. At the local level, a common method is known as the "kitchen-table conversation," which resembles a focus group with some regulatory negotiation elements. Water board functionaries or local politicians employ this method vis-à-vis individual stakeholders. The purpose is to discuss future plans and foreseeable consequences with respect to the participants' land, homes, and surroundings. The first visits may have a mutually informing character; during subsequent visits, elements for negotiations may be brought up.

Another method, popular in the 1990s, is the organization of integrated regional processes (see Glasbergen 1996). This involves bottom-up collaborative planning, aimed at combining several policy goals, instruments, and funds in such a way as to generate a surplus value for the district. As a starting point, a vision for the desired future of the district is developed in collaboration with the province, local authorities and water boards, nongovernmental organizations, local farmers, and inhabitants. In later phases, stakeholders formulate an action program, negotiate on package deals, and make settlements with respect to coresponsibility for implementation (see, e.g., Ovaa 1999).

A relatively new method that is becoming increasingly popular in water management practices is the interactive design atelier, which enables authorities and public participants to combine different kinds of knowledge and gain insights into the spatial and hydrological consequences of various choices. On the basis of multiple designs, the authorities and stakeholders discuss preferable scenarios, strategies, and packages of measures to take. In the Netherlands, this method has been employed in the national river reconstruction project called Room for the River.

A last method is the open planning process, which involves a number of consultative rounds. At successive stages of the process, this method invites a broad selection of the public—in public hearings and workshops—to bring forward their ideas and share their reactions. At first they are asked to relate relevant problems, in a second round to discuss ideas, in a later phase to comment on a first draft, and so forth. This type of method is predominantly employed for large-scale, multi-issue, long-term planning problems. The Netherlands' Fourth National Policy Memorandum on Water Management, for example, was developed using this method (see Koolhaas et al. 1998).

CASE STUDIES: FOCUS GROUPS AND A CITIZENS' JURY

In order to illustrate how public participation methods play out in the field of water management and what goals they can serve, this section details our experience with two particular public participation methods in the IJsselmeer region: the focus group and the citizens' jury.[6] Using the design parameters, both methods are described in terms of their methodology, application in the IJsselmeer case, and outcomes. The IJsselmeer is a lake located in the heart of the Netherlands, bordered by the provinces of Friesland, North Holland, and Flevoland, although the name is often used for the area encompassing both the IJsselmeer and Markermeer lakes (both lakes are separated by a dike). At the end of this section, we evaluate and compare the methods with respect to the five goals of public participation described earlier.

The Focus Group Method

A focus group can best be described as an informal discussion among selected individuals about a specific topic. There are many variations on the basic method, but in general, a focus group involves one or more group discussions in which participants focus collectively on a topic selected by the initiator, usually presented to them as a small set of questions (Wilkinson 1998, *182*). The main aim of this method is to gain insight into people's perceptions, experiences, and beliefs concerning a specific issue (Morgan 1998a).

Regarding the *authorities assigned to the participants*, the outcomes of a focus group are not binding for policy; focus groups do not have decisionmaking power. The participants do have some authority with respect to the issues they wish to discuss. The focus group is guided by a moderator who is a well-trained professional and works from a predetermined set of discussion topics (Morgan 1998a). These are usually rather general, and the participants are allowed to raise other topics that they consider to be important and thereby influence the outcomes of the process.

In terms of the *conditions of access* to the process, focus groups are small, typically ranging in size from six to ten participants, although the number may vary. Focus groups are often fairly homogeneous, sometimes consisting of preexisting communities (e.g., members of a farmer group), but a heterogeneous mix of participants may be brought together from different communities specifically for the purpose of a focus group (Morgan 1998b). It is important to note that this method is not aimed at either involving all relevant actors or capturing a representative sample of the population, thus implying that certain relevant groups can be excluded and the process manipulated.

With regard to the *flows of information*, focus groups generally rely on the knowledge that is available within the group of participants. The discussion is rarely influenced by scientific information, allowing for a sound impression of the viewpoints and opinions of those in the group. It is most important that the participants feel at ease with each other to speak freely, which is more difficult when they meet for the first time.

As for the issue of *costs*, focus groups require little commitment and preparation on the part of the participants. Focus groups are usually held near where the participants live (e.g., a community center), and the average duration of the meetings is 1.5 to 2 hours. As the focus group method generally relies on the knowledge that the participants already have, not much time, if any, is needed for preparation.

Focus Groups in the IJsselmeer Region. The aim of the IJsselmeer focus group was to gain insight into the views held by various types of users of the lake with regard to water management. From May to June 2003, nine focus groups were held in the IJsselmeer region. In an effort to articulate the views and perceptions of particular types of users, each group was fairly homogenous with regard to the participants' profession or interest in the lake. Of the nine groups, two consisted of farmers (Friesland and North Holland), two of ordinary citizens (Friesland and Almere), and one each of fishermen, recreational users of the lake, nature conservationists, homeowners, and public officials.

Figure 12.1 shows that the willingness to participate of those approached for the study varied from 24% to 100%. The 100% score for the agricultural group was strongly influenced by the fact that we received a list of names of active farmers from their representative organization. The willingness to participate of the other groups ranged from 24% to 44%. On one hand, it could be said that this is very high, given the fact that people had to give up spare time, usually for an evening session. On the other hand, one could say that the percentage is rather low, precisely because it took only one evening and required little to no preparation. The reasons for not wanting to participate were generally very pragmatic, such as lack of time or interest.

In an effort to stimulate debate on water management, the project team devised a list of 15 questions related to issues of water management and the environment in a broad sense. Additionally, the participants were asked to reflect on two newspaper clippings about the water quality and level of the IJsselmeer.

Outcomes of the Focus Groups. The project team drew up reports on each of the focus groups. These reports present a number of interesting views and perceptions of the different types of users. For instance, water quality was a universal topic of interest and concern for all focus groups. Most equated good water quality with clarity and the absence of mosquitoes, algae, and litter, and almost all were aware of a notable improvement in water quality in recent decades. Only the fishermen reported a decrease in water quality, related to the fact that the lake's nutrient load has diminished because of various policy measures, including the use of nonphosphate detergents and improved wastewater treatment. This implies less food for the

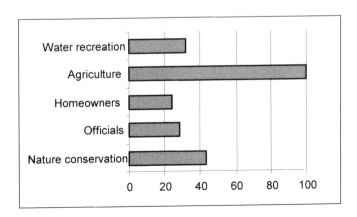

Figure 12.1 *Percentages of people who were willing to participate per focus group*

fish and therefore a decline in their numbers. The environmental NGOs agreed that the water quality should be improved, indicating that the IJsselmeer still contains too many chemical substances such as PCBs as well as phosphates. They complained that water quality improvement efforts are aimed mainly at parameters relevant for human consumption (drinking water) and recreation (swimming water), whereas they should be aimed at improving ecological conditions. Diametrically opposed to this view were the citizens of the city of Almere, who argued that water quality is important only from the perspective of human uses.

The water level in the IJsselmeer and, more specifically, flood safety are important concerns for the water managers but were issues that did not automatically come up in any of the focus groups. This could be a reflection of the more general attitude of the Dutch public that this issue is more or less under control and need not be worried about. Although participants saw an increasing European influence in water management as unavoidable and probably for the better of all, there was clear sense that something would get lost in the process. For the citizens of Friesland and the farmers, the process of scale enlargement of the Dutch water boards was already a point of concern. They felt that under the newly established water board, money was being wasted on bureaucracy and housing, and contact with the region was diminishing and would be lost altogether. For the policymakers, the increased role of the EU seemed to especially imply a loss in flexibility of regulations.

The Citizens' Jury Method

A citizens' jury consists of a group of randomly selected citizens who attend a series of meetings in order to learn about and discuss a specific issue, and then make their recommendations public (Crosby 1995). At the start, the jury gets a "charge," which is a question they have to answer or topic they must address. The jury then hears "witnesses" whom they selected to represent different, perhaps conflicting, viewpoints on the topic under consideration. Essentially, the participants (the jurors) hear evidence, question witnesses, discuss the issues raised, and then make an informed judgment with regard to the charge (Kuper 1996).

In terms of the *authorities assigned to the participants*, the jury verdict often carries the weight of a recommendation to the commissioning body. Jurors are normally allowed to alter the agenda slightly; however, the broad agenda tends to be determined by the commissioning body. The jurors can influence the process through the selection and questioning of witnesses. A jury normally tries to make decisions based on consensus, but if one cannot be reached, each juror can influence the outcomes by means of voting.

In terms of the *conditions of access*, the number of participants can vary from 12 to 24. The citizens are selected via a quota system in such a way as to represent a microcosm of the community from which they are drawn. Typically, the criteria include demographics such as age, gender, and education or else rely on balancing the number of jurors with various attitudes on the question under consideration so that they are representative of their community. Certain groups tend to be overrepresented among the volunteers, for which the system usually compensates by introducing minimum quotas for various types of jurors (e.g., no less than 40% women).

In contrast to a focus group, a citizens' jury is characterized by multiple *flows of information*. Several experts, such as scientists or other stakeholders, play the role of witnesses. They give presentations and are questioned by the jurors, sometimes individually, sometimes more than one at the same time, which gives the jurors the opportunity to confront the witnesses on their viewpoints. Furthermore, the citizens' jury includes at least one day of deliberation, in which the jurors discuss and contemplate among themselves the various viewpoints and information gathered, with the aim of formulating recommendations for policymakers.

With respect to *costs*, citizens' juries are quite demanding for the participants in the sense that they require a good deal of preparation, tend to last several days, and demand substantive concentration. As a result, more effort is needed in attracting citizens to participate in a jury versus a focus group. Jury members often receive a limited amount of money to compensate for lost labor time or pay for childcare.

The Markermeer Citizens' Jury. The citizens' jury in our case study focused on a part of the IJsselmeer called the Markermeer. The jury received the charge "What should be the points of attention in the policy that the government carries out with regard to the quality of the water in the Markermeer?" To answer this question, the jury was organized into a three-day event, with two evenings dedicated to preparation and one to evaluation (see also Huitema et al. 2004). The preparation evenings were spent on training the jurors in issues relevant to water management as well as the skills required for being a juror, such as asking the right questions. On one of the evenings, jurors were invited to an information market, where, on their own initiative, they could freely walk around and talk to four experts who were present. During the first two days of the process, the jurors collected information through questioning the witnesses. The third day was devoted to jury deliberation and formulation of recommendations. The organizers wrote out the ensuing recommendations in a report that was discussed and then accepted for approval by the jurors in a separate evening session. Eventually these documents were submitted to the authorities during a session held a few weeks later.

A common procedure for participant recruitment is to mail invitation letters, flyers, and reply cards to a large number of addresses; in this case, they were sent out to 2,000 residents in Lelystad, the capital city of Flevoland. The addresses were chosen randomly from files that were (again randomly) selected by the Dutch National Post. The eventual jurors were selected from the 61 people who responded positively, a response rate of 3.05%. This percentage is lower than most of the response rates mentioned in the literature.[7] A possible explanation is that people participating in the jury were expected to give up three full days and a number of evenings, and to do so without any financial compensation, which was not the case in many other juries.[8]

Figure 12.2 highlights three demographic characteristics of those who were willing to participate in the jury, as compared with the general population of Lelystad. The figure also shows the characteristics of the people that were actually selected for the jury. Two facts stand out: the great majority of the prospective jurors were

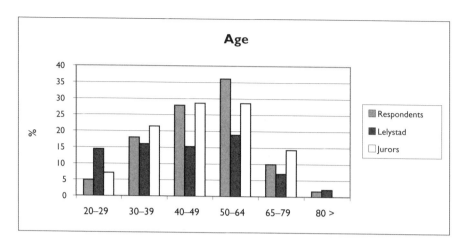

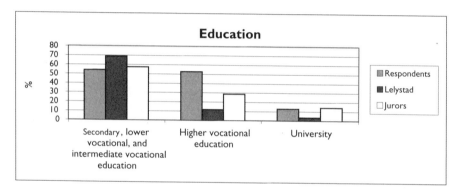

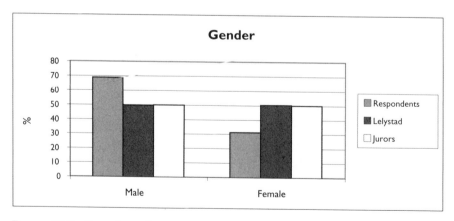

Figure 12.2 *Overview of age, education, and gender characteristics of the respondents, the population of Lelystad, and the jurors*

males, and the age group 20 to 29 was underrepresented in the group of candidates and, as a result, also in the actual jury.

Outcomes of the Citizens' Jury. The citizens' jury reached a conclusion after three days of meetings and discussions. Concerning the Water Framework Directive, an important step in its implementation would be the designation of a status to the Markermeer as either a natural or a human-influenced water basin. From this basic distinction would flow a range of decisions, the bottom line of which is that water quality standards are more ambitious for natural than for human-influenced water basins. In this light, it was very significant that the jury decided the Markermeer should be assigned the "heavily influenced by humans" status, and standard setting should proceed from there.

The jury acknowledged that the earlier protracted and now completed discussion about whether to turn the lake into polder land still had an influence on its situation. Because the Markermeer had been officially designated as a subject of reclamation for decades (roughly from the 1920s to the 1970s), and the official government policy toward reclamation was very much in limbo from the 1970s until about 1995, little consideration had been given to the values and possibilities of the lake as a stretch of *open water* now and in the future. The jury fully recognized these values and possibilities, for the flora and fauna as well as for humans, and therefore developed a vision they all agreed on: the Markermeer should remain an open water body (prohibiting land reclamation in the corners of the lake), with considerably more biodiversity than at present, moderate transitions between land and water, greater access to nature for recreation, and a role of diminished importance for agriculture and the fishing industry (by reducing the use of water for agriculture and emissions from that sector and by banning professional fisheries). According to this vision, the lake thereby would also become suitable for the possible extraction of drinking water in the future. In order to realize this vision, cooperation, not only within the government, but also between the government and the private sector, would have to be improved. The public had to become more aware of the possibilities the lake offers, and the local residents needed to be more involved in any planning.

Evaluation of the Focus Groups and Citizens' Jury

This section evaluates the capacity of the focus groups and citizens' jury to contribute to the goals of public participation presented above. With respect to *raising public awareness* among the wider audience, no miracles should be expected from a focus group or citizens' jury. Because their membership is limited, both processes involve few people. In the case of the jury, though, the method does teach these few people a lot. Raising awareness in the wider audience depends on various other mechanisms, including the degrees to which the media pick up the issue and the participants share their experience. The jury may have greater potential for media attention, but this was not the case for the Markermeer jury, except for an article in the local newspaper and brief items on the regional radio and TV stations. This was because of the nature of the topic and the status of the citizens' jury. The jury initially attracted the attention of national TV news reporters, but they lost interest as soon as they found out that there was no urgent problem with water management of the lake and the citizens' jury was not going to make real decisions.

For those who expect focus groups and citizens' juries to provide the policy process with new factual insights that can actually lead to *improved decisions*, the capacity of these two methods is modest. For the knowledgeable observer of policy development in the IJsselmeer region, not many new "facts" were heard in the recommendations of either the citizens' jury or the focus groups. On the other hand, both the jury recommendations and the focus group outcomes did give insight into the normative aspects of water management and showed the *citizens'* viewpoint on what should be the priorities of water management, the kinds of choices that should be made, and the feasibility of policy measures. This may be an important insight for water managers. It also was interesting and informative to hear the questions the jurors asked, sometimes very fundamental ones about understandings and agreements that insiders know about and take for granted, but that may seem confusing to the average citizen.

With regard to *legitimacy*, the focus groups did not achieve this goal, but they were not intended to. The degree to which the jury attains legitimacy depends in part on the role its recommendations play in further policy formulation, especially with regard to the WFD, which is still in the early stages. The jury method is still quite new in the Netherlands, however, so perhaps legitimacy of recommendations cannot yet be ascertained.

Concerning *accountability*, this did not occur in the focus groups, but it was not supposed to. As the focus groups mainly aimed to gain insight into users' problem perceptions rather than provide recommendations for policy, they did not interact with the policy process, and the outcomes of the focus groups were not presented to politicians with the request to respond (as was the case with the citizens' jury). Accountability did occur to some extent in the jury, but it was limited to the jurors and other people who came to the hearings. One of the most frequently heard remarks among the jurors was that their participation in the jury had increased their understanding of the complexities of governmental decisionmaking. Whether the jury has any coresponsibility is hard to say, as this depends on various factors, including the degree to which the jury's recommendations will now play a role in the policy process. Also important is how involved the jurors remain in water policymaking. A possible indication for a sharing of responsibilities is that one of the jury members started to visit the meetings of the group that prepares the river basin management plan under the WFD for the Delta Rhine Central region, of which the Markermeer is a part.

As to *collective learning*, two conclusions can be drawn. The first relates to the dimension of *collective*. Neither the jury nor the focus groups resulted in collective management plans in which the various user groups and public officials would work closely together to manage the water of the IJsselmeer basin or in the development of a collective vision in the community, but this was by design. Both methods did, however, lead to a collective vision among the participants, particularly in the citizens' jury. As organizers, we did not seek to alter current government decisionmaking procedures that allow ordinary citizens only a limited role. The consequence is that the recommendations of the jury, which are aimed to some extent at influencing the policy process, are their own product, and the government parties do not necessarily share the jury's opinions. The second conclusion relates to the dimension of *learning*. In this respect, the jurors learned quite a bit from their involvement. For the focus groups, however, the learning effect was more modest (see Huitema et al. 2004). The learning effect for policymakers was greater in the case of the citizens' jury than that of the focus groups; this did not involve new factual information, however, but mainly insight into the citizens' viewpoints on water management.

CONCLUSIONS

This chapter has addressed the issue of public participation in water management within the context of the Netherlands. It has been suggested that a water manager organizing a participatory process should not be obsessed with the degree to which participants will gain power over representative democracy. Although this is a very relevant aspect of public participation, other issues need to be considered, such as the flow of information, conditions of access, and costs.

A variety of methods for public participation in water management are directly available, from public hearing and opinion poll to citizens' jury and referendum. With such a wide range to choose from, it is remarkable that the legally prescribed methods are so uniform and limited in number. Given the well-known limitations of the favorite instrument for participation under Dutch law, the public hearing, it should not be a surprise that the practice of interactive policymaking subsequently evolved. Although the introduction of the WFD offers an opportunity for expanding the tool kit even more, it is still an open question whether that will actually happen.

From a functional perspective, we suggested five goals of public participation that the water manager can pursue and use to evaluate participation processes: awareness raising, improvement of decisions, increased legitimacy, greater accountability, and learning. In order to show how certain public participation methods score against these goals, we discussed two methods that are novel to the Netherlands in the sense that they are not legally prescribed and have not been experimented with often: the focus group and the citizens' jury, both used in the IJsselmeer area. It must be noted that our focus on these two methods is more a consequence of our combined experience than an outcome of a careful attempt to select case studies. This, combined with the fact that we described only single applications of these two methods, means that a comparison between the experiences can only be explorative and tentative in nature.

Nevertheless, we can draw some conclusions with regard to strengths and weaknesses of the two methods in the Dutch setting, and possibly elsewhere as well. These strengths and weaknesses can be related to the goals the water manager may have in using the methods. Of the two methods, the citizens' jury is better in *raising awareness*, but the effect remained limited to the direct participants. This suggests that raising awareness among the wider public probably requires further measures. The citizens' jury succeeds better in increasing *legitimacy* and *accountability*, mainly because it has a distance-reducing effect, giving water managers an opportunity to be responsive to the public and enhancing access to government.

Although surrounded with uncertainties, neither of the two methods seems to have resulted in undiluted support for measures. Perhaps not surprisingly, collective learning among the participants is the best served purpose for each of the methods. The focus group, although not scoring very positively in many respects, does achieve a certain purpose here, which compares well to its low costs. The citizens' jury performs well. For both methods, however, the goal of achieving a shared vision in the entire relevant community remains elusive, which is one reason why these methods should probably be used *within* the framework of representative democracy rather than seen as an alternative to it.

We conclude by pointing out that the water managers' functional perspective is not the only valid viewpoint for discussing public participation. Other, very relevant, perspectives are those of stakeholders and citizens. Ridder et al. (2005) suggested that the criteria these groups apply to judge public participation methods may be different. Important for them are openness, protection of core values, speed, and substance of the debate. Far too often, participatory processes tend to be set up in a way that ignores the expectations of participants. Organizing such processes conveys a certain responsibility onto the water manager to be a good host. This means structuring the discussion process well, organizing the meetings at times appropriate for citizens (evenings and weekends, if need be), and a clear indication of what will be done with the outcomes of the process. This chapter aims to have contributed to an increased desire on the part of water managers to organize participatory methods and a greater resolve to be good hosts to the participants. The social capital generated in that way will likely be one of the better results from the investments that water managers can make.

NOTES

1. Many sessions at the 2006 World Water Forum in Mexico City were devoted to public participation in water management. Good practice in public participation was an important theme.

2. For overviews of participatory methods, see Creighton et al. (1998); Mayer (1997); Olsen (1982); Rowe and Frewer (2000); van Asselt and Rijkens-Klomp (2002); and van de Kerkhof (2004).

3. In environmental licensing procedures in the Netherlands, for example, the more sensitive the nature of the information that is being discussed (e.g., company secrets), the smaller the circle of people involved.

4. See Staatsblad 1992, *315*. The act is comparable to the Administrative Procedures Act in the United States.

5. Staatsblad 2005, *303*.

6. These were organized as part of the project River Dialogue, financed under the EU Fifth Framework Program, contract RPAM-2002-00057. For more information, see www.riverdialogue.org.

7. Renn and Tyroller (2003) reported a willingness to participate in citizens' forums varying from 5% to 40%. For more response rates, see Huitema (2003).

8. Interesting to note is that the positive response rate for taking part in an Internet panel in the province of Flevoland was 20%. Apparently people consider it much easier to commit to such a process than to one where they physically meet at set times and dates.

REFERENCES

Arnstein, S.R. 1969. A ladder of citizen participation. *Journal of the American Institute of Planning* 35 (4): 216–24.

Birch, A.H. 1993. *The concepts and theories of modern democracy.* London: Routledge.

de Boer, J., H. Goosen, and D. Huitema. 2003. *Bewust werken aan waterbewustzijn: Studie naar de rol en relevantie van het begrip waterbewustzijn voor het waterbeleid* [*Consciously working on water consciousness. Study of the role and relevance of the concept of water awareness for water policy*]. Amsterdam: IVM (Institute for Environmental Studies).

Bressers, J.Th.A., D. Huitema, and S.M.M. Kuks. 1995. Policy networks in Dutch water policy. In *Networks for water policy: A comparative perspective*, ed. J.Th.A Bressers, L.J. O'Toole, and J.J. Richardson, 24–51. London: Frank Cass.

Coenen, F.H.J.M., D. Huitema, and L.J. O'Toole. 1998. *Participation and the quality of environmental decision making.* Dordrecht, Netherlands: Kluwer Academic Publishers.

Cooke, B., and U. Kothari. 2001. *Participation: The new tyranny?* London: Zed Books.

Creighton, J., J. Delli Priscoli, and C. Dunning. 1998. *Public involvement techniques: A reader of ten years experience at the Institute for Water Resources.* Alexandria, VA: Institute for Water Resources.

Crosby, N. 1995. Citizens juries: One solution for difficult environmental questions. In *Fairness and competence in citizen participation: Evaluating new models for environmental discourse*, ed. O. Renn, T. Webler, and P. Wiedemann, 157–74. Dordrecht, Netherlands: Kluwer Academic Publishers.

Downs, A. 1972. Up and down with ecology. *Public Interest* 28:38–45.

Drafting Group. 2002. *Guidance on public participation in relation to the Water Framework Directive: Active involvement, consultation, and public access to information.* Copenhagen: Drafting Group.

Glasbergen, P. 1996. Learning to manage the environment. In *Democracy and the environment*, ed. W.M. Lafferty and J. Meadowcroft, 175–93. Cheltenham, UK: Edward Elgar.

Huitema, D. 2002. *Hazardous decisions: Hazardous waste facility siting in the UK, Netherlands and Canada: Institutions and discourses.* Dordrecht, Netherlands: Kluwer Academic Publishers.

———. 2003. *How to organize a citizens' jury.* Amsterdam: IVM (Institute for Environmental Studies).

Huitema, D., and S.M.M. Kuks. 2004. Harboring water in a crowded European delta. In *Integrated governance and water basin management: Conditions for regime change towards sustainability*, ed. J.Th.A. Bressers and S.M.M. Kuks, 61–100. Dordrecht, Netherlands: Kluwer Academic Publishers.

Huitema, D., M. van de Kerkhof, R. Terweij, M. van Tilburg, and F. Winsemius. 2004. *Exploring the future of the IJsselmeer: Report to the river dialogue project on the Dutch citizens' jury.* Amsterdam: IVM (Institute for Environmental Studies).

Huitema, D., M. van de Kerkhof, and G.M. van Tilburg. 2005. De burgerjury en de dilemma's van interactieve beleidsvorming [The citizens'jury and the dilemmas of interactive policymaking]. *Bestuurskunde* 14 (6): 23–32.

Kaijser, A. 2002. System building from below: Institutional change in Dutch water control systems. *Technology and Culture.* 43:521–48.

Koolhaas, E., S. Kroon, M. de Kruijk, and M. Thieme. 1998. *Procesevaluatie NW4. Eindrapportage procesevaluatie Regeringsvoornemen Vierde Nota Waterhuishouding* [Process evaluation Fourth National Policy Memorandum on Water Management, Final Report]. The Hague: B&A Groep.

Kuper, R. 1996. Citizens juries: The Hertfordshire experience. Working paper series no. 26. Hatfield, UK: University of Hertfordshire Business School.

Mayer, I. 1997. *Debating technologies: A methodological contribution to the design and evaluation of participatory policy analysis.* Tilburg, Netherlands: Tilburg University Press.

Morgan, D. 1998a. *The Focus Group Guidebook*. Focus Group Kit, vol. 1. Thousand Oaks, CA: Sage.

———. 1998b. *The Focus Group Guidebook*. Focus Group Kit, vol. 2. Thousand Oaks, CA: Sage.

Noordegraaf, M., T. Brandsen, and D. Huitema. 2006. Fragmented but forceful: Dutch administrative sciences and their institutional evolution. *Public Administration* 48: 989–1006.

Olsen, S. 1982. *Group planning and problem-solving: Methods in engineering management*. New York: John Wiley and Sons.

Ovaa, E. 1999. *Gebiedscontracten. Een nieuwe kijk op sturing van regionaal landgebruik en waterbeheer [Area contracts. A new vision on the management of regional land use and water management]*. Wageningen, Netherlands: Wageningen University.

Ovaa E., and B. Ottow. 2006. *Actieve betrokkenheid van maatschappelijke partijen bij de implementatie van KRW/WB21. Evaluatie van de voorgestelde werkvormen [Active involvement of societal parties in the implementation of the WFD and WB21. Evaluation of proposed work forms]*. Lelystad, Netherlands: RIZA.

Pahl-Wostl, C. 2002. Towards sustainability in the water: The importance of human actors and processes of social learning. *Aquatic Sciences* 64:394–411.

Renn, O., and A. Tyroller. 2003. Citizens' juries within the River Dialogue project: Recommendations for the practice. Stuttgart (unpublished paper).

Ridder, D., E. Mostert, and H.A. Wolters. 2005. *Learning together to manage together: Improving participation in water management*. Osnabrück, Germany: University of Osnabrück.

Rorty, R. 1999. *Contingency, irony, and solidarity*. Cambridge: Cambridge University Press.

Rowe, G., and L.J. Frewer. 2000. Public participation methods: A framework for evaluation. *Science, Technology and Human Values* 25 (1): 3–29.

Schumpeter, J. 1942. *Capitalism, socialism and democracy*. New York: Harper and Row.

Seley, J. 1983. *The politics of public facility planning*. Lexington, MA: Lexington Books.

Smith, G., and C. Wales. 2000. Citizens' juries and deliberative democracy. *Political Studies* 48:51–65.

van Asselt, M., and N. Rijkens-Klomp. 2002. A look in the mirror: Reflection on participation in integrated assessment from a methodological perspective *Global environmental change* 12:167–84.

van de Kerkhof, M. 2004. *Debating climate change: A study of stakeholder participation in an integrated assessment of long-term climate policy in the Netherlands*. Utrecht, Netherlands: Lemma Publishers.

———. 2006. A dialogue approach to enhance learning for sustainability: A Dutch experiment with two participatory methods in the field of climate change. *Integrated Assessment Journal. Bridging Sciences & Policy* 6 (4): 7–34.

van de Kerkhof, M., and D. Huitema. 2004. Public participation in river basin management: A methodological perspective. In *Information to support sustainable water management: From local to global levels*, ed. J.G. Timmerman, H.W.A. Behrens, F. Bernardini, D. Daler, P. Ross, K.J.M. van Ruiten, and R.C. Ward, 141–48. Lelystad, Netherlands: RIZA.

Vandersmissen, H., and J. den Hengst. 1998. *Het woelige water. Water management in Nederland [Turbulent waters. Water management in the Netherlands]*. Wormer, Netherlands: Inmerc.

Webler, T., and O. Renn. 1995. A brief primer on participation: Philosophy and practice. In *Fairness and competence in citizen participation: Evaluating models for environmental discourse*, ed. O. Renn, T. Webler, and P. Wiedemann, 17–33. Dordrecht: Kluwer Academic.

Wilkinson, S. 1998. Focus group methodology: A review. *International Journal of Social Research Methodology* 1 (3): 181–203.

CHAPTER 13

Conclusions
Lessons from Dutch Integrated Water Management

Stijn Reinhard and Henk Folmer

THE CHAPTERS THAT make up this volume have shown that Dutch water management provides important lessons for other countries. Both developing and industrialized countries can benefit from the Dutch experiences and avoid some of the pitfalls that the Dutch have gone through.

One key lesson is to adopt *integrated water management* in as early a stage as possible so as to avoid the inefficiencies emerging from path dependencies. Integrated water management means putting all the pieces together. Social, environmental, and technical aspects must be considered. This book has illustrated multiple aspects of Dutch integrated water management. One of the main aspects has been flood risks from both the *sea* and *inland rivers*. As de Jonge discussed in Chapter 1, from the 1950s until the mid-1990s, flood protection in the Netherlands was primarily aimed at the sea. Threats from the Rhine and Meuse rivers in 1993 and 1995, however, led to a reformulation of water management and policy objectives, with protection from flooding caused by rivers becoming a major objective next to that of a very strong sea defense.

The *water basin dimension* is a second important aspect of integrated water management. In addition to extreme precipitation, other main causes of extremely high water levels in the Netherlands in the 1990s were deforestation and canalization in upstream countries. For the Dutch situation, the water basin dimension led to international aspects of water management. A third dimension is *quality control* in addition to quantity control, which had been the main objective of water management in the Netherlands up to the 1960s. Water quality did not get a lot of attention before, because water quantity problems had a greater catastrophic impact in the short term. Quality control is relevant not only for drinking water, but also for recreational purposes and the preservation of environmental quality. In this context again the international water basin dimension is crucial, because sources of water pollution are often located in upstream countries.

A fourth dimension is the integration of water management and *spatial planning*. As described by Voogd and Woltjer in Chapter 10, water management in the Netherlands was formerly sectoral. It initially focused on flood control and, at a later stage, water quality control, while ignoring the interdependencies with spatial planning. Various types of land use, such as housing, agriculture, recreation, and nature preservation, impose conditions on water quantity and quality, and vice versa: water quantity and quality restrict land uses such as the application of pesticides and the location of residential areas. Moreover, some types of land use, such as agriculture and nature preservation, may lead to conflicting water quality and quantity demands. Regulation of groundwater tables as required by agriculture usually has negative impacts on the protection of nature. In this context, *numerical hydrological models* are important tools for system analysis and policymaking. In Chapter 2, Heijkers and van Bakel presented the conceptual framework and a brief overview of this type of models, which can be used to weigh different interests and cope with the mutual interdependencies of the various forms of land use. Conflicting water quality and quantity demands may arise not only from different types of land use, but also from different types of water use. In Chapter 3, Piersma analyzed the *conflict between fisheries and nature preservation* in the Dutch Wadden Sea, particularly the impacts of mechanical dredging for shellfish on the shorebird populations dependent on these food resources.

A second essential lesson concerns a paradigm shift related to *catastrophic floods*. Disturbances such as floods are likely to cause major disruptions in Dutch society for several reasons: the Netherlands has a high population density, four times the EU average; more than a quarter of its land area is below sea level, and this area is home to 60% of the population; the country has an extensive industrial and infrastructural network; and natural conditions have altered as a result of climate change. These developments have induced shifts in the approach toward water management and dealing with the threat of major floods. Traditional technology-based approaches such as raising the dikes are no longer sufficient. In Chapter 4, Bočkarjova et al. discussed policy options when, as a result of a catastrophic flood, parts of the economic and social networks fail for a considerable period of time. The authors presented an approach that would redistribute the available resources among various categories of sources and destinations in a way that would minimize the impacts of the interruption. In this context, the authors argued for a system that would shift the balances between public and private domains in favor of a model of sharing responsibilities such that the problem would become a matter of interactions between private and public interests.

The application of *economic principles* is a third significant lesson. Rouwendal showed in Chapter 6 that although water is a basic need for human life, the common belief that it should be made available for free or at negligible prices leads to *inefficiencies*. Instead, water supply and sewage treatment should be viewed as scarce rather than free commodities. Water supply and sewage treatment are public utilities in the Netherlands, as public control is thought necessary to ensure their availability for everyone at all times, and because the network structures hamper competition. The author presented some guidelines for pricing and capacity in this setting. He demonstrated that in the Netherlands, regulation has been successful in preventing monopolistic prices, and that capacity should not be chosen such that its limits will never be exceeded. Moreover, the prices should be set such that revenues are sufficient to cover the complete capacity cost as well as the variable cost. Such pricing limits the cost of capacity and realizes maximal downward pressure on peak demand. In Chapter 5, Brouwer and van der Veeren discussed the application of economic principles in Dutch integrated water policy analysis. Specifically, they analyzed the *costs and benefits* of various long-term flood control policies in the Lower River Delta and presented a new *institutionalized integrated water and economic information system*, which links economic activities to water use (e.g., abstraction and emission of water-polluting substances).

The development of *wastewater treatment technology* holds a fourth valuable lesson. Whereas in the past, wastewater was viewed as an unwanted product to dispose of, it is now increasingly seen as a valuable resource of water, energy, and nutrients that must be harvested and reused. Euverink et al. showed in Chapter 7 that the development of new wastewater treatment technology or the improvement of existing ones requires investment in long-term multidisciplinary research. The authors also argue that government, industry, and households need to cooperate in the context of advanced wastewater treatment. Particularly, improved treatment plants put requirements on the type of wastewater they receive, which in its turn necessitates separation at the source and hence commitment of households and industry as well as a change of infrastructure.

A fifth lesson relates to *governance*. van Leussen and Lulofs described in Chapter 9 the *evolution of water management* in the Netherlands from self-governance during a period of weak central government and lack of a national administration (1200–1798), to hierarchical governance during a period of a strong central government (1798–2000), to cogovernance during the present period of integrated water management, with its full attention to the relationships with other policy fields. In this context, in Chapter 8, Kuks detailed the evolution of *water boards*, which are responsible for water management in the Netherlands. The water boards have developed from very small-scale, local institutions for drainage and flood protection into "all-in" organizations at the size of tributary water basins. The author also discussed their full cost recovery tax system.

Cogovernance requires *public participation*. In this setting, Huitema et al. described in Chapter 12 several participation methods, including the focus group, citizens' jury, and social learning group, and compared them in terms of raising awareness, improvement of decisions, legitimacy, accountability, and learning. Through analysis of case studies, they concluded that none of the methods stood out as uniformly best on all criteria. Therefore, the choice of method should be guided by the importance of the objectives.

The EU Water Framework Directive (WFD), with the objectives of achieving good status for all waters and a river basin approach, has encouraged further development of the integrated and international dimensions of Dutch water management. Van Rijswick pointed out in Chapter 11 that the WFD is directed at many more policy areas than just water. Consequently, implementing the directive requires great effort in fields such as environmental and ecological management, spatial planning, agriculture, traffic, and transport. From the author's analysis, it also follows that the integrated approach requires proper regulation and legislation, on both the European and national levels.

Integrated water management in the Netherlands started as integration of water quantity and quality management. The concept has extended from the formerly sectoral water management to a more interdisciplinary approach based on strong relations with spatial planning, taking into account different types of water and land use within the water basin. Technology-based approaches such as dikes are no longer sufficient; a paradigm shift based on other disciplines is necessary, for instance, to minimize the impacts of floods from the sea or rivers. Economic principles such as water pricing and cost–benefit analysis prevent imprudent water use and stimulate wastewater treatment. Governance has to change accordingly to facilitate the development of real integrated water management; for example, public participation is a condition of cogovernance and international cooperation in the implementation of the European Union Water Framework Directive.

Index

[Cultural, Regulatory
  provisioning, Supply services.]

Aichi Biodiversity Targets - 2020

EUROPE 2020: SMART, SUSTAINABLE + INCLUSIVE
                                        GROWTH.

Eng : Natl cmt Wlt Ppn

Eng
 CFMP
 SMP
 SWMP
 LFRMS
 FRMP
 MAFP
 RBMP

Millenium Ecosystem Assesst
                    MEA 2005,
Natl Ecosystem Assesst
                    UK NEA 2011.
The Economics of Ecosystems +
        Biodiversity TEEB 2010 *
RANGE OF MANAGT OPTIONS.

Conclusions

growth.   Kasper Kerte

benefits people derive from natl ent.

E.S. Approach = STRATEGY INTEGRATED
MANAGT OF LAND, WTR, & LIVING RESOURCES
; promotes conservation + sust use in equitable
way, for people.

ESA key policy obj of EU + UK.
criteria for assests.

Adv: cross agency working interdisc.
   C+BA
   Sustainable solns optimise multiple benefits.
   systematic understanding of ecosyst change + envt.
                    effect on people
   engaging with stakeholders ?. tool.
   Provide solns that fit with local priorities

Approach: (1) tiered assesst approach.
   (scale + controversy) * quantitative assessmnt/
                       monetary value.

   (2) expert based assessment of change in
       ecosystem service delivery under
       alternative mangt options = V. USEFUL
       Quick - simple. OK for maintenance issues

Challenge + Barriers. time, res, team challenges
              cc working, philosophical issues, practicals

For capital works projects + some maintenance?
? ESYS + WFD. combine both assessments.

   - operational guidelines.
   - training + training,
   - more costs + benefits.
   LINK F CRM + WFD/RBM ply processes

965